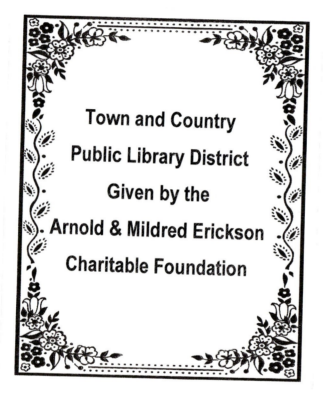

CRITICAL INSIGHTS

The House on Mango Street

by Sandra Cisneros

CRITICAL INSIGHTS

The House on Mango Street

by Sandra Cisneros

Editor
María Herrera-Sobek
University of California, Santa Barbara

Salem Press
Pasadena, California   Hackensack, New Jersey

Published by Salem Press

© 2011 by EBSCO Publishing
Editor's text © 2011 by María Herrera-Sobek
"The *Paris Review* Perspective" © 2011 by Chloë Schama
for *The Paris Review*

Library of Congress Cataloging-in-Publication Data
The house on Mango Street, by Sandra Cisneros / María Herrera-Sobek, editor.
    p. cm. — (Critical insights)
Includes bibliographical references and index.
ISBN 978-1-58765-717-7 (v. 1 : alk. paper)
1. Cisneros, Sandra. House on Mango Street. I. Herrera-Sobek, María.
PS3553.I78H627 2011
813'.54—dc22

2010030198

PRINTED IN CANADA

Contents_____

The Book and Author_____

Critical Contexts_____

Critical Readings_____

Resources

About This Volume

María Herrera-Sobek

Sandra Cisneros's *The House on Mango Street* is without a doubt the most written about novel in Chicano literary production, discussed by Chicano/a critics as well as by other scholars. Featured in this volume are some of the most outstanding essays written on Cisneros's work—a good number already published and others commissioned specifically for this reader.

The volume is divided into three sections. The first section, focusing on the work and its influences, features my introductory editor's essay, a biography on Cisneros by Gloria A. Duarte-Valverde, and an essay by Chloë Schama, on behalf of *The Paris Review*, that elaborates on Cisneros's strong desire and need to write as well as to provide a voice for her community.

The second section centers on the critical contexts in which *The House on Mango Street* developed, such as its midwestern roots, which are delineated by Amelia María de la Luz Montes, and the history of the critical reception of the novel, which is detailed by Amy Sickels. Felicia J. Cruz further expands on the intricacies of reception theory-based approaches to *Mango Street* and aesthetic response theory. Her essay examines the various responses to the novel, including those from middle-class readers and those from Latino/Chicano audiences, and finds that both groups often miss the significant complexity of the novel.

Catherine Leen proffers an excellent comparative analysis between Cisneros's work and Toni Morrison's *The Bluest Eye* and demonstrates how two authors from radically different cultural traditions find a commonality through their focus on patriarchal structures and the negative effect they have on the lives of the novel's women protagonists.

The essays in the "Critical Readings" section feature various approaches to the reading and hermeneutics of *Mango Street*. Three of the critical essays focus on gender and feminist literary criticism; three concentrate on border theory and the various border crossings of the novel; two center their critical lens on the topic of "a room of one's own" as essential for writing and how *Mango Street* navigates this issue; two essays examine *Mango Street* from the perspective of the bildungsroman; one examines the natural environment of Mango Street; and one applies mythic literary criticism.

Gender issues are of paramount concern in Leslie Petty's article "The 'Dual'-ing Images of la Malinche and la Virgen de Guadalupe in Cisneros's *The House on Mango Street*." Petty explores the dichotomy of the Virgin of Guadalupe and the Malinche and demonstrates how Cisneros's work goes beyond this stereotypical duo to fashion strong and resilient women characters. Catrióna Rueda Esquibel offers, in "Memories of Girlhood: Chicana Lesbian Fictions," new and original insights into the female friendships inscribed in *Mango Street* and characterizes them as instances of lesbian desire. The last article focusing mainly on gender issues is Michelle Scalise Sugiyama's "Of Woman Bondage: The Eroticism of Feet in *The House on Mango Street*." In this perceptive essay, Sugiyama points out how, within some of Cisneros's vignettes, sexuality is inscribed in the subject of shoes and tiny feet.

The theoretical construct of the border, which encompasses a variety of borders such as gender, sexual orientation, social class, genre, language, and so forth, is prominent in Robin Ganz's "Sandra Cisneros: Border Crossings and Beyond." In her essay, she provides an overview of Cisneros's early life, her introduction as a writer, and her ability to navigate different "borders." Equally interested in border theories and border crossings as applicable to *Mango Street* is Stella Bolaki, whose essay in this volume is titled "'This Bridge We Call Home': Crossing and Bridging Spaces in Sandra Cisneros's *The House on Mango Street*," and Maria Karafilis, who gives us "Crossing the Borders of Genre: Revisions of the *Bildungsroman* in Sandra Cisneros's *The House on Mango Street* and Jamaica Kincaid's *Annie John*."

Karafilis's essay could just as well fit within the next category of critical articles since she also focuses on the bildungsroman structure of *Mango Street*. Annie O. Eysturoy's "*The House on Mango Street*: A Space of Her Own" and Delia Poey's "Coming of Age in the Curriculum: *The House on Mango Street* and *Bless Me, Ultima* as Representative Texts" both tackle this subject. Eysturoy focuses on how Cisneros is able to transform a Eurocentric, individualistic, and male-centered structure, such as the bildungsroman, or novel of development and maturation, into a form able to encompass a young girl's coming-of-age in a community-oriented Mexican American environment. Poey explores the problematics related to the status of *Mango Street* and Anaya's *Bless Me, Ultima* as "representative" texts within the context of multiculturalism and related debates.

Two more essays, Maria Antònia Oliver-Rotger's "Homeplaces and Spaces of Their Own" and Jacqueline Doyle's "More Room of Her Own: Sandra Cisneros's *The House on Mango Street*," focus on the house and its relation to creativity as expounded by French theorist Gaston Bachelard and the dictum, expressed by Virginia Woolf, that "a room of one's own" is indispensable for the act of creating. Both Oliver-Rotger and Doyle discuss how these articulations play out in the pages of *Mango Street*.

James R. Giles, in his "Nature Despoiled and Artificial: Sandra Cisneros's *The House on Mango Street*," discusses the novel in terms of the city in which it is set, Chicago, and the natural or, more specifically, unnatural environment surrounding the lives of the characters. In this sense, his analysis can be linked to ecological literary criticism. He posits that, although Cisneros's view of Chicago cannot be as positive as one coming from a middle-class writer, her depiction of nature in the various vignettes in *Mango Street* yields yet another perspective on her very innovative literary work.

Reuben Sánchez's "Remembering Always to Come Back: The Child's Wished-For Escape and the Adult's Self-Empowered Return in Sandra Cisneros's *House on Mango Street*" uses mythic criticism to discuss Cisneros's transformation and incorporation of myth in her work.

All of the aforementioned articles collectively and individually illuminate Cisneros's splendid novel and provide a multiplicity of critical approaches to, perspectives on, and insights into *The House on Mango Street*. The often brilliant and incisive analyses of the novel by this volume's contributors afford the reader a deeper understanding of Cisneros's work as well as a greater appreciation and enjoyment of it.

THE BOOK
AND
AUTHOR

On *The House on Mango Street*

María Herrera-Sobek

Sandra Cisneros's novel *The House on Mango Street*, published in 1984, heralded the new literary boom in Chicana/Latina authors that exploded in the 1980s. The decade witnessed the introduction and success of such literary luminaries as Ana Castillo, Helena María Viramontes, Denise Chávez, Julia Alvarez, and Gloria Anzaldúa. This success continued into the 1990s and on to the twenty-first century. *The House on Mango Street* was the literary gem that cracked the doors opened to both Chicanas/os as well as Latinas/os and ushered them into mainstream publishing houses. Before the publication of *The House on Mango Street*, the Chicano literary scene was dominated by male authors such as Rudolfo Anaya, Rolando Hinojosa, Tomás Rivera, Alejandro Morales, Miguel Méndez, Oscar Zeta Acosta, Ron Arias, José Antonio Villarreal, Luis Valdez, and Alurista. But even these Chicano literary stars were generally published by small presses and ignored by mainstream national ones. Cisneros's success with *Mango Street* was instrumental in attracting the attention of major publishing houses, which soon began viewing this ethnic group as viable authors for the national marketplace.

The House on Mango Street celebrated its twenty-fifth anniversary in 2009 with a special edition and a flurry of literary activities such as conferences, radio talk shows, television appearances, lectures, library readings, and so forth. Chicago, Cisneros's birthplace, picked the novel for its sixteenth One Book, One Chicago selection. The novel has done exceptionally well commercially, having sold out its first printing in 1984 soon after publication, and this success has led to its being reprinted repeatedly. It was in the same year, 1985, that *Mango Street* won the prestigious American Book Award from the Before Columbus Foundation. The award gave the novel a new round of publicity, and reprints continued to be issued by Arte Público Press. By 1992, Vintage Press, a subsidiary connected to the powerhouse publishing firm Random House, obtained the rights to print it. The book has attained "classic" status and is read throughout the U.S. educational system; from grade schools to high schools and from community colleges to four-year colleges and universities in the United States, *Mango Street* can easily be found in the classroom.

Extensive discussions regarding *Mango Street*'s classification within traditional academic canonical genres have taken place among literary critics. Several scholars in this volume note the border crossing characteristics of Cisneros's work and its ambiguous position within established literary genres. The work has been classified variously as a novella, a collection of short stories, a novel, a collection of vignettes, a fictional autobiography, an experimental novel, and an autobiography. Most commonly, though, it is classified as a novel or collection of vignettes. This definition of "novel" offered by *The American College Dictionary* (third edition) is typical: "A fictional prose narrative of considerable length, typically having a plot that is unfolding by the actions, speech, and thoughts of the characters." The same dictionary describes the vignette as "a short, usually descriptive literary sketch" or "a short scene or incident, as from a movie." Nevertheless, most literary critics, including the ones featured in this volume, classify or refer to *Mango Street* as a novel, given that its principal protagonist, Esperanza Cordero, links the forty-four vignettes into one unit; also, the work's consistent setting is an urban street in Chicago, and secondary characters reappear throughout the narrative. Cisneros herself has called *Mango Street* a collection of "lazy poems" because of the narrative episodes' original connection to her poetry. Thus *Mango Street*, by crossing boundaries between short stories, vignettes, the novel, and poetry, challenges established conceptualizations of rigid borderlines between genres.

Why has *Mango Street* been so successful? What is it in the novel that makes it so universally appealing to readers? Readers and critics constantly return to these two questions. They have been answered in various ways, and some of these answers are included in the essays presented in this volume. Nevertheless, I am positing that it is both the "simplicity" as well as the "complexity" of Cisneros's novel that appeals to a wide spectrum of readers, from elementary school children to sophisticated university professors and literary critics. The simplicity lies in the linguistic register offered by Cisneros via Esperanza—that of a young girl, perhaps a preadolescent of eleven or twelve years of age. The dialogue and narrative is structured in simple language so that anyone can read the work at one level. But therein lies the complexity of *Mango Street*, since at a deeper, more profound level are inscribed the politics of gender, race, and class—it is indeed a hard-hitting novel deceptive in its linguistic simplicity and choice of vocabulary. One of Cisneros's brilliant strokes of genius is her skillful manipulation of language, which has led to her splendid structuring of metaphor and simile. Below are but a few examples taken from the 1984 *Mango Street* edition:

Their strength is their secret. They send ferocious roots beneath the ground. They grow up and they grow down and grab the earth between their hairy toes and bite the sky with violent teeth and never quit their anger. (71)

[He] just went crazy, he just forgot he was her father between the buckle and the belt. (86)

The family that spoke like guitars. (87)

There were big green apples hard as knees. (87)

Dead cars appeared overnight like mushrooms. (88)

The ceiling smooth as wedding cake. (95)

Inscribed in the "simple" metaphors and similes of these quotes are issues of urban rage and poverty, hints of incest and the physical abuse of a young daughter by her father, linguistic differences, urban decay, and marital entrapment.

Much has been written about the central character, Esperanza, and her name. The translation of her name as "hope" and all the ramifications the English and Spanish versions of her name imply have been frequently discussed. However, Esperanza's last name, Cordero, never seems to attract the attention of critics. Esperanza's last name is extremely interesting given the classification of the novel by many critics as belonging to the bildungsroman category due to its structure. Cordero, a Spanish word, means lamb, which, of course, is the opposite of what Esperanza is but, on the other hand, it also means Lamb of God or the Savior, that is, Jesus. Esperanza positions herself as coming back to Mango Street to help those who cannot get out. In this sense, Esperanza is a God-like figure in the form of a female—that is to say, a female savior. Again Cisneros crosses borders by making her God-like figure a woman and not a man. We can also see that Cordero encodes the English word "cord," as in umbilical cord, which again links Esperanza to her origins, her beginnings in Mango Street.

Likewise, the name of the street in Cisneros's novel has not been properly, if at all, analyzed by critics: mango (which is a Spanish word) is a sweet, exotic fruit that grows in Mexico and other tropical areas. In Spanish popular speech, "mango" refers to an extremely handsome, sexually attractive man. The two syllables that combine to make up the Spanish word "mango" are also the two English words "man" and "go." "Mango" can be decoded as "man get out," which, keeping in mind the feminist tenor of the book, is quite elucidating. All of this only points to the deceptiveness of the supposed "simplicity" of *Mango Street* and how excavating into its deeper meanings yields surprising results.

After the publication of *The House on Mango Street,* Cisneros continued to produce works of exceptional literary merit. She has published several collections of poetry, including *Loose Woman* (1994) and *My Wicked, Wicked Ways* (1987), as well as a children's book,

Hairs = Pelitos (1984). Her collection of short stories, *Woman Hollering Creek, and Other Stories* (1991), has received considerable critical attention. In this collection, Cisneros centers her attention, once again, on gender issues such as spousal abuse and betrayal. The short story "Woman Hollering Creek" in particular details the hardships and disillusionment of a young Mexican bride, Cleófilas, who leaves her home in Mexico to join her new husband in Texas. Cleófilas, in a similar manner to several of the female characters appearing in *Mango Street*, is trapped in an abusive relationship. The young bride's inability to speak English and her isolation from others leaves her particularly vulnerable. Cleófilas's husband begins to abuse her physically, and, after their baby is born, she enlists the help of other women to escape back to Mexico and to her family.

Equally critically acclaimed is Cisneros's most recent novel, *Caramelo* (2002). In a manner analogous to her work in *Mango Street* and the stories in *Woman Hollering Creek*, Cisneros literally employs issues of border crossing (from Chicago to Mexico City and back) and introduces them metaphorically by using two languages in the novel, Spanish and English. Concerns with feminist issues are also of paramount importance in this novel, as is Cisneros's incorporation of folklore and popular culture, which are rendered in a highly creative and original manner.

Sandra Cisneros's *The House on Mango Street* was a trailblazer in many respects: it broke genre boundaries both with respect to form and content (i.e., the novel and the bildungsroman), challenged patriarchal structures, introduced into the canon marginalized women characters, opened the doors to mainstream publishing houses for Chicanos/as, challenged stereotypical conceptualizations of race and class, and introduced into the general American consciousness the coming-of-age of a Mexican American girl heretofore never read about. We look forward to future novels, short stories, and poetry from this talented and brilliant American author. Her work will be enjoyed for many generations to come.

Works Cited

Acosta, Oscar Zeta. *Autobiography of a Brown Buffalo*. San Francisco: Straight Arrow Press, 1972.

Alurista. *Floricanto en Aztlán*. Los Angeles: University of California, Chicano Studies Cultural Center, 1971.

Alvarez, Julia. *How the García Girls Lost Their Accent*. New York: Plume, 1991.

Anaya, Rudolfo. *Bless Me, Ultima*. Berkeley, CA: Quinto Sol, 1972.

Anzaldúa, Gloria. *Borderlands/La Frontera. The New Mestiza*. San Francisco: Spinsters/Aunt Lute Press, 1987.

Arias, Ron. *The Road to Tamazunchale*. Reno, NV: West Coast Poetry Review, 1975.

Castillo, Ana. *The Mixquiahuala Letters*. Binghamton, NY: Bilingual Review Press, 1986.

Chávez, Denise. *The Last of the Menu Girls*. Houston: Arte Público Press, 1986.

Cisneros, Sandra. *Caramelo*. New York: Alfred A. Knopf, 2002.

_____. *The House on Mango Street*. 1984. New York: Random House, 1992.

_____. *Loose Women*. New York: Random House, 1994.

_____. *My Wicked, Wicked Ways*. Berkeley, CA: Third Woman Press, 1987.

_____. *Woman Hollering Creek, and Other Stories*. New York: Vintage Books, 1991.

Hinojosa, Rolando. *Estampas del Valle y otras obras*. Berkeley, CA: Quinto Sol, 1973.

Méndez, Miguel. *Peregrinos de Aztlán*. Tucson, AZ: Editorial Peregrinos, 1974.

Morales, Alejandro. *Caras viejas y vino nuevo*. Mexico City: Editorial Joaquín Mortiz, 1975.

Rivera, Tomás. . . . *y no se lo tragó la tierra/. . . and the earth did not part*. Berkeley, CA: Quinto Sol, 1971.

Valdez, Luis. *Actos*. San Juan Bautista, CA: Cucaracha, 1971.

Villarreal, José Antonio. *Pocho*. New York: Doubleday, 1959.

Viramontes, Helena María. *The Moths, and Other Stories*. Houston: Arte Público Press, 1985.

Biography of Sandra Cisneros_____

Gloria A. Duarte-Valverde

Sandra Cisneros was born in Chicago in 1954 to a Mexican father and a Mexican American mother. She grew up in a working-class family with six brothers; her family expected her to follow the traditional female role. Her lonely childhood growing up with six males and the family's constant moving contributed to her becoming a writer. The family moved frequently—from house to house and from Chicago to Mexico City—which caused constant upheavals. She felt trapped between the American and the Mexican cultures, not belonging in either one. Understandably, Cisneros withdrew into a world of books. The family finally settled down in a Puerto Rican neighborhood on the north side of Chicago. This setting provided Cisneros with the inspiration for her first novel, *The House on Mango Street*, and the characters who appear in it.

Cisneros attended Loyola University in Chicago and graduated in 1976 with a B.A. in English. She was the only Hispanic majoring in English at the time, a unique situation which isolated her from her peers. During her junior year at Loyola, she came in contact with her cultural roots and the Chicago poetry scene, influences she would later appreciate and return to in her writings.

Cisneros moved to Iowa, where she earned a master's degree in creative writing at the University of Iowa Writers' Workshop in 1978. During her two years there, she felt lonely and displaced. A particularly unsettling experience occurred, one that ultimately helped her find her narrative voice and her writing subjects. During a seminar discussion of Gaston Bachelard's *The Poetics of Space* (1957), Cisneros discovered that his use of "house" as a metaphor differed radically from her understanding. She realized that Bachelard and her classmates shared a communal understanding of "house," one that she did not possess. Recognizing her otherness, she decided to write about subjects and memories close to her life but foreign to her classmates: third-floor flats, fear of rats, drunk and abusive husbands, all unpoetic subjects. At the same time, she found her literary voice, one which had been there but she had suppressed. Cisneros began writing autobiographical sketches about her life experiences and continues to write about "those ghosts that haunt [her], that will not [let] her sleep."

Bad Boys, Cisneros's first published work, appeared in 1980. The series of seven poems depicts childhood scenes and experiences in the Mexican American ghetto of Chicago. In these early poems, Cisneros was more concerned with sound and timing than with content. Although Cisneros has written four volumes of poetry, it is her fiction for which she is best known. *The House on Mango Street* received the 1985 Before Columbus American Book Award. This work, which took her five years to complete, provides a feminine perspective on growing up. The collection of forty-four narratives relates the experiences of Esperanza Cordero, the Hispanic adolescent narrator. The sketches describe her experiences as she matures and discovers life in a poor Hispanic urban ghetto. The house on Mango Street symbolizes her search for self-identity as she yearns for "a house all [her] own."

My Wicked, Wicked Ways, Cisneros's third volume of poetry, which includes "The Rodrigo Poems," is her revised and expanded master's thesis. It collects sixty poems on various subjects, including encounters with friends, travels, amorous experiences such as the monologues by women romantically involved with Rodrigo, and the guilt associated with a Mexican and Catholic upbringing. Supported by a 1982 National Endowment for the Arts grant, Cisneros traveled through Europe and worked on poems describing brief encounters with men she met during her travels. The poems in this collection tell Cisneros's own life story from a more mature voice. As the title suggests, the major emphasis is on the author's dealing with her own sexuality and feelings of guilt associated with her "wicked" ways. *Woman Hollering Creek, and Other Stories* appeared in 1991. Its twenty-two narratives, or *cuentitos*, focus on Mexican American characters who live near San Antonio, Texas. Cisneros surveys the Mexican American woman's condition, which is at once individual and universal. She addresses contemporary issues associated with stereotypical roles, minority status, and cultural conflicts.

Loose Woman consists of sixty love poems that verge on the erotic and cover a broad spectrum of emotions. The poems are organized into three sections: "Little Clown, My Heart"; "The Heart Rounds up the Usual Suspects"; and "Heart, My Lovely Hobo." In these poems, Cisneros breaks loose from feelings of guilt and celebrates her womanhood.

Caramelo marked Cisneros's return to long fiction, with a more conventional novelistic form than her previous works. The dominant metaphor for this multigenerational story is the rebozo, or traditional Mexican shawl, owned by the main character's grandmother. As with all of Cisneros's fiction, there is a strongly autobiographical aspect to her heroine, Celaya, who travels between her nuclear family home in Chicago and the extended family home in Mexico City, and who grows up to become a poet.

Before developing her career as a writer, Sandra Cisneros worked as a teacher, counselor, and arts administrator. She is internationally recognized for her poetry and fiction, in which she intermingles English and Spanish. Her poetry and short stories, though not copious, have earned for her recognition as an outstanding Chicana writer.

From *Cyclopedia of World Authors, Fourth Revised Edition.* Pasadena, CA: Salem Press, 2004.

Bibliography
Brady, Mary Pat. "The Contrapuntal Geographies of *Woman Hollering Creek, and Other Stories*." *American Literature* 71 (March, 1999): 117-150. Shows how Cisneros's narrative techniques challenge various spatial representations and lay bare hidden stories. Claims that Cisneros explores the various subtleties of violence in changing spatial relations.

Cisneros, Sandra. "On the Solitary Fate of Being Mexican, Female, Wicked, and

Thirty-three: An Interview with Writer Sandra Cisneros." Interview by Pilar E. Rodríguez Aranda. *Americas Review* 18, no. 1 (1990): 64-80. In an enlightening interview, Cisneros discusses her identity as a Chicana, her development as a writer, and her use of poetry and modern myth in her fiction. The interview focuses on the collections *My Wicked, Wicked Ways* and *The House on Mango Street*.

_____. "Sandra Cisneros: Conveying the Riches of the Latin American Culture Is the Author's Literary Goal." Interview by Jim Sagel. *Publishers Weekly* 238 (March 29, 1991): 74-75. In this informative interview, Cisneros speaks about the influence that her childhood had on her writing. The interview touches on the personal side of the writer and includes a brief description of the genesis of the collection *Woman Hollering Creek, and Other Stories*.

Cruz, Felicia J. "On the 'Simplicity' of Sandra Cisneros's *The House on Mango Street*." *Modern Fiction Studies* 47, no. 4 (2001): 910-946. Studies the varieties of representation in Cisneros's novel.

Doyle, Jacqueline. "More Room of Her Own: Sandra Cisneros's *The House on Mango Street*." *MELUS* 19 (Winter, 1994): 5-35. Discusses *The House on Mango Street* as a transformation of the terms of Virginia Woolf's vision in *A Room of One's Own* (1929). Asserts Cisneros's work provides a rich reconsideration of the contemporary feminist inheritance as influenced by Woolf.

Griffin, Susan E. "Resistance and Reinvention in Sandra Cisneros' *Woman Hollering Creek*." In *Ethnicity and the American Short Story*, edited by Julie Brown. New York: Garland, 1997. Discusses the role that Mexican popular culture and traditional Mexican narratives play in limiting women's sense of identity. Focuses primarily on the negative effects of popular romances in Mexico and televised soap operas.

Madsen, Deborah L. *Understanding Contemporary Chicana Literature*. Columbia: University of South Carolina Press, 2001. A close study of the work of Bernice Zamora, Ana Castillo, Sandra Cisneros, Denise Chávez, Alma Luz Villanueva, and Lorna Dee Cervantes. Includes an extensive bibliography.

Matchie, Thomas. "Literary Continuity in Sandra Cisneros's *The House on Mango Street*." *Midwest Quarterly* 37 (Autumn, 1995): 67-79. Discusses how *The House on Mango Street* uses Mark Twain's *Adventures of Huckleberry Finn* (1884) and J. D. Salinger's *The Catcher in the Rye* (1951) as literary models of adolescents growing up in a culturally oppressive world. Like Huck and Holden, Cisneros's protagonist is innocent, sensitive, and vulnerable, and she grows mentally in the process of the narrative.

Miriam-Goldberg, Caryn. *Sandra Cisneros: Latina Writer and Activist*. Berkeley Heights, N.J.: Enslow, 1998. A biography in a series on Hispanic writers.

Mullen, Harryette. "'A Silence Between Us Like a Language': The Untranslatability of Experience in Sandra Cisneros's *Woman Hollering Creek*." *MELUS* 21 (Summer, 1996): 3-20. Argues that Spanish as a code comprehensible to an inside group and as a repressed language subordinate to English are central issues in *Woman Hollering Creek*.

Olivares, Julián. "Sandra Cisneros' *The House on Mango Street*, and the Poetics of

Space." *Americas Review* 15, nos. 3/4 (1987): 160-170. This essay is an in-depth analysis of the stories of *The House on Mango Street* in terms of Cisneros's distinctive use of the metaphor of a house situated in a Latino neighborhood. Contains bibliographical references pertinent to *The House on Mango Street*.

Sanborn, Geoffrey. "Keeping Her Distance: Cisneros, Dickinson, and the Politics of Private Enjoyment." *Publications of the Modern Language Association* 116, no. 5 (2001): 1334-1348. Analyzes Cisneros's use of a poem by Emily Dickinson in *The House on Mango Street* as a means of evoking the pleasures of withdrawal from face-to-face sociality.

Thompson, Jeff. "'What Is Called Heaven?' Identity in Sandra Cisneros's 'Woman Hollering Creek.'" *Studies in Short Fiction* 31 (Summer, 1994): 415-424. States that the overall theme of the stories is the vulnerability of the female narrators. The vignettes should be read as symptomatic of a social structure that allows little cultural movement and little possibility for the creation of an identity outside the boundaries of the barrio.

Wyatt, Jean. "On Not Being La Malinche: Border Negotiations of Gender in Sandra Cisneros's 'Never Marry a Mexican' and 'Woman Hollering Creek.'" *Tulsa Studies in Women's Literature* 14 (Fall, 1995): 243-271. Discusses how the stories describe the difficulties of living on the border between Anglo-American and Mexican cultures and how the female protagonists of the stories struggle with sexuality and motherhood as icons that limit their identity.

The *Paris Review* Perspective _____

Chloë Schama for *The Paris Review*

"Why did I work so hard to buy a house with a furnace so she could go backwards and live like this?" Sandra Cisneros's father exclaimed when confronted with her first apartment, warmed only by a space heater. "*Mija*," he asked her every week, "when are you coming home?"

Why do writers choose to be writers? Parental pressures are often deterrent forces; with good intentions, mothers and fathers conspire to inform their children of the hardships of the writer's life—the solitude, the poverty, the inescapability of the work. The necessary deprivations of the young writer's life are a cause of explicit sorrow, and the felt importance of writing, compared to professions directly addressing obvious worldly suffering, adds another layer of insecurity.

"Should she give up writing and study something useful like medicine?" Cisneros wondered in her early years, recalled in the introduction to the twenty-fifth anniversary edition of the still-moving and spirited *The House on Mango Street*. To make a living, the young Cisneros taught students who had dropped out of high school but were pursuing their diplomas, students who managed to make it to her classroom only by skirting gangs, avoiding abusive boyfriends, and convincing their parents that a degree was worth more than a minimum-wage income. "Should she be teaching these students to write poetry when they need to know how to defend themselves from someone beating them up?" she asks. Could writing be any more sensible for her?

Writing the fragments that would evolve into *The House on Mango Street,* Cisneros sat alone in her drafty apartment "under the circle of light from a cheap metal lamp clamped to the kitchen table . . . with paper and pen and pretends she's not afraid. She's trying to live like a writer." That effort was driven not only by ambition but also by a feeling of necessity. In her twenties, Cisneros would gather with other writers who shared a "sense that art should serve our communities," a sense that well-being is not confined to physical safety but extends to the ability to communicate. Together with these writers, Cisneros published a collection of writing, *Emergency Tacos*, titled to invoke the *taquería* that fueled their nightly work and also the urgency of their endeavor. They completed this writing because, as she puts it, "The world we live in is a house on fire and the people we love are burning."

In *The House on Mango Street,* it is the women and girls, in particular, who are in danger of going up in flames—having their spirits extinguished by confinement and male control. That plight is embodied by the figure of a woman looking out the window, removed from the world but longing to take part in it. A young neighbor is "still young but getting old from leaning out the window" since her husband won't let her out of the house. The narrator's grandmother "looked out the window her whole life, the way so many women sit their sadness on an elbow." This figure has deep roots, ranging from Penelope to Shakespeare and Tennyson's Mariana, but Cisneros's women are her own. Sally, a girl with "eyes like Egypt" and raven-black hair, is so eager to get away from her bully father that she marries a marshmallow salesman and runs away to "another state where it's legal to get married before eighth grade," then spends the rest of her life looking at the linoleum roses printed on her kitchen tiles—an even more two-dimensional view than the "glooming flats" that greeted Tennyson's heroine.

The political imperatives of *The House on Mango Street* have come to be among its most celebrated characteristics. Perpetually popular and widely translated, the novel has become an emblem of the shifting and broadening of the American canon, which has embraced, in the years since the book was first published, a growing number of female writers and developed, as a perhaps more personal credit to Cisneros, an increasing emphasis on the Chicano voice. Such status, however, can be both a blessing and a curse. Symbols of political movements date much faster than great works of literature.

But along with the polemical and feminist elements of *Mango Street*, its urgency has a less complicated and more universal basis; it is driven by the urge to capture fleeting moments of beauty, comedy, and unassuming strength. *The House on Mango Street* celebrates the rarity of these moments and gives the impression that ordinary life, even in a crowded house on a gritty urban street, is packed full of them. On Mango Street there are the two little black dogs that "don't walk like ordinary dogs, but leap and somersault like an apostrophe and comma," trees that "grow up and . . . grow down and grab the earth between their hairy toes and bite the sky," and a cloud overhead that looks like a "sphinx winking." The narrator, Esperanza, is not the only one attuned to such pleasures in the everyday. "The moon is beautiful like a balloon," says the hapless Ruthie. When there is no moon, there are silly dogs, inspiring trees, and mysteries in the sky. "Butterflies are too few and so are flowers and most things that are beautiful," writes Cisneros. "Still, we take what we can get and make the best of it."

There is a third component to the felt urgency of *Mango Street*. While Cisneros could try to ignore her disapproving father, she could not vanquish the voices in her head that compelled her to write. As a child she desired a house that was bigger and better than the house on Mango Street; as an adult she desired a place where she could "be quiet and still and listen to the voices inside herself." Her young narrator experiences the same perpetual internal narration. "I like to tell stories," she states; "I tell them inside my head. I tell them after the mailman says, Here's your mail. Here's your mail, he said." Writers do this for practice; they do it because it captures reality, and because it improves on reality. A jumping dog becomes a comma in the air; scraggly trees become pillars of strength; a brown shoe an evocation of disappointment. "I make a story for my life," writes Cisneros, "for each step my brown shoe takes. I say, 'And so she trudged up the wooden stairs, her sad brown shoes taking her to the house she never liked.'"

"You must keep writing. It will keep you free," says Esperanza's aunt in *The House on Mango Street*. This is the advice that the adult Cisneros took to heart, seeking out a room of her own, despite her father's objections, to craft her stories. The novel is a bildungsroman for a young writer, exploring the tension between comfortable confinement and expressive liberty, charting how one girl approaches the knowledge that the alternative to staring sadly out the window involves listening for quiet voices, seeking the "too few" moments of beauty, and looking at a blank piece of paper in search of an infinite vista.

CRITICAL CONTEXTS

Midwest Raíces:
Sandra Cisneros's *The House on Mango Street*_____
Amelia María de la Luz Montes

In 2005, Garrison Keillor, best known for his radio program *A Prairie Home Companion*, launched a radio series called *Literary Friendships* as a way to showcase well-known authors and place a spotlight on literature. "Inspired by famous literary companions such as F. Scott Fitzgerald and Ernest Hemingway or Gertrude Stein and Thornton Wilder," Keillor, according to the *Los Angeles Times*, designed each episode to feature "two noted writers who are also close friends, discussing their craft," as well as how their friendship has strengthened their writing. He intended the show to shatter the stereotype of the lone writer working in isolation from his or her peers. Among the show's participants was Sandra Cisneros, who had chosen the Muscogee poet and musician Joy Harjo to join her. The two had been friends for more than twenty years.

Cisneros led the conversation by discussing how she and Harjo had met when they were students at the prestigious Iowa Writers' Workshop at the University of Iowa. Keillor was quite interested in their experiences and lauded the workshop as the best in the country. However, Cisneros recounted the difficult experiences both she and Harjo endured at Iowa. Cisneros remarked:

> Well, it was like . . . when you said something in class, there was a silence in the room. [to Harjo] Do you remember that? I came with all the courage I had. I didn't have any feelings to feel defensive. But when I said something, there'd be this absolute silence. And you just felt like: Did I say something wrong?

Keillor, assuming that Cisneros's and Harjo's classmates were all from the Midwest, suddenly took their side. He chided: "We may be like that in the Midwest, however."

Cisneros took a breath, then quietly said, "Well I thought *I* was from the Midwest. I come from Chicago" (*Literary Friendships*).

The audience roared with laughter at Keillor's obvious mistake and applauded Cisneros's defense of her midwestern heritage. Yet, did the audience really understand the irony here or were they laughing and applauding at the mistake many people make about who counts as a midwesterner? Does Cisneros's black hair and brown skin, which is often adorned with silver jewelry and colorful rebozos, point to what is considered midwestern? "I thought *I* was from the Midwest," she said to the hundreds of people listening in on the program that day. The greatest irony in this exchange is the fact that Cisneros's most well-known book, *The House on Mango Street*, is clearly set in the Midwest—in Chicago. And this irony underlines the mistake often made regarding the character and racial background of the typical midwestern American. This essay places a careful lens on the geographic location of *The House on Mango Street* and Cisneros's Latino characters who inhabit this space in order to reveal how the novel's interrelated stories create a specific midwestern "house" with universal themes regarding class, race, and gender.

Theorists and scholars such as Catrióna Rueda Esquibel, Leslie Petty, and Monika Kaup have explored issues of friendship, homosocial relations, and female sexuality against the backdrop of Cisneros's multiple meanings of "house." Petty writes:

> It is Esperanza's dream for a house, a dream inextricably linked with her poetry. . . . In such a metaphorical space, Esperanza can create for herself an identity that reconciles the violation and pain that she associates with Mango Street as well as the responsibility she feels to nurture and aid her community. (130)

Petty's essay resonates with Esquibel's, which investigates the way characters such as Sally and Esperanza negotiate their friendship within a heterosocial working-class environment that causes tension and painful moments between them. The social and familial expectations of normative behavior hinder characters such as Sally from becoming fully actualized individuals. These expectations become an oppressive "house" for them. It is Esperanza who observes them with a keen eye and a desire that her future not duplicate such a "household" environment. Kaup takes a more political view. She points out that Cisneros's "house" is a central location for Chicano literature to investigate not only issues of identity but also questions of nationalism:

> With the transition from the heroic mode of Chicano nationalism of the early seventies to the more ironic and contingent mode of the present, a shift in symbols has occurred in which we find that the focus has passed from land, a central symbol of Chicano nationalism indebted to the notions of *tierra* and Aztlán (the Chicano homeland), to houses. (363)

In all of these essays, the question of house, identity, and friendship is explored but without really articulating it from the vantage point of geographic location.

In their article "Latinos and the Changing Demographic Fabric of the Rural Midwest," Jorge Chapa and his colleagues write:

> Since the 1980s, the Midwest has received substantial migration of Mexican Americans from the Southwest, as well as increasing immigration directly from Mexico (Saenz and Cready 1996). Census data show that the rate of immigration to the Midwest is increasing. At the time of the 2000 census, 47 percent of immigrants in the Midwest had arrived in the United States in the past 10 years. (49)

Yet though these were new immigrants—and though Cisneros's work was not published until 1984—Latinos had long before been present in the Midwest and on the Great Plains and even appeared in literature set in the Midwest. Jim Burden, a character in Nebraska writer Willa

Cather's novel *My Ántonia*, remembers learning about the Spanish explorer Coronado coming to the Midwest:

> A farmer in the county north of ours, when he was breaking sod, had turned up a metal stirrup of fine workmanship, and a sword with a Spanish inscription on the blade. . . . Father Kelly, the priest, has found the name of the Spanish maker on the sword, and an abbreviation that stood for the city of Cordova. (236)

Cather, in effect, describes a Spanish colonizer on Midwest lands. Yet Mexicans and Latinos to arrive at the turn of the twentieth century—mestizos—would be considered quite differently from Coronado. Chicano scholar Rafael Grajeda, in his article "Chicanos: The Mestizo Heritage," writes:

> It is more than a curiosity of history that the two entrances into the Central Plains by the Spanish speaking people were so strikingly dissimilar. . . . That the original explorers of the Central Plains were Spanish conquistadores, and the later immigrants were Mexican mestizos, is—in its irony—further instructive, for the very conditions of the poor in Mexico—those conditions which to a large degree "pushed" these people to the north—can be traced to the conquest and later colonization of that country by the very same conquistadores. (51)

It is this "mestizo" history that Cisneros inherits growing up in Chicago, and it is her experience of this history that gives rise to an articulation and creation of a Mango Street that illustrates one of many contemporary mestizo experiences in the Midwest. *The House on Mango Street* shatters the myth that Latinos live only on the East or West Coast. Yet if even well-known media commentators such as Garrison Keillor make such glaring mistakes in thinking Latinos like Cisneros are not midwestern, there is still more education to be done to shatter such myths.

Scholars Ann V. Millard, Jorge Chapa, and Eileen Diaz McConnell challenge myths regarding Latinos within the United States. In an article describing "ten myths about Latinos," they trace the twentieth-century Latino presence in the Midwest:

> The sugar beet migration to the Midwest occurred from 1917 to 1929. . . . The Bracero Program followed, recruiting workers from Mexico for agricultural work throughout the United States (1943-1964). . . . The Immigration Reform and Control Act of 1986 offered legal residency. . . . During the 1990s, the U.S. Immigration and Naturalization Service was commanded not to deport Latinos who lacked authorization as long as they held jobs. Mexican migration to the Midwest thus has continued for over a century, has usually occurred as a result of vigorous recruitment by employers, and has often contributed to economic growth in the region. (23)

By establishing a historical preface regarding Latino presence in the Midwest, we can then proceed to investigate how Cisneros weaves her Mango Street characters into a specific midwestern urban landscape many literary critics have continued to ignore. By foregrounding this specific landscape that Cisneros recalls and creates, the individual struggles and poignant moments each character experiences contribute to the larger canon of Midwest stories.

Cisneros begins her book with a description of the neighborhood around Mango Street, because the narrator, Esperanza, has lived on many other streets, such as Loomis, Keeler, and Paulina. Her neighborhood is based on the actual Chicago working-class neighborhood where Cisneros grew up: Humboldt Park, which hosts the Puerto Rican Day Parade and Mexican Independence Day as well as the Irish Pride Parade. At Esperanza's house on Mango Street, "There is no front yard, only four little elms the city planted by the curb. Out back is a small garage for the car we don't own yet and a small yard that looks smaller between the two buildings on either side" (4).[1] The four elms appear at the beginning and toward the end of the book. According to horticulturist and photographer Susan A. Roth, the healthy elm's "tall, stout trunk splits into several leaders that grow upward. . . . This tree's high, spreading canopy makes it ideal for shading streets because traffic can flow easily beneath its branches" (299). However, the elms in the chapter titled "Four Skinny Trees" are far from "stout." Esperanza describes them as "four skinny trees with skinny necks and pointy elbows like mine. Four who do not belong here but are here. Four raggedy excuses planted by the city" (74). Yet despite their "raggedy" appearance, despite Esperanza's observations that they "do not belong" the way she does not belong, Esperanza proclaims their power:

> Their strength is secret. They send ferocious roots beneath the ground. They grow up and they grow down and grab the earth between their hairy toes and bite the sky with violent teeth and never quit their anger. This is how they keep. Let one forget his reason for being, they'd all droop like tulips in a glass, each with their arms around the other. Keep, keep, keep, trees say when I sleep. They teach. (74-75)

The reader, then, is placed within a working-class midwestern neighborhood—urban, poor, "raggedy"—and yet Esperanza, even in the midst of all the painful stories happening up and down the block and around the circumference of these trees, finds in her neighborhood the beauty and potency of the natural world. Sally, Minerva, Rafaela, and Mamacita are all like the trees—at times hardly surviving, struggling at best, yet holding on to each other.

In his article "Keeping Her Distance: Cisneros, Dickinson, and the Politics of Private Enjoyment," Geoffrey Sanborn points out the stark differences between Cisneros's descriptions of her natural environment and those of the nineteenth-century poet Emily Dickinson. Sanborn writes:

Cisneros turns our attention from the easily idealized survival strategies of natural objects . . . to the compromised struggles of human beings. When Dickinson communes with antiteleological existence, the objects of her attention are usually . . . things outside human society. . . . Dickinson sustains the mystification of race and class privileges and . . . her private poetic project is disengaged from meaningful political action. (1344-45)

After Sanborn's argument, how interesting, then, it is to return to Cisneros's appearance on Garrison Keillor's show, when she described how her classmates at the Iowa Writers' Workshop became silent when Cisneros tried to contribute to the conversation. These were students, Cisneros later explains, who were privileged and could not relate to her. In interviews with Chicano scholar Hector A. Torres, Cisneros has elaborated on how these difficult class discussions led her to begin writing *The House on Mango Street*. At one point in her studies there, the class was reading Gaston Bachelard's book *The Poetics of Space*. Cisneros recalls reacting to her classmates' excited discussion about the book:

I remember my face feeling hot. . . . Even though you're brown, you feel browner . . . and it occurred to me . . . that there was something about me that was different from everyone in the room and the thing that triggered it was that they were talking about houses. They were talking about the house of their memory, the attic of their memories, and the basement of their childhood. Well, I don't want to talk about the basement of my childhood because there were rats there! [Laughing] I don't want to go near those basements and we lived in third-floor flats and we didn't have attics. Who in the hell had an attic! And then all of a sudden it occurred to me in that moment that I don't have a house of childhood. All I have are some apartments. . . . It suddenly occurred to me . . . that whatever they wrote about, I'd write about the opposite. If they wrote about swans then I would make sure I'd write about a rat in my poem. If they wrote about a cupola, then I was going to write about a porch to counter them. That's when I found my voice. (199-200)

Cisneros's reaction to the predominantly white and privileged students helped her develop descriptions of the Chicago working-class neighborhoods with which she was familiar. She began to write what she knew—the spaces within and outside of the Chicago midwestern working-class house.

Looking more closely at *The House on Mango Street,* outside of the house, the narrator, Esperanza, observes more than the trees. In the piece titled "Laughter," Esperanza feels that one of the houses in their neighborhood is like the houses she has seen in Mexico. Here she makes a link to her American *and* Mexican heritage. Rachel and Lucy do not believe her. But it is Nenny, Esperanza's sister, who agrees with her observation, creating a moment of familial solidarity, of sisterhood, while creating symbolic comparisons across borderlands. In "Meme Ortiz" Esperanza notices how much smaller her house looks from Meme's huge tree in his backyard, a tree that holds "many families of squirrels" and towers over "mostly dirt, and a greasy bunch of boards" (22). This tree is a house of refuge that also portends danger: a fall from its protective limbs would break a bone. The tension in each story is emphasized with looks, descriptions, dialogue, a tragic action or simply by watching the clouds.

Descriptions of clouds and the sky in two consecutive chapters, "Darius and the Clouds" and "And Some More," again connect to distinctly human concerns, such as security and happiness. "Here there is too much sadness and not enough sky," Esperanza tells us. "Still, we take what we can get and make the best of it" (33). The beauty Esperanza notices is often not far from what is unsavory or ugly. For example, Esperanza notices the "flowerboxes Edna paints green each year," in the piece "The Earl of Tennessee," but along with these flower boxes is a cockroach Tito saw "with a spot of green paint on its head" (70). The appearance of a cockroach is often a cliché in descriptions of poor neighborhoods, but here the cockroach seems to portend growth and beauty. It, too, has caught a bit of paint, slightly transforming it as if it could somehow too become a thing of beauty. This is the backdrop to the Earl who brings prostitutes home to his dark apartment. Esperanza and her friends think he's married, but they cannot agree on what his wife looks like since most nights he comes home with a different woman. The children's innocence beautifies Earl's loss of innocence.

The contrasts between beauty and the grotesque, wealth and squalor, kindness and violence in just a few lines of description or dialogue create a complex and rich midwestern landscape and characters who are far from any homogenous description. This is certainly not Emily Dickinson's world even though, at times, Esperanza is provided a glimpse of such a life. In "Bums in the Attic," Papa takes the family up the hill where he goes to work. It is not clear what Papa does. Is he a landscaper for these wealthy people's gardens or does he clean the inside of their homes? Esperanza writes:

> I want a house on a hill like the ones with the gardens where Papa works. . . . People who live on hills sleep so close to the stars they forget those of us who live too much on earth. They don't look down at all except to be content to live on hills. They have nothing to do with last week's garbage or fear of rats. (86-87)

And in dreaming of such a life, Esperanza more than once says, "I won't forget who I am or where I came from" (87). Esperanza will have an attic like the attics of Cisneros's classmates described at Iowa, but, unlike anyone else, she will open her door to the homeless and make her space into a shelter for others. "Some days after dinner, guests and I will sit in front of a fire. Floorboards will squeak upstairs. The attic grumble. Rats? They'll ask. Bums, I'll say, and I'll be happy" (87).

Finally, Cisneros places the most emphasis on the natural world in "The Monkey Garden," in which she describes at length the kinds of flowers, insects, and small mammals she and her friends find in the garden: "There were sunflowers big as flowers on Mars and thick cockscombs bleeding the deep red fringe of theater curtains. . . . Thorn roses and thistle and pears. Weeds like so many squinty-eyed stars and brush that made your ankles itch and itch" (94-95). The cockscomb she describes is specifically the crested celosia, which "look[s] like big brain corals," according to gardener Frances Manos, who was born in Chicago and now lives an hour west of the city in Saint Charles (100). The crested celosia is just as Cisneros describes it in her piece: the flowers are velvety, brightly colored waves, the "deep red fringe of theater curtains." It is a hardy plant that would certainly grow in an unruly yard between crumbling buildings alongside "thorn roses and thistle" and weeds. In Cisneros's Monkey Garden are also "dusty hollyhocks thick and perfumy like the blue-blond hair of the dead" (95). Like the crested celosia, hollyhocks are hardy and can survive with little maintenance. As it does on Mango Street, life continues on in this garden where dead mice are found and abandoned cars suddenly appear, making it an ideal setting for the testing of Esperanza's love for Sally. Among the disheveled foliage and blooms and the hulls of old autos, Esperanza takes a brick to hurl at the boys who are threatening to kiss her Sally; yet, before she can throw it, she sees both them and Sally laughing at her and she learns the hard truth about deception.

Esquibel, a theorist and literary scholar, best explains the tension between Esperanza and Sally:

Sexuality—heterosexuality—however it is naturalized, defined, and promoted, remains outside the realm of Esperanza's understanding. . . . The joke is heterosexuality: it's fun, it's funny, it's a game they all know. And yet, like Nenny singing her childish rhyme, oblivious to the advantages of hips, Esperanza lives in a world that does not accommodate such things. Heterosexuality is, throughout the novel, a brutal intrusion into the world of girls. (655)

In the end, Sally marries before entering high school and becomes enclosed in a house, disengaged completely from the outside world unless her husband allows her to go out. She has the furniture and requisite cooking utensils, but Cisneros paints a sad picture of her life. For

Esquibel, it is in this story (as well as "Red Clowns") that Esperanza "passes out of adolescence, not in the patriarchal sense of 'being made a woman' through intercourse with a man, but because she is passed over in favor of a male and then subsequently used for male pleasure" (657). The garden is no longer a site for play, only painful memories. And each flower described in the garden symbolizes the beauty and pain that come with Esperanza's coming-of-age in a working-class midwestern neighborhood. Yet, in this neighborhood, and in many others like them near city centers and downtowns across the country, the working class are being pressured to leave. Hints of gentrification are apparent in Cisneros's book.

Latina scholar Mérida M. Rúa's work on gentrification in Chicago reveals that the neighborhood Cisneros describes in her book—Humboldt Park—is slowly being transformed. Rúa writes, "Today, the city is viewed less and less as a place for working poor and working-class Latinos and other people of color" (87). The population being forced out by gentrification and settling in suburban areas is largely people of color; it is a mostly white, young adult population that is moving into the city centers and encouraging large condominium-type housing. Rúa's study of urban development and gentrification led her to interview a number of Latinos in and around Humboldt Park. One of the Latinas she interviewed was Valeria Girón. Rúa writes:

> A former Palmer Square resident, Valeria Girón was a tenant for over twenty years of the building on Humboldt Boulevard and Shakespeare. . . . She received a letter from the new property owner notifying her that she had a year to find other housing accommodations because the building was to undergo renovations. With renovations complete, "affordable" apartments are currently advertised at a range from $1100 to $1800 a month. The lowest priced apartments rent at slightly less than double the amount Valeria paid as a tenant. . . . Not able to find reasonable rental property in the area, Valeria purchased a bungalow style home in a far Northwest neighborhood following a Latino trend westward. (81-82)

Cisneros's *The House on Mango Street* may more obviously portray the Humboldt Park of working-class neighborhoods in the Midwest, but it also points to the disruption of people's lives due to hasty city planning, developers hungry to buy old buildings, rebuild on the cheap, and sell new housing for a much higher price. In Cisneros's stories, the "house" is a slippery sign that marks a personal identity as well as a variety of shifting social and psychological landscapes: childhood and adulthood; the working class and middle class; sexual freedom and sexual regulation. In *Extinct Lands, Temporal Geographies*, Mary Pat Brady emphasizes, "The processes of producing space, however quotidian or grand, hidden or visible, have an enormous effect on subject formation—on the choices people can make and how they conceptualize themselves, each other, and the world" (7-8). Cisneros has recorded these effects with a keen eye.

Interestingly, when *The House on Mango Street* was first published by Arte Público Press its cover more closely matched the story's Chicago's urban framework. The 1989 cover superimposes an illustration of two little girls' faces over an illustrated neighborhood street. The four flimsy elm trees Cisneros describes in the first story are to the left of the picture and above Cisneros's name. The girls' faces are slightly elongated, as if they have been caught running by a high-speed camera, giving a feeling of movement. Coming down the street is the CTA, or L Train, and, to the right, are the many tall apartment buildings packed like sardines one after the other, some leaning one way, others imposing and dark. Rusty reds, greens, and yellows give the drawing a humid, afternoon tone, as if the sun were about to set. The artist, Alejandro Romero, is a Latino muralist who has studied in Mexico, Paris, New Mexico, and the Art Institute of Chicago. While in Chicago, he lived in the Pilsen neighborhood, not far from Humboldt. His drawing reflects his own lived experience near the South Side of Chicago.

In contrast, on the cover of the 1991 Vintage edition of *The House on Mango Street* is a much more stylized painting of three women by

Nivia Gonzalez. The women's eyes are closed, and one drapes a veil over another. Somber but powerful and emphasizing the women's solitude, it seems entirely suitable for Federico García Lorca's play about enclosed domestics: *La casa de Bernarda Alba*. The mood is much more peaceful and serene; the three women are clearly not children, and there is no hint that the story is set in Chicago. Unlike Romero, Gonzalez was born and raised in the United States, in San Antonio, Texas; she attended Cooper Union in Greenwich Village and later received her master's degree in art at the University of Texas at Austin.

When I teach the book in undergraduate courses, I often show students the two covers and ask them for their opinions about the two artists' interpretations of the novel. More often than not, the students choose to discuss at length Romero's cover. They point to its playfulness, and, more often than not, they argue that Romero is speaking from a sense of place, a knowledge of a geographic space: the working-class neighborhood of Chicago's South Side. Had this cover stayed on *The House on Mango Street*, perhaps readers would have a more literal picture to go along with the very visual and poetic language Cisneros offers. Then maybe someone such as Garrison Keillor would not have made such a glaring mistake about Cisneros's geographic background. More important, Romero's cover emphasizes what Cisneros learned from her days at Iowa—to create from what you know. Esperanza's world begins with what Cisneros knew, and, in Cisneros's brilliant hands, it takes on a more universal language and symbolism. The Midwest, while remaining a particular place, takes on universal import.

In "Born Bad" Esperanza describes visiting her blind aunt who "never saw the dirty dishes in the sink. She couldn't see the ceilings dusty with flies, the ugly maroon walls, the bottles and sticky spoons" (60). Nevertheless, Esperanza goes to visit her and reads her library books, one of which is Charles Kingsley's *The Water-Babies*, a British novel. In it, a working-class boy saves an upper-class girl and, in saving her, falls into the river and dies. He becomes a water-baby and embarks on a moral education, and, through his life and education,

Kingsley questions British child labor laws and criticizes how the poor are treated in England. Esperanza loves the story and so does her aunt. In many ways, Cisneros has spent her writing life doing just the same: daring to and successfully articulating the world from which one Latina has emerged. She has created a midwestern space that readers can interpret as also theirs.

Note

1. All quotations in the text from *The House on Mango Street* are from the 1991 Vintage Books edition.

Works Cited

Betancur, John J. "The Settlement Experience of Latinos in Chicago: Segregation, Speculation, and the Ecology Model." *Social Forces* 74.4 (1996): 1299-1324.

Brady, Mary Pat. *Extinct Lands, Temporal Geographies: Chicana Literature and the Urgency of Space.* Durham, NC: Duke UP, 2002.

Cather, Willa. *My Ántonia.* 1918. Ed. Charles Mignon. Lincoln: U of Nebraska P, 1994.

Chapa, Jorge, Rogelio Saenz, Refugio I. Rochín, and Eileen Diaz McConnell. "Latinos and the Changing Demographic Fabric of the Rural Midwest." *Apple Pie and Enchiladas: Latino Newcomers in the Rural Midwest.* Ed. Ann V. Millard and Jorge Chapa. Austin: U of Texas P, 2004. 47-73.

Cisneros, Sandra. *The House on Mango Street.* 1984. Houston: Arte Público Press, 1989.

_____. *The House on Mango Street.* 1984. New York: Vintage Books, 1991.

Esquibel, Catrióna Rueda. "Memories of Girlhood: Chicana Lesbian Fictions." *Signs* 23.3 (1998): 645-82.

"Garrison Keillor Celebrates Literary Pals." *Los Angeles Times.* 18 Nov. 2004. 12 Apr. 2010. http://articles.latimes.com/2004/nov/18/news/wk-quick18.

Grajeda, Rafael. "Chicanos: The Mestizo Heritage." *Broken Hoops and Plains People.* Lincoln: Nebraska Curriculum Development Center, 1976.

Kaup, Monika. "The Architecture of Ethnicity in Chicano Literature." *American Literature* 69.2 (1997): 361-97.

Literary Friendships with Garrison Keillor. Air date 17 May 2005. 12 Apr. 2010. http://literaryfriendships.publicradio.org.

Manos, Frances. *Midwest Cottage Gardening.* Boulder, CO: Trails Books, 2004.

Millard, Ann V., Jorge Chapa, and Eileen Diaz McConnell. "En Pocas Palabras [In a Few Words] I: Ten Myths About Latinos." *Apple Pie and Enchiladas: Latino Newcomers in the Rural Midwest.* Ed. Ann V. Millard and Jorge Chapa. Austin: U of Texas P, 2004. 22-25.

Petty, Leslie. "The 'Dual'-ing Images of la Malinche and la Virgen de Guadalupe in Cisneros's *The House on Mango Street." MELUS* 25.2 (2000): 119-32.

Roth, Susan A. *Taylor's Guide to Trees.* New York: Houghton Mifflin Harcourt, 2001.

Rúa, Mérida M. "Claims to the City: Puerto Rican Latinidad Amid Labors of Identity, Community, and Belonging in Chicago." Ph.D. dissertation, University of Michigan, 2004.

Sanborn, Geoffrey. "Keeping Her Distance: Cisneros, Dickinson, and the Politics of Private Enjoyment." *PMLA* 116.5 (2001): 1334-48.

Saenz, Rogelio, and Cynthia M. Cready. "The Southwest-Midwest Mexican American Migration Flows, 1985-1990." Paper presented at the annual meeting of the Rural Sociological Society, Des Moines, Iowa, 1996.

Torres, Hector A. "Sandra Cisneros: Two Interviews." *Conversations with Contemporary Chicana and Chicano Writers.* Albuquerque: U of New Mexico P, 2007.

The Critical Reception of
*The House on Mango Street*_____

Amy Sickels

While Sandra Cisneros was enrolled in the master of fine arts program in fiction at the prestigious University of Iowa Writers' Workshop in the late 1970s, she, in her words, for the first time "felt the other" ("Ghosts and Voices" 72) when she noticed that the majority of her classmates were middle-class and Caucasian. Cisneros's ethnicity and background as a Mexican American raised in a working-class Latino neighborhood in Chicago set her apart; she felt insecure about her differences and tried to fit in by emulating the writing of her professors and classmates. Then, during her second year in the program, Cisneros had an epiphany that helped her develop as a writer and also led her to the stories of *The House on Mango Street*. She and her classmates were assigned Gaston Bachelard's *The Poetics of Space*, and during their discussion of the book, as her classmates spoke fondly of their childhood homes, Cisneros realized, "I don't have a house of childhood. All I have are some apartments. That's when everything slammed into me at that moment. I decided then that I didn't even like the stuff they were writing and trying to imitate" (Torres 199). The place where she was from flashed in her mind: "The metaphor of a house—a house, a house, it hit me. What did I know except third-floor flats. Surely my classmates knew nothing about that" ("Ghosts and Voices" 73). She recounts, "It was at that moment I realized I had a lot of stuff to write about" (Torres 200). While at Iowa in 1977, she wrote some of the earliest sketches that would inform *The House on Mango Street* and then wrote the majority of the vignettes between 1979 and 1981.

After three years of writing, rewriting, and revising the vignettes, Cisneros sent them Nicolás Kanellos, founder and editor of Arte Público Press, a small press affiliated with the University of Houston. The press published *The House on Mango Street* in 1984 and announced its new emphasis on women's literary writing at the National

Association for Chicano Studies Conference, where *The House on Mango Street*, along with four other books by Chicana writers, was featured. At that point, outside of small Chicano literary circles, nobody had heard of Cisneros, and few even knew about the press. *Mango Street* won the Before Columbus Foundation's American Book Award in 1985 and had gone into its third printing by 1987. In 1991, Vintage Contemporaries reissued the book, drawing more publicity and an even wider readership. Nearly twenty years later, *Mango Street* has sold more than two million copies and is commonly found on grade school, high school, and college reading lists. Cisneros is one of today's most prominent Chicana writers. Her publications include three collections of poetry as well as the acclaimed short-story collection *Woman Hollering Creek, and Other Stories* and a novel, *Caramelo*, both of which were reviewed widely in newspapers across the United States. By the mid-1990s, although her publication list was not large, Cisneros was well established in the literary world. *The House on Mango Street* has received more critical attention than any other Chicana novel and is Cisneros's most widely read book. In the spring of 2009, a twenty-fifth anniversary edition was released, generating a new round of publicity for the book.

Critical discussion of *Mango Street* started slowly but took off in the 1990s with the emergence of multiculturalism and as debates about the literary canon grew prominent in academic discourse. The initial response to *Mango Street* came primarily from Chicano/a critics, but in a short time, as *Mango Street* grew in popularity, the critical response expanded across academia. Today a search of the MLA database for scholarly articles on *Mango Street* will return more than one hundred articles from both English- and Spanish-language journals. In twenty-six years of overwhelmingly positive criticism, feminists, Latino studies scholars, and literary scholars with interests in feminism and cultural studies have written the majority of the scholarship on *Mango Street*. The bulk of this criticism focuses on the protagonist's understanding of her identity and how it relates to questions of gender, class, and ethnicity. The novel's universal themes, combined with a narrative built on the specificity of gender and ethnic identity, has made *Mango Street* both a representative text for multicultural literature and also a rich text for critical examination. This chapter examines the history and current state of the critical reception to *Mango Street* while highlighting the main topics that the two and a half decades of scholarship address.

In order to understand fully the significance of *The House on Mango Street*'s popular and critical success, one must look briefly at the context and time of its publication. Before Arte Público Press published Cisneros, only a few Chicano authors were known in the United States, all of them male. Tomás Rivera, Rudolfo Anaya, and Raymond Barrio, for example, were all a part of the Chicano canon, which came out of the Chicano movement of the 1960s and early 1970s, an extension of the Mexican American civil rights movement. The Chicano movement had inspired Chicano social and political activism, cultural pride, and the development and recognition of Chicano art and writing. However, although women were deeply involved in the movement, the Chicano canon consisted only of male authors. By the mid-1970s, Chicana feminists, in reaction to this exclusion and influenced in part by the women's movement, were beginning to publish their work in journals and newsletters, advocating *la nueva chicana*, or the new Chicana. As Ramón Saldívar explains, much of this writing, in addition to critiquing the dominant American culture, was critical of the patriarchal aspects of Mexican American culture: "Contemporary Chicana writers challenge not only the ideologies of oppression of the Anglo-American culture that their Chicano brothers confront, but they also challenge the ideologies of patriarchal expression evinced by Chicano writers and present within Chicano culture itself" (173). This critique was controversial, as some feared that it would break apart the movement. Yet by the 1980s, Chicana writers were leaving a mark that could not be ignored, and, as Carmen Haydée Rivera has observed, the Chicano canon began to grow and "shift from a male-centered ideology emphasizing race, class, and political struggle to a female subjectivity that stressed a new politicized personal identity" (3).

Throughout the 1980s and 1990s, as Latino studies became more accepted in universities, critics and writers examined the emergence of Chicana literature and attempted to articulate and define Chicana poetics. *Mango Street* was regarded as a text that exemplified and popularized the most significant themes of Chicana literature. As Rivera states:

> By bringing gender issues and questions of sexuality and female oppression to the forefront, Chicana writers broadened the thematic space of Chicano/a literature. In portraying and interrogating gender specific roles for women in Latina/o culture, Chicanas introduced a new dimension to the concept of resistance. (3)

The Chicana writers' work not only expanded the voice of Chicano literature but also garnered popular and critical support that extended beyond Chicano circles. The work of Chicano feminist writers began appearing on reading lists for Chicano, Latino, and feminist studies, and, by the late 1980s, the most recognized authors of Chicano literature were women. Other authors, in addition to Cisneros, who were being noticed by critics and who continue to be read today include Ana Castillo, Helena María Viramontes, Cherríe Moraga, and Gloria Anzaldúa. These Chicana authors, like their male counterparts, examined the oppressions and ideologies of race and class, but they also challenged the ideologies of patriarchal oppression and brought to the forefront questions about what Chicana feminist critic Gloria Anzaldúa calls the "borders"—the boundaries of gender, race, and class. With *Mango Street*, explains critic Alvina E. Quintana, Cisneros "flung down the gauntlet, challenging, at the least, accepted literary form, gender inequalities, and the cultural and economic subordination of minorities" (55).

When *Mango Street* was first published in 1984, only a few brief reviews appeared; critical response was also minimal. It was not until two years later that academics began to take notice of the novel with essays focused on the innovation of its form; by 1988, academics were examining Cisneros's feminist and cultural poetics. *The House on Mango Street* grew in popularity during the 1990s during the height of the controversy over multiculturalism and also as Latino/a authors were transitioning from small presses to major publishing houses. Oscar Hijuelos's *The Mambo Kings Play Songs of Love*, which won the Pulitzer Prize in 1990, brought new attention to Latino/a authors, and as Latino/authors expanded beyond Spanish speakers and Latino audiences, they also began to receive more critical attention.

At the same time, university English departments around the country were expanding to include feminist and cultural studies, and more academics were working to legitimate the work of women and minority writers as worthy of scholarly attention. Feminist and cultural literary critics embraced *Mango Street* for depicting a marginalized community rarely presented in American literature and for its sympathetic portrayal of a strong, perceptive young Chicana narrator. Certainly, the bulk of the critical response to *Mango Street* during the 1990s emerged from these fields. Throughout the decade, articles on the novel appeared in critical monographs and collections focused on Chicana literature or ethnic studies, such as *Chicana Creativity and Criticism: Charting New Frontiers in American Literature* (1988), edited by María Herrera-Sobek and Helena María Viramontes; *Breaking Boundaries: Latina Writing and Critical Readings* (1989), edited by Asunción Horno-Delgado and others; *Chicano Narrative: The Dialectics of Difference* (1990), by Ramón Saldívar; *Home Girls: Chicana Literary Voices* (1996), by Alvina E. Quintana; *Daughters of Self-Creation: The Contemporary Chicana Novel* (1996), by Annie O. Eysturoy; *Ethnicity and the American Short Story* (1997), edited by Julie Brown; and *The Latino/a Condition: A Critical Reader* (1998), edited by Richard Delgado and Jean Stefancic. A wide array of feminist monographs and essay collections also included studies on *Mango*

Street, such as *Haunting the House of Fiction: Feminist Perspectives on Ghost Stories by American Women* (1991), edited by Lynette Carpenter and Wendy K. Kolmar; *Anxious Power: Reading, Writing, and Ambivalence in Narrative by Women* (1993), edited by Carol J. Singley and Susan Elizabeth Sweeney; *Speaking the Other Self: American Women Writers* (1997), edited by Jeanne Campbell Reesman; and *Creating Safe Space: Violence and Women's Writing* (1998), edited by Julie Sharp and Tomoko Kuribayashi.

Important early articles that addressed *Mango Street* as a Chicana feminist text include Julián Olivares's "Sandra Cisneros's *The House on Mango Street,* and the Poetics of Space," which appeared in *Chicana Creativity and Criticism*, and María Elena de Valdés's "In Search of Identity in Cisneros's *The House on Mango Street*" (1992), which appeared in the *Canadian Review of American Studies.* Olivares takes a structural and thematic approach to the novel, arguing that Cisneros's house is constructed on Chicana feminist ideology, a different kind of space from Bachelard's house, which is built on patriarchal ideology; Valdés examines the poetics of a Chicana identity by looking at the novel's narrative voice and structure. Both of these articles were written at a time when critics and writers were developing a Chicana canon and addressing the complexities of Chicano/a ideology and poetics. They held up works by Castillo, Anzuldúa, and Cisneros as examples of narratives that wrestle with the ideological tensions of gender, race, class, nationality, ethnicity, sexuality, and education. An important contribution to this debate over Chicano/a poetics is Ramón Saldívar's *Chicano Narrative*, in which he argues that all of these ideological tensions must be taken into account before Chicana literature can be fully theorized. He includes a chapter examining *Mango Street*, along with work by Isabella Rios and Cherríe Moraga, as a new and crucial development in Chicano literature that disrupts and challenges hegemonic ideologies.

Feminist and cultural critical approaches often inform and overlap with each other, and the criticism on *Mango Street* is no exception. As critics recognize *Mango Street* for its unique presentation of a coming-of-age story of a young Chicana girl, and for its resistance of patriarchy and gender roles, they also praise it for challenging social, racial, and cultural borders. For many critics, as critic Yvonne Yarbro-Bejarano explains in her definition of Chicana feminist criticism, feminism and cultural criticism are bound up with each other: "The Chicana's experience as a woman is inextricable from her experience as a member of an oppressed working class racial minority and a culture which is not the dominant culture . . . elements of gender, race, culture and class coalesce" (213). According to Ramón Saldívar, *Mango Street* is a novel of resistance that "speak[s] to the harsh oppressiveness, an oppression within oppression, that women face in the day-to-day world of male-centered Mexican American society as they live out between worlds, cultures, and histories" (175).

In order to understand the growing presence of feminist and Chicana criticism in the 1990s, it is important to look back at the development of minority writing and its readership. It wasn't until the 1970s that both small and large publishing houses began to publish more minority writers, and with these publications critical response and scholarship also expanded. Yet the diversification of curriculum during the 1970s was met in the 1980s by conservative backlash that advocated a return to the classics and denounced multiculturalism as politically motivated. Alan Bloom's *The Closing of the American Mind* (1987) and E. D. Hirsch's *Cultural Literacy: What Every American Needs to Know* (1987), which both railed against the inclusion of noncanonical texts in high school and college curricula, were best sellers, and politicians and the media also jumped into the fray. In the midst of these "culture wars," even more minorities and women were being published, and many academics argued for their inclusion into the canon. Thus the scholarly interest in *Mango Street* came at a time when feminists and ethnic studies scholars, often within English departments, were developing the tenets of multiculturalism and trying to legitimate minority writers as a crucial part of the landscape of American literature.

An important early essay regarding *Mango Street*'s relation to the literary canon, Ellen McCracken's "Sandra Cisneros' *The House on Mango Street*: Community-Oriented Introspection and the Demystification of Patriarchal Violence," can be found in *Breaking Boundaries*. At the time of the essay, *Mango Street* was, within academia, still little known outside of Chicano circles, and McCracken, using a Marxist and feminist lens, describes how the book opposes the ideology of male-centered texts; according to her, the book was being ignored by traditional American literary critics because of its frank portrayal of patriarchal violence and its depiction of a poor Chicana girl who opposes this oppression and rises to a deeper understanding of herself and society. She explains, "In bold contrast to the individualistic introspection of many canonical texts, Cisneros writes a modified autobiographical novel, or *Bildungsroman*, that roots the individual self in the broader socio-political reality of the Chicano community" (63-64). Similarly, in an article published in the *English Journal* in 1992, Dianne Klein points out that Chicana coming-of-age stories were excluded from the American literary canon, which, until a shift in the late 1990s, was predominantly composed of white, heterosexual males. Klein shows how *Mango Street,* as a coming-of-age story with a female protagonist, differs from both white and Chicano male coming-of-age stories. This concept of "difference" is a major thread of *Mango Street* criticism, which in some ways parallels Cisneros's initial impetus behind the book: to define herself in opposition to her classmates. Yet, at the same time, *Mango Street* possesses universal appeal.

A principal way in which *Mango Street* is both different and yet similar to the "universal" themes of literature is in its narrative focus on identity—a topic of interest to critics of diverse perspectives. *Mango Street* is essentially a coming-of-age story, or bildungsroman. The bildungsroman is a literary genre that arose during the German Enlightenment and typically features a young male character searching for his identity and for his place in the world. These novels typically concern the relationship between self and society and the protagonist's psychological and emotional growth. Critics have examined *Mango Street* as both an exemplification and critique of the bildungsroman, which is historically associated with the white male experience.

Feminist and Chicano/a critics claimed *Mango Street* as a new kind of bildungsroman—one that features a marginalized character whose experiences of class, race, ethnicity, and gender are specific to her identity and development. In one of the earliest critical essays, "Growing Up Chicano: Tomás Rivera and Sandra Cisneros" (1985), Erlinda Gonzales-Berry and Tey Diana Rebolledo contrast *Mango Street* with Tomás Rivera's 1971 novel . . . *y no se lo tragó la tierra/. . . and the earth did not part*. They argue that, while the coming-of-age story is a common theme in Chicano literature, *Mango Street* is unique because of its feminism. Comparisons between *Mango Street* and Rivera's novel are common, in part because both are narratives about an adolescent's maturation and both tell their stories through vignettes. Chicana critic Alvina E. Quintana has argued, however, that these comparisons are problematic because they exemplify "the tendency to categorize women's literary production by measuring it against what has been deemed the universal (generally masculine) standard" (55). A significant development that rose out of feminist and cultural critical discourse was the insistence that critics stop imposing "universal" critical lenses on works by minority writers; yet, often, according to Delia Poey, critics and teachers still look for the universal: "Even as a revision of the genre, *Mango Street* offers a veneer of familiarity in its association with coming-of-age books" (212). Critic Dianne Klein contrasts *Mango Street* with another coming-of-age narrative from the Chicano canon, *Bless Me, Ultima* (1972), and finds both texts representative of contemporary Chicano literature. However, she notes, *Mango Street*, with its female protagonist, follows a path different from *Ultima*'s: "Unlike the traditional bildungsroman, the knowledge with which she emerges is not that of regeneration, but a painful knowledge, the knowledge of betrayal and physical violation" (25). Numerous comparative essays address *Mango Street*'s coming-of-age theme, including Poey's "Coming of Age in the Curriculum: *The House on Mango Street* and *Bless Me, Ultima* as Representative Texts" (1996), Maria Karafilis's "Crossing the Borders of Genre: Revisions of the *Bildungsroman* in Sandra Cisneros's *The House on Mango Street* and Jamaica Kincaid's *Annie John*" (1998), and Christina Rose Dubb's "Adolescent Journeys: Finding Female Authority in *The Rain Catchers* and *The House on Mango Street*" (2007).

The majority of the novel's critical reception has focused on its bildungsroman elements, acknowledging both its universal qualities and its differences from the traditional novel—a double lens that exemplifies how *Mango Street* straddles the line between the mainstream and the marginalized. Feminist critics focus on how *Mango Street* subverts, revises, or challenges the bildungsroman. In a departure from this approach, Thomas Matchie, in "Literary Continuity in Sandra Cisneros's *The House on Mango Street*" (1995), situates *Mango Street* as part of an American literary tradition, comparing Esperanza's coming-of-age to those of Huck Finn and Holden Caulfield. Though Matchie acknowledges the importance of gender in Cisneros's coming-of-age narrative, he does not see *Mango Street* as differing wildly from other American coming-of-age stories: "So in a general way Cisneros's novel belongs to a female tradition in which culture and literary quality are important. But for her, far more significant as literary models are Huck Finn and Holden Caulfield, primarily because they are adolescents growing up in culturally oppressive worlds." He sees her coming-of-age story "in the tradition of, but distinct from Huck and Holden."

Feminist and Chicana critics also argue that *Mango Street* is different from a traditional bildungsroman because community plays such an important role in the development of Esperanza's identity. "This shift from an individual to a communal perspective marks a significant turn away from the highly individualist tradition," notes Leslie S. Gutiérrez-Jones (309). *Mango Street* is dedicated "A las Mujeres/To the women," and many consider the community of women crucial to Esperanza's growth. Poey explains, "*Mango Street* negates the ideology of individualism in several ways, the most notable being that even as the narrative remains constant, the text is comprised of 44 vignettes describing and expressing the interiority of a wide spectrum of characters who make up the Mango Street neighborhood" (214). The focus of the traditional bildungsroman is on the protagonist—and the community is separate from his or her identity, but in *Mango Street*, writes Annie O. Eysturoy, "The narrative itself centers on the community of women on Mango Street who form part of Esperanza's *Bildungs* process" (111). Eysturoy's essay "*The House on Mango Street*: A Space of Her Own" focuses on how Esperanza's creativity helps her survive and overcome oppression and examines the ways that community and place contribute to her narrative construction.

In *Mango Street*, Cisneros portrays a community of women who are isolated, abused, and trapped, but Esperanza learns from them by observing their situations and by listening to them. Esperanza is sympathetic toward the women but also realizes she wants a different kind of life; over the course of the book, she develops into a strong, independent young woman who will be able to find her own path. In her *Home Girls*, Quintana argues, "The book's episodes challenge societal and cultural codes by emphasizing the protagonist's refusal to accept prescribed gender limitations" (56). Many critics see Esperanza as someone who develops herself in opposition to her surroundings, but Nicholas Sloboda, in "A Home in the Heart: Sandra Cisneros's *The House on Mango Street*" (1997), argues against what he considers to be a typical reading of Esperanza, in which she is considered "exclusively as a voice of opposition to dominant-culture practices of oppression and hegemony" (89). He agrees that Esperanza develops self-resilience and self-acceptance but argues that positive experiences in the community also develop her: "While this character has become an important figure in the development and expression of female subjectivity in recent Mexican American fiction, all too often she is read exclusively as a voice of opposition to dominant-culture practices of oppression and hegemony" (89).

Critics have noted that the community of women and the neighborhood in which they live are both intrinsic to Esperanza's narrative and to the formation of her identity. Analysis of the barrio and of the homes, which often entrap the women, makes up a significant portion of the critical response on *Mango Street*. The metaphor and symbolism of the idea of a home connect to Esperanza's search for her identity as a woman, as a Chicana, and as a writer, another a key topic in discussions of the novel. The title of the vignette "A House of My Own" alludes to Virginia Woolf's seminal extended essay *A Room of One's Own* (1929), in which she argues that women, because of their financial and social dependence on men, have been denied the opportunities for artistic development afforded to men. In order to write, she claims, a woman needs the independence money confers, "a room of her own." In her "More Room of Her Own: Sandra Cisneros's *The House on Mango Street*" (1994), Jacqueline Doyle considers not only how woman writers have been excluded from the canon but also how class, ethnicity, and race have determined this exclusion: "While feminists . . . have expanded the literary canon in the past two decades, too many have ignored questions of race, ethnicity, and class in women's literature" (5). *Mango Street*, she finds, expands Woolf's ideal to incorporate race and class: "By engaging *A Room of One's Own* in *The House on Mango Street*, Cisneros opens a dialogue. Preserving Woolf's feminist architecture, she enlarges and even reconstructs Woolf's room to make space for her own voice and concerns" (40).

Feminist readings of *Mango Street* often view the text as a revisionist and reconstructive work. Leslie Petty, in "The 'Dual'-ing Images of la Malinche and la Virgen de Guadalupe in Cisneros's *The House on Mango Street*" (2000), argues that Cisneros revises "the significance of the Chicana archetypes of la Malinche and la Virgen de Guadalupe through her characterization of females in the book. By recasting these mythical stories from the female perspective, Cisneros shows how artificial and confining these cultural stereotypes are" (131). Kelly Wissman, in "'Writing Will Keep You Free': Allusions to and Recreations of the Fairy Tale Heroine in *The House on Mango Street*"

(2007), explores how Cisneros rewrites traditional fairy tales in which the heroines are often passive or victims.

Although feminist approaches to *Mango Street* have been among the most popular critical approaches, some critics have argued that it is crucial that the text not be forced into a white feminist framework. Delia Poey states, "As important as establishing the text in a feminist context maybe be, it is also imperative to locate it within a Chicano critique of the genre" (213). Quintana explains that contemporary Chicana literature "bring[s] home the point that Chicano/a is the embodiment of multiplicity" (12). Esperanza's identity as a Chicana is the backbone of her story, and in the late 1990s more critics began to address the ways in which Esperanza's ethnicity both oppresses and empowers her, a theme that continues with current criticism. This criticism stresses the need to challenge borders and boundaries, a significant thematic concern of Latina literature. Carmen Haydée Rivera notes that borders are "social, cultural, racial, and linguistic divisions that often circumscribe and limit human interaction and creative/artistic expression" (7). In "The Chicana Girl Writes Her Way In and Out: Space and Bilingualism in Sandra Cisneros' *The House on Mango Street*" (1998), Tomoko Kuribayashi characterizes Esperanza as a "a bilingual and bicultural being" who is able to move through and across boundaries (173). Kuribayashi explains that, being "nonwhite, poor, and female," Esperanza

> draws her strength from the very sources of her oppression. Her ability to speak two languages with equal fluency and her compassion for the socially weak and neglected, especially women of her community and of other ethnic origins, give her a unique spatial vision which enlivens her imagination as a writer and as a social critic. Having mastered two languages, Esperanza knows the two different worlds that the two languages construct and represent. She is able to travel back and forth between the two languages and the two worlds, creating, in the process, new space for herself and for the people she wishes to help out—women, the poor, and minorities, with whom she has something in common. (165)

Maria Szadziuk's "Culture as Transition: Becoming a Woman in Bi-Ethnic Space" (1999) looks at the role of culture in the development of identity, and, in "The Bicultural Construction of Self in Cisneros, Alvarez, and Santiago" (1998), Ellen C. Mayock examines the strength that comes from understanding multiple cultures and identities. Beth Brunk, in "*En Otras Voces*: Multiple Voices in Sandra Cisneros' *The House on Mango Street*" (2001), focuses on structure and narrative voice, how Esperanza's voice is informed by her status as a child, a Latina, and a woman, and how voice empowers her to give recognition to the marginalized. In *Border Crossings* (2009), Rivera asserts that "one of the greatest accomplishments of Cisneros' narrator . . . is the balancing act she performs, straddling two cultures, languages, and histories, placing herself within the crux of her community while at the same time maintaining a sense of individuality and control" (31).

This theme of hybridity and multiplicity also pertains to the text itself. From its first appearance, critics were not sure how to describe *The House on Mango Street*—was it a novel, a collection of short stories, prose poems, or vignettes, or a blend of all of these? Some critics see the forty-four loosely connected, lyrical vignettes as a hybrid between poetry and prose. Cisneros explains that she "wanted to write a collection which could be read at any random point without having any knowledge of what came before or after. Or that could be read as a series to tell one big story. I wanted stories like poems, compact and lyrical and ending with reverberation" ("Did You Know Me" 78). Poet Carol Muske describes the stories as "long soliloquies, dense and startlingly musical" (para. 24) and "Like a haiku, each vignette distills an emotion" (para. 26). Critics have also differed over whether the book ought to be approached as fiction or as autobiography. Though Cisneros has maintained that it is a work of fiction, she has acknowledged that some of the story lines in *Mango Street* stem from her own experiences and childhood memories.

Sometimes the book is categorized as juvenile literature, and other times it is regarded as adult literature; the narrator's simple childlike voice has appealed to a wide audience while also attracting critics. Ellen McCracken argues that the voice of Esperanza is an opposition to "the complex, hermetic language of many canonical works" (64). The "simplicity of children's speech" has the advantage of "making the text accessible to people with a wider range of reading abilities" (64). Similarly, Rivera explains that the simple voice allows Cisneros "to expose and critique the cultural, social, and economic subordination of confined and abused women through a seemingly naïve, childlike perspective" (35). However, in "In Search of the Latino Writer," which appeared in the *New York Times* in 1990, Earl Shorris describes Cisneros's style as "a retreat from the sophistication of Tomás Rivera." He states, "The narrator of the sketches . . . speaks in an almost simpleminded voice, which unfortunately points to one of the continuing problems of Latinos, especially in works about Mexican-Americans: the stereotype of the simple peasant" (BR1).

Though majority of reviews and scholarship on *Mango Street* have been positive, several critics disagreed with the general assessment during the 1980s and early 1990s. Some felt that the novel cast Mexican Americans in a negative light or sent the wrong message. For example, in a 1984 review in the *Austin Chronicle*, Juan Rodríguez claimed that Esperanza ultimately rejects her Mexican culture and that Cisneros advocates assimilation. Other critics have refuted this argument, such as Rivera: "What Esperanza wants to leave behind are the culturally inscribed gender roles imposed by patriarchy and manifested through the lives of the women in her neighborhood . . . [but she] make[s] a promise to return and speak for family and friends in the barrio [she] left behind" (35). In "Una Nueva Voz," (1991) Mexican American essayist and cultural commentator Ilan Stavans writes that *Mango Street* became "a hot item" only because its author is a Mexican American woman. His description of the novel is lukewarm: "The content is at times amateurish" but, overall, the novel is "a pleasurable read," and Cisneros's "style is candid, engaging, rich in language."

But, he complains, "Its major flaw . . . is that she [Cisneros] bases most of her cast on stereotypes" (524).

Today multiculturalism is accepted in America as a pedagogical tool, and diverse texts are incorporated into curriculum of English departments. *Mango Street* is required reading in grade schools, high schools, and universities, and much of the critical literature has focused on the teaching of *Mango Street*. For example, in *Teaching American Ethnic Literatures* (1996), Julián Olivares provides an analysis of *Mango Street*, along with suggestions on how to teach it. Myrna-Yamil González also gives suggestions for teaching in "Female Voices in Sandra Cisneros' *The House on Mango Street*" (2000). In "Teaching *The House on Mango Street*: Engaging Race, Class, and Gender in a White Classroom," Kathleen J. Ryan advocates using *Mango Street* as a way to engage students in a dialogue about class and cultural privileges. Critic Felicia J. Cruz, in her essay "On the 'Simplicity' of Sandra Cisneros's *House on Mango Street*" (2001), notes that in classes predominantly composed of Caucasian middle-class students, the students tend to overlook the ethnic and racial themes of the book, while predominantly Chicano classes have often articulated very different perceptions of the novel. Cruz addresses *Mango Street*'s complex status as a representative multicultural text, its popular appeal, and the multiple and divergent readings it provokes among critics and students. "The widespread appeal of *Mango Street* raises the question of *why*," she writes, "one might ask whether the general process of reading this book adds up to a matter of different readers differentially ascribing meaning" (913). That *Mango Street* is known as a representative multicultural text incites many questions. Delia Poey has examined how the work is often appropriated as a multicultural text in the classroom, and Jane Juffer has argued that anthologies often feature *Mango Street* or stories from *Woman Hollering Creek* that are also told from a child's perspective as a way to sanitize Cisneros. Jane Juffer asserts that editors and critics "find it easier to focus on the more 'universal' coming-of-age themes and stories that present ethnic role models than those texts that represent the sometimes angry and disenchanted, frankly sexual, often ambiguous and always complicated adult Chicana that speaks in much of Cisneros's work" (para. 1).

Similarly, Quintana explains that "because *Mango Street* can be read from a variety of non-threatening positions, it has been used in many universities as a primer for raising consciousness about gender oppression" (73), yet she also argues that a close reading reveals the narrator's resistance to and exposure of "cultural and economic subordination" (74). It is also important to realize that, although the canon debates have died down since the 1990s, not all scholars have accepted *Mango Street* as an example of American literature. As Rivera observes:

> Despite critical discussions on the tenets of multiculturalism, the increasing debates over literary canon formation, and the groundbreaking work of writers, scholars, and instructors in the field of multiethnic studies, there continues to be a degree of skepticism and refusal to engage in readings and/or analyses of texts written by multiethnic authors. (98)

Yet, overwhelmingly, *The House on Mango Street's* broad appeal continues to reach generations of readers. No full-length analytical study of Cisneros's work has yet been published, but scholarly articles on her work appear often in journals, anthologies, and studies of Chicano and feminist literature. The scholarly response to *Mango Street* also reaches beyond Latino and feminist-focused publications to include general literary journals such as the *English Journal, College Literature*, and the *Journal of the Midwest Modern Language Association*. Of the three published Cisneros biographies, the most recent, part of the Women Writers of Color Biography Series and titled *Border Crossings* (2009), is a combination of biography and analysis.

Cisneros's work has helped shape both Chicana and feminist literature. Though her works are not numerous, *Mango Street* has helped to establish Cisneros as a major figure in contemporary American literature. In a sense, the critical reception of *Mango Street* is still in its infancy, and it is difficult to predict what readers and academics will think of the work fifty years from now; however, given the scholarly reception of the book thus far and its steady popularity, it is likely that *Mango Street* will remain an important part of the contemporary American literature canon.

Works Cited

Brown, Julie, ed. *Ethnicity and the American Short Story*. New York: Garland, 1997.

Brunk, Beth. "*En Otras Voces*: Multiple Voices in Sandra Cisneros' *The House on Mango Street*." *Hispanófila* 133 (Sept. 2001): 137-50.

Carpenter, Lynette, and Wendy K. Kolmar, eds. *Haunting the House of Fiction: Feminist Perspectives on Ghost Stories by American Women*. Knoxville: U of Tennessee P, 1991.

Cisneros, Sandra. "Do You Know Me?" *Americas Review* 15.2 (Jan. 1987): 77-79.

_____. "Ghosts and Voices: Writing from Obsession." *Americas Review* 15.2 (Jan. 1987): 69-73.

Cruz, Felicia J. "On the 'Simplicity' of Sandra Cisneros's *House on Mango Street*." *Modern Fiction Studies* 47.4 (Winter 2001): 910-46.

Delgado, Richard, and Jean Stefancic, eds. *The Latino/a Condition: A Critical Reader*. New York: New York UP, 1998.

Doyle, Jacqueline. "More Room of Her Own: Sandra Cisneros's *The House on Mango Street*." *MELUS* 19.4 (Winter 1994): 5-35.

Dubb, Christina Rose. "Adolescent Journeys: Finding Female Authority in *The Rain Catchers* and *The House on Mango Street*." *Children's Literature in Education* 38.3 (Sept. 2007): 219-32.

Eysturoy, Annie O. *Daughters of Self-Creation: The Contemporary Chicana Novel*. Albuquerque: U of New Mexico P, 1996.

_____. "*The House on Mango Street*: A Space of Her Own." *Daughters of Self-Creation: The Contemporary Chicana Novel*. Albuquerque: U of New Mexico P, 1996. 89-112.

González, Myrna-Yamil. "Female Voices in Sandra Cisneros' *The House on Mango Street*." *U.S. Latino Literature: A Critical Guide for Students and Teachers*. Ed. Harold Augenbraum and Margarite Fernández Olmos. Westport, CT: Greenwood Press, 2000. 101-12.

Gonzales-Berry, Erlinda, and Tey Diana Rebolledo. "Growing Up Chicano: Tomás Rivera and Sandra Cisneros." *Revista Chicano-Riqueña* 13.3-4 (1985): 109-19.

Gutiérrez-Jones, Leslie S. "Different Voices: The Re-*Bildung* of the Barrio in Sandra Cisneros' *The House on Mango Street*." *Anxious Power: Reading, Writing, and Ambivalence in Narrative by Women.* Ed. Carol J. Singley and Susan Elizabeth Sweeney. Albany: State U of New York P, 1993. 295-312.

Herrera-Sobek, María, and Helena María Viramontes, eds. *Chicana Creativity and Criticism: Charting New Frontiers in American Literature.* 1988. 2nd ed. Albuquerque: U of New Mexico P, 1996.

Horno-Delgado, Asunción, et al., eds. *Breaking Boundaries: Latina Writing and Critical Readings.* Amherst: U of Massachusetts P, 1989.

Juffer, Jane. "Sandra Cisneros' Career." *Modern American Poetry.* 16 Apr. 2010. http://www.english.illinois.edu/maps/poets/a_f/Cisneros/career.htm.

Karafilis, Maria. "Crossing the Borders of Genre: Revisions of the *Bildungsroman* in Sandra Cisneros's *The House on Mango Street* and Jamaica Kincaid's *Annie John.*" *Journal of the Midwest Modern Language Association* 31.2 (Winter 1998): 63-78.

Klein, Dianne. "Coming of Age in Novels by Rudolfo Anaya and Sandra Cisneros." *English Journal* 81.5 (Sept. 1992): 21-26.

Kuribayashi, Tomoko. "The Chicana Girl Writes Her Way In and Out: Space and Bilingualism in Sandra Cisneros' *The House on Mango Street.*" *Creating Safe Space: Violence and Women's Writing.* Ed. Julie Sharp and Tomoko Kuribayashi. Albany: State U of New York P, 1998. 165-77.

McCracken, Ellen. "Sandra Cisneros' *The House on Mango Street*: Community-Oriented Introspection and the Demystification of Patriarchal Violence." *Breaking Boundaries: Latina Writing and Critical Readings.* Ed. Asunción Horno-Delgado et al. Amherst: U of Massachusetts P, 1989. 62-71.

Matchie, Thomas. "Literary Continuity in Sandra Cisneros's *The House on Mango Street.*" *Midwest Quarterly* 37.1 (Autumn 1995): 67-79.

Mayock, Ellen C. "The Bicultural Construction of Self in Cisneros, Alvarez, and Santiago." *Bilingual Review* 23.3 (Sept.-Dec. 1998): 223-29.

Muske, Carol. "Breaking Out of the Genre Ghetto." *Parnassus: Poetry in Review* 20.1-2 (1995): 409-11, 417-23.

Olivares, Julián. "Entering *The House on Mango Street.*" *Teaching American Ethnic Literatures.* Ed. John R. Maitino and David R. Peck. Albuquerque: U of New Mexico P, 1996. 209-36.

_____. "Sandra Cisneros's *The House on Mango Street,* and the Poetics of Space." *Chicana Creativity and Criticism: New Frontiers in American Literature.* 2nd ed. Ed. María Herrera-Sobek and Helena María Viramontes. Albuquerque: U of New Mexico P, 1996. 233-44.

Petty, Leslie. "The 'Dual'-ing Images of la Malinche and la Virgen de Guadalupe in Cisneros's *The House on Mango Street.*" *MELUS* 25.2 (Summer 2000): 119-32.

Poey, Delia. "Coming of Age in the Curriculum: *The House on Mango Street* and *Bless Me, Ultima* as Representative Texts." *Americas Review* 24.3-4 (1996): 201-17.

Quintana, Alvina E. *Home Girls: Chicana Literary Voices.* Philadelphia: Temple UP, 1996.

Reesman, Jeanne Campbell, ed. *Speaking the Other Self: American Women Writers.* Athens: U of Georgia P, 1997.

Rivera, Carmen Haydée. *Border Crossings and Beyond: The Life and Works of Sandra Cisneros.* Santa Barbara, CA: Praeger, 2009.

Rodríguez, Juan. "*The House on Mango Street*, by Sandra Cisneros." *Austin Chronicle* 10 Aug. 1984.

Ryan, Kathleen J. "Teaching *The House on Mango Street*: Engaging Race, Class, and Gender in a White Classroom." *Academic Exchange* (Winter 2002): 187-92.

Saldívar, Ramón. *Chicano Narrative: The Dialectics of Difference.* Madison: U of Wisconsin P, 1990.

Sharp, Julie, and Tomoko Kuribayashi, eds. *Creating Safe Space: Violence and Women's Writing.* Albany: State U of New York P, 1998.

Shorris, Earl. "In Search of the Latino Writer." *New York Times* 15 July 1990: BR1, BR27-29.

Singley, Carol J., and Susan Elizabeth Sweeney, eds. *Anxious Power: Reading, Writing, and Ambivalence in Narrative by Women.* Albany: State U of New York P, 1993.

Sloboda, Nicholas. "A Home in the Heart: Sandra Cisneros's *The House on Mango Street.*" *Aztlán: A Journal of Chicano Studies* 22.2 (Spring 1997): 89-106.

Stavans, Ilan. "Una Nueva Voz." *Commonweal* 118.15. (13 Sept. 1991): 524-25.

Szadziuk, Maria. "Culture as Transition: Becoming a Woman in Bi-Ethnic Space." *Mosaic* 32.3 (Sept. 1999): 109-29.

Torres, Hector A. *Conversations with Contemporary Chicana and Chicano Writers.* Albuquerque: U of New Mexico P, 2007.

Valdés, María Elena de. "The Critical Reception of Sandra Cisneros's *The House on Mango Street.*" *Gender, Self, and Society: Proceedings of the IV International Conference on the Hispanic Cultures of the United States.* Ed. Renate von Bardeleben. New York: Peter Lang, 1993. 287-300.

_____. "In Search of Identity in Cisneros's *The House on Mango Street.*" *Canadian Review of American Studies* 23.1 (Fall 1992): 55-72.

Wissman, Kelly. "'Writing Will Keep You Free': Allusions to and Recreations of the Fairy Tale Heroine in *The House on Mango Street.*" *Children's Literature in Education* 38 (2007): 17-34.

Yarbro-Bejarano, Yvonne. "Chicana Literature from a Chicana Feminist Perspective." *Chicana Creativity and Criticism: Charting New Frontiers in American Literature.* 2nd ed. Ed. María Herrera-Sobek and Helena María Viramontes. Albuquerque: U of New Mexico P, 1996. 213-19.

On the "Simplicity" of Sandra Cisneros's
House on Mango Street_____

Felicia J. Cruz

As I perused the back cover of a recent Vintage Books edition of *The House on Mango Street* a short while ago, I read that it has been translated worldwide and that it has become a "classic" work in the canon of coming-of-age novels. This prompted me to think about whether this edition of *Mango Street*—which appeared identical to my personal copy (an earlier, 1991 Vintage Books edition)—sought to interpellate similar, if not the same, groups of readers that contributed to the consolidation of the unwavering popularity of Cisneros's rite-of-passage book.[1] Consequently, upon returning home, I retrieved my copy of *Mango Street* and saw that its back cover declares that the novel "signals the emergence of a major literary talent." The appeal of *Mango Street* clearly remains unabated in both the real and literary worlds.[2] Yet, the fact that this book, within six years after its publication in 1984 by the small, Hispanic publishing house Arte Público, had attracted enough attention to prompt its publication by a mainstream publisher warrants further consideration of the circumstances surrounding its seemingly meteoric rise within the US publishing industry.

According to Alvina Quintana, 1984 was a watershed year that "witnessed a revitalized interest in Chicana literature." Explains Quintana, "Although the National Association for Chicano Studies had organized annual conventions for eleven years, not until 1984 at the twelfth national conference in Austin, Texas, were scholars sanctioned by the theme of the convention—*Voces de la Mujer* (women's voices)—to address issues related to an emergent Chicana feminist movement" (54).[3] Quintana refers to the Chicana reading and book signing sessions sponsored by Arte Público as the highlight of the conference, identifying Cisneros in particular as the standout among a group of writers that included Pat Mora, Evangelina Vigil, and Ana Castillo: "Only [her] *Mango Street* defied the poetic form previously privileged by many Chicana writers. [. . .] Cisneros defined a distinct Chicana literary space [. . .], challenging, at the least, accepted literary form, gender inequities, and the cultural and economic subordination of minorities" (55). Further, Ramón Saldívar included Cisneros among the Chicana writers whose work, produced in the 1970s and 1980s, represented "the most vibrant new development in Chicano narrative" (171). These writers were impressive, according to Saldívar, because of their active engagement within "the ongoing disruption of the absolute fusion of hegemonic ideologies and the status quo" (199). Echoing Saldívar, Nicolás Kanellos, the founding publisher of Arte Público, identified Cisneros as one of the "new" generation of college-educated Chicano writers whose works were endorsed by prestigious foundations (two of which awarded fellowship grants to Cisneros: the NEA and the MacArthur Foundation) and were published by mainstream publishers:

> [These writers] inscribed themselves on the published page precisely at the time when literary publishing was [. . .] opening up to women as writers and intellectuals [. . .]. It was this generation, very much aware of the business of writing, of the industry's networks, and of the norms of language, metaphor, and craft protected by the academy, that was able to break into commercial and intellectual circles and cause a stir. (xix)

Since its initial publication in 1984, the readership of *Mango Street* has expanded beyond the pale of Chicano and Latino communities to include families and students of all ages and ethnicities.[4] According to María Elena de Valdés, a 1988 essay on Chicano criticism marked "a turning point in Cisneros's criticism, moving [. . .] into the richer context of North American literature and out of the limited area of ethnic writing." Valdés continues, "1989 and 1990 criticism no longer [had] to explain the barrio or the author's relation to it or what it means to be a Chicana writer" ("Critical Reception" 290). Another critic, Delia Poey, points out that *Mango Street* is not only frequently assigned in

American literature courses, but is also regularly incorporated into courses on women's and multicultural literatures (216). The specific focus of Poey's study is the nature of the appropriation in multicultural classrooms and literary anthologies of *Mango Street* as a "representative" work of Chicano or Latino writing.[5] Post 1990 studies of *Mango Street* extrapolate from Saldívar's focus on the marginalized situation of enunciation of Chicano writing, to Maria Szadziuk's consideration of Cisneros's book through the lens of "postnational, multicultural" societies in the US (109).[6] Speaking to feminist approaches to Cisneros's book, Andrea O'Reilly Herrera claims that *Mango Street* "raises disturbing questions regarding both female nature and the realities and fictions of development for women in general, and Chicanas in particular" (199). The drawing power of *Mango Street* indeed encompasses both "students of life" and literature.

In light of the reception trajectory of *Mango Street*, it is not surprising that during the summer of 1991 the college one of my sisters attended sent her a copy to read (before the start of classes); Cisneros's book appeared to have acquired elite status as a "representative" work of multicultural literatures in the curricula of high schools and colleges.[7] When my sister arrived on campus in September, she participated in one of various small-group discussions on the novel. A couple of years later, I saw the book on one of her bedroom shelves and asked her if she'd liked it. Almost apologetically, she nodded her head in dissent and replied, "Not as much as I'd hoped to." At the same time, however, she indicated that many of her peers and the faculty members who had led the campus-wide discussions had been quite taken by it. My sister's comments brought to mind the collective reaction of my own students to Cisneros's novel during the spring of 2000; students from both the English and Spanish departments at the university where I teach had lavished enthusiastic praise on the book: some admired its lyrical, albeit "simplistic" tone, while others related to the trials and tribulations of the novel's young female protagonist.[8] Their positive appraisals of *Mango Street*, moreover, concurred with the positive assessment of various critics in the United States and beyond, in countries such as Spain, Italy, Germany, France, Hungary, and Denmark.[9]

Still, the widespread appeal of *Mango Street* raises the question of *why*. To put the question one way, if this novel, as Poey has suggested, has become a "representative" selection in anthologies of American and Multicultural Literatures, what, exactly, can be said about its range of "representativity" (202)? Can it be that my younger sister and my stepmother (who did not like the book either) did not come across anything in *Mango Street* that moved them enough to sustain their interest in it? Further, had one or both of them brought unrealistic expectations to a book that they had both known, prior to reading it, was famous?[10] In light of the divergent opinions among not only my students but also among critics regarding *Mango Street*'s content, and, ultimately, its meaning, one might ask whether the general process of reading this book adds up to a matter of different readers differentially ascribing meaning. If this is the case, perhaps it remains to be asked, does *Mango Street* mean whatever one wants it to?

It's Not That Simple

Teaching *Mango Street* after a hiatus of six years dredged up questions and textual ambiguities that had not only surfaced the first time I had read it, but had also remained unresolved and/or unsatisfactorily addressed the first time I taught it in 1994. As I pondered both my students' reactions to and assessment of the novel and compared these to the opinions of various critics, it struck me that whereas both groups had consistently pinpointed the "simplicity" (Quintana 57; Saldívar 181), "accessibility" (Reuben Sánchez 222) and seeming directness of Cisneros's novel and had continually remarked on its poignancy and "poetic" force (Quintana 150), in reality, each group had actualized the book in different ways. In other words, each group of readers had engaged, had been thinking—and thinks—about *different* aspects of *Mango Street*, both textual and contextual. This in turn affects and effects varied opinions about what it "means." Thus the overarching concern of the rest of this essay will be to look in greater detail at the nature of the book's ostensible simplicity. On the one hand, doing so will permit me to identify some of the aspects and areas of the novel through which readers *differentially* ascribe meanings to it. On the other hand, consideration of some of the *referentially* ascribed meanings of *Mango Street* avails the opportunity to underline that few of its numerous critical readings pay sufficient respect and/or attention to one of the book's preeminent themes, what Iser calls "fictionalizing acts" ("Representation" 218). Hopefully, the final portions of this essay will be able to account for or accommodate such varied reader responses as, "it is about growing up," to "it's about a Chicana's growing up," to "it is a critique of patriarchal structures and exclusionary practices." Before proceeding, however, a few caveats are in order.

On a personal level, if not from a reception theory-based approach to the book (*rezeptionstheorie*), *Mango Street* has remained enigmatic for me from the standpoint of "aesthetic response theory" (*wirkungstheorie*). The latter, in my opinion, begs for closer scrutiny. Reception theory, as Wolfgang Iser reminds us, has to do with following and delineating the "history of judgments" of a literary work's readers. By contrast, aesthetic response theory has its "roots in the text," and "focuse[s] on what happens to us through [the literary work]" (Iser, *Act of Reading* preface x). However, having to focus on the processes of what happens to individuals as they read Cisneros's book presents a challenge, given the "multivalent," "incomplete" and "open" (Poey 205) nature not only of language, but of literary texts. Regarding the thorny question of intentionality and speech, for example, James Edie reminds us that "[u]ltimately, what one means to say will always remain incomplete and unsatisfactory" (148). Further, given the purported "conversational," "dialogic" tone of *Mango Street*, the fact that it is *not* rendered through speech makes discussing its meaning(s) even more complex. Among other critics, Poey underlines the slippery quality of both spoken and written discourse, as she defers to the discipline of linguistics: "[A]ll units of language are necessarily incomplete or open. No utterance or written text is free of ambiguity. In the case of the written text, undecidability is further complicated in that body language or physical expressions are absent as contextual clues, and clarification on the part of the speaker is simply not an option" (205). Edie emphasizes, moreover, that finding meaning is neither tantamount to "the act of referring" nor to discerning "mental images" or "clear, distinct ideas open to introspective inspection" (141).

Overall, in light of the wide range of responses to Cisneros's book, it seems reasonable to assert that all readers appropriate aspects of *Mango Street* in differential, subjective ways. As Jody Norton sees it, *Mango Street* communicates in highly personal ways; it therefore evokes highly personal responses. *"To use a text as literature is,"* as Norton remarks, *"to read it responsively*—to read oneself through it, in a double sense, with a concentration, at once of empathy and self-reflexivity, that enables one to experience the text conjunctively from without and from within—that is, aesthetically" (590).

The Novel as *Vox Populi*

For various readers, the novel briefly recounts the straightforward story of Esperanza, a young girl who desires and embarks on a quest for the American dream. In the introduction to the Knopf edition of *Mango Street*, published a decade after the novel's initial publication, Cisneros draws attention to the reflexivity with which readers have viewed her novel—the neighborhood, plot, and life experiences portrayed therein—as a mirror of (their) reality: "I've witnessed families buying my book for themselves and for family members, families for whom spending money on a book can be a sacrifice. [...] And there are letters from readers of all ages and colors who write to say that I have written their stories" (Introduction xix). These comments, in addition to others that Cisneros makes, underline the popularity, and personal, strong, emotional impact it has had on members of the general public, across ethnic-, gender-, and generational lines: "Often [families] bring a mother, father, sibling, or cousin along to my readings, or I am introduced to someone who says their son or daughter read my book in class and brought it home for them. [. . .] The raggedy state of my books that some readers and educators hand me to sign is the best compliment of all" (Introduction xix).

Besides signifying the popular appeal of her book, Cisneros's comments proffer possible explanations for why *Mango Street* seems so accessible. Among the reasons she gives are its nonintellectual themes and its rebellious, colloquial, even antiliterary tone. Concerning the novel's themes Cisneros admits to "'search[ing]' for the 'ugliest' subjects [she] could find, the most un-'poetic'—slang, monologues in which waitresses or kids talked their own lives." Cisneros's iconoclasm is further confirmed in the admission that she "was trying the best [she] could to write the kind of book [she] had never seen in a library or in a school, the kind of book not even professors could write" (Introduction xv). Central to this task, indicates Cisneros, was language itself. "It's in this rebellious realm of antipoetics," remarks Cisneros, "that I tried to create a poetic text with the most unofficial language I could find." She adds that "[t]he language in *Mango Street* is based on speech," and is "very much an antiacademic voice—a child's voice, a girl's voice, a poor girl's voice, a spoken voice, the voice of an American-Mexican" (Introduction xv). Hence, the colloquial tone and antiliterary inflection of her novel.

Cisneros's remarks additionally point out the novel's deliberate deployment of child-like speech, which presents readers the opportunity to eavesdrop on the innocent, earnest, youthful thoughts that the protagonist Esperanza draws out within and across the vignettes she depicts. For Quintana, the child-like naiveté and simplistic conversational tone of *Mango Street* serve as a counterpoise to the "somber realities" to which it speaks (such as rape, incest, and cultural, racial, sexual prejudice) (57). Notwithstanding the gravity of these realities, the childlike ingenuousness of Esperanza serves as a buffer to the real world. Moreover, Cisneros's use of first-person narrative seems to impart to Esperanza's tales a sense of immediacy and intimacy between the book's characters and readers (implied and actual). Consequently, *Mango Street* might at first glance seem to be an "easy" read.

However, reflexive readings of *Mango Street*, such as relating to it as if it were live speech, may encourage "the naive notion that a literary text is a kind of transcript of the living voice of a real man or woman addressing us" (Eagleton 120). It is thus not surprising that correlative to the common tendency to view the content of *Mango Street* in mimetic fashion, as a direct reflection of reality, is the impulse to view Esperanza *as* Cisneros. Cisneros has considered the phenomenon of conflating the standpoint of *Mango Street*'s narrator with her own views. Responding to the issue of whether or not her book is "about her," she acknowledges the autobiographically-inclined beginnings of *Mango Street*: "When I began [it, in 1977, as a graduate student in Iowa City], I thought I was writing a memoir. By the time I finished it, [in 1982], my memoir was no longer memoir, no longer autobiographical" (Introduction xi-xii). Yet, in consideration of the perennial question concerning whether or not "she is Esperanza," Cisneros evasively responds, "Yes. And no. And then again, perhaps maybe" (Introduction xix).[11]

Quintana further confirms *Mango Street*'s "tendency to conflate the two perspectives [the point of view of the author and the standpoint of the narrator]," which, she indicates, "has led some critics to argue that Esperanza's narrative (and, by implication, Cisneros's politics) simply illustrates an individual's desire for a house outside the barrio" (58). Consequently, for some Chicanos, whose writing and criticism in large part begins from the premise of collective resistance to mainstream institutions, values, and behavior, Cisneros's novel sends out the transparent message that individualistic pursuits are tantamount to the betrayal of one's community. For example, in an early review of *Mango Street*, Juan Rodríguez took its protagonist and, by extension, its author, to task for her "assimilationist" stance (qtd. in Quintana 59). Rodríguez equated Esperanza's choice to leave Mango Street, "her social/cultural base," with becoming more "Anglicized" and individualistic (qtd. in Quintana 150), and judged her desire to become a writer in terms of betrayal: "that she chooses to move from the real to the fantasy plane of the world as the only means of accepting and surviving the limited and limiting social conditions of her barrio becomes problematic to the more serious reader" (qtd. in Quintana 150-51).

Setting aside the thorny issue of defining "the more serious reader" and distinguishing her or him from other (less serious?) readers, Rodríguez's comments underline the tendency of certain, if not all, readers to conflate their own agenda, their personal horizons of experience, and their own expectations regarding Cisneros's book with their opinions about the politics and/or probable intentions of Cisneros herself. Among others, Reuben Sánchez warns that this type of criticism is limited, if not counterproductive. For him, Rodríguez's comments present an example "of what can happen when one does not evaluate a literary text on its own terms and on the terms appropriate to the genre, when one complains instead of analyzes" (231). He suggests, furthermore, that "[t]he literary value of [Cisneros's book] is [. . .] suspect for Rodríguez," and admonishes that "his conclusions seem based on whether [the author] espouses a particular ideology" (230). Valdés concurs with Sánchez, stating that such reviews are themselves an "ideological response to the challenge of the creative power of the text" (294). She adds that "[t]he most limited and useless responses are those that use the text in order to express the ideological posture of the commentator" (294). Turning back to Rodríguez's critique of Esperanza, and, by extension, of Cisneros, Sánchez suggests that he "does not recognize that [her] text is political *and* serious in that she writes about oppression (political, economic, sexual) and the way her protagonist might free herself from that oppression" (230-31). Like Valdés, Sánchez points to the source of Rodríquez's contention: "[Cisneros's] politics just do not happen to be his politics" (231).

Still, Cisneros herself has noted that even when Latina/o readers do not condemn Esperanza for wanting to be alone and/or leave, nevertheless, some, especially Latinas, are puzzled by her resolve to set herself apart from others. In an interview with Martha Satz fifteen years after the publication of *Mango Street*, Cisneros remarked, "According to their perspective, to be alone, to be exiled from the family, is so anti-Mexican" ("Return" 182). Cisneros alluded to her own feelings of guilt in terms of betrayal: "For a long time—and it's true for many writers and women like myself who have grown up in a patriarchal culture, like Mexican culture—I felt great guilt betraying that culture. Your culture tells you that if you step out of line, if you break [. . .] norms, you are becoming anglicized [. . .]" ("Return" 170). It is interesting to note that in its allusion to the prospect of "becoming [a]nglicized," Cisneros's voice appears to resonate with Rodríguez's, albeit not with the condemnatory tenor that his evinces. Cisneros seems to be speaking within the fold of her perception of the collective Chicano community, which commonly emphasizes group unity over individuality. The general stance of this community, and other disenfranchised groups, is resistance to and self-definition vis-à-vis mainstream institutions and values, not having had equal access to economic and educational opportunities, nor a political voice (which has been recognized by the powers that be) or equal participation in mainstream-controlled institutions and policymaking. As such, from within this group, which so intensely focuses on collectivity, one would likely have difficulties conceiving of, much less making, the decision to break away from the community, in order to tend to individual concerns and/or pursue individual goals. Nonetheless, Cisneros's protagonist does draw attention to and underscores the heterogeneity within her perception of the Chicano community, constantly pointing to, for example, inequity between the two sexes ("Boys and Girls"), between different generations within the same family ("My Name," "Alicia Who Sees Mice," "A Smart Cookie"), and between different ethnic communities presiding in the same general vicinity ("Cathy, Queen of Cats," "Those Who Don't").

At this point, in order to underline Cisneros's and some other Chicana/o writers' simultaneous inclusion and exclusion in both mainstream and ethnic (for lack of a better term) cultures, it might be useful to emphasize what Gloria Anzaldúa referred to in 1987 as the "bordered" condition or "interstitial" (20) situation of enunciation that Chicanas, women of color, and other groups embody and occupy. As Rosaura Sánchez points out, "[various] ethnic groups in this country [. . .] suffer both inclusion and exclusion. Ideologically, thanks to the media and to our educational system, [Chicanos] will probably all have swallowed the same myths and yet, materially, be excluded from the lifestyle, goods and services that characterize the life of middle classes in the US" (81). From an autobiographical standpoint, Cisneros's experience in the prestigious Iowa Writers' Workshop underlines the extent to which even the apparent attainment of the myth does not result in the happily-ever-after. On one hand, she alludes to the privileged position in which she found herself: "[U]nlike many young writers I've met in the barrio [. . .], I was born at a time when there were government grants that allowed me to pursue higher education. I was able to attend an undergraduate program that had a writer in residence, and he [. . .] took a great interest in my work and recommended me to the University of Iowa. [. . .] I entered rather naively [. . .]" ("Return" 169). At the same time, Cisneros acknowledges her discomfiture, her feelings of being neither-here-nor-there within academia. She reveals that while she was physically present in class, emotionally she felt totally out of it: "Coming from a working class background, an ethnic community, an urban community, a family that did not have books in the house, I just didn't have the same frames of reference as my classmates. It wasn't until [I] realized and accepted that fact that [I] came upon the subjects [I] wanted to write about." Her voice, "a street child's voice," would, in reality, emerge at the antipodes of the "very distilled writing" of her middle-class classmates, once she had rebelled. "[A]s an attempt to move far away from their style," she concedes, "I stumbled upon the voice that predominates in the *House on Mango Street* [. . .]" ("Return" 169).[12]

Cisneros's comments, spoken at a far chronological and geographical remove from the origins of the writing of her novel, seem to epitomize the experience of the displaced individual or displaced ethnic community that, being rooted in or tied to a larger culture (the US), to a large extent has been indoctrinated with (and has appropriated) mainstream Western values. Cisneros's protagonist, Esperanza, gives voice to this very issue. Initially, she acknowledges that her ideal house consists of a private dwelling with "real" stairs, "like the houses on T.V.," a house like "the [one] Papa talked about when he held a lottery ticket," and "the [one] Mama dreamed up in the stories she told us before we went to bed" (4). Mango Street, however, bears no resemblance to Esperanza's dream house: "The House on Mango Street is ours, and we don't have to pay rent to anybody, or share the yard with the people downstairs, or be careful not to make too much noise, and there isn't a landlord banging on the ceiling with a broom. But even so, it's not the house we thought we'd get" (3). Even before her family manages to procure a house of their own, Esperanza, as Cisneros in graduate school, is made painfully aware of her difference, and exclusion from "others":

Once when we were living on Loomis, a nun from my school passed by and saw me playing out front. [. . .]
Where do you live? she asked.
There, I said pointing up to the third floor.
You live *there*?
There. I had to look to where she pointed—the third floor, the paint peeling, wooden bars Papa had nailed on the windows so we wouldn't fall out. You live *there*? The way she said it made me feel like nothing. *There*. I lived *there*. I nodded. I knew then I had to have a house. A real house. One I could point to. (5)

Esperanza, as Rosaura Sánchez and Quintana stress, actually experiences concurrent inclusion in *and* exclusion from mainstream society. "On an ideological level, [she] dreams the American dream; [but] on a material level, like all in her community she remains systematically excluded from it" (Quintana 57).[13] Extrapolating from the theme of practices of exclusion in mainstream culture, Reuben Sánchez points out the significance of the gender of *Mango Street*'s protagonist for the Chicano community as a whole. Sánchez remarks:

> The Chicana's concern with 'place'—a house, or room of one's own is a reaction against the patriarchal myth that denies the Chicana a place of her own. [. . .] The reality the Chicana addresses, [. . .] is the reality of her restriction to the urban setting—particularly the house or the room. That setting is Esperanza's past and her present in [the novel]; she recognizes that it might very well be her future as well." (229)

Whereas Esperanza's resolve to distance herself from her family and community has struck and strikes readers in some communities as puzzling, if not reprehensible, for other individuals, solitude, striking it out on one's own, and breaking away from one's family constitute the very steps needed for growing up, even for becoming part of the "real world." My undergraduate seminar students, for example, viewed Esperanza's desire to acquire a house and her vow to become independent and self-sufficient as universal ideals that somehow correspond to a *natural* right which—in the liberal democratic spirit of the Founding Fathers—is, or should be available to *all* American citizens. These readers, who uncritically, if not unconsciously, identify with mainstream views, inscribed Esperanza's dream in a foundational democratic rhetoric and declaration (that the pursuit of freedom, liberty, and happiness is the right of all American citizens); they did so reflexively, in the naive, albeit earnest belief that an iron will and *individual* hard work (that is, the Protestant work ethic) *would* eventually lead her to her dream. What, then, can we make of the diametrically opposed perceptions of some working-class Chicanos and those of my middle-class Caucasian students regarding the textual phenomenon of Esperanza's desire for self-sufficiency and individualism?

If, on the one hand, the uncritical transcription of Esperanza as the "voice" of Cisneros is carried out by both students and scholars in both Latino/a and non-Latino/a communities, there may be on the other hand a marked difference among each group's perception of what the novel's prevalent themes and/or issues are. For example, the majority of my undergraduate students overlooked the regional specificity of the novel, sidestepping its pointed focus on the relation between issues of ethnicity and class and the novelistic representation of ideologies of exclusion based on the protagonist's Chicana background and working-class roots.[14] The students focused instead on feelings of alienation, discomfiture, and solitude that they themselves had experienced as children.[15] Speaking to the issue of the indelible nature of childhood trauma, Norton asserts, "Because most of us have our own memories of a moment when our preadolescent reality seemed suddenly to have shifted to one side without telling us [. . . ,] it is easy to engage Cisneros's poignant (because simple and frank) account, and to make literary experience through the intertextual relation of Cisneros's fiction and our own emotional past" (595).

Even after they were asked to identify and analyze specific vignettes that treated particularly harsh incidents and issues, the students by and large spoke to instances in the book that are gender- and family-centered; not a single student drew attention to any of the vignettes centered on class and ethnicity. Perhaps because they have either never experienced or witnessed the sorts of discrimination reflected in the novel, or because they genuinely believe or would like to believe that all Americans are *equal* American citizens with equally strong chances and opportunities to garner "success," it was very difficult for my students to apprehend, much less feel, the extent to which Esperanza— and, by extension, her community—exists at a far remove from white, middle-class standards and styles of living. These students, not unlike readers who are unable and/or unwilling to accommodate a Chicana's

(Esperanza's) individualism, were even less likely to come to the realization that their reality, and, by extension, the world is not homogeneous (that is, it is *not* the same for all).

The selective vision of my students mirrors a general tendency among formalist critics to overlook the very contextual lenses—ethnicity, race, gender, and class—through which other scholars, namely resistance-inclined critics (including Chicanas and Latinas) routinely focus their writing. How can the respective foci of these groups of readers be so diverse, now universal-inflected, now barrio-bent?[16] Perhaps in reference to universalist critics, Quintana partially attributes the wide-ranging appeal of *Mango Street* to its capacity to speak to non-ethnic and/or mainstream readers in a "dispassionate" tone (72). For Quintana, Cisneros's novel—in contrast to other, more openly aggressive, angry works by other female writers of color—extends textual accessibility to readers, men and women alike, in a "non-threatening" way (73). Poey, moreover, discerns in *Mango Street* a high level of language- and content-based "intelligibility," which she defines as "the degree to which a given text is accessible to a given community of readers based on that community's prior knowledge and expectations deployed in making meaning and assigning value." As Cisneros's own comments suggest, one need not be Chicano or Latino to find meaning in *Mango Street*. Why? As Poey states, "The negotiation of [the] meaning [of a literary work] is removed from the speaking or writing subject and transferred to the text, so that the interaction is contextualized through the reader's prior experience [. . .]" (205). As such, the process of making meaning is tied to a dialectic involving the contextualization of aspects/themes of a literary work according to one's personal views and experiences. It might appear, then, that to a certain extent, the literary work *can* "mean" what and how readers want it to.

Yet, there are some common themes and aspects of *Mango Street* that numerous readers recognize, if even briefly. Reuben Sánchez focuses on the book's treatment of the common need/desire to escape or have some other place to go: "Why Esperanza wishes to escape Mango

Street and why she must return are issues Cisneros addresses by means of the home versus homeless theme. In doing so, she has created a narrative account of 'a condition we all recognize'—a narrative, further, accessible to both the adult reader and the child reader" (228). O'Reilly Herrera (195-96) and Poey both draw attention to the ease with which various readers (in my opinion, including students, scholars, and mainstream publishing houses) relate to and classify Cisneros's book as a bildungsroman or "novel of youth or apprenticeship" (Poey 206).[17] Additionally, Norton identifies "the trauma of exclusion" experienced during childhood as an especially poignant "specific paradigm of structurally significant experience" (593), since youth "is the location of personality formation." As such, continues Norton, any narrative "that explores this existential chronotope speaks to us about the single most structurally significant portion of our lives" (594). Further, given that *Mango Street*'s protagonist, by contrast to those of classical bildungsroman narratives, is a young girl, various critics also extrapolate from the book's criticism of patriarchal structures and ideology. These studies work with what they see as *Mango Street*'s feminist resonance with Virginia Woolf's concept, "a room of one's own."[18] From a yet more contextually specific perspective, however, I continue pondering how students like the ones I have had can persist in apparently *not* seeing what seem to be for me obvious markers of racial, ethnic, class, and cultural conflict in Cisneros's novel.

If we turn to Iser's claim that most if not all people try to establish consistency while reading, or, in other words, if we agree that sense-making—ordering, harmonizing, and movement toward closure—is "essential to all comprehension" (*Act of Reading* 16), then answering this question seems less daunting.[19] Iser stresses that the search for meaning, in contrast to the common notion that it seems "natural" or "unconditional" (3), is, in actuality, "considerably influenced by historical norms," namely classical norms of interpretive criticism, such as harmony, order, symmetry, unity, coherence, and completeness. Endeavors to find symmetry and make connections are, to Iser's thinking, tantamount to "grappling with the unknown": "Symmetry relieves one from the pressure of the unfamiliar by controlling it within a closed and balanced [and familiar] system." In his opinion, the "debt" owed by New Criticism (through which several of my students were taught) to the "classical norm of interpretation" is none other than "[t]he harmonization and eventual removal of ambiguities," which is frequently accompanied by an exclusive focus on aesthetic technique or concern for interpreting the "intrinsic elements" of a literary work (*Act of Reading* 15). (The result is an abundance of decontextually-centered assessments of *Mango Street*'s poetic, lyrical, although childlike, style). Conceivably, as Rosario Ferré has suggested in an article on translation between Spanish and English language and culture, the particular issues, instances, and themes to which my students did not speak proved to be "lacunae" evinced by "missing cultural connotations" (162). As such, it is possible that these New Critically inclined students simply overlooked issues that other (Latino) reader-critics emphasize, choosing instead to trace and connect threads and stories that had safe and/or immediate relevance in, or significance to, their own lives. Poey implies, for instance, that unless readers come to a literary work already believing that it is "significant," they "will work toward making meaning in a more limited way since [they are] more uncertain about the potential payoff of [their] effort[s]" (208).

To be fair, I do not mean to give the impression that my students were wholly oblivious to the racial and ethnic strains in Cisneros's book. Several of them had, after all, demonstrated or professed that they believed in multiculturalism per se and felt they were more culturally and politically liberal than conservative. Perhaps this particular group of students could be counted as proponents or constituents of what Goldberg conceives as "weak multiculturalism," which "consists of a strong set of common, universally endorsed, centrist values to which everyone—every reasonable person irrespective of the divisions of race, class, and gender—can agree." Weak multiculturalism, in Goldberg's opinion, admits and "[is] combined with a pluralism of ethnic insight and self-determination provided no particularistically promoted claim is inconsistent with the core values" (qtd. in Poey 209). In light of this, perhaps my students, after all, found no need to harp on the cultural, regional specificity of *Mango Street*, given that its heroine ultimately seemed to want what they do: a space of her own, and the freedom to go there. Unfortunately, the cost of decontextualized, generalized readings of Cisneros's novel, might be, as Poey intimates, the blunting of its revisionary edge. "It is not the text [. . . itself that is] problematic," she states, insisting that the book does "engage in layered critiques and proposes [its] own aesthetics. Rather, it is [its] acceptance as representative that is troubling, given that [this provides] opportunities for easy incorporation which erases [the book's] transformative possibilities" (215).

Aspects of weak multiculturalism are, not surprisingly, also applicable to the discursive text on the back cover of my edition of *Mango Street* (1991 Vintage Books). On the one hand, the textual blurb generalizes that the book is about the story of "a young girl growing up in the Hispanic quarter of Chicago." It is not acknowledged that there may be more than one "Hispanic" community in the Windy City. Additionally, the back cover betrays bildungsroman-like obstacles, such as "a desolate landscape of concrete and run-down tenements" in which Esperanza brushes against the hard knocks of the life that her kind typically encounters: "the fetters of class and gender, the specter of racial enmity, the mysteries of sexuality, and more." (One cannot help but think of reviews for movies and television programs, both of which try to appeal to mass audiences by offering sensationalistic somethings-for-everyone.) Finally, though, the back cover alludes to the American dream, namely, an implied happy ending in which the protagonist "is able to rise above hopelessness," to create a "'room all her own,'" in spite of "her oppressive surroundings." In short, conveyed in a politically correct multicultural framework, this lead-in to *Mango Street*, while handwaving to racial-, class-, and gender-related strife, ultimately distills into the barest of generalized (generic?) plots: Hispanic girl heroically strives for and thrives because of the American dream. Is this not, after all, one of the basic premises for Jessica Alba's new television series, *Dark Angel*? Is it not true that she, the epitome of stereotypic Latin sexiness, persists in learning to become more of an individual, thereby continually deferring chances to return home with her part-automaton brethren?[20]

Despite the fact that students and critics relate easily to the book, in my opinion, most of the readers that I have considered have essentially rendered Cisneros's book transparent. They have read *Mango Street* primarily in mimetic fashion, ordering and simplifying in order to make Esperanza's story cohere. On the whole, no single group seems inclined to focus on the book's "simple," "direct" language and messages as part of Cisneros's complex arsenal of sophisticated literary devices and nuanced rhetorical strategies. In their persistent view of *Mango Street* as a "mirror of life," the groups I have pointed out have generally failed to take into account the book's ideological *and* narrative intricacies. The remainder of this essay thus hinges on my argument that as the *Mango Street* narrative coils back to the question of the act of narration, readers may or may not, if they choose to throw on blinders, come away unsettled, since the book's final vignette self-consciously heralds the *fictional* character of Esperanza's story. What remains for consideration, then, is the book's status as a *literary* work, which, "in the act of apparently describing some external reality, is secretly casting a sideways glance at its own processes of construction" (Eagleton 105).

Mango Street does to, as much as it *recounts for*, readers. As alluded to throughout this essay, *Mango Street* cannot speak directly, in unmediated fashion, to the reader. "A work," states Eagleton, "is not actually a 'living' dialogue or monologue," but "a piece of language which has been detached from any specific 'living' relationship [. . .]" (119). Further, as Iser asserts, "the text represents a potential effect realized in the reading process" (*Act of Reading* ix). Hence, while it may be tempting for readers to presume that literature describes "reality," Eagleton warns that "its real function is 'performative': it uses language within certain conventions in order to bring about certain effects in a reader," and "achieves something *in* the saying: it is language as a kind of material practice in itself [. . .]" (118).[21] As a case in point, consider the first and last vignettes of *Mango Street*, where the reader apparently sees the beginning in the end, and the end in the beginning. Since this juncture will be closely read further on, suffice it to point out that the repetition of "We didn't always live on Mango Street" in both the initial and final chapters of the book does *not* suggest closure. As Reuben Sánchez remarks, "The narrative, in fact, is not self-enclosed; rather, it is open-ended and encourages the reader to consider what will become of [the protagonist] after the book has ended" (223).

Given that the reading process, as described by Norton (alluding to Iser, Jauss, and Bakhtin), is "a dialectic between the text and the idiosyncratic mind of the reader" (590), any meaning ascribed to the literary work will, of necessity, be proteic and personal because contingent on the experiences, beliefs, expectations, and will of individual readers. Sánchez's and Norton's statements thus underscore that determining what a literary work means pivots on the reciprocal, live interaction between individual readers and the literary work at hand. Turning back to Edie, for whom making meaning can neither be linked to mere acts of referring, nor to discerning clear and "distinct ideas open to introspective inspection" (141), and to Iser, for whom the literary work awaits "actualization" (*Act of Reading* 18) by readers, one can better apprehend the literary work as an elusive, ever in-process, and therefore incomplete entity and signifying system. How is this embodied in Cisneros's book? What, moreover, does *Mango Street do* as it recounts the story of Esperanza?

Cisneros's novel dissembles, bringing together multiple voices and life experiences in the character of Esperanza. For Renato Rosaldo, Esperanza "inhabits a border zone peopled with multiple subjectivities and a plurality of languages and cultures" (85).[22] Her name alone is multivalent: "Moving between English and Spanish, [Esperanza's] name shifts in length [. . .], in meaning (from hope to sadness and waiting), and in sound (from being as cutting as tin to being soft as silver)" (Rosaldo 85). Esperanza's naiveté and innocence can thus be viewed as part of the sophisticated, intricate narrative strategies deployed by Cisneros to "introduce a variety of political concerns that confront Chicano/a communities in the United States" (Quintana 57). In this sense, contrary to popular belief, Esperanza is *not* a monolith, but rather an "ideological foil" (Quintana 56). Cisneros confirms the macaronic character of her novel: "I arranged and diminished events on Mango Street to speak a message, to take from different parts of other people's lives and create a story like a collage" (Introduction xvii-xviii). She, in effect, places into relief the self-conscious performative nature of writing her book: "I merged characters from my twenties with characters from my teens and childhood. I edited, changed, shifted the past to fit the present. I asked questions I didn't know how to ask when I was an adolescent [. . .]" (Introduction xvii-xviii). "Cisneros's novel is," as Valdés succinctly puts it, "an explicit composition" (292). "The author," she continues, "has designed, redesigned, written and rewritten the discursive system of the text. Names, places and situations have been organized into a specific structure. Emplotment has worked at every level of configuration as the writers strive to give the right balance of determinate and indeterminate features" (292). In short, *Mango Street* is anything but a passively ingestible mirror of life. On the contrary, it is a stage.

Of paramount importance in the consideration of performative representation (*darstellung*) is, as Iser indicates, accounting for the circumstances surrounding the "fictionality" of a literary work: "To conceive of representation not in terms of mimesis but in terms of performance makes it necessary to dig into the structures of the literary text, laying bare the levels and conditions out of which the performative quality arises" ("Representation" 218).[23] Understanding that language retains its denotative function at the same time it speaks connotatively, is, moreover, pivotal in laying bare aspects or factors that bring about performative, "doubling" action in literature. "[T]he sentence [in literary works]," remarks Iser, "does not consist solely of a statement [. . .] but aims at something beyond what it actually says" ("Reading Process" 78). Iser's comments extrapolate from Mikhail Bakhtin's notion of "dialogic" discourse (*Problems* 182-85), in which words are "double-voiced" (*Problems* 195) and possess a "sideward glance" (205): they are "directed both toward the referential object of speech . . . and toward *another's discourse*, toward *someone else's speech*" (*Problems* 205); that is, they are bound up with an awareness and consideration of another's words.[24] In short, our own words, inflected with the voices of others, become meaningful in relation to other and others' words. For Bakhtin, novelistic discourse is made up of "heteroglossia," which he defines as "the social diversity of speech types" (*Dialogic* 263). Novelistic discourse is, moreover, dialogic:

Heteroglossia, once incorporated into the novel [. . .], is *another's speech in another's language*, serving to express authorial intentions but in a refracted way. Such speech constitutes a special type of *double-voiced discourse*. [. . .] In such discourse there are two voices, two meanings and two expressions. And all the while these two voices are dialogically interrelated, they—as it were—know about each other (just as two exchanges in a dialogue know each other and are structured in this mutual knowledge of each other); it is as if they actually hold a conversation with each other. Double-voiced discourse is always internally dialogized. (*Dialogic* 324)[25]

In what sense, then, can heteroglossia be detected in Cisneros's *Mango Street*?

Re-thinking the Literary Text: In the End Is the Beginning?

Heteroglossia and staging, which, according to Iser, is one of the ways in which doubling in fiction is achieved, play a central role in the last vignette of Cisneros's novel, "Mango Says Goodbye Sometimes." This vignette, which alludes to Esperanza's departure from her community, is most likely the one responsible for bringing about the extrapolations of readers who "actualize" the implied realization of her dream. The beginning of *Mango Street*'s final vignette "stages" the nature of storytelling as it discloses the fictionalized nature of Esperanza's story:

> I like to tell stories. I tell them inside my head. I tell them after the mailman says, Here's your mail. Here's your mail he said.
>
> I make a story for my life, for each step my brown shoe takes. I say, "And so she trudged up the wooden stairs, her sad brown shoes taking her to the house she never liked."
>
> I like to tell stories. I am going to tell you a story about a girl who didn't want to belong.
>
> We didn't always live on Mango Street. Before that we lived on Keeler. Before Keeler it was Paulina, but what I remember most is Mango Street, sad red house, the house I belong but do not belong to. (109)

This vignette seems abrupt when compared to the one it follows, "A House of my Own," which presents the last in a series of ideal homes that Esperanza has described throughout the book. Further, the narrative "I" of this portion of the last vignette alludes to aspects particular to the craft of storytelling in general. Third, when one juxtaposes the second paragraph in this section of the vignette with the last two paragraphs, the reader is suddenly drawn back into the story posited in the opening passage of the book. In other words, the end of *Mango Street* casts a "sideward glance" at its beginning, thereby reactivating one's familiarity with the story told by Esperanza. At first glance, it seems easy to process the conclusion of Cisneros's novel.

On further examination, however, the final vignette's selection and incorporation of details and a passage from earlier in the novel combine to raise questions about what the text is, after all, about. Ultimately, the familiar passage, which appears in the first vignette, and re-appears in the last one, yields two different passages:

> We didn't always live on Mango Street. Before that we lived on Loomis on the third floor, and before that we lived on Keeler. Before Keeler it was Paulina, and before that I can't remember. *But what I remember most is moving a lot.* (3, emphasis added)

> We didn't always live on Mango Street. Before that we lived on Loomis on the third floor, and before that we lived on Keeler. Before Keeler it was Paulina, *but what I remember most is Mango Street, sad red house, the house I belong but do not belong to.* (109, emphasis added)

Comparing the text (here not limited exclusively to written discourse) that precedes and follows the "we-didn't-always-live" sequence of the novel's last vignette with the text that follows the "we-didn't-always-live" sequence of *Mango Street*'s opening chapter renders a gap in the narrator's story. Clearly, the content and possible message of Esperanza, who at the outset states, "What I remember most is moving a lot" (3), are different from the focus and possible message of Esperanza when she comments, "What I remember most is Mango Street, sad red house, the house I belong but do not belong to" (109). The latter remarks concurrently connote Esperanza's acknowledgement and self-distancing of herself as a part of the Mango Street community. The transmogrified focus of the narrator from start to finish may in turn alter the reader's perception of what Cisneros's book is about.[26] In effect, subsequent retrieval and comparison of the first and penultimate vignettes of *Mango Street*, besides reminding us that "[t]he act[s] of selection [and combination] [. . .] [are] integral to fictionality [and are forms] of doubling" (Iser, "Representation" 218), foregrounds the non-coincidence between, on one hand, Esperanza at the beginning of the novel, and on the other, Esperanza at the end of the book. Let us take a closer look into some possible ramifications of her transformation.

Notwithstanding the "immediacy" of the two passages from *Mango Street* cited in the paragraph above, Eagleton reminds us that literature is not a "living" dialogue or monologue but rather "a piece of language which has been detached from any specific 'living' relationship" (119). As such, books are "thus subject to the 'reinscriptions' [. . .] of many different readers" (Eagleton 119). Hence, by the end of *Mango Street*, the "meaning(s)" of "Esperanza's" story will likely shift, since, in Iser's view: "Each text makes inroads into extratextual fields of reference and by disrupting them creates an eventful disorder, in consequence of which both structure and semantics of these fields are subject to certain deformations and their respective constituents are differently weighted according to the various deletions and supplementations" (Iser, "Representation" 218). To complicate matters further, the respective texts resulting from the combination and selection of the common passage ("We didn't—always—live on Mango Street") do not blend harmoniously together; neither text stands in autonomous isolation:

> [T]he doubling process becomes [. . . more] complex, for the texts alluded to and the segments quoted begin to unfold unforeseeably shifting relationships both in respect to their own contexts and to the new ones into which they have been transplanted. Whatever the relationships may be like, two different types of discourse are ever present, and their simultaneity triggers a mutual revealing and concealing of their respective contextual references. From this interplay emerges semantic instability, which is exacerbated by the fact that the two sets of discourse are also contexts for each other, so that each in turn is constantly switching from background to foreground. The one discourse becomes the theme viewed from the standpoint of the other, and vice versa. (Iser, "Representation" 219)

Moreover, as Eagleton notes in reference to poetry, the repetition of a word or image contributes to semantic instability: "A particular meaning [derived initially] [. . .] will cause us retrospectively to revise what we have learnt already," since the reappearance of the word-image signifies something other than what it had previously connoted (116). Thus, with respect to Espeanza's recollection of Mango Street at the beginning and end of the book, one might do well to refrain from thinking that the image "means" what it did initially, since "[n]o event occurs twice" (Eagleton 116). In fact, it might be wise not to impose closure at all, that is, not to think in circular terms. Instead, perhaps one might mull over Iser's insistence that "the literary work is to be considered not as a documentary record of something that exists or has existed, but as a reformulation of an already formulated reality, which brings into the world something that did not exist before" (*Act of Reading* x).

Still, after noting *Mango Street*'s title and opening the book, many readers have initially come away with the notion that the "sad red house" is its primary focus. On one hand, the first vignette, bearing the same title as the novel, raises the question of whether or not the narrator will acquire another house. However, the last four paragraphs of the final vignette insinuate that the primary focus of the book has been or is, actually, Esperanza:

> I put it down on paper and then the ghost does not ache so much. I write it down and Mango says goodbye sometimes. She does not hold me with both arms. She sets me free.
>
> One day I will pack my bags of books and paper. One day I will say goodbye to Mango. I am too strong for her to keep me here forever. One day I will go away.
>
> Friends and neighbors will say, What happened to that Esperanza? Where did she go with all of those books and paper? Why did she march so far away?
>
> They will not know that I have gone away to come back. For the ones I left behind. For the ones who cannot out. (109-10)

Because of this, the plot no longer appears to hinge solely on the question of whether or not she manages to acquire another house. Further, although memories of Mango Street are still present, it is made clear that it is *she* who ultimately has the upper hand; Esperanza controls Mango Street, contrary to the claim: "She does not hold me with both arms. She sets me free" (110).

In fact, much about the final four paragraphs of the novel is ambiguous, in large part because of abrupt shifts in time and space, on the one hand, and, on the other, a marked change in the disposition of the last of three narrative "I"s present in "Mango Says Goodbye."[27] Shifts in verb tenses, from the present to the future to the simple past, mark the spatial, temporal, and psychological distance between the story-telling narrator at the beginning of the last vignette and the apprentice-writer narrator of the middle of it, and, finally, the more mature, community-oriented narrator projected in the last paragraph of the book. This last narrative "I" is situated at a far remove—ideologically, temporally, and geographically—not only from the child-like narrative "I" in the first vignette, but also from the child-like, albeit more confident, authoritative voice that begins the last one. Hence, despite the brevity and seemingly direct statements made in the last vignette, and despite its endeavors to relieve the tension between the ingenuousness of its young protagonist and narrator, this chapter nonetheless underscores the distinction between the act of *narration*, the storytelling that Esperanza has engaged from start to finish, and *narrative*: what has ultimately been recounted.[28]

Another reason for which the last chapter, "Mango Says Goodbye Sometimes," makes the implications and meaning(s) of the novel difficult for readers to pin down is that, with the exception of one of its sections, set off and marked by quotation marks ("And so she trudged up the wooden stairs, her sad brown shoes taking her to the house she never liked" [109]), this chapter, like virtually all of the other tersely rendered vignettes, lacks conventional markers that would guide readers and clarify the text(s). The "gap" between the last four paragraphs of the final vignette and the rest of the book's vignettes has the capacity to leave readers feeling addled, if not altogether ambivalent. If, for instance, one juxtaposes the last four paragraphs of the final vignette with all of the first vignette—which ends with the narrator's feelings of shame, longing, and general dissatisfaction with her house—the trajectory and outcome of Esperanza make logical sense: she disliked her house, she longed for another, and—we are to presume—she will surely leave. At the same time, the final paragraph of the last vignette ("They will not know I have gone away to come back. For the ones I left behind. For the ones who cannot out.") appears to transport Esperanza back to her origins, effecting her return and pulling her into the fold of her community.

Still, the projected reunion, or reconciliation of Esperanza with her community has not, in reality, proven to be all that convincing to certain readers. According to the way it is framed in "Mango Says Goodbye," Esperanza's story appears to end *and* continue, which, as Iser might suggest, may cloud her tale: "Ending and continuing are basic forms of life, but when they are both present simultaneously in one [person's] consciousness, they begin to invalidate each other. Continuing robs the end of its uniqueness, which would otherwise be a consolation. But from the standpoint of a finite individual, endless continuation is both aimless and beyond [their] control" (Iser, "Representation" 230). The applicability of Iser's statement (made in reference to *King Lear* and *Macbeth*) to *Mango Street* concerns the following predicament in which Esperanza seems to be: No matter how hard the narrative strives through the opinions of other characters to "naturalize" how gifted she is, how clearly destined she is for writerdom, and how *certain* it appears that she *will* retain her ties to her community,[29] ultimately, the last paragraph of the book does not manage to convey the impression that Esperanza's resolve to reintegrate or, as some readers might see it, finally integrate herself into the Mango Street community is rooted in selflessness, that is, in the philanthropic desire to mingle with and serve her community.

Consequently, actual readers, such as Rodríguez, may come away with the impression that even though Esperanza has "returned," she has done so because, in accordance with messages imparted in such vignettes as "The Three Sisters," and "Alicia and I," *she will have had to*. That is to say, in the way of filial obligation to one's parents, as the "daughter" of her community, Esperanza is eternally indebted to Mango Street (her origins): she can no sooner "forget" Mango Street than she can "disown" her parents. Furthermore, what Esperanza writes and has written is based, parasitically, on memories of a *formative* reality. As such, no matter how displeasurable this has been, and/or unpalatable it still is, whether she likes it or not (to echo the attitude of her friend Alicia) Mango Street *is* Esperanza, and vice versa. More than this, Mango Street provides the fodder for both her books and her "writerly" persona.

If one traces Esperanza's wish to reinvent herself throughout chapters such as "My Name," "A Rice Sandwich," "Born Bad," "Bums in the Attic," "Beautiful and Cruel," "A House of My Own," alongside her desire for freedom, it is easier to view her story in terms of an odyssey directed at self-knowledge (and, presumably, self-acceptance). Whereas in "Beautiful and Cruel" Esperanza resolves to become more strong and independent—"I am one who leaves the table like a man, without putting back the chair or picking up my plate" (89); whereas in "Alicia and I Talking on Edna's Steps, "she persists in strong denial of her ties to Mango Street; and whereas "A House of My Own" represents her ongoing, wistful longing for a "real" house, the abrupt appearance of the final vignette, which on the surface conveys Esperanza's deep concern for her community, seems all the more conspicuous, if not altogether incongruous.

In effect, by the end of *Mango Street*, it cannot with certainty be said that Esperanza knows, much less accepts, herself. This may be because the last vignette, as literature, "is not an explanation of origins; it is a *staging* of the constant deferment of explanation [. . .]" (Iser, "Representation" 228, emphasis added). And staging, to reiterate, brings about the "suspension" of language's denotative function. Hence, "what [staging] designates is no longer meant to represent a something to which it refers, but serves as an analogue instead, through which a wordless desire may find expression or a response-inviting appeal may be signaled," (Iser, "Representation" 229). Has the author, Cisneros, deployed the story Esperanza conveys in the last chapter as a persuasive device aimed at drawing the attention of *Mango Street*'s initial implied readers—Chicanos/as–*away* from the original, basic rift in herself, a division which, on one hand, fueled her desire to be alone to write, and, on the other, triggered her claim to simultaneously desire to want to be in, and serve her community?[30]

Taking a closer look at the spread of statements made by "Esperanza" in the last vignette draws attention to and underlines its heteroglossic nature—"I like to tell stories. I am going to tell you the story about a girl who didn't want to belong" (109); "We didn't always live on Mango Street, [. . .] but what I remember most is Mango Street, sad red house, the house I belong but do not belong to" (109-10); "I put it down on paper and then the ghost does not ache so much" (110); "One day I will pack my bags of books and paper. [. . .] One day I will go away"; "Friends and neighbors will say What happened to that Esperanza? [. . .] Why did she march so far away?"; "They will not know I have gone away to come back. For the ones I left behind. For the ones who cannot out" (110). Heteroglossia, one may recall, "is *another's speech in another's language*, serving to express authorial intentions but in a refracted way" (*Dialogic* 324). The "refracted way" in this case is a "loophole" in Esperanza's discourse on leaving. A loophole is defined by Bakhtin as "the retention for oneself of the possibility for altering the ultimate, final meaning of one's own words" (*Problems* 233). Hence, while on the one hand, the final vignette contains Esperanza's "confessional self-definition"—the "story" told about the "girl who didn't want to belong" turns out to be about herself—on the other hand, the last chapter also endeavors to record her resolve to return. Esperanza's last words—"They will not know I have gone away to come back. For the ones I left behind. For the ones who cannot out"— glance sideways, at her prospective critics ("friends and neighbors" of the community she will have left behind). Ultimately, however, Esperanza's words in this last vignette may not be all that convincing: "An anticipated and obligatory vindication by the other merges with self-condemnation, and both tones begin to sound simultaneously in that voice, resulting in abrupt interruptions and sudden transitions" (*Problems* 234).

In the end, Bakhtin's summary assessment about confessional self-definitions with loopholes might appear rather convincing: "the confessional self-definition with a loophole [. . .] is [. . .] an ultimate word about oneself, a final definition of oneself, but in fact it is forever taking account internally the responsive, contrary evaluation of oneself made by another. The [heroine] who repents and condemns [herself] actually wants to provoke praise and acceptance by another" (Bakhtin, *Problems* 233). Such a loophole, moreover, can make the heroine "ambiguous" and "elusive" not only to others, such as readers, but also to herself (Bakhtin, *Problems* 234). Curiously, Esperanza's self-affirmation in the final vignette of *Mango Street* could go unvalidated, since "[her] affirmation of self" may strike some readers "like a continuous hidden polemic [. . .] with some other person on the theme of [herself]" (*Problems* 207).

From Iser's perspective, it is during narrative moments like the Esperanza-centered polemic, when coherence begins to fray and meaning starts to collapse, that the "aesthetic dimension" of a work comes forth:

> It is such transformations that give rise to the aesthetic dimension of the text, for what had seemed closed is now opened up again. The more one text incorporates other texts, the more intensified will be the process of doubling induced by the act of selection. The text itself becomes a kind of junction, where other texts, norms, and values meet and work upon each other; as a point of intersection its core is virtual, and only when actualized—*by the potential recipient*—does it explode into its plurivocity. ("Representation" 219, emphasis added)

At this point, the evasive words of Cisneros regarding the autobiographic resonance in *Mango Street* begin to make more sense. "One thing I know for certain," she states, "you, the reader, are Esperanza." Such a revelation nudges the implied readers of her novel to actualize on their own its elusive messages and/or myriad meanings (Introduction xix).

Viewing the final vignette of the novel as an intertextual, intradiscursive "junction" which at once incorporates and alters others has, hopefully, allowed readers to see in clearer fashion that what at the beginning of the novel appeared to be the recollection of the narrator's neighborhood, ends up transforming itself into an ambiguous diary-like entry about Esperanza's "reality" and experience as a writer. More than this, "Mango Says Goodbye" suggests that the primary referent of Esperanza's collective tales might be the fictionalizing act itself. As such, readers may be left to mull over the implication of this. "In looking at 'constative' propositions, statements of truth or falsity," states Eagleton, "we tend to suppress their reality and effectivity as actions in their own right; literature [therefore] restores us to this sense of linguistic performance in the most dramatic way, for whether what it asserts as existing actually exists or not is unimportant" (118-19).

Consequently, one could be left pondering whether the focus of critics should, as Iser has suggested, be more—rather than less—inclined toward the question of what narrative representation can "*tell us about ourselves.*" After all, "[t]he work itself cannot 'foresee' its own future history of interpretations, cannot control and delimit these readings as we can do, or *try* to do [. . .]" (Eagleton 119, emphasis added). What, then, are we, the readers, to do with and about the houses that are all Mango Street?

From *Modern Fiction Studies* 47, no. 4 (Winter 2001): 910-946. Copyright © 2001 by the Purdue Research Foundation. Reprinted with permission of The Johns Hopkins University Press.

Notes

1. Arte Público Press published the novel in 1984, 1985, and 1986. In 1989, Arte Público published a slightly altered edition of *Mango Street*. Subsequently, in 1991 Vintage Books, a division of Random House Publishers, published the revised 1989 edition of the book. Knopf followed suit in 1994. Unless otherwise noted, all quotes from the novel are taken from the Vintage Books edition, 1991.

2. The fact that Cisneros's book continues to attract the attention of scholars and critics in several disciplines can be seen in the number of articles that have been written on her and/or *Mango Street* from the mid 1980s through 2000. An online search of the MLA Bibliography in January 2001 returned more than 40 articles.

3. Poey's comments point to long-standing marginalization of Chicana writers (females) within the larger collectivity of Chicano writers and the Chicano community (which consists of both males and females). Ramón Saldívar addresses the marginality of Chicano narrative, within mainstream US culture, stating that "it is to the margins [of American literature] that Chicano literature has been consigned [. . .]" (10). Saldívar also underlines the more extreme marginalization of Chicana writers and women in general within circles of both Chicano and mainstream American culture:

> Contemporary Chicana writers challenge not only the ideologies of oppression of the Anglo-American culture that their Chicano brothers confront, but they also challenge the ideologies of patriarchal oppression evinced by Chicano writers and present within Chicano culture itself. [. . .] [T]he literature produced by Chicana authors is counterhegemonic to the second power, serving as a critique of critiques of oppression that fail to take into account the full range of domination. (173)

Within my paper, the term "Chicano community" encompasses both Mexican-American men and women; "Chicano writers" refers to men only. At the same time, the use of "Chicana," to designate writers and/or the community, refers to Mexican-American women.

4. Whereas I have distinguished between Chicana writers and the Chicana community, on one hand, and, on the other, Chicano writers and the Chicano community, I intend a similar distinction between Latina writers and the Latina community, on one hand, and Latino writers (males) and the Latino community (males and females). Latina writers encompass women writers of Hispanic origin, including Mexicans, Cubans, Argentines, Chileans, Dominicans, Puerto Ricans, and others. Latina writers, like Chicanas, have also been marginalized within both the larger collectivity of Latino writers and Latino culture, on one hand, and mainstream US culture, on the other. In addition to Saldívar, see Rosaura Sánchez and Gloria Anzaldúa.

5. Poey views *Mango Street* together with Rudolfo Anaya's *Bless Me, Ultima*, in an effort to gauge "how and to what extent [they] are incorporated as additives to the already established canonical tradition as well as the logic behind their promotion as documented, legal trespassers into the academic landscape" (202). Poey maintains that

the term representative does not imply that they speak or stand for the "complete representation of Chicano or Latino literary expression" (204); she further stresses that Anaya's and Cisneros's books have "become representative [. . .] by often being the only Latina/o works assigned in a relatively broad spectrum of courses" (204).

6. Szadziuk maintains that

[C]ulture can no longer be regarded as a static entity but must be viewed instead as something dynamic [. . .]. In the case of Western American societies, this need to regard culture as an on-going process may be seen especially in the emergence of studies concerned with the border between the United States and Mexico [. . .] which focus on the crosscultural indeterminacy of this meeting ground rather than on either of the two cultures in isolation. (109)

See also Poey and Saldívar.

7. Since 1994 students have periodically informed me that they had already read *Mango Street* in high school. See also Poey.

8. Students in my spring undergraduate seminar (2000) were given the task of speaking from the perspective of Cisneros, in order to summarize what the book dealt with and ascertain which audiences it seemed to target. Several students underlined the independence of the female author who, they believed, spoke primarily to women; two students singled out the "independence" of *Mango Street*'s "Mexican-American" author, who, in their opinion, seemed to be addressing a Chicana or Latina readership. Only one student abstained from positing an ideal community of readers exclusively comprised by women. Proclaiming his open admiration and extremely high regard for the book, this student refused to formulate any reductive, facile hypothesis concerning the latter. Neither group of students—neither those who planned to major or minor in English, nor those with plans to major or minor in Spanish—could arrive at a consensus regarding what they perceived as the primary themes and messages of the book.

9. My remark on the crosscultural appeal of the novel is based on the numerous essays indexed in the MLA Bibliography and on the commentary of book covers and prefaces/afterwords of several printings of the book published by Arte Público, Random House, and Knopf.

10. This paper obviously ascribes to particular aspects of reception theory, such as the concept of horizons of experience and expectation of both authors and readers. It thus presumes that "meanings" in and of a literary work are actively produced, at once internally derived and externally influenced. See for example, Jauss; Eco; Ingarden; Iser, *The Act of Reading: A Theory of Aesthetic Response*; Suleiman and Crosman.

11. Although her response seems elusive, it is important to keep in mind that *Mango Street* was written over the span of more than five years, a period during which Cisneros not only attended graduate school but also taught in inner-city schools. Cisneros stresses that the story lines in *Mango Street*, if initially inclined toward autobiography, at a certain point metamorphosed into a collective—thus multidiscursive, multivalent—story not only about her life, but about the lives of others, over a range of time, and across different places (Introduction xi-xii).

12. According to Bakhtin, "Language becomes 'one's own' only when the speaker populates it with his [sic] own intention, his own accent, when he appropriates the word, adapting it to his own semantic and expressive intention" (*Dialogic* 293).

13. See "The House on Mango Street," "Cathy Queen of Cats," "A Rice Sandwich," "Bums in the Attic," "Alicia and I Talking on Edna's Steps," "A House of My Own."

14. In his essay, "Race under Representation," David Lloyd identifies "exclusion" as one of the predominant terms that has been commonly deployed in anti-racist cultural politics and discourse in recent years. Among the other terms cited by Lloyd are "euro-" and "ethnocentrism," "marginalization," and the critical categories "orientalism" and the "West," expressions which, in his view, share the common trait of being "spatial" terms (62).

15. My students' sensitivity to and/or sympathy for gender- and family-related issues addressed in *Mango Street* might be related to the fact that the class consisted primarily of white, middle-class women, several of whom had identified themselves as liberal and feminist and/or had taken classes that had incorporated feminist approaches to literature. All students, including the lone male, expressed sympathy for the plight of Esperanza, primarily on the basis that they, as children, had experienced or encountered similar situations.

16. For examples of, in my opinion, limited formalist approaches to Cisneros's writing, see Klein, Kolmar, and Thomson. For a sample of Chicano/a perspectives of *Mango Street*, see Olivares; Rosaldo, 84-93; Quintana, 54-74; Saldívar, 171-99; Valdés, 287-300; and "In Search of Identity in Cisneros's *The House on Mango Street*;" and Yarbro-Bejarano. Although this body of criticism does not suffer from decontextualized readings, some of these critics view the language in *Mango Street* as a transparent medium that mimetically renders reality.

17. Poey states that she appropriates the term *Bildungsroman* as it has been seen and used in English literary studies, not as it is viewed and defined in Germanic studies (206).

18. In addition to Norton, see, for example, Doyle.

19. The need for establishing consistency stems from the fact that at any given moment, a reader's grasp of the story at hand is partial. The novel, according to Iser, "[c]annot be continually 'present' to the reader with an identical degree of intensity" (*Act of Reading* 16).

20. Referring to overgeneralized readings of *Mango Street*, Poey comments: "By isolating [the text] from [its] discursive and historical contexts, [the literary work] can also function as [a mirror] of the hegemonic and [confirm . . .] stereotypic representations" (215).

21. According to J. L. Austin, language is not merely descriptive: it can *do* something, even as it appears to make a statement (12), as in the case of a "performative sentence" (6). States Austin, "The name is derived [. . .] from 'perform,' the usual verb with the noun 'action': it indicates that the issuing of the utterance is the performing of an action—it is not normally thought of as just saying something" (6-7). Austin focuses on instances "in which to say something is to *do* something; or in which *by* saying or *in* saying something we are doing something" (12). For him, it is "illocutionary"

speech acts that do something *in* the saying, and "perlocutionary" acts that achieve an effect *by* saying. Illocutionary acts include "informing, ordering, undertaking [. . .], i.e. utterances which have a certain (conventional) force" (108). Perlocutionary acts are "what we bring about *by* saying something, such as convincing, persuading, deterring, and even [. . .] surprising or misleading" (108).

22. Simon Dentith's discussion of Voloshinov's notion of the "multiaccentual" nature of the sign (and, by extension, language) elucidates Rosaldo's reference to the polyvalence of Esperanza's name in Spanish and English: "[T]he signs of language (words, above all), bear different accents, emphases, and therefore meanings with different inflections and in different contexts. Meanings emerge in society and society is not a homogeneous mass but is itself divided by such factors as social class; signs do not therefore have fixed meanings but are always inflected in different ways to carry different values and attitudes" (22-23). Regarding the question of translation from Spanish to English, for example, Rosario Ferré speaks to the impossibility of transcribing one cultural identity into another: "As I write in English, I am inevitably translating a Latin American identity, still rooted in pre-industrial traditions and mores, with very definite philosophical convictions and beliefs, into a North American context" (157). Although Ferré's comments refer to Puerto Rican reality, her comments can be applied to Chicana/o writers like Cisneros, who created a protagonist whose name, Esperanza, connotes different things in the two languages and cultures in and through which she endeavors to define herself: North American and Mexican American.

23. Speaking to the confusion that surrounds the term "representation" in the English language, Iser states that representation and mimesis have become "interchangeable notions in literary criticism," the result of which is the concealment of "[. . .] the performative qualities through which the act of representation brings about something that hitherto did not exist." He emphasizes, moreover, that *darstellung* is more "neutral and does not necessarily drag all the mimetic connotations in its wake," and should therefore not be mistaken with mimesis, which does refer to a "given" object assumed to exist "prior to the act of representation" ("Representation" 217).

24. In *Problems of Dostoevsky's Poetics* ("Discourse of Dostoevsky") Bakhtin remarks, for example, that the "attitude" the hero has towards himself [sic] "is inseparably bound up with his attitude toward another, and with the attitude of another toward him. His consciousness of self is constantly perceived against the other's consciousness of him—'I for myself' against the background of 'I for another.' Thus the hero's words about himself are structured under the continuous influence of someone else's words about him" (207). See also pages 182-84.

25. Regarding Bakhtin's notion of dialogism in language, Dentith states, "Language appears here as the site or space in which dialogic relationships are realized; it manifests itself in discourse, the words oriented towards another" (34). Of heteroglossia Dentith comments, "it is a word [Bakhtin] coins [. . .] to allude to the multiplicity of actual 'languages' which are at any time spoken by the speakers of any 'language.' These are languages of social groups and classes, of professional groups, of generations, the different languages for different occasions that speakers adopt even within these broader distinctions" (35).

---

26. According to Eagleton:

> [A] literary work can be seen as constructing what have been called 'subject positions' (119). [. . .] To understand a [literary text] means grasping its language as being 'oriented' towards the reader from a certain range of positions: in reading, we build up a sense of what kind of effects this language is trying to achieve ('intention'), what sorts of rhetoric it considers appropriate to use, what assumptions govern the kinds of poetic tactics it employs, what attitudes towards reality these imply. (120)

Additionally, in "The Reading Process" Iser, referring to Roman Ingarden, remarks that

> Once we are immersed in the flow of *Satzdenken* (sentence-thought), we are ready, after completing the thought of one sentence, to think out the "continuation," also in the form of a sentence—and that is, in the form of a sentence that connects up with the sentence we have just thought through. In this way the process of reading goes effortlessly forward. But if by chance the following sentence has no tangible connection whatever with the sentence we have just thought through, there then comes a blockage in the stream of thought. This hiatus is linked with a more or less active surprise, or with indignation [. . .]. (79)

Iser accounts for the prospective "exasperation" of the reader by drawing attention to Ingarden's assumption that all readers—in the spirit and shadow of classical aesthetics—expect and thus follow the seamless "flow" of a work, from beginning to end. In contrast to Ingarden, Iser maintains that "literary texts are full of unexpected twists and turns, and frustration of expectations," and adds that gaps avail readers the chance to engage their own faculty for "establishing connections" whereby textual indeterminacies are filled in (79).

27. See Valdés, "The Critical Reception of Sandra Cisneros's *The House on Mango Street*," for a nuanced analysis of the way that the narrative brings about the conjunction in the last vignette of the socio-historical context of Cisneros's novel, at the same time that it underlines the "narrative unfolding of discourse" (292-94).

28. See for example, Genette.

29. See the chapters "Born Bad," "Edna's Ruthie," "Bums in the Attic," "A Smart Cookie," "The Three Sisters," "Alicia and I Talking on Edna's Steps," "A House of My Own," and "Mango Says Goodbye Sometimes."

30. According to Cisneros's recollection of the period between the time she started her book and published it, her encounters with and feelings of ineffectiveness at helping her students availed her the opportunity to mend a self-perceived rift in her character, one which she had hitherto believed was irreconcilable. She refers to the part of her that wanted to actively participate and make a difference in her community, and she alludes to the more individualistic part of her that longed for seclusion, in hopes of nurturing and pursuing her goal of becoming a writer (Introduction xi-xii; xvii-xviii).

Works Cited

Anzaldúa, Gloria. *Borderlands/La Frontera: The New Mestiza*. San Francisco: Spinsters, 1987.

Austin, J. L. *How to Do Things with Words*. Ed. J. O. Urmson. New York: Oxford UP, 1962.

Bakhtin, Mikhail. *The Dialogic Imagination: Four Essays*. Trans. Caryl Emerson and Michael Holquist. Ed. Michael Holquist. Austin: U of Texas P, 1981.

_____. *Problems of Dostoevsky's Poetics*. Trans. and Ed. Caryl Emerson. Minneapolis: U of Minnesota P, 1984.

Cisneros, Sandra. *The House on Mango Street*. New York: Vintage, 1991.

_____. Introduction. *The House on Mango Street*. New York: Knopf, 1994. xi-xx.

_____. "Return to One's House: An Interview with Sandra Cisneros." Interview with Martha Satz. *Southwest Review* 82.2 (1997): 166-85.

Dentith, Simon. "Voloshinov and Bakhtin on Language." *Bakhtinian Thought*. Ed. Simon Dentith. London: Routledge, 1995. 22-40.

Doyle, Jacqueline. "More Room of Her Own: Sandra Cisneros's *The House on Mango Street*." *MELUS* 19.4 (1994): 5-35.

Eagleton, Terry. *Literary Theory: An Introduction*. Minneapolis: U of Minnesota P, 1983.

Eco, Umberto. *The Role of the Reader*. Bloomington: Indiana UP, 1979.

Edie, James. *Speaking and Meaning: The Phenomenology of Language*. Bloomington: U of Indiana P, 1976.

Ferré, Rosario. "On Destiny, Language, and Translation." *The Youngest Doll*. Lincoln: U of Nebraska P, 1991. 153-65.

Genette, Gerard. *Narrative Discourse*. Trans. Jane Lewin. Ithaca: Cornell UP, 1980.

Ingarden, Roman. *The Literary Work of Art*. Evanston: Northwestern UP, 1973.

Iser, Wolfgang. *The Act of Reading: A Theory of Aesthetic Response*. Baltimore: The Johns Hopkins UP, 1978.

_____. "The Reading Process: A Phenomenological Approach" (1974). *Modern Literary Theory*. Eds. Philip Rice and Patricia Waugh. 2nd ed. London: Edward Arnold, 1993. 77-83.

_____. "Representation: A Performative Act." *The Aims of Representation: Subject/Text/History*. Ed. Murray Krieger. New York: Columbia UP, 1987. 217-32.

Jauss, Hans Robert. "Literary History as a Challenge to Literary Theory." Trans. Elizabeth Benzinger. *New Literary History* 2 (1970): 7-37.

Kanellos, Nicolás. Introduction. *The Hispanic Literary Companion*. Ed. Nicolás Kanellos. Detroit: Visible Ink, 1997.

Klein, Dianne. "Coming of Age in Novels by Rudolfo Anaya and Sandra Cisneros." *English Journal* (September 1992): 21-26.

Kolmar, Wendy. "'Dialectics of Connectedness': Supernatural Elements in Novels by Bambara, Cisneros, Grahn, and Erdrich." *Haunting the House of Fiction*.

Eds. Lynnette Carpenter and Wendy Kolmar. Knoxville: U of Tennessee P, 1991. 236-49.

Lloyd, David. "Race Under Representation." *Oxford Literary Review* 13.1-2 (1991): 62-94.

Norton, Jody. "History, Rememory, and Transformation: Actualizing Literary Value." *The Centennial Review* 38.3 (1994): 589-602.

Olivares, Julián. "Sandra Cisneros's *The House on Mango Street*, and the Poetics of Space." *Americas Review* 15.3-4 (Fall 1987): 160-70.

O'Reilly Herrera, Andrea. "'Chambers of Consciousness': Sandra Cisneros and the Development of the Self and the BIG *House on Mango Street*." *Bucknell Review* 39.1 (1995): 191-204.

Poey, Delia. "Coming of Age in the Curriculum: *The House on Mango Street* and *Bless Me, Ultima* as Representative Texts." *Americas Review* 24.3-4 (1996): 201-17.

Quintana, Alvina E. *Home Girls: Chicana Literary Voices*. Philadelphia: Temple UP, 1996.

Rodríguez, Juan. "*The House on Mango Street*, by Sandra Cisneros." *Austin Chronicle* 10 August 1984.

Rosaldo, Renato. "Fables of the Fallen Guy." *Criticism in the Borderlands*. Eds. Calderón and José David Saldívar. Chapel Hill: Duke UP, 1994. 84-93.

Saldívar, Ramón. *Chicano Narrative: The Dialectics of Difference*. Madison: U of Wisconsin P, 1990.

Sánchez, Reuben. "Remembering to Always Come Back: The Child's Wished-For Escape and the Adult's Self-Empowered Return in Sandra Cisneros's *House on Mango Street*." *Children's Literature* 23 (1995): 221-41.

Sánchez, Rosaura. "Ethnicity, Ideology, and Academia." *Americas Review* 15.1 (1987): 80-88.

Suleiman, Susan, and Inge Crosman, eds. *The Reader in the Text: Essays on Audience Interpretation*. Princeton: Princeton UP, 1980.

Szadziuk, Maria. "Culture as Transition: Becoming a Woman in Bi-ethnic Space." *Mosaic* 32.3 (1999):109-29.

Thomson, Jeff. "'What is Called Heaven': Identity in Sandra Cisneros's *Woman Hollering Creek*." *Studies in Fiction* 31.3 (1994): 415-24.

Valdés, María Elena de. "The Critical Reception of Sandra Cisneros's *The House on Mango Street*." *Gender, Self, and Society*. Ed. Renate von Bardeleben. Frankfurt: Peter Lang, 1993. 287-300.

Yarbro-Bejarano, Yvonne. "Chicana Literature From a Chicana Feminist Perspective." *Chicana Creativity and Criticism*. Ed. María Herrera-Sobek. Houston: Arte Público, 1988. 139-45.

Stories from the "Hem of Life":
Contesting Marginality in Sandra Cisneros's *The House on Mango Street* and Toni Morrison's *The Bluest Eye*_____

Catherine Leen

With the publication of the twenty-fifth anniversary editions of *The House on Mango Street* in 2009 and *The Bluest Eye* in 1993, Sandra Cisneros and Toni Morrison both wrote essays for the new editions in which they look back on their first novels. Cisneros recalls that, as a twenty-three-year-old aspiring writer, her aim was to "write stories that ignore borders between genres, between written and spoken, between highbrow literature and children's nursery rhymes, between New York and the imaginary village of Macondo, between the U.S. and Mexico" (xvi-xvii). Cisneros refers to a Mexican and Pan-Latin American heritage as the inspiration for her work, although her main intent was to communicate her experience as a Mexican American woman growing up in Chicago through language that transcends literary conventions and political borders. Similarly, in her essay, Morrison discusses her attempts to portray her distinct culture through her writing, commenting on her bid to articulate her meditation on internalized racism by means of a narrative that both reached and represented her community. Morrison notes that her use of a distinctive language "as well as my attempt to shape a silence while breaking it are attempts to transfigure the complexity and wealth of Black-American culture into a language worthy of the culture" (172).

Both writers show a keen awareness of the fact that to tell their stories, which have few precedents, they must create a distinct literary style, and their desire to write about their communities stems partly from their sense of exclusion from Euro-American literary texts. Cisneros has mentioned on numerous occasions the isolation she experienced as a student at the University of Iowa when she and her classmates were asked to read and comment on Gaston Bachelard's *The*

Poetics of Space, and she could not relate to her classmates' stories of houses with attics and basements: "Well, I don't want to talk about the basement of my childhood because there were rats there! [Laughing] I don't want to go near those basements and we lived in third-floor flats and we didn't have an attic. Who in the hell had an attic!" (Torres 199). Morrison, like Cisneros, was inspired to write her first novel as a reaction to a literary tradition that did not represent her experience: "There were no books about me, I didn't exist in all the books I had read" (Matus 37). The adolescent narrators of *The House on Mango Street* and *The Bluest Eye* are acutely aware of their marginal positions in relation to mainstream U.S. society. Early in *The Bluest Eye*, Claudia MacTeer observes that she and her sister, Frieda, move about "on the hem of life" as a consequence of being "a minority in both caste and class" (11). Similarly, Esperanza Cordero exposes outsiders' racist attitudes toward her Mexican American neighborhood: "They think we're dangerous. They think we will attack them with shiny knives" (28). By forming and transforming narratives based on the distinct languages of their cultures, these young female narrators learn to articulate their own identities and break a tradition of silence about the abuse of women in their cultures. Cisneros has commented that she sought to write about the "'ugliest' subjects [she] could find, the most un-'poetic'" (Cruz 915). Morrison's pronouncement on the importance of rejecting language that marginalizes minority groups is more definitive still. She observes in her 1993 Nobel Prize lecture, "Oppressive language does more than represent violence; it is violence; does more than represent the limits of knowledge; it limits knowledge" (in Peterson 269).

Virginia Woolf's *A Room of One's Own* looms large as an influence for women writers attempting to tell their stories. Woolf's treatise on the relationship between women's poverty and their lack of a literary tradition has been criticized, however, for its lack of attention to class differences and almost complete neglect of women of color. In fact, one critic has suggested that Cisneros's protagonist, Esperanza, a young girl growing up in a poor Chicago *barrio*, may well have been prevented from finding her voice as a writer by "Woolf's class and ethnic biases" (Doyle 7). Chicana writer and theorist Gloria Anzaldúa rejects Woolf's premise entirely, urging women to write no matter what their circumstances: "Forget the room of one's own—write in the kitchen, lock yourself up in the bathroom. Write on the bus or the welfare line, on the job or during meals, between sleeping and waking" (170). Woolf's privileged position notwithstanding, however, her insistence on the importance of recording the minutiae of women's lives continues to resonate with contemporary writers:

> All the dinners are cooked; the plates and cups washed; the children sent to school and gone out in the world. Nothing remains of it all. All has vanished. No biography or history has a word to say about it. And the novels, without meaning to, inevitably lie. All these infinitely obscure lives remain to be recorded. (89)

Morrison has clearly been influenced to some extent by Woolf's work, as she wrote her master's thesis on the theme of suicide in the writings of Woolf and William Faulkner (Peach 3). Although Cisneros had not read Woolf before writing *The House on Mango Street*, she nevertheless, like Woolf, used the metaphor of the house to represent physically the female writer's claim for space in the literary world.

In the early 1980s, Francisco A. Lomelí wrote that Chicana writers had "been generally ignored or misunderstood and stigmatized as being less rigorous in their approach to producing literature" (29). In his analysis of the reasons for the eventual crossover success of *The House on Mango Street*, Manuel M. Martín-Rodríguez observes that marketing strategies packaged Chicana and Chicano texts in book covers with a graphic style that "accentuates the childish, the nice, the colourful" (131), thus presenting them as unthreatening and pleasingly exotic. The use of such marketing strategies is complicated by the frequently contestatory and complex nature of the narratives themselves, however, which "give voice to unexpected and uncontainable social problematics that break through the pleasing veneer of the ideal Latina postmodern commodity" (McCracken 39). Cisneros has noted that she has found reviews of her first novel that dismiss it because it is told from a child's perspective frustrating, adding, "It's really a book about the author's search for identity and gender and class and ethnicity even though the persona is a young girl, twelve or so" (Torres 232-33). Moreover, Cisneros does not avoid the controversial topics of poverty, exclusion, and the abuse of women in a patriarchal society. As Norma Klahn notes, her writing continues a feminist tradition led by Chicanas in the 1960s who "asserted their right within the radicalized struggles for democracy and social justice to voice their experiences outside the laws of the fathers" (117). Read as a metafiction, Esperanza Cordero's quest to find her voice and tell her story becomes a metaphor of the struggle of Chicana writers to be recognized and valued. Morrison also tells her story mainly from the viewpoint of a young girl, Claudia, but her novel, too, is far from childish and breaks a silence about contentious and even taboo subjects, such as domestic abuse, racism, and incest. On a metafictional level, *The Bluest Eye* also marks a sea change in African American literature in its shift away from portraying the African American community as a unified group. Like other black women writers who speak of the violence toward women in their communities, Morrison has had hostile reactions from many African American men, who see her engagement with difficult subjects as "sowing the seeds of division in what should be perceived, from a black nationalist perspective, as a homogenous community in the face of white oppression" (Peach 45). Thus Claudia's narrative, which is inextricably interwoven with those of the women around her, becomes "an artistic, often poetic, exploration of the complex relations between individual and community" (Tirrell 13).

In each novel, the outcome of the story is less important than the manner in which it is recounted. The story outlined at the outset of each novel is essentially complete, so that it is not its conclusion that is important, but the manner in which it unfolds: "Since why is difficult to handle, one must take refuge in how" (Morrison 4). *The House on Mango Street* opens with narrator Esperanza's expression of disappointment at the latest house her family inhabits. Esperanza had longed for a "real house" with "stairs inside like the houses on T.V. And we'd have a basement and at least three washrooms. . . . Our house would be white with trees around it, a great big yard and grass growing without a fence" (4). She refuses to accept her parents' assurances that their situation is temporary, saying, "I know how these things go" (5). Her cynicism proves well founded, for her dream of an ideal house is not realized by the end of the novel. Similarly, in *The Bluest Eye* Claudia presents a succinct summary of the story of Pecola Breedlove that leaves no doubt as to how it concludes:

> There were no marigolds in the fall of 1941. We thought, at the time, that it was because Pecola was having her father's baby that the marigolds did not grow. . . . What is clear now is that all of that hope, fear, lust, love, and grief, nothing remains but Pecola and the unyielding earth. Cholly Breedlove is dead; our innocence too. (4)

Esperanza and Claudia struggle to make sense of the world around them by negotiating the conversations they hear and the events they witness. By piecing together parental instructions, gossip, stories, advice from peers and elders, and other narratives, they attempt to find their own voices and document unrecorded histories and overlooked lives. In this chapter, I examine how the authors, by weaving together fragmented narratives and taboo themes and by using language in radical new ways, negotiate their position of marginality.

The fact that Cisneros's novel speaks both to Chicana writers' efforts to claim a literary space and to the adolescent protagonist's desire to find a way of being means that the way in which Cisneros tells the story, what Claudia terms the "how," is central to the understanding of her text. What at first appears to be an adolescent's straightforward account of her and her neighbors' lives is, in fact, a carefully crafted narrative that is conversational but does not cite dialogues or report them in a direct manner. A close reading of the novel reveals countless markers of reported speech, with Cisneros insistently using the word "says," which thus foreground Esperanza's creation of her own narrative style by repeating, questioning, or dismissing conversations that she hears and engages with, leading to "a conceptual juxtaposition of action and reaction where the movement itself is the central topic" (Valdés 165-66). Esperanza is cast as much as a listener, and sometimes a reader, as she is as a narrator. Her image of the much longed-for ideal house that represents the realization of the American Dream is, in fact, filtered through her parents' stories and dreams: "They always told us that one day we would move into a house, a real house" (4); "This was the house Papa talked about" (4); "This was the house Mama dreamed up" (4). The house on Mango Street, however, is "not the way they told it at all" (4). Esperanza's deep disappointment at the gap between the imagined house of her and her family's stories and dreams and the decrepit reality leads to her disillusionment with her parents' narratives and her refusal to accept their reassurances that the house is a temporary measure.

Not only must Esperanza navigate a polyphony of voices and diverse, sometimes conflicting, points of view, but, as her reaction to her circumstances becomes more nuanced and mature, she must also decide to what extent she will accept the various versions of the stories she hears. The adults' speech in the novel is generally portrayed as confusing, especially when they talk about sexuality. In "Hips," Esperanza and the other girls explain the reason for the maturation of their bodies in an unintentionally humorous manner, with Rachel commenting that hips are "good for holding a baby when you're cooking," while the younger Nenny believes that "if you don't get them you may turn into a man" (49). Their confusion over sexuality and maturity is compounded by the dearth of positive role models in their community. The women in Mango Street are trapped, often literally, in abusive marriages or have such limited opportunities that marriage is their only hope for changing their lives. Marin longs to work downtown, because you "can meet someone in the subway who might marry you and take you to live in a big house far away" (26). This dream of escape through marriage is never realized in any of the stories Esperanza hears, however. Ruthie, whose marriage has broken up, is forced to return home and reverts to a second childhood of excessive dependence on her mother (68). Rafaela, meanwhile, is the victim of an obsessively possessive husband who locks her in their house for fear that "she will run away since she is too beautiful to look at" (79).

The danger of being too beautiful is echoed in the story of Esperanza's most important peer role model, Sally. Sally's versions of events are perhaps the ones that are most explicitly and consistently called into question. Her father beats her because "to be this beautiful is trouble" (81), yet for a time she displays a defiance that fascinates Esperanza, painting her eyes and pulling up her skirt at school until she prepares to return home as "a different Sally" (82). To escape her violent father, Sally marries a husband who is equally controlling and abusive. In the only vignette that directly refers to telling stories, "What Sally Said," the repetition of the words "said" or "say" undermine the credibility of the excuses Sally makes for the bruises left by her father's beatings: "He never hits me hard. She said her mama rubs lard on all the places where it hurts. Then at school she'd say she fell" (92). Although Sally is clearly the victim of her father's violence, Esperanza is fascinated by her precocious sexuality and longs to emulate it by wearing black like her. Significantly, however, Esperanza's mother sounds a warning note about Sally's behavior, "my mother says to wear black so young is dangerous" (82), which will prove prophetic. In the vignette "Red Clowns," Esperanza is betrayed by her friend, who leaves her alone with a group of boys that sexually abuse her. This experience is so traumatic that for the first time Esperanza does not want to narrate it, "Please don't make me tell it all" (100). She situates her friend's misleadingly positive stories about boys within the romantic myths perpetuated by popular culture:

Sally, you lied. It wasn't what you said at all. What he did. Where he touched me. I didn't want it, Sally. The way they said it, the way it's supposed to be, all the storybooks and movies, why did you lie to me? (99)

When considered within the context of Sally's betrayal, the vignette in which Esperanza tells of Sally's abusive marriage has more than a hint of bitterness: "She is happy, except sometimes her husband gets angry . . . she sits at home because she is afraid to go outside without his permission" (101-02). Sally maintains the tradition of silence about violence and domestic abuse upheld by her own parents and by other women in the novel. There is a strong element of disappointment if not judgment here, as Esperanza realizes that Sally has succumbed to a world of confinement and lies and that she must find other role models. It is at this point that she turns to writing as both a means of communicating her experience and a way of escaping the oppression that dominates the lives of the women in her neighborhood. From here on, her role models are women who are writers or who appreciate writing, and it is through their encouragement that she finds the courage to prepare to leave Mango Street, though she acknowledges that she will always carry it with her in her writing.

In *The Bluest Eye*, Claudia also attempts to find her way in a complex, often threatening world by weaving a story that will help her make sense of her experiences. She is a more obviously self-conscious narrator than Esperanza, for she looks back on her childhood from an adult's perspective and directly comments on her efforts to shape adults' comments into a cohesive narrative: "We . . . considered all speech a code to be broken by us, and all gestures subject to careful analysis" (150). The adults in Claudia's world deal sternly with children, "Adults do not talk to us—they give us directions. They issue orders without providing information" (5). Not surprisingly, their messages are frequently misunderstood, sometimes to hilarious effect. Maureen Peal, the "high-yellow dream child" (47) who inspires ferocious jealousy in Claudia, attempts to imitate her teacher's authority by dismissing their classmate Bay Boy as "incorrigival" (51). Similarly, the sudden arrival of Pecola's first period is confidently explained by Claudia's older sister Frieda as "ministratin'" (19). The girls are so utterly confused by sexuality that when they learn that Pecola is pregnant by her own father, Cholly, they are not shocked: "The process of having a baby by any male was incomprehensible to us—at least she knew her father" (149-50). Disturbingly, what most strikes them about the overheard snippets of adult conversation about Pecola's plight is the utter lack of compassion for her: "They were disgusted, amused, shocked, outraged, or even excited by the story. But we listened for the one who would say, 'Poor little girl,' or, 'Poor baby,' but there was only head-wagging where those words should have been" (149).

The disappointments or unreliability of adults' narratives is a salient theme in the novel. When Claudia and Frieda see their beloved lodger, the charming and generous Mr. Henry, consort with the prostitutes the Maginot Line and China in their home, they are well aware that his explanation that they are members of his Bible class is not to be believed, as it is prefaced by "the grown-up getting-ready-to-lie laugh. A heh-heh that we knew well" (61). The girls have learned that the women are pariahs in their community, as Claudia observes that the Maginot Line was "the one my mother said she 'wouldn't let eat out of one of her plates.' That was the one church women never allowed their eyes to rest on" (60). Claudia and Frieda depend more on the way in which the stories are told than on the words with which they are told for clues as to how to interpret them, since they "do not, cannot, know the meanings of all their words, for we are nine and ten years old. So we watch their faces, their hands, their feet, and listen for truth in timbre" (10). When Frieda is sexually molested by Mr. Henry, she, like Esperanza, struggles to describe the experience to her puzzled sister:

"Did you get a whipping?"

She shook her head no.

"Then why you crying?"

"Because."

"Because what?"

"Mr. Henry."

"What'd he do?"

"Daddy beat him up." (76)

Sexuality and sex are almost unspeakable, and the only possible reaction to Mr. Henry's abuse is violence, thus suggesting a cycle of violence and abuse taken to the extreme by Cholly. The sexual trauma he suffered as an adolescent by being spied on and mocked by white men during his first sexual encounter leads him to express his inability to communicate with his daughter by raping her, "What could he do for her—ever? What give her? What say to her?" (127).

The girls take the narratives they overhear and blend them into their own discourse with their peers. Pecking orders of respectability based on moral codes segue into those based on race. The self-directed racism embodied by Geraldine, who asserts that "colored people were neat and quiet; niggers were dirty and loud" (67), is reflected in the children's awareness of racially determined hierarchies of beauty. Maureen tells Pecola that the light-skinned star of the ironically titled film *Imitation of Life* "hates her mother 'cause she is black and ugly" (52). This summary is doubly ironic, as Maureen recounts a plot based on racist notions of beauty to Pecola in an effort to cheer her up after she has been viciously taunted by boys chanting, "Black e mo Black e mo Ya daddy sleeps nekked" (50). Despite her attempts to be kind to Pecola, Maureen instinctively resorts to racist epithets when she falls out with Claudia and Frieda, shouting, "I *am* cute! And you ugly! Black and ugly black e mos" (56). Unlike *The House on Mango Street*, which ends on a note of hope as Esperanza overcomes the unreliable, contradictory, and sometimes damaging narratives that she negotiates,

Pecola's story ends in tragedy. She succumbs to madness after the death of her baby and is unable to use words to escape her trauma, instead constructing imagined dialogues that underline her mental collapse. She believes that she has realized her dream of having blue eyes and interprets her mother's inability to look directly at her as jealousy: "Ever since I got my blue eyes, she look away from me all of the time" (154). If words cannot save Pecola, however, Claudia's narrative breaks the silence surrounding the devastating effects of marginalization, racism, and sexual abuse and thus means that the pattern of abuse represented by her story will be exposed.

Besides the fragmented nature of their narratives and their controversial themes, *The House on Mango Street* and *The Bluest Eye* are notable for their use of nonstandard and nonliterary language. Having convinced her mother to let her eat her lunch in the school canteen, Esperanza reproduces the letter of permission in which her mother asks the Sister Superior to excuse her from going home "because she lives too far away and she gets tired. As you can see she is very skinny. I hope to God she does not faint" (45). While the inappropriate language and overly familiar tone of the letter is comic, the letter also points to Esperanza's mother's lack of education, which is confirmed later in the novel when she tells her daughter that she did not finish school because she was ashamed of her poor clothes (91). A key aspect of the novel's nontraditional language lies in its use of Spanish, or code-switching. Esperanza's mother "can speak two languages" (90), and when Esperanza's father tells her that her grandfather has died, he says, "Your *abuelito* is dead," referring to his father in Spanish and using the diminutive form "*ito*" to convey his love for him (56). While Esperanza's father's use of Spanish suggests how integral it is to communication and identity among Chicano families, outside the home the use of Spanish speaks of exclusion and difference. As Ilan Stavans points out, "Even though *el español* is very much a U.S. tongue and its increasing political power is unquestionable, entrance into the American Dream requires a fluency, however limited, in Shakespeare's language" (163).

In "Geraldo No Last Name," Marin witnesses the death of a recently arrived immigrant in a hit and run. She describes him as a "wetback" and a "brazer" (66), a corruption of "bracero," the term used to describe Mexican migrant workers who moved to the United States during World War II. Her pejorative descriptions of Geraldo indicate her reluctance to be associated with someone from a group doubly marginalized by the members' ethnicity and undocumented status. Perhaps the most poignant vignette to deal with the difficulties of language is "No Speak English," which centers on the recently arrived Mamacita, whose English is limited to "*He not here* for when the landlord comes, *No speak English* if anybody else comes" (77). The isolation and loneliness that result from her inability to understand or speak the dominant language intensify at the end of the vignette. Horrified to hear her baby son singing along to a Pepsi commercial, Mamacita repeats her phrase: "No Speak English, she says to the child who is singing in the language that sounds like tin" (78). Terrified that her isolation will be complete if she cannot communicate with her son, her declaration becomes a plea.

A final noteworthy aspect of the novel's unconventional use of language lies in its intertextual references. Esperanza repeatedly refers to stories that are not normally considered to be literary, such as lullabies or skipping rhymes. The vignette "There Was an Old Woman She Had so Many Children She Didn't Know What to Do" appropriates the title of the children's rhyme and recasts the story in a contemporary environment devoid of charm or fantasy, as the woman in question becomes Rosa Vargas, "who is tired all the time from buttoning and bottling and babying, and who cries every day for the man who left without even leaving a dollar for bologna or a note explaining how come" (29). When Esperanza and her friends wear high-heeled shoes for the first time, they compare themselves to Cinderella (40), while Rafaela "leans out the window and leans on her elbow and dreams her hair is like Rapunzel's" (79). Following Martín-Rodríguez, it is clear that the numerous parallels drawn between the women of Mango Street and fairy-tale characters directly or obliquely underline the women's confinement and subaltern role in their society (77). More importantly, however, they constitute a defiant statement that popular cultural and folkloric sources can be just as resonant and multifaceted as the "highbrow literature" Cisneros refers to in her twenty-fifth anniversary essay.

One of the most vibrant aspects of *The Bluest Eye* is Morrison's ability to capture the distinctive colloquial language of her characters. The earthy, lively dialogues that pepper the text lend much-needed humor to her darkly pessimistic account of poverty and sexual abuse. One of the earliest dialogues overheard by Claudia conveys the reactions of the women in the community to the news that Della Jones's husband left her because she was too clean: "Old dog. Ain't that nasty!" "You telling me. What kind of reasoning is that?" "No kind. Some men just dogs" (8). The social hierarchies the community rigidly imposes on itself, which deem homelessness to be the worst possible indicator of dysfunction, doom Pecola from the outset. She comes to live with the MacTeer family because, as Claudia explains, "Mama didn't know 'what got into people,' but that old Dog Breedlove had burned up his house, gone upside his wife's head, and everybody, as a result, was outdoors" (11). As well as gossip, a frequently cited source is biblical language. Cholly's Aunt Jimmy, overcome by illness, "nodded in drowsy appreciation as the words from First Corinthians droned over her" (106). Language—such as folkloric traditions maintained through the telling of ghost stories and, above all, the musical heritage passed down through the singing and playing of jazz and blues—also leads to a sense of social cohesion. Music even manages to bridge the divisions between churchgoing women, such as Claudia's mother, and the prostitutes.

The range of intertextual references in the novel is far-reaching, including the aforementioned songs, biblical references, and films. While Morrison mentions some canonical literary texts, such as *Hamlet* and *Othello*, the most notable use of another text is the reference to a children's primer about the ideal American family. Even before the novel's opening passage, the dream of an ideal family has been deconstructed and destroyed as the story of Mother, Father, Dick, and Jane playing happily against the backdrop of a pretty green and white house with a red door collapses into a jumble of letters so chaotic the story becomes almost impossible to read. The neat, clear description of the ideal home is rendered meaningless. Thus the chasm between the American Dream represented by the primer and the harsh reality that Pecola inhabits is thrown into sharp relief from the beginning, just as Esperanza's dream of a perfect house is never realized.

The fragmented narratives woven together by Morrison's and Cisneros's narrators are radical in content and form. Carol Clark D'Lugo's comments on twentieth-century Mexican literature provide a useful framework for understanding the work of both authors: "The nation's fragmented social and political reality is consistently exposed in novels that dramatize a lack of cohesion, urban atomization, or disparities in class, race and gender" (1). Both *The House on Mango Street* and *The Bluest Eye* focus on characters written out of Euro-American literature because of their marginalization as women of color living in disadvantaged areas. And both authors express this condition of alienation from the mainstream though fragmented texts that represent a history that has barely been noted and that engage the reader in a process of rewriting history "by turning the passive experience of reception into an activity" (Tyrkkö 277). The use of the vernacular and nonliterary texts to articulate this experience of isolation and marginalization constitutes a rejection of the supremacy of Western texts, for, as Henry Louis Gates, Jr., has noted, while African American literature shares some features of these texts, "Black formal repetition always repeats with a difference, a black difference that manifests itself in the specific language use. And the repository that contains the language that is the source—and the reflection—of black difference is the black English vernacular tradition" (xxii-xxiii). Similarly, in her analysis of Latina/o writing, Lourdes Torres observes, "Using Spanish in an English language text serves to legitimize the much-maligned practice of mixing codes in vernacular speech" (76). The use of popular language thus challenges what Bourdieu has termed "a sort of censorship of the expressive context" found in the so-called high culture represented by museums, opera, and theatre (34). Cisneros and Morrison celebrate the uniqueness of their culture but they also, to borrow Cherríe Moraga's term, insist on the "specificity of the oppression" faced by women of color (Moraga and Anzaldúa 29). *The House on Mango Street* challenges the abuse of women that results from the upholding of Mexican patriarchal norms, while *The Bluest Eye* rejects the self-directed racism that is a legacy of slavery. Paradoxically, by facing these oppressions head-on, Cisneros and Morrison show how subjects considered to be the antithesis of poetic expression become a source of inspiration for transformative texts that make the margin the center and forge a new type of literary discourse.

Works Cited

Anzaldúa, Gloria. "Speaking in Tongues: A Letter to Third World Feminists." *This Bridge Called My Back: Writing by Radical Women of Color.* 2nd ed. Ed. Cherríe Moraga and Gloria Anzaldúa. New York: Kitchen Table/Women of Color Press, 1983.

Bourdieu, Pierre. *Distinction: A Social Critique of the Judgement of Taste.* Cambridge, MA: Harvard UP, 1987.

Cisneros, Sandra. *The House on Mango Street.* 1984. New York: Vintage Books, 2009.

Cruz, Felicia J. "On the 'Simplicity' of Sandra Cisneros's *House on Mango Street.*" *Modern Fiction Studies* 47.4 (2001): 910-46.

D'Lugo, Carol Clark. *The Fragmented Novel in Mexico: The Politics of Form.* Austin: U of Texas P, 1997.

Doyle, Jacqueline. "More Room of Her Own: Sandra Cisneros's *The House on Mango Street.*" *MELUS* 19.4 (1994): 5-35.

Gates, Henry Louis, Jr. *The Signifying Monkey: A Theory of African-American Literary Criticism.* New York: Oxford UP, 1988.

Lomelí, Francisco A. "Chicana Novelists in the Process of Creating Fictive Voices." *Beyond Stereotypes: The Critical Analysis of Chicana Literature.* Ed. María Herrera-Sobek. Tempe, AZ: Bilingual Press/Editorial Bilingüe, 1985.

Klahn, Norma. "Literary [Re]Mappings: Autobiographical [Dis]Placements by Chicana Writers." *Chicana Feminisms: A Critical Reader.* Ed. Gabriela F. Arredondo et al. Durham, NC: Duke UP, 2003. 114-45.

McCracken, Ellen. *New Latina Narrative: The Feminine Space of Postmodern Ethnicity*. Tuscon: U of Arizona P, 1999.

Matus, Jill. *Toni Morrison*. Manchester: Manchester UP, 1998.

Moraga, Cherríe, and Gloria Anzaldúa, eds. *This Bridge Called My Back: Writing by Radical Women of Color*. 2nd ed. New York: Kitchen Table/Women of Color Press, 1983.

Morrison, Toni. *The Bluest Eye*. 1970. New York: Vintage Books, 1999.

Peach, Linden. *Toni Morrison*. New York: Macmillan, 2000.

Peterson, Nancy J., ed. *Toni Morrison: Critical and Theoretical Approaches*. Baltimore, MD: Johns Hopkins UP, 1997.

Stavans, Ilan. *The Hispanic Condition: The Power of a People*. New York: HarperCollins, 2001.

Tirrell, Lynne. "Storytelling and Moral Agency." *Toni Morrison's Fiction: Contemporary Criticism*. Ed. David Middleton. New York: Garland, 1997.

Torres, Hector A. *Conversations with Contemporary Chicana and Chicano Writers*. Albuquerque: U of New Mexico P, 2007.

Torres, Lourdes. "In the Contact Zone: Code-Switching Strategies by Latino/a Writers." *MELUS* 32.1 (2007): 75-96.

Tyrkkö, Jakka. "Kaleidoscope Narratives and the Act of Reading." *Theorizing Narrativity (Narratologia)*. Ed. John Pier and Ángel García Landa. Berlin: Walter de Gruyter, 2008.

Valdés, María Elena de. *The Shattered Mirror: Representations of Women in Mexican Literature*. Austin: U of Texas P, 1998.

Woolf, Virginia. *A Room of One's Own*. 1929. London: Penguin Classics, 2000.

CRITICAL READINGS

The "Dual"-ing Images of la Malinche and la Virgen de Guadalupe in Cisneros's *The House on Mango Street*_____

Leslie Petty

In "And Some More," a story from Sandra Cisneros's *The House on Mango Street*, two young girls discuss the nature of snow:

> There ain't thirty different kinds of snow, Lucy said. There are two kinds. The clean kind and the dirty kind, clean and dirty. Only two.
>
> There are a million zillion kinds, says Nenny. No two exactly alike. Only how do you remember which one is which? (35)

At first glance, the girls' conversation appears to be a bit of childish nonsense, and, on a surface level, it is. Read in a broader context, however, Nenny and Lucy's debate highlights a conflict that is at the heart of Cisneros's work: the insistence on culturally defining the world by a rigid set of black/white, good/bad, clean/dirty dualities, versus the reality of individuality, uniqueness, and infinite differentiation. Cisneros comments on the difficulties inherent in this clear-cut dichotomy, and she relates this binary specifically to the Mexican influences in her life and writing:

> Certainly that black-white issue, good-bad, it's very prevalent in my work and in other Latinas. We're raised with a Mexican culture that has two role models: La Malinche y la Virgen de Guadalupe. And you know that's a hard route to go, one or the other, there's no in-betweens. (Rodríguez-Aranda 65)

According to Cisneros, then, females, like the snow, are not seen in Latino culture as unique individuals but are labeled as either "good" women or "bad" women, as "clean" or "dirty," as "virgins" or "*malinches*."

Cisneros is not the first writer to acknowledge the difficulties in dealing with this duality nor the cultural archetypes upon which it is based. As Luis Leal observes, "the characterization of women throughout Mexican literature has been profoundly influenced by two archetypes present in the Mexican psyche: that of the woman who has kept her virginity and that of the one who has lost it" (227).[1] These archetypes, embodied in the stories of la Malinche, the violated woman, and la Virgen de Guadalupe, the holy Mother, sharply define female roles in Mexican culture based on physical sexuality; however, as historical and mythical figures, these two archetypes take on both political and social significance that also influence perceptions of femininity in the Latin American world.

As the Mexican manifestation of the Virgin Mary, la Virgen de Guadalupe is the religious icon around which Mexican Catholicism centers. Consequently, versions of her historic origin are prevalent throughout the national literature. Although several variations of the story of the Virgin's initial apparitions exist, Stafford Poole identifies the version published in 1649 by the Vicar of Guadalupe, a priest named Luis Laso de la Vega, as the definitive source (26). According to Poole's translation of de la Vega,[2] la Virgen de Guadalupe originally appeared to a converted Indian, Juan Diego, in 1531, on the hill of Tepeyac, identifying herself as "mother of the great true deity God" (27). The Virgin tells Juan Diego that she "ardently wish[es] and greatly desire[s] that they build my temple for me here, where I will reveal . . . all my love, my compassion, my aid, and my protection" (27). Diego immediately proceeds to the bishop in Mexico City, but he is greeted with disbelief. On his second visit, the bishop asks Diego for proof of the apparition. The Virgin sends Diego to the top of the hill, where he gathers "every kind of precious Spanish flower," despite the fact that these flowers are out of season and do not grow on that hill, and the Virgin places them in his cloak (27). When Diego visits the bishop, the bishop's servants try to take some of the blossoms, but they turn into painted flowers. Finally, when Diego sees the bishop and opens his cloak, the flowers fall out, and an imprint of the Virgin is left on the lining of the cloak. The bishop becomes a believer, begs for forgiveness, and erects the shrine to la Virgen de Guadalupe on the hill of Tepeyac.

Several elements of this story are important in the development of the cult of la Virgen de Guadalupe that spread rapidly in Mexico after this apparition. As Octavio Paz observes, "The Virgin is the consolation of the poor, the shield of the weak, the help of the oppressed. In sum, she is the Mother of orphans" (76). In addition to her religious importance, Paz and others recognize the political significance of this nurturing aspect of the Virgin in the formation of a Mexican national identity. First, in *Quetzalcóatl and Guadalupe*, Jacques Lafaye makes the case that la Virgen de Guadalupe is a Christian transformation of Tonantzin, the pagan goddess who was originally worshipped on the hill of Tepeyac (216). This link with Aztec culture is important because it distinguishes the Mexican symbol from its Spanish counterpart, la Virgen de Guadalupe de Estremadura.[3] Therefore, as Leal notes, la Virgen de Guadalupe de Tepeyac is "an Indian symbol," and she is "identified with what is truly Mexican as opposed to what is foreign" (229). She is the "protector of the indigenous" (Leal 229). Appropriately, the image of the Virgin was used on banners promoting independence during the Mexican Revolution, and today she is revered as the "Queen of Hispandidad" (Lafaye 230), giving la Virgen de Guadalupe a political designation in Latin American tradition in addition to her religious significance.

The shrine of La Virgen de Guadalupe is a haven for the indigenous population of Mexico. As the incarnation of the Virgin Mary, Guadalupe represents the passive, pure female force. According to Paz, "Guadalupe is pure receptivity, and the benefits she bestows are of the same order: she consoles, quiets, dries tears, calms passion" (76). As such, she represents the holy, chaste woman, the embodiment of feminine purity as well as the virtues of nurturing and self-sacrifice. Thus, she is venerated in Mexican culture as the proper symbol for womanhood.

The antithesis of the pure maternal image of la Virgen de Guadalupe in the Mexican "dual representation of the mother" (Paz 75) is la Malinche, Cortés's interpreter and mistress during the conquest of Mexico. Like the Virgin, the popular perception of La Malinche is based more on legend than historical accuracy, and is therefore often romanticized and contradictory. Even her name is a source of contention. While Spanish accounts refer to her as "Doña Marina" or "Marina," indigenous Mexicans refer to her as "la Malinche," a name that implies the mythical persona as much as the historical woman. In "Marina/Malinche: Masks and Shadows," Rachel Phillips tries to deflate this myth as much as possible by using the small amount of historical documentation available to reconstruct a more factual account of Marina's life.[4] To begin with, while historians and contemporaries idealize Marina, identifying her as an "Indian Princess," Phillips shows that although she was from an indigenous Mexican tribe, she was far from royalty. Born in Painala, she grew up speaking Nahuatl and was either sold or given away as a child; therefore, she was enslaved by another tribe and moved to Tabasco where she learned to speak Mayan.

As a young woman, she was given to Cortés, along with nineteen other Indian slave women, as gifts from local Indian leaders. When Monteczuma's envoys came to Tabasco to find out information about Cortés, they spoke only Nahuatl while Cortés's Spanish translator spoke only Mayan. Marina was used to provide the missing link by translating the Nahuatl into Mayan. Marina soon learned Spanish and became Cortés's primary translator. Contemporary paintings and accounts show that Marina was near Cortés at all times and that her skill as a translator helped him defeat Monteczuma, furthering the cause of the Spanish conquest in Mexico. In addition to her role as translator, historical writings confirm that Cortés and Marina had a sexual relationship; she gave birth to his son, Martín. The last bit of information available about Marina is that some time after this birth, on an expedition to Honduras, Cortés gave her to one of his captains, Juan Jaramillo, to marry.

Although the historical facts about Marina are scant, the mythic implications of La Malinche in the Mexican psyche are just as complex and powerful as those of la Virgen de Guadalupe. Octavio Paz explains:

> If the Chingada[5] is a representation of the violated Mother, it is appropriate to associate her with the Conquest, which was also a violation, not only in the historical sense, but also in the very flesh of Indian women. The symbol of this violation is doña Malinche, the mistress of Cortés. It is true that she gave herself voluntarily to the conquistador, but he forgot her as soon as her usefulness was over.[6] Doña Marina becomes a figure representing the Indian women who were fascinated, violated, or seduced by the Spaniards. And, as a small boy will not forgive his mother if she abandons him to search for his father, the Mexican people have not forgiven La Malinche for her betrayal. (77)

Paz exposes the ambivalence that Mexicans feel for the la Malinche figure. While he equates her with the violated Mother at the beginning, he accuses her of betrayal at the end. The paradox is that Malinche embodies both the passivity and violation associated with the fallen woman while simultaneously representing the powerful act of treason as one who "betrays the homeland by aiding the enemy" (Leal 227). Both Malinche's betrayal and her violation threaten the Mexican concept of the Male; she either openly challenges his authority or is not saved by his protection. This dual threat makes her the symbol of the female sexuality that is both denigrated and controlled in Mexican society.

The work of a Chicana writer is threatened in a different way by the la Malinche archetype, a way that makes the role model of la Virgen de Guadalupe just as dangerous. For Cisneros, the dilemma is creating a role model for herself and other Chicanas that is neither limited by this good/bad duality ingrained in Mexican culture, nor too "Anglicized" (Rodríguez-Aranda 65) to adequately represent their experience.

When interviewing Cisneros, Pilar E. Rodríguez-Aranda observes, "the in-between is not ours. . . . So if you want to get out of these two roles, you feel you're betraying you're [sic] people" (65). In response to this dilemma, Cisneros claims that she and other Chicana women must learn the art of "revising" themselves by learning to "accept [their] culture, but not without adapting [themselves] as women" (66).

The House on Mango Street is just such an adaptation. The author "revises" the significance of the Chicana archetypes of la Malinche and la Virgen de Guadalupe through her characterization of females in the book. By recasting these mythical stories from the female perspective, Cisneros shows how artificial and confining these cultural stereotypes are, and through her creation of Esperanza, imagines a protagonist who can embody both the violation associated with la Malinche and the nurturing associated with la Virgen de Guadalupe, all the while rejecting the feminine passivity that is promoted by both role models. Therefore, Esperanza transcends the good/bad dichotomy associated with these archetypes and becomes a new model for Chicana womanhood: an independent, autonomous artist whose house is of the heart, not of the worshiper, nor of the conqueror.

María Elena de Valdés observes that in *The House on Mango Street*, Esperanza is "drawn to the women and girls [in the story] as would-be role models" (59). Not surprisingly, Esperanza does not find many lives that she would like to emulate. Her rejection of these role models stems from each character's close alliance with one of the two Mexican archetypes. Cisneros shows how being culturally defined by either of these two roles makes for an incomplete, frustrated life. While the Virgin Mother is a venerated role model, Cisneros complicates this veneration through her characterization of other maternal figures, most notably, Esperanza's mother and her aunt, Lupe.

In "Hairs," Cisneros paints an intimate picture of Esperanza's relationship with her mother, whose hair holds "the smell when she makes room for you on her side of the bed still warm with her skin, and you sleep near her" (6). Like the Virgin, Esperanza's mother is a protector, a haven for her daughter during the rain. This idealized memory is marred somewhat in "A Smart Cookie," in which it is clear that Esperanza's mother is very talented, that she can "speak two languages" (90), and "can sing an opera" (90), but that she is not contented with her life. Mother says, "I could've been somebody, you know?" (91). Apparently, being the nurturing, self-sacrificing mother whose hair "smells like bread" is not sufficient to make Esperanza's mother's life complete. Instead of being a dependent female, Esperanza's mother tells her daughter that she has "got to take care all your own" (91), alluding to a culture that desires virgin-like women, but which does not reward the desired passivity with the care and adoration also reserved for the Virgin; instead, Mother mentions several friends who have fulfilled their roles as mothers but have consequently been left alone. Mother encourages her daughter to reject this self-sacrificing path that Mexican culture sees as noble, like the Virgin, and to choose instead to "study hard" (91) in school in order to prepare herself for independence.

A more forceful rejection of the Virgin archetype is evident in the characterization of Esperanza's aunt, Guadalupe. Like the mythic character for whom she is named, Aunt Lupe is a passive woman in a shrine, but in "Born Bad," this connection is corrupted with images of sickness, stagnation, and helplessness. Unlike Paz's assertion that "through suffering, our women become like our men: invulnerable, impassive and stoic" (30), there is nothing idyllic or positive about Cisneros's portrayal of a suffering woman. Instead of living in a resplendent holy place, Cisneros's Guadalupe lives in a cramped, filthy room with "dirty dishes in the sink" (60), and "ceilings dusty with flies" (60). The passivity of Lupe is the result of a debilitating illness that has caused her bones to go "limp as worms" (58). Guadalupe is chaste[7] like the Virgin, but her lack of sexual activity is not a sign of her moral superiority; it is again caused by her illness and associated with the frustration and longing of "the husband who wanted a wife again" (61).

Aunt Lupe, like Esperanza's mother, does provide a haven of sorts for the young protagonist, even though Esperanza "hate[s] to go there alone" (60). Esperanza says that she likes her aunt because "she listen[s] to every book, every poem I ever read her" (60). Aunt Lupe's home gives Esperanza a safe place to explore her passion for writing and her aspirations as a poet, and this protection is the most positive connection that Cisneros makes between Aunt Lupe and the Virgin. Aunt Lupe encourages Esperanza to "keep writing" because "[i]t will keep [her] free" (61). Ironically, the life that Aunt Lupe encourages Esperanza to follow is not one of passivity and self-sacrifice associated with the Holy Mother; instead Lupe gives Esperanza a push towards independence much like the one that the adolescent girl receives from her own mother. After Aunt Lupe dies, Esperanza begins to "dream the dreams" (61) of pursuing her education and her artistic aspirations.

While the primary female characters associated with the Virgin in *The House on Mango Street* are adult figures, and therefore distant and revered, the females aligned with la Malinche are adolescents, making them more accessible to Esperanza in her search for role models. The images of la Malinche are more widespread in Cisneros's book than those of the Virgin; in fact, images of the violated, abandoned, or enslaved woman are scattered from beginning to end, indicating that the unfortunate reality of Malinche/Marina's life is a more likely scenario for women in the barrio than that of being worshipped as the ideal mother. Rosa Vargas, a woman with unruly children, "cries every day for the man who left without even leaving a dollar" (29); the abandonment seems to be the reason she is such a distracted, ineffective mother. The husband of another character, Rafaela, locks her "indoors because [he] is afraid [she] will run away since she is too beautiful to look at" (79). In this story, Rafaela, like Malinche, is enslaved because she and her sexuality are viewed as threats that must be contained. Another character, Minerva, who "is only a little bit older than [Esperanza]" (84), has already been abandoned by her husband, who leaves her to raise two children alone. Like Esperanza, Minerva is a poet, but her fate as a "*chingada*" makes her always sad, and her potential as an artist is consumed by her unlucky fate. As a young, frustrated writer, Minerva's story represents the probable path of Esperanza's life if she were to become inscribed in one of the typical roles for Mexican-American women.

While all of these women represent aspects of the Malinche archetype, perhaps the most sustained exploration of that archetype in *The House on Mango Street* can be found in the character of Marin, who, like Aunt Lupe, shares the name of the mythical figure she represents. By reading Marin's story through the lens of the la Malinche archetype, one gains insight into the pitfalls of this culturally proscribed role. In "Louie, His Cousin & His Other Cousin," the description of Marin immediately aligns her with the darker, more sexual side of Chicana femininity; she wears "dark nylons all the time and lots of makeup" (23) and is more worldly than Esperanza and the other girls. Like Malinche, Marin is living with people who are not her family, and in a sense, she is enslaved; she "can't come out—gotta baby-sit with Louie's sisters" (23).

It is Marin's aspirations, however, that most closely align her with Malinche. Marin says that,

> she's going to get a real job downtown, because that's where the best jobs are, since you always get to look beautiful and get to wear nice clothes and can meet someone in the subway who might marry you and take you to live in a big house far away. (26)

Like Malinche, Marin could be perceived as betraying her family and culture. By "getting a job downtown," she is leaving her neighborhood and her duty as babysitter to go where the "better jobs" are, in the more Anglo-oriented downtown area. However, Marin does not see her actions as an act of betrayal; she is hoping for self-improvement. Just as Malinche's position as translator for the powerful Cortés seems logically preferable to being a slave who "kneads bread"[8] for those in her own country, Marin's desire to escape her circumstances are justifiable. But, for Marin, and Malinche, this escape is inextricably tied to dependence on a man. The dream of marriage and a "big house far away" are Marin's sustaining thoughts, but the reality of her focus on sexuality leads to a denigration much like that of Malinche. While Marin believes that "what matters . . . is for the boys to see us and for us to see them" (27), this contact only provides a space for lewd sexual invitations from young men, who "say stupid things like I am in love with those two green apples you call eyes, give them to me why don't you" (27). Finally, Marin, like Malinche, is sent away because "she's too much trouble" (27).

Through these connections, Cisneros's text appropriates the Malinche myth, showing that this type of dependence on men for one's importance and security is what leads to violation and abandonment. The danger of Marin's "waiting for . . . someone to change her life" (27) lies in the possible result of this passivity. Paz comments on this potential for downfall: "This passivity, open to the outside world, causes her to lose her identity: she is the Chingada. She loses her name; she is no one; she disappears into nothingness; she is Nothingness. And yet she is the cruel incarnation of the feminine condition" (77). Cisneros seems to suggest that this "nothingness" is almost inevitable for women in the barrio.

Perhaps no one in *The House on Mango Street* more fully embodies the "cruel incarnation of the feminine condition" than Esperanza's friend, Sally. At different times in the book, Sally can be aligned with both la Malinche and la Virgen de Guadalupe, and her story reveals both the objectification and confinement associated with each archetype. In "Sally," her description, like Marin's, suggests a link with physical sexuality and desirability. She has "eyes like Egypt and nylons the color of smoke" (81), and her hair is "shiny black like raven feathers" (81). Unfortunately, Sally's attractiveness is the source of much unhappiness. Because her looks are perceived as a sign of promiscuity, she is stigmatized in her school; the boys tell stories about her in the coatroom, and she has very few female friends. More damaging, though, is the reaction of her father, who "says to be this beautiful is trouble" (81), and confines Sally to her room. Like la Malinche, Sally's sexuality is doubly threatening to her father's masculinity. Not only could she betray him by being promiscuous, but her beauty might also entice a man to violate her, which would threaten the father's role as protector. This perceived threat causes her father to erupt in horrific displays of violence, hitting his daughter until her "pretty face [is] beaten and black" (92) because "[h]e thinks [she's] going to run away like his sisters who made the family ashamed" (92). Sally's father uses force to deform her and to contain her threatening sexuality.

To get away from her father's abuse, Sally marries a marshmallow salesman, "young and not ready but married just the same" (101). Sally "says she's in love, but . . . she did it to escape" (101). Sally perceives marriage as the path for leaving behind the "bad girl" image that links her to la Malinche as well as the violence she associates with this connection. As a wife she gains respectability and a propriety of which her culture approves; her sexuality has been contained within the proper confines of marriage, and now she has the potential to recreate the Virgin's role as nurturer and worshipped love.

In "Linoleum Roses," Cisneros again juxtaposes the reality of the female situation with its mythic counterpart. Significantly, the image of the "linoleum roses on the floor" echoes the story of Juan Diego's flowers that heralded the need for a house of worship for the Virgin. Similarly, Sally's roses are proof of her status as a "good" female. Like the Virgin, Sally gets the home that she wants, but again the house functions more like a prison than a shrine. As Julián Olivares argues, the linoleum roses are a "trope for household confinement and drudgery, and an ironic treatment of the garden motif, which is associated with freedom and the outdoors" (165). Sally "sits at home because she is afraid to go outside without [her husband's] permission" (102). Her only consolation is looking at the roses and the other "things they own" (102). Sally has not gained much from her crossing from one extreme to the other of the good/bad dichotomy that classifies

Chicana women. The house of her husband is just as limiting as the house of her father.

Dianne Klein has observed that in the stories that Esperanza tells of women in her barrio, the house functions as a place of confinement (23), and this sense of imprisonment exists whether the female is associated with la Virgen de Guadalupe, whose "house" is supposed to be a shrine, or la Malinche, who is enslaved in the metaphorical "house" of Cortés and the Spanish conquerors; Aunt Lupe is just as imprisoned in her home as Marin is in hers. Only Esperanza has a different vision for the house that she wants to inhabit, one that she says is "not a man's house. Not a daddy's" (108), but a "house all my own" (108). Esperanza's quest for a house is crucial in understanding how her character transcends the Malinche/Virgen de Guadalupe duality that defines and confines the other females in *The House on Mango Street*. As Valdés states, "the house she seeks is in reality her own person" (58), one that is labeled neither "good" nor "bad" by her society. This radical characterization unfolds in a series of vignettes in which Esperanza is alternately aligned with la Virgen de Guadalupe and la Malinche, finally fusing elements of the two archetypes at the end of the text. While Esperanza retains a connection to these myths, her art becomes the key to her transcendence of them.

The most obvious connection made between Esperanza and either of these archetypes is the protagonist's desire for a house, which resonates with la Virgen de Guadalupe's charge to Juan Diego that "they build my temple for me here" (Poole 27). In "Bums in the Attic," Esperanza, like the Virgin, wants "a house on a hill like the ones with the gardens" (86). Esperanza's hill is connected to the hill of Tepeyac, the location of la Virgen de Guadalupe's shrine, and the reference to the garden is easily associated with the flowers on the hill that the Virgin made grow as a sign of her divinity. Perhaps a more significant connection between the Virgin and Esperanza is Esperanza's plan for her house:

One day I'll own my own house, but I won't forget who I am or where I came from. Passing bums will ask, Can I come in? I'll offer them the attic, ask them to stay, because I know how it is to be without a house. (87)

Esperanza's promise to take care of the bums is important for two reasons. First, it echoes the Virgin's promises to give "aid and . . . protection" to her followers, and to "hear their weeping . . . and heal all . . . their sufferings, and their sorrows" (Poole 27). Furthermore, Esperanza promises not to forget "where [she] came from," establishing a connection with her society that is reminiscent of the Virgin's position as the "truly Mexican" symbol. While some critics mistakenly interpret Esperanza's desire for a house as a betrayal of her heritage that is more in line with the negative aspects of the la Malinche myth,[9] her attitude toward the "bums" shows that she is not blind to the needs of those in her community, nor will she neglect her responsibility to that community. Although Esperanza's desire for a house is prompted by her desire for security and autonomy, it also encompasses a degree of compassion and nurturing that represents the noblest qualities of the Virgin archetype.

Esperanza's alignment with the Virgin, however, is complicated in the next story, "Beautiful and Cruel." Esperanza says she has "decided not to grow up tame like the others who lay their necks on the threshold waiting for the ball and chain" (88). Instead, she wants to be like the "beautiful and cruel" female in the movies, whose "power is her own" (89). Accordingly, Esperanza has "begun [her] own private war. . . . [she is] the one who leaves the table like a man" (89). In this story, Esperanza rejects the passivity associated with all women in her culture, whether they emulate the Virgin or Malinche. Instead, she imagines herself as Paz's "*mala mujer,*" the woman who "comes and goes, . . . looks for men and then leaves them," whose "power is her own" (31). Paz sees this woman as the female equivalent to the Mexican "macho": "hard, impious and independent" (31). Still, this power is based on the mysterious, threatening existence of female sexuality that links Esperanza with la Malinche. While applauding Esperanza's refusal to be passive, the reader senses that if Esperanza relies on being "beautiful and cruel" to achieve her independence, she will follow a self-destructive path that will inscribe her on the "bad" side of Chicana femininity.

Not until "Red Clowns" is the heroine linked with the violation and forced passivity that are at the root of the la Malinche myth. While Esperanza waits for Sally at the carnival, she is raped by a male with a "sour mouth" who keeps repeating "I love you, Spanish girl, I love you" (100). Overcome with emotion while relating the story, Esperanza begs, "Please don't make me tell it all" (100), and then accuses Sally, saying "You're a liar. They all lied" (100). Like Malinche, Esperanza has been violated by someone outside her own culture, indicated by the rapist calling her "Spanish girl," which perhaps suggests that he himself is not Hispanic. The sad irony is that, also like Malinche, Esperanza is not Spanish, but Mexican, and this taunt falsely identifies her with a culture that is not her own.

This story also connects Malinche and Esperanza through a reference to language: Esperanza's saying, "Please don't make me tell it all" demonstrates just how painful recounting the story of one's own violation can be. As Cortés's translator, Malinche, too, was forced to "tell all" of the words that led to the violation of her country, and her son Martín was a nonverbal admission of the personal violation that Malinche herself suffered. Esperanza, like Malinche, understands the harsh reality of being a *chingada*. María Herrera-Sobek claims that Esperanza's accusations at the end of the story refer to this harsh reality and are directed at "the community of women who keep the truth [about female sexuality] from the younger generation of women in a conspiracy of silence" (178). This truth, according to the female characterizations in *The House on Mango Street*, is that, whether a woman follows the example of the Virgin, or of la Malinche, being reduced to either side of the good/bad dichotomy entails confinement, sacrifice, and violation.

It is Esperanza's dream for a house, a dream inextricably linked with her poetry, that keeps her from succumbing to her culture's demand that she be identified with one of these archetypes. Olivares interprets Esperanza's house as a "metaphor for the house of storytelling" (168). In such a metaphorical space, Esperanza can create for herself an identity that reconciles the violation and pain that she associates with Mango Street as well as the responsibility she feels to nurture and aid her community, the place in which she "belong[s] but do[es] not belong to" (110). Esperanza imagines:

> One day I will pack my bags of books and paper. One day I will say good-bye to Mango. I am too strong for her to keep me here forever. One day I will go away.
>
> Friends and neighbors will say, What happened to that Esperanza? Where did she go with all those books and papers? Why did she march so far away?
>
> They will not know I have gone away to come back. For the ones I left behind. For the ones who cannot out. (110)

Elements of la Malinche and the Virgin are fused in Esperanza's plan. Like Malinche, Esperanza goes off into the world of the "conqueror," the more affluent, anglicized society outside the barrio, and also like Malinche, her motivations will be questioned. However, like the Virgin, Esperanza will return to support, protect, and aid those that need her within the barrio. Esperanza imagines herself as a bridge between these two worlds, and her writing is the tool that helps her create this connection: "I make a story for my life" (109). According to Wendy Kolmar, the "vision at the end of *The House on Mango Street* can only be achieved by the narrative's resistance of boundaries, separations, and dualisms" (246), and the most significant dualism that Esperanza rejects is the division of "good" versus "bad" females in her culture. Esperanza is neither "good" nor "bad"; she encompasses traits of both the Virgin and la Malinche, but she refuses passively to accept the label of either one. Instead, she sees her life, like her dream house, as a space "clean as paper before the poem" (108), with potential for creativity, autonomy, and most importantly, self-definition.

Not surprisingly, this self-definition is also a goal of Sandra Cisneros as a woman, as well as an author. In her essay, "Guadalupe the Sex Goddess: Unearthing the Racy Past of Mexico's Most Famous Virgin," Cisneros relates her own attempt to redefine what it means to be a Chicana artist by merging dichotomous images of the female: "To me, la Virgen de Guadalupe is also Coatlicue, the creative/destructive goddess. . . . Most days, I too feel like the creative/destructive goddess Coatlicue, especially the days I'm writing. . . . I am the Coatlicue-Lupe whose square column of body I see in so many Indian women. . . . I am obsessed with becoming a woman comfortable in her own skin" (46).

This essay first appeared in *MELUS: Journal of the Society for the Study of the Multi-Ethnic Literature of the United States*, issue 25.2 (Summer 2000), pages 119-132, and is reprinted by permission of the journal. Copyright © 2000 by *MELUS*.

Notes

1. Leal's article traces manifestations of the violated woman and the chaste woman in Mexican literature, dealing with some historical accounts from the 1660s, but focusing on works written between the 1860s and the 1960s. The author labels the various transformations of the stereotypes with terms such as "the available girlfriend" and the "pure sweetheart." Although Leal makes a convincing case for the existence of this duality, he does not develop a theory as to its significance, saying only that "Mexican literature, like all other literatures, reflects the prejudices of the ages and creates types that are remolded within the limits of these prejudices, most of them derived from the past" (241).

2. My summary of this apparition is based almost exclusively on Poole's translation because it corresponds with and elaborates on the details of the apparition that are found in other sources, such as those given by Leal and Lafaye.

3. Interestingly, Cortés and his troops venerated this Spanish icon (Lafaye 217); perhaps this explains the Mexican insistence on distinction between the two.

4. I use "Marina" consistently in this summary because that is the name Phillips uses.

5. Paz gives a detailed definition of the usage of this term (67-71).

6. Because of her status as a slave, it would seem that Paz's assertion that Marina acted voluntarily is a matter of conjecture.

7. While "chaste" is often used to designate virginity, *The American Heritage College Dictionary* lists "celibacy" as a third definition. While Lupe is obviously not virginal, all signs indicate that she is currently, and permanently, celibate.

8. Phillips's article includes an eyewitness account that claims this was Marina's original job as a slave (103).

9. In her synthesis of the critical reception of *The House on Mango Street*, Valdés criticizes Rodríguez's interpretation that "Cisneros's novel expresses the traditional ideology of the American Dream, a large house in the suburbs and being away from the dirt and dirty of the *barrio* is happiness," and that accuses Esperanza of losing her ethnic identity (289).

Works Cited

Cisneros, Sandra. *The House on Mango Street*. New York: Vintage, 1991.

_____. "Guadalupe the Sex Goddess: Unearthing the Racy Past of Mexico's Most Famous Virgin." *Ms*. July-August 1996: 43-46.

Herrera-Sobek, María. "The Politics of Rape: Sexual Transgression in Chicana Fiction." *The Americas Review* 15. 3-4 (1987): 171-88.

Klein, Dianne. "Coming of Age in Novels by Rudolfo Anaya and Sandra Cisneros." *English Journal* 81.5 (1992): 21-26.

Kolmar, Wendy K. "'Dialectics of Connectedness': Supernatural Elements in Novels by Bambara, Cisneros, Grahn, and Erdrich." *Haunting the House of Fiction: Feminist Perspectives on Ghost Stories by Women*. Ed. Lynette Carpenter and Wendy K. Kolmar. Knoxville: U of Tennessee P, 1991. 236-49.

Lafaye, Jacques. *Quetzalcóatl and Guadalupe*. Chicago: U of Chicago P, 1976.

Leal, Luis. "Female Archetypes in Mexican Literature." *Women in Hispanic Literature: Icons and Fallen Idols*. Ed. Beth Miller. Berkeley: U of California P, 1983. 227-42.

Olivares, Julián. "Sandra Cisneros' *The House on Mango Street*, and the Poetics of Space." *The Americas Review* 15. 3-4 (1987): 160-70.

Paz, Octavio. *The Labyrinth of Solitude*. Trans. Lysander Kemp. 1961. London: Penguin, 1967.

Phillips, Rachel. "Marina/Malinche: Masks and Shadows." *Women in Hispanic Literature: Icons and Fallen Idols*. Ed. Beth Miller. Berkeley: U of California P, 1983. 97-114.

Poole, Stafford. *Our Lady of Guadalupe*. Tucson: U of Arizona P, 1995.

Rodríguez, Juan. "*The House on Mango Street*, by Sandra Cisneros." *Austin Chronicle* (August 10, 1984). Cited in María Elena de Valdés. "The Critical Reception of Sandra Cisneros's *The House on Mango Street*." *Gender, Self and Society*. Ed. Renate von Bardeleben. Frankfurt: Peter Lang, 1993. 287-300.

Rodríguez-Aranda, Pilar E. "On the Solitary Fate of Being Mexican, Female, Wicked and Thirty-three: An Interview with the Writer Sandra Cisneros." *The Americas Review* 18.1 (1990): 64-80.

Valdés, María Elena de. "The Critical Reception of Sandra Cisneros' *The House on Mango Street*." *Gender, Self, and Society*. Ed. Renate von Bardeleben. Frankfurt: Peter Lang, 1993. 287-300.

Memories of Girlhood:
Chicana Lesbian Fictions_____

Catrióna Rueda Esquibel

> To link families with four sisters who would be friends longer than their
> lifetimes, through children who would bond them at baptismal rites.
> *Comadres.* We would become intimate friends, sharing coffee, gossip, and
> heartaches. We would endure the female life-cycle—adolescence, mar-
> riage, menopause, death, and even divorce, before or after menopause, be-
> fore or after death.
>   I had not come for that. I had come for her kiss.
>
> —Pérez 1996, 13

In my research of Chicana literature, I have found a series of stories
in which girlhood provides a space, however restrictive, for lesbian desire. Within the socially sanctioned system of *comadrazgo*, young
Chicanas are encouraged to form lifelong female friendships, and it is
the intimacy of these relationships that often provides the context for
lesbian desire. Specifically, I consider the representation of girlhood
friendships in four novel-length works by Chicana authors: Sandra
Cisneros's *The House on Mango Street* (1991), Denise Chávez's *The
Last of the Menu Girls* (1987), Terri de la Peña's *Margins* (1992), and
Emma Pérez's *Gulf Dreams* (1996). Of these, only the lesbian-
authored texts—those by de la Peña and Pérez—are generally perceived as "lesbian" fiction. By including *Mango Street* and *Menu Girls*
in my study, I argue that they too are Chicana lesbian texts, not because
the characters (or their authors) self-consciously claim a lesbian identity, but because the texts, in their literary construction of such intense
girlhood friendships, inscribe a desire between girls that I name "lesbian."

In this, I participate in lesbian textual criticism, which has discussed
at length the question, What is a lesbian text? Bertha Harris has defined
lesbian texts thus: "If in a woman writer's work a sentence refuses to

do what it is supposed to do, if there are strong images of women and if there is a refusal to be linear, the result is innately lesbian literature" (1976; cited in Smith 1982, 164). Such a definition seems to use *lesbian* as a metaphor for *feminist* or *woman-identified*. Barbara Smith implicitly demonstrates the exceedingly broad scope of Harris's definition when she applies it to Black women's writing. Indeed, Smith argues that according to Harris's definition, the majority of Black women's literature is lesbian, "not because the women are lovers, but because they are its central figures, are positively portrayed and have pivotal relations with one another" (1982, 164). While I concur that such a definition likewise encompasses most contemporary Chicana literature, so defining all Chicana literature as lesbian would hardly enhance an understanding of either Chicana literature in general or Chicana lesbian literature in particular.

However, in her well-known reading of *Sula*, Smith gestures toward a more nuanced description of lesbian fiction: "[*Sula*] works as a lesbian novel not only because of the passionate friendship between Sula and Nel, but because of [its] consistently critical stance toward the heterosexual institutions of male/female relationships, marriage, and the family. Consciously or not, Morrison's work poses both lesbian and feminist questions about Black women's autonomy and their impact upon each other's lives" (165). Seemingly, Smith's use of the term *lesbian* to describe a critique of heterosexual institutions is both metaphoric and utopic.[1] Because she seems to use *lesbian* and *lesbian feminist* interchangeably, both the passionate friendship and the critique of institutionalized heterosexuality are necessary to her definition of *lesbian*. However, if one applies Smith's description of "both lesbian and feminist" respectively to the "passionate friendship" and critique of heterosexual institutions, one comes closer to a usage of *lesbian* that is neither metaphoric nor interchangeable with *feminist*. Thus the critique of heterosexual institutions makes *Sula* feminist (in a nonheterocentric sense), while the "passionate friendship" invites a lesbian reading.

It is important, I think, to differentiate *lesbian* from other homo-social relations between women and from female desire in general, lest the latter two erase the former, as has been the case with many applications of Adrienne Rich's "Lesbian Continuum." In *The Practice of Love* (1994), Teresa de Lauretis unravels *lesbian* from its metaphoric and political applications to define it in quite specific terms:

> Whatever other affective or social ties may be involved in a lesbian relationship—ties that may also exist in other relations between and among women, from friendship to rivalry, political sisterhood to class or racial antagonism, ambivalence to love, and so on—the term *lesbian* refers to a sexual relation, for better or for worse, and however broadly one may wish to define sexual. I use this term . . . to include centrally—beyond any performed or fantasized physical sexual act, whatever it may be—the conscious presence of desire in one woman for another. (284)

De Lauretis argues that *lesbian* is not equivalent to woman-identified or feminist but derives from desire that is not simply female desire but desire in one woman (or girl) for another. I feel that Smith was invoking just such an understanding of desire between women in her discussion of Sula and Nel's "passionate friendship;" which Lorraine Bethel has characterized as expressing "a certain sensuality in their interactions" (Bethel 1976; cited in Smith 1982, 166).

Yet, extending de Lauretis's definition to girlhood raises other interpretive questions, for what constitutes "the conscious presence of desire" in girlhood stories? As Bonnie Zimmerman has noted, "Lesbian writers of retrospective narratives often claim to have felt themselves to *be* lesbian from birth or age two, or certainly from puberty and thus always to have had a lesbian perspective" (1993a, 136). Thus, as retrospectives, girlhood stories in particular are "products of the very perspective that they purport to explain." By this logic, *lesbian* girlhood stories are those that retroactively construct adult lesbian identity, but this too is a subjective definition; "for example, a woman might focus on the fact that she was intimate friends with Sally at age six and fail to note that so were a dozen other girls, none of whom became lesbians" (Zimmerman 1993a, 136).[2] In the interplay between reader and text, it occurs to me that this retroactive construction might work both ways: a story of being "intimate friends with Sally" might appear to some readers to be a simple girlhood story, with no implications about sexuality outside of gender identity, while to others it would be a specifically lesbian girlhood story. Thus for many readers, *The House on Mango Street* and *The Last of the Menu Girls* would constitute lesbian girlhood stories because the readers identify with the protagonist and her feelings of loss for her friend, while other readers, approaching these stories from a heteronormative stance, would emphatically refute such a reading for precisely the same reasons.

Zimmerman claims that "if a text lends itself to a lesbian reading, then no amount of . . . 'proof' ought to be necessary to establish it as a lesbian text" (1993b, 39). As I undertake a lesbian reading of all four of these texts, I hope that my readers, while they may hold themselves unconvinced, will yet acknowledge that I am not "demanding a plot . . . that the writer has not chosen to create" but am "picking up on hints and possibilities that the author, consciously or not, has strewn in the text" (Zimmerman 1993a, 144). While both Cisneros and Chávez depict the cultural structures of institutionalized heterosexuality, neither fixes a heterosexual ending for her protagonist; each is alone at the end of the text, with many possibilities open to her.

In Chicana/o literature, tales of girlhood and adolescence provide a glimpse into the construction of sexual identity when "the girls come . . . face to face with . . . their prescribed roles" in Chicana/o (hetero)sexual economies (Saldívar 1990, 184). The stories show how and what the young female characters learn about sexuality and the sense they make of it. The girls are frequently perceived as asexual, since they are not sexually active, or more specifically, not (yet) heterosexually active. They are discouraged—by mothers, family, community, and religion— from recognizing or exploring their sexuality. At the same time, the cultural role of *comadres*, which raises lifelong friendships to the status of kinship, is both encouraged and recognized. In this article, I focus on the representation of desire as it develops between girlhood friends and on the ways in which that desire, and any explicitly sexual perception of it, is masked by the presumed sexlessness of adolescent girls.[3]

In *The House on Mango Street, The Last of the Menu Girls, Margins*, and *Gulf Dreams*, girlhood friendships have a very specific relationship to institutionalized heterosexuality. These texts critique the limited and heterosexual roles open and indeed prescribed to young Chicanas, as well as the ways in which female friendships are less valued than heterosexual relationships. However, I have chosen these texts neither for their critique of heterosexual institutions nor for their depiction of the role of girlhood friendships within their respective Chicana/o communities, but because they locate certain erotic elements in girlhood friendships.[4] Chicana/o literary criticism has not yet discussed these texts in terms of lesbian sexuality.[5] While more scholarship on Chicana lesbian literature is being produced, most criticism focuses on the two best-known Chicana lesbian writers, Cherríe Moraga and Gloria Anzaldúa. As the coeditors of the 1981 anthology *This Bridge Called My Back: Writings by Radical Women of Color*, Moraga and Anzaldúa were instrumental in the circulation of writings by lesbians of color. Many of their subsequent individual works have been widely anthologized, often several times over. While both have taken pains to develop and promote the work of other writers—through editing, teaching, and work-shopping—they are often taken as representative of Chicana lesbians in general and thus are published in lieu of other Chicana lesbian writers. Because of the prominence of these two authors, criticism on Chicana lesbian writers has focused mainly on the genres of drama and nonfiction prose. In looking at girlhood friendships, I hope to broaden the scope of Chicana lesbian literary criticism, both by bringing attention to less well known writings and authors and by reevaluating Cisneros's and Chávez's works in light of the explicit representation of lesbian desire in girlhood in the novels of de la Peña and Pérez, and thus to expand Chicana lesbian literature beyond the writings of lesbian-identified authors. In my readings, I dwell on the "passionate friendships" between girls that other scholars have been at pains to ignore, rationalize, or misrepresent.

The House on Mango Street

Sandra Cisneros's *The House on Mango Street* was first published in 1984 by Arte Público, a small press out of the University of Houston featuring the works of Latino writers in English and Spanish. In 1991, the third edition was published by Vintage and has been an international best-seller. It is frequently referred to as a "novel-in-stories"; it is, in fact, a series of forty-four vignettes that feature the same narrative voice and cast of characters. Alvina Quintana takes exception to the tendency to classify *Mango Street* as a novel, which she sees as a means of incorporating Cisneros's work into traditional forms: "Cisneros defined a distinctive Chicana literary space—oh so gently she flung down the gauntlet, challenging, at the least, accepted literary form, gender inequities, and the cultural and economic subordination of minorities. Theoretically speaking, this little text subverts traditional form and content in a way that demonstrates how conventional applications of literary genre and the social construction of gender undermine a 'feminist aesthetic'" (1996, 55). Ironically, in spite of its being classified as a novel, critical discussions of *Mango Street* (Herrera-Sobek 1987; Saldívar 1990) often approach it as a collection of separate stories, with little effort to appreciate the complex relationships among the characters as they develop throughout the work. As a departure, then, I examine one relationship as it is developed in five of the vignettes: "Sally," "What Sally Said," "The Monkey Garden," "Red Clowns," and "Linoleum Roses." These stories focus on the developing relationships between Esperanza, the narrator, and Sally, with whom she shares a particular friendship.

All the stories (or vignettes) in *Mango Street* are told by the adolescent Esperanza in first person. She discusses the other inhabitants of Mango Street, at some times giving her own views on people, at others repeating what she has been told. Most of the secondary characters are also girls: her younger sister Nenny; her friends across the street, Lucy and Rachel; the older girls in the neighborhood, Marin, Alicia, and Sally. In this community, an adult woman is one who has a house, and women are classified by whether they have a husband or whether their husband has died or has left them. Women are viewed primarily in relation to men, in heterosexual terms. The narrator begins describing herself by explaining her name, "Esperanza," which means both "hope" and "waiting." She does not want to wait for a man to change her life; she wants to write her own changes. Esperanza seeks an alternative to the options presented to her: options prescribed by sexism and institutionalized heterosexuality. One of Esperanza's dilemmas is how to reconcile her desires with her opportunities. She looks forward to having her own house, without a husband to lock her in or leave her lonely. Such a thing is unheard of on Mango Street, where women are confined to the home, where a woman is alone not by her choice but by necessity or by a man's choice. Thus Esperanza, who looks for something more, must look beyond Mango Street.

Ramón Saldívar (1990) discusses *Mango Street* at length in his chapter "Gender and Difference in Ríos, Cisneros and Moraga." Like many other critics, including Julián Olivares (1987), Quintana (1996), and Renato Rosaldo (1991), he focuses on the space of Mango Street, the houses, gender roles, and the confinement of women. Ironically, while addressing the limited roles made available by the patriarchal structure, he becomes caught up in its discourse, defining women in relation to men and thus missing the significant relationships between girls that occur in the novel. Saldívar places the intense friendship Esperanza feels for her friend Sally solely in the realm of emulation or shared experience and does not differentiate it from Esperanza's other friendships, such as those with Rachel and Lucy, who are nearer her own age, or the significant but less charged older-girl/younger-girl friendships she enjoys with Marin and Alicia.

For Esperanza and for her world, adulthood—that is, womanhood—is defined by men. In "The Family of Little Feet," Esperanza, Lucy, and Rachel are given three pairs of fancy high-heeled shoes by a neighbor lady.[6] They practice walking and running up and down the street with them, and then

> Down to the corner where the men can't take their eyes off us . . .
>
> Mr. Benny at the corner grocery puts down his important cigar: Your mother know you got shoes like that? Who give you those?
>
> Nobody.
>
> Them are dangerous, he says. You girls too young to be wearing shoes like that. Take them shoes off before I call the cops, but we just ran. (40-41)

The shoes enact one transformation on the girls and on the men another. On the one hand, the shoes make the girls into desirable objects; they see their own legs becoming long and shapely because of the high heels: "The truth is it is scary to look down at your foot that is no longer yours and see attached a long long leg" (40). On the other hand, the men, through their desiring gaze, make the girls into women: here, clearly, to be a woman is to be an object of desire to heterosexual men. The male attention places the girls in the adult world; they are solicited by the men and finally run away home to hide the shoes for another day because they "are tired of being beautiful." But that other day never comes, and they leave the shoes hidden, to be thrown away later by a cleaning mother.

"The Family of Little Feet" is a good example of the ways in which Esperanza keeps coming up against adulthood, womanhood—which actually means adult heterosexuality—and her resistance to that change. At the same time, Esperanza distinguishes herself from her younger sister Nenny, who is firmly in the realm of childhood. In "Hips," Esperanza, Lucy, and Rachel are discussing their desire to grow hips, what hips mean, and what they are for. As they jump rope, each girl makes up a rhyme about hips. Nenny does not understand the conversation: "Everybody is getting into it now except Nenny who is still humming *not a girl, not a boy, just a little baby.* She's like that" (51).[7] Instead of making up her own song about hips, Nenny uses standard jumping rhymes, like "Engine, engine number nine" and "My mother and your mother were washing clothes," even when the other girls tell her she is not playing right. In contrast to Nenny, who is a child, and Esperanza, Lucy, and Rachel, who are adolescents, the older teenage girls in the stories are constantly circulating in the male sexual realm. Whether under the control of their fathers, meeting with boys at dances, fulfilling the roles of absent mothers, or marrying and being confined to the house, Marin, Sally, and Alicia are clearly situated within adult heterosexuality. While Esperanza is friends with most of these older girls, one in particular—Sally—has a transformative effect on her. Esperanza admires Sally, and desires her, although that desire is not explicitly sexual. Through Sally, Esperanza comes to understand the value system in which female friendships are relegated to childhood while adulthood is reserved for heterosexuality.

"Sally," the first of the stories to depict Sally and Esperanza's relationship, introduces "the girl with eyes like Egypt and nylons the color of smoke" (81). Esperanza describes Sally first as Sally's father perceives her—"to be this beautiful is trouble"—and then as Esperanza's mother sees her—"to wear black so young is dangerous"—both parents implying that Sally's sexual desirability will bring her grief. Indeed this is already the case, as she has no best friend, "not since [Cheryl] called you that name" (82), that is, presumably, since Cheryl labeled her as sexually dirty. While it attracts males, Sally's sensuality creates a barrier between herself and other girls. She is judged to be fast or dirty or ill fated and is thus left alone. Furthermore, Sally seems afraid to go home and attempts to "clean herself up" before entering her house: "You pull your skirt straight, you rub the blue paint off your eyelids. You don't laugh, Sally. You look at your feet and walk fast to the house you can't come out from" (82). Both Saldívar and Quintana look at the story "Sally" as being primarily about the danger of sexuality. Yet they do not contextualize this story with the other Sally stories but see it as one of a series of introductions, not as part of a larger narrative about this one character. Cisneros introduces Sally between "Rafaela Who Drinks Coconut and Papaya Juice on Tuesdays," a view of a young married woman locked up in her house, and "Minerva Writes Poems," the story of a friend "only a little bit older than me but already she has two kids and a husband who left" (84). The Sally stories are unique within *Mango Street* because they are not isolated vignettes but chart the development of the character Sally and her relationship with Esperanza. The stories dealing with Lucy and Rachel, for example, could be read in any order, whereas the Sally stories chronicle the growing intimacy between Esperanza and Sally, the ending of that intimacy, and the subsequent distance from which Esperanza perceives Sally.

Saldívar argues that "Esperanza wishes to be like Sally, wishes to learn to flick her hair when she laughs, to 'paint [her] eyes like Cleopatra,' and to wear black suede shoes and matching nylons as Sally does" (185). Yet Esperanza's desire to be taught how to paint her eyes "like Egypt" is less about being *like* Sally than it is about being *with* Sally.[8] It is intertwined with the desire to lean against the fence with Sally and share her hairbrush, to hear Sally's dreams. Esperanza then goes on to articulate a world for Sally-like Esperanza's own dreams for a "real" house, far away from the barrio and the limits of Mango Street—a world where Sally keeps walking to a quiet, middle-class neighborhood, where she can dream her dreams, where her desire for desire is innocent and not damning, and where her desire for love is not "crazy" but the most normal thing in the world.

Quintana is most interested in the way the depiction of Sally and her desires "illuminates the contradictions in an ideology whose primary objective is masculine gratification" (69). The negative opinions of Sally, such as those voiced by Esperanza's mother and Sally's father, and "the stories the boys tell in the cloakroom" are clear evidence of the contradiction that women face: they must reproduce themselves for a desiring male gaze, but in doing so, they incur censure. Although she labels this ideology "heterosexist" (69), Quintana does not herself go beyond a heterosexual framework, and in my view she fails to appreciate Sally the character and her significance for Esperanza fully. Esperanza's descriptions of Sally are poetic and appreciative, although when she describes Sally as pretty she does so in reference to male approval: "The boys at school think she's beautiful because her hair is shiny black like raven feathers and when she laughs, she flicks her hair back like a satin shawl over her shoulders and laughs" (81). In her own mind she poses questions to Sally, in a bantering, flirting tone quite unlike Esperanza's usual form of address: "Sally, who taught you to paint your eyes like Cleopatra? And if I roll the little brush with my tongue . . . will you teach me?" Here she goes on to articulate a desire to be like Sally, to have shoes and nylons like hers, but again her means of expressing this indicates how much it is Sally she desires. Precisely because they do not read "Sally" in conjunction with the other four Sally stories, Quintana and Saldívar miss the development of Esperanza and Sally's relationship throughout the book. Perhaps they see no reason to privilege female friendships or to consider lesbian desire in their critique of the gender limitations within *Mango Street*. Instead, they see "Sally" as merely one of a sequence of character introductions, between Rafaela and Minerva.

Of all the characters, however, it is Sally that Esperanza desires, and it is Sally who betrays her. In "The Monkey Garden," Esperanza is torn between running with the children and talking to the boys with Sally. "Play with the kids if you want to," Sally says, from the circle of a boy's arms, "I'm staying here" (96). In their sexual banter, the boys take Sally's keys and refuse to return them unless she gives each of them a kiss, and the group enters the garden to accomplish this:

> One of the boys invented the rules. One of Tito's friends said you can't get the keys back unless you kiss us and Sally pretended to be mad at first but she said yes. . . .
>
> I don't know why, but something inside me wanted to throw a stick. Something wanted to say no when I watched Sally going into the garden with Tito's buddies all grinning. It was just a kiss, that's all. A kiss for each one. So what, she said.
>
> Only how come I felt angry inside. Like something wasn't right. (97)

Esperanza is incensed at this manipulation of her friend. Confused by Sally's compliance, she interprets it as passivity and attempts to interfere with the male coercion. She first complains to the mother of one of the boys, who tells her, in effect, that boys will be boys. Frustrated, Esperanza decides she has the responsibility to rescue Sally.

> I . . . ran back down the three flights to the garden where Sally needed to be saved. I took three big sticks and a brick and figured this was enough.
>
> But when I got there Sally said go home. Those boys said leave us alone. I felt stupid with my brick. They all looked at me as if I was the one that was crazy and made me feel ashamed. (97)

Esperanza is shown that her assistance is neither required nor desired. In fact, her aggression, if you will, her refusal to accept this male sexual barter as "justo y necesario" is precisely what marks Esperanza as "childish" rather than "womanly."[9] Furthermore, Sally not only demonstrates that she thinks Esperanza is childish for resisting, but she is quite clear in expressing her preference for Tito's company over Esperanza's. Sally, articulating her adult sexuality (heterosexuality), mocks Esperanza and signifies her as infantile both for her active role (attempting to rescue the seemingly passive Sally) and for her perception of male sexuality and heterosexuality as dangerous. It is this rejection by Sally that affects Esperanza so strongly that she feels sick and angry and "wrong." She hides herself in the monkey garden, weeping and praying for death: "I wanted to will my blood to stop, my heart to quit its pumping. I wanted to be dead, to turn into the rain, my eyes to melt into the ground like two black snails. I wished and wished. I closed my eyes and willed it, but when I got up my dress was green and I had a headache" (97-98). The violence of her reaction demonstrates the depth of her feeling for Sally and the pain of betrayal. Yet her feelings, her love, are clearly of little value in comparison to male attention. Although Esperanza frequently expresses feelings of rebellion and resistance toward the limited gender roles available to girls, in this instance she resents heteronormativity as well as sexism, because it limits not merely what she can do but whom she can love and how. Sexuality—heterosexuality—however it is naturalized, defined, and promoted, remains outside the realm of Esperanza's understanding. "They were laughing. She was too. It was a joke I didn't get" (96). For Sally and Tito and the other boys, the joke is heterosexuality: it's fun, it's funny, it's a game they all know. And yet, like Nenny singing her childish rhyme, oblivious to the advantages of hips, Esperanza lives in a world that does not accommodate such things. Heterosexuality is, throughout the novel, a brutal intrusion into the world of girls.

In Chicana contexts, girlhood is a space and time before the imposition of normative heterosexuality and, as such, provides a site for texts to stage lesbian desires, such as those of Esperanza, whose feelings for Sally go beyond those of simple friendship. According to the institutions of heterosexuality Esperanza's reluctance to enter into (hetero)sexuality is both validated by and a symptom of her sexual immaturity. Because she is a child, she is repulsed by the mature reality of heterosexuality. When she is older, she will get the joke. Yet, throughout *The House on Mango Street*, Esperanza resists this forced heterosexualization. In "Red Clowns," she is violently initiated into heterosexuality by a boy who says, "I love you, Spanish girl." She and Sally are at a carnival, and it is while she is waiting for Sally, who has gone off with another boy, that she is forced into sex. She cries out against the act, which is not like the stories of her girlfriends, or the songs, or the movies, but is painful and unpleasant and a manifestation of male desire that has little to do with her as a person. Esperanza's resistance constitutes what Smith would describe as the text's "critical stance toward the heterosexual institutions of male/female relationships, marriage and the family" (1982, 165). And yet, what moves *Mango Street* into the realm of lesbian text is Esperanza crying out to Sally, "Sally Sally a hundred times" (100). As in "The Monkey Garden," Sally chooses male company over Esperanza, leaving the latter confused and vulnerable. Esperanza very clearly voices her desire for Sally and the ways in which she perceives it to differ from male desire: "And anyway I don't like carnivals. I went to be with you because you laugh on the tilt-a-whirl, you throw your head back and laugh. I hold your change, wave, count how many times you go by. Those boys that look at you because you're pretty. I like to be with you, Sally" (99). Esperanza is attempting to articulate a desire for Sally that she differentiates from the mere physical attraction of "those boys that look at you because you're pretty." She is, however, unable to find words to express that differentiation and thus falls back on the acceptable description of female intimacy: "You're my friend." Saldívar misses the nuances of this story, stating only, "Waiting to meet Sally at an amusement park, Esperanza is assaulted by three white boys" (186).[10] Esperanza's love for Sally and Sally's preference for a boy are precisely what has placed Esperanza in this vulnerable position; Sally's action represents not merely "complicity in embroidering a fairy-tale-like mist around sex" (Herrera-Sobek 1987, 178) but the further betrayal of Esperanza's love for her.

What stand out about both "Red Clowns" and "The Monkey Garden" are the ways in which Esperanza relates to heterosexuality, not through boys, but through Sally. Sally desires male attention, while Esperanza desires Sally's attention. She wants to be Sally's friend and confidante, to stand by her when others do not. Instead she is rejected and left waiting while Sally chooses to kiss the boys. It is Esperanza's desire for Sally, both in the way that it differs from her friendships with

Lucy and Rachel and in the way that it pushes Esperanza into hetero-sexuality, that makes this a lesbian girlhood story. I do not mean that Esperanza chooses heterosexuality, but merely that she is violently initiated into it because of her desire to be with Sally, who does not prefer to be with her. "Linoleum Roses," which follows "Red Clowns," effectively brings Sally's narrative, and Esperanza's involvement in her life, to a close. Sally is married and locked away in a man's house. Although he is prone to violence, Sally says her new husband is "okay. Except he won't let her talk on the telephone. And he doesn't let her look out the window. And he doesn't like her friends" (101-2). Thus Sally is lost to Esperanza, who is not allowed "to visit her unless he is working." Not even able to gaze at roses outside the window, Sally can view only those printed on her linoleum floor.

The Sally stories, and "The Monkey Garden" and "Red Clowns" in particular, have a transformative effect on both the narrator and the text. They are situated near the end of the collection and suggest "a change in Esperanza's attitude" (Quintana 1996, 65).[11] In these stories Esperanza passes out of adolescence, not in the patriarchal sense of "being made a woman" through intercourse with a man, but because she is passed over in favor of a male and then subsequently used for male pleasure. These traumatic events are marked off, as is Esperanza's perception of her self. "I looked at my feet in their white socks and their ugly round shoes. They seemed far away. They didn't seem to be my feet anymore. And the garden that had been such a good place to play didn't seem mine either" (98). Esperanza's world, her self, and the way she views everything have dramatically shifted as a result of the loss of Sally's friendship. However, while the world in which Esperanza moves is exclusively heterosexual, she is not recuperated by heterosexuality at the end of the book. The ending, in fact, raises more questions about Esperanza's future than it answers.

Friends and neighbors will say, What happened to that Esperanza? Where did she go with all those books and paper? Why did she march so far away? They will not know I have gone away to come back. For the ones I left behind. For the ones who cannot come out. (110)[12]

Perhaps Esperanza will come back one day for Sally, the one "who cannot come out."

The Last of the Menu Girls

Denise Chávez's 1987 work, *The Last of the Menu Girls*, has enjoyed moderate success for a small-press book. Like *The House on Mango Street*, *The Last of the Menu Girls* is a series of interrelated stories about an adolescent female character negotiating her womanhood. Also like Cisneros's work, *Menu Girls* resists easy classification. While the seven stories are distinct, their depiction of Rocío Esquibel, the primary narrator, demonstrates the depth and movement of her character. Several of the stories were originally published individually, yet as a collection the stories achieve a certain unity that informs the minor aspects of the individual stories.[13] However, Rocío's world is very different from Esperanza's: women are not defined by men or dependent on them for identity or support. Rocío herself comes from a household of women, although traces of her mother's two husbands can be found in dusty corners.

The stories are set in the area of Las Cruces, New Mexico, which borders El Paso, Texas, which in turn borders Ciudad Juárez, Mexico. They are generally told from the perspective of Rocío, who lives with her younger sister, Mercy, and their mother, Nieves, a schoolteacher. Her father, Salvador, has deserted the family and is working up north, and Ronelia, her elder sister, has left home to marry. Although she is looking back on her adolescence and captures the bluntness of that period, Rocío clearly speaks as an adult through most of the stories. In *The Last of the Menu Girls*, I am primarily interested in Chávez's portrayals of the relationships among girls and between girls and women, and in the way that Rocío's eroticism and desire focus on women. Chávez is quite frank in depicting the sensual dynamics of these relationships, and in fact it is the sensual dimension that causes Rocío to question herself continually. Rocío is a challenging narrator, for unlike Esperanza of *Mango Street*, who holds little back, Rocío is often coy and evasive, providing only hints of her true feelings.

The book begins with the title story, which describes Rocío's first job, delivering menus to patients at the local hospital. Being in the presence of the "sick and dying" reminds her of caring for her dying great-aunt Eutilia four years earlier. Following a multitude of visceral images of Eutilia's illness, Rocío recalls dancing "around her bed in my dreams, naked, smiling, jubilant. It was an exultant adolescent dance for my dying aunt. It was necessary, compulsive. It was a primitive dance, a full moon offering that led me slithering into her room with breasts naked and oily at thirteen" (14). This "full moon offering," charged with imagery of female sexuality, is not solely self-expression. In her mind, Rocío performs not merely in the presence of Eutilia, but for Eutilia:

> Down the steps I leaped into Eutilia's faded and foggy consciousness where I whirled and danced and sang. . . . Eutilia stared at me. I turned away.
>
> I danced around Eutilia's bed. I hugged the screen door, my breasts indented in the meshed wire. In the darkness Eutilia moaned, my body wet, her body dry. Steamy we were, and full of prayers. (15)

While one could perhaps read this scene as solely a fantastic healing ritual, it seems clear that Rocío herself sees it as distinctly sexual. Renato Rosaldo describes this dance in terms of "sexuality and danger" and acknowledges a "bodily sexual connection" between Rocío and Eutilia, but does so, perversely, without considering the implications of that "sexual" connection being between women. Instead he reads it exclusively as an aspect of her familial ties to generations of women (1991, 89-90).[14] However, this fantasy of Rocío's offering her own oiled breasts, pressing them against the screen door that separates her from Eutilia, the contrast of "my body wet, her body dry," Eutilia's stare—which simultaneously draws Rocío and drives her away—and Eutilia's moans mark this not merely as female sexuality but as sexuality between women.

Throughout the stories, Rocío's sexuality is expressed most profoundly in relation to other women. Although Rocío does not identify as a lesbian—and she does know lesbians—she repeatedly expresses complex desires for other female characters. For example, Rocío describes a significant week:

> When Arlene took a short vacation to the Luray Caverns, I became the official menu girl. That week was the happiest of my entire summer.
>
> That week I fell in love.
>
> ELIZABETH RAINEY (Chávez 1987, 26)

The name "Elizabeth Rainey" marks a section break within the story. The previous sentence, "That week I fell in love," sets up an expectation that Rocío will tell of her first boyfriend, perhaps of an awkward courtship, or a romantic one. Instead, she describes Elizabeth Rainey, an elegant young Anglo patient at the hospital, who impresses Rocío with her beauty and sorrow.

> I ran out, frightened by her pain, yet excited somehow. She was so beautiful and so alone. I wanted in my little girl's way to hold her, hold her tight and in my woman's way never to feel her pain, ever, whatever it was. (27)

> It was this woman in her solitary anguish who touched me the most deeply. How could I, at age seventeen, not knowing love, how could I presume to reach out to this young woman in her sorrow, touch her and say, "I know, I understand." (27)

Elizabeth Rainey has an aura of sexuality, for she "was in for a D and C. I didn't know what [that] was, but I knew it was mysterious, and to me, of course, this meant it had to do with sex" (26). This is another example of the difference from *Mango Street*, where, although girls may marry before high school or leave home because of pregnancy, they do not get abortions.[15]

Elizabeth Rainey is indeed marked by sexuality but not treated kindly by it: "She looked fragile, and yet her face betrayed a harsh indelicate bitterness" (26). Although her hospital room is full of flowers, there is no tender lover to greet her, to inquire anxiously how she is feeling. Instead there is only a seventeen-year-old menu girl, fascinated and yearning but unable to act: "As long as I live I will carry Elizabeth Rainey's image with me: in a creme-colored gown she is propped up, her hair fanning pillows in a room full of deep sweet acrid and overspent flowers. Oh, I may have been that summer girl, but yes, I knew. I understood. I would have danced for her . . . had I but dared" (28). Yet in spite of foreshadowing the week of Elizabeth Rainey as "the week I fell in love," Rocío avoids actually saying that she has fallen in love with Elizabeth. Rather, she articulates those qualities that attract her to Elizabeth Rainey—her beauty, her pain—and then her own inability to reach out, to give the comfort or understanding expected of the Florence Nightingales of the hospital. Although she expresses her desire in terms of nurturing, she also dwells on her desire to dance naked for Elizabeth Rainey as she dreamed of doing for Eutilia. Yet, while she was able to fantasize quite explicitly about that dance for Eutilia, something—perhaps the fact that Elizabeth Rainey is marked by sexuality—keeps Rocío from actively fantasizing that dance for her; instead she regrets her lack of daring.

Here and elsewhere in *Menu Girls*, Rocío attempts to explain her desire away in terms of identification. "I shrank back into myself and trembled behind the door. I never went back in her room. How could I? It was too terrible a vision, *for in her I saw myself*, all life, all suffering. What I saw both chilled and burned me. I stood long in that darkened doorway, confused in the presence of human pain. I wanted to reach out . . . I wanted to . . . But *how*?" (27; ellipses in original, first emphasis added). However, "it is important to consider that identification and desire can coexist, and that their formulation in terms of mutually exclusive oppositions serves a heterosexual matrix" (Butler 1991, 26). One need not choose either to identify with a person or to desire that person (see Butler 1993, 99). Such an argument seems to refute the distinction de Lauretis makes between (lesbian) desire for a woman and "'intrafeminine' self-directed, narcissistic 'fascinations'" (120), which she sees as "quintessentially heterosexual." However, within the cultural contexts of both *Mango Street* and *Menu Girls*, the narrators are unable to articulate desire for females except through socially acceptable identification.

Unlike *Mango Street*, which does not include the possibility for women-loving women, Rocío's world is inhabited by lesbians—quite a few lesbians, in fact, such as "the Nurses González and González—Esperanza, male, and Bertha, female" (28).[16] "Esperanza the dyke" is the head nurse of the surgical floor (32). She is bossy, prejudiced against immigrant Mexicans, and wholly unsympathetic, in stark contrast to the feminine women to whom Rocío is attracted. Far from identifying with this lesbian character, Rocío seems quite repulsed by this "Esperanza of no Esperanzas" (32), who is "without hope" both because of her own aggressive belligerence and because, looking back from the future, Rocío knows of her early death in a car accident: "Later when Esperanza was killed my aunt said, 'How nice. In the paper they call her lover her sister. How nice!'" (32). This incident marks both the visibility and invisibility of lesbian relationships. Everyone knows that Esperanza and Bertha are lovers. The author of the newspaper obituary recognizes the significance of that relationship by claiming Bertha as "sister," that is, as the closest legitimate female kin. Yet that same claim simultaneously erases their lesbianism by conflating it with the nonsexual blood ties. Anyone not personally acquainted with González and González will merely see that a woman has died in a car accident and was survived by her sister. Meanwhile, the ending of the story links Rocío back to Esperanza the dyke because her summer also ends with a car accident, although not a fatal one. Like Elizabeth Rainey, she is installed in a hospital room full of flowers, and she curses her own stupidity, which has brought her to such a pass. While Chávez thus creates a chain of signification from Esperanza to Rocío and back to Elizabeth Rainey, Rocío is at pains to distance herself from Esperanza, and thus from lesbianism. The subsections of this story are named for the characters who are most prominent in them (Mr. Smith, Arlene Rutshman, Elizabeth Rainey, and Dolores Casaus). This section should logically be named "Esperanza González"; instead, it is named for a rather minor character, Juan María—an undocumented Mexican worker disfigured in a barroom brawl—as if Rocío is afraid to put too much emphasis on Esperanza the dyke. In the stories dealing with Rocío's desires for women, Chávez repeatedly invokes lesbian figures, who stand simultaneously for lesbian potential and the denial of that potential. The lesbian serves as a marker, as if to say, "Something queer is going on here," and yet, because of her unsympathetic portrayal, that queerness is never claimed for Rocío. Instead, the narrator chooses to rearticulate that desire for women as an identification.

"Shooting Stars," the third story of the collection, deals at length with Rocío's relationship to other girls, specifically her friend Eloisa, who is sixteen and "already a woman" in comparison to the still girlish Rocío. During her annual summer visit with relatives in Texas, Rocío discovers that Eloisa is a cousin, of sorts: "Her aunt wore men's shirts and pants and bound her breasts with rags. One day I found that Eloisa's mother and aunt (half men to me) were relatives! This made Eloisa, too, part of my mother's family. Most of them were a queer, unbalanced lot" (55). Eloisa's nameless "aunt" is clearly a butch lesbian. The earlier euphemistic representation of González and González as sisters provides a certain ambiguity as to whether Eloisa's mother is the "aunt's" lover rather than her sister. That Eloisa's mother is included in the designation "half men to me" seems to support the possibility that the two women are lovers. These queer women serve to introduce Rocío's relationship with Eloisa, whose "womanliness" or maturity makes her desirable to Rocío and at the same time contains the rejection of that desire. "How I admired Eloisa! How grateful I was for allowing me into her magical woman's world. Eloisa and I were bright girls, mature girls. . . . Later, after the nightly watermelon, I would fall asleep under the stars thinking about Eloisa. She was Venus, I myself was a shooting star. The two of us were really one. We were beautiful girls, bright beautiful girls spitting out watermelon seeds. We were coyotes calling out to the moon" (56). Representing Eloisa as Venus, the bright planet and also the goddess of love, Rocío again emphasizes identification with her: "The two of us were really one." Yet the title, "Shooting Stars," emphasizes the ephemeral quality of their relationship.

Rocío's love for Eloisa, like Esperanza's for Sally in *Mango Street*, eventually comes up against socially sanctioned heterosexual relationships. Rocío's reverential love for Eloisa is destroyed when she sees her at a movie theater, smoking lasciviously and allowing some faceless man to paw her. Eloisa, then, implicitly rejects Rocío's love through her desire for a man, and Rocío retaliates by withdrawing entirely and curtailing their rambling walks together. This new image of Eloisa as fast, as wanton and decidedly heterosexual, produces a physical revulsion in Rocío, who feels "sick with nicotine, faint with its smell . . . sick to my heart . . . faint with disappointment" (56), just as Esperanza was sick in the monkey garden. Even after her return to New Mexico, Texas and Eloisa continue to haunt Rocío, taunting her to make sense of her feelings and her memories: "To me, Texas signified queer days, querulous wanderings, bloody fairy tales, hot moon-filled nights. . . . Texas was women to me: my fading grandmother, my aunt dying of cancer, my mother's hunchbacked aunt and Eloisa. All laughing, laughing. . . . When I lay in the solemn shade of my father's study, I thought of myself, of Eloisa, of all women. The thoughts swirled around like the rusty blades of our swamp cooler. . . . Perhaps someday when I grow older, I thought, maybe then I can recollect and recount the real significance of things in a past as elusive as clouds passing" (57). Rocío specifically expresses her desire for women, always placing it in the context of exploring womanliness. Thus as she conjures up images of women she has loved from the patterns in the stucco walls, she wonders, "What did it mean to be a woman? To be beautiful, complete? Was beauty a physical or a spiritual thing, was it strength of emotion, resolve, a willingness to love? What was it then that made women lovely?" (53).

Rocío's next "crush" is on Diana, an occasional domestic worker in the Esquibel household. She cleans and acts as older sister for Rocío, whose sister Ronelia left home to marry. Diana is a beautiful innocent, "unlike her Texas counterpart," and for Rocío she was "first and foremost: a friend who could never betray, no never. Nor could she see the possibility of betrayal. In this assumption of hers and mine lies all the tragedy of young womankind" (58). Diana's loyalty clearly constitutes one part of Rocío's attraction: she is still smarting from Eloisa's betrayal. She attempts to articulate what it was about Diana that attracted her, whether it was her beauty, her body, her laughter, which "crossed the fields and fogged all consciousness" (58). She then swiftly sidesteps any suggestion of lesbianism by asserting that "in observing Diana, I observed myself" (58). This is in spite of the fact that Diana and Rocío are not otherwise represented as similar. Diana is not a fully formed character or yet a fully formed person. Her speech, always formal and polite, always yielding gracefully, nevertheless takes the form of "monosyllabic utterings of someone dependent upon the repetitious motions of work, the body and its order." When she speaks she is "naïve, a little girl" (58). Her "weakness of spirit" separates her from Rocío, as she marries, has children, and is neglected by her straying husband. She thus ultimately accomplishes another kind of betrayal— a betrayal of Rocío's image of her, Rocío's hopes for her. When she becomes a good wife to a bad husband, Diana's youth, her beauty, and her laughter fade to a yellowed shell. Rocío cannot even recognize "Diana the huntress" in the wrinkled, whiskered woman with sad eyes whom her mother points out at church. She feels a strong sense of loss for the beautiful Diana.

The perceived betrayals by Eloisa and Diana, and Rocío's subsequent rejection of them, are ultimately refigured as their unsuitability as "role models." In actuality, of course, within the cultural constraints of institutionalized heterosexuality, they are unsuitable objects of desire. Thus Rocío tells herself to "let them go." She thinks about "*loving* women. Their beauty and their doubts, their sure sweet clarity. Their unfathomable depths, their flesh and souls aligned in mystery" (63). However, given the apparent fact that women are destined for heterosexual relations, Rocío sternly puts this thought from her mind, supplanting it with the image of her sister Ronelia, a more suitable (heterosexual) role model. Yet, inevitably the thought of them comes back to her: "Women. Women with firm, sure flesh of that age in time. In dreams. Let them go. . . . They were clouds, soft bright hopes. Just as quickly as they were formed, they dissolved into vast pillows. Their vague outlines touched the earth and then moved on" (65). This passage from the end of "Shooting Stars" articulates very carefully that one should not love women precisely because of an inherent flaw: their propensity for betrayal. This awareness is charged with regret and nostalgia for Rocío, as if to say: Who can help loving women, even if there is no future to it?

The final story, "Compadre," demonstrates the different ways in which Rocío expresses desire toward women and toward men. Her repulsion for the large daughters of Regino Suárez (her mother's *compadre*) clearly does not extend to all members of the family: "The car was being driven by Eleiterio, Regino's only son. Handsome, handsome young man, with Regino's dark skin and bright eyes, he was the embodiment of whatever passion there was in the union between Braulia and Regino" (150). Later, Rocío thinks she has seen Eleiterio cruising Main Street, pachuco-like, but convinces herself that she has not: "I imagined things. Almost always imagined things, and only once or twice with Eleiterio. *Su apá era adventista*" (159).[17] While Rocío is conscious of a desire for Eleiterio, she speaks of him very briefly. His younger sister Zianna, however, draws Rocío's sustained attention during an unplanned visit to the Suárez family. Unlike her sisters, Zianna is slender and attractive.

> Zianna, the darkest, loveliest flower in the Suárez garden. A hose in hand, fingers laced over the hose head, Zianna watered the roses that grew near the street side of the house. She stood between the tame and the untamed worlds, that of her father's constant laborings and that of her mother's rampant, uncontrollable life.
>
> Zianna's face, lovely as a dark brown, dusky rose, was lit with natural highlights. Her neck was long, her small proud head balanced by a full, fleshed mouth. Her luminescent eyes shielded themselves against the elements and luxuriated in the absence of explanations.
>
> Full, lush and firm, her breasts were carefully rounded swells of female flesh, flowerets full of awakening fragrance. Zianna stood straight, her face in the direction of her thirsty charges. Her feet were planted firmly on the grateful grass. (154)

Rocío dwells on the "lush" curves of Zianna's body as the girl stands in the garden watering flowers. After the scene in which Rocío thought she had seen Eleiterio cruising, she fantasizes about Zianna:

> Ssssmmosh. MMMMmmmmmm. Patter, patter, patter, patter. Black bird, blackbird, *what are you thinking?* Zianna stood nearby, a part of the landscape. She was too wild for the garden's cultivation, yet too refined for the wildness of the Suárez home. She was a small, silent black bird on the nearest branch.
>
> Sssssmooosh. Mmmmmmmm. Patter, patter, patter . . .
>
> I imagined Zianna standing in the grass, watering wearing [my] squash dress. That dress will be hers. Dark girl in the sunshine, seeking shade. (159; emphasis and ellipsis in original)

The language used to describe Zianna, in direct contrast to that used for Eleiterio, is wholly unrestrained and exults in Zianna's physical beauty, her flesh, and the eroticism she inspires in Rocío. Rocío imagines Zianna in her own dress (the Esquibels generally give their old clothes to Zianna's family) and dwells on how well it will suit her and on the visual pleasure of Zianna: "Zianna would get her dress wet; she never wore pants like the other girls. She stood on the grass barefooted, with no shoes on and in a wet dress and never caught cold" (158).

While critics such as Rosaldo are quite vocal about the sexual energy of *Menu Girls*, and even direct attention to many of the same examples I draw from the text, they completely avoid the possibility that Rocío actually desires these women. Rosaldo recognizes the "bodily, sexual connection" with other women but considers only the context of female desire without respect to its object. Quintana does not examine the intimate relationships between Rocío and the different women; she sees them (as she did in *Mango Street*) as merely "a catalogue of female characters . . . a variety of female options for solving the riddle of female self-fashioning" (104). Such themes are certainly present in the book, and even Rocío herself offers them as explanations for her interest in women, but they are not the whole story. Although Rocío is attracted occasionally to men, her most passionate, sexual desire is directed toward a series of feminine women. It is that desire I name "lesbian."

Margins

Terri de la Peña's 1992 novel, *Margins*, is sometimes incorrectly identified as "the first Chicana lesbian novel." If this means a Chicana lesbian-authored text with Chicana lesbian characters, then that honor more properly belongs to Sheila Ortiz Taylor's *Faultline* (1982). However, Ortiz Taylor, de la Peña, and Pérez all prepared their manuscripts for publication conscious of the scarcity of fiction focusing on Chicana lesbians. De la Peña initially published a series of short stories imagining a community of Chicana lesbians from the West Los Angeles area, while at the same time creating an audience for the novel to come.[18] Like *Margins* itself, the majority of these stories were published in mainstream lesbian anthologies and journals and are concerned with positive representation of Chicana lesbians in relationships with one another.[19] *Margins* is primarily a coming-out novel, emphasizing lesbian identity, coming out to family, and adult relationships with lesbian-identified women.[20] I concentrate on how this novel deals with the subject of lesbian girlhood, as it recalls the first lesbian love relationship of the main character, Veronica Melendez.

The novel opens as Veronica is recovering from an automobile accident that killed her "best friend," Joanna Nuñez. Veronica and Joanna had been best friends since girlhood, and their relationship had become sexual during adolescence. They lived together as "roommates" throughout their college years and lived a closeted life, without participating in a lesbian community or referring to themselves as lesbians outside of their relationship. And yet throughout their girlhood, adolescence, high school, and college years, both their families were accepting of their "particular friendship" without perceiving the possibility of sexuality or homosexuality. That Veronica and Joanna could carry on a sexual relationship for more than ten years without anyone else noticing demonstrates both the cultural validation of same-sex friendships for girls and the heterosexual structure within which those relationships are presumed to exist. When Isabel, Joanna's mother, explains her own oblivion to the sexual aspect of the relationship, she dwells on the perceived sexlessness of girlhood friendship:

> "Roni, I'm not sure *I* understand. I had favorite girlfriends too. We just never—"
> "Joanna and I were so close that loving each other came easily, too."
> "I remember how you girls could practically read each other's minds. . . . I thought that was friendship, nothing else. . . . I never thought of you two— that way. I knew Joanna and you were always together, and had been for years, but I thought she was close to you because she didn't have a sister. . . .

All the time you girls were growing up, I was always glad Joanna had you for a friend. You're such a good student, a nice quiet girl—never in trouble."

"You have to watch those quiet ones," Veronica quipped.

Isabel ignored that modest attempt at levity. "I thought you were a good influence on her." (111-13)

Although she comes to accept the truth, Isabel initially insists on the perceived "innocence" of the girls' friendship, echoing literary critics' discussions of *Mango Street* and *Menu Girls*. She later tries to reestablish this narrative of innocence when Steve, a young teenage boy, begins displaying pornographic pictures of lesbian sex and telling both Isabel's younger sons and Veronica's nephew Phil that Veronica and Joanna used to "do that." Isabel exclaims, "Oh, Roni. It isn't your fault. You and Joanna loved each other in an innocent way. It wasn't like—in that magazine" (180). This narrative is further developed by other family members, including Veronica's older sister Lucy, a Carmelite nun: "You're the baby of the family. I think Mama wanted to keep you inocente [*sic*] as long as she could. . . . You loved Joanna from the day you met her in kindergarten. Everyone knew that. We just never looked beyond the friendship" (248). Veronica's relatives rely on the idea that there is an innocence, a sexlessness, to young Chicanas that by definition precludes the possibility of homosexuality. This becomes clearly marked in the novel when rumors of the sexual aspect of Veronica and Joanna's relationship begin to spread. When Phil is asked to explain to his grandparents his argument with the boy who showed him the magazine, he does not reveal the discussion of lesbianism; instead, the topic of conversation becomes his own (hetero)sexuality:

"And what were you y Steve arguing about?"

"Some girl," Phil murmured.

"Ay, que muchachos! You're too young for that, Philly."

"Sara, he's old enough to shave." Joe offered his grandson a conspiratorial smile. "Just be careful next time, Phil." (146)

This "boys will be boys" discussion makes it clear that, while the four-teen-year-old boy is perceived as a sexual being, his twenty-four-year-old aunt is not. The issue of female sexuality is further complicated because there are no women in the family, other than Veronica, who claim an active sexuality. Her mother, Sara, clearly thinks of sex as dirty, and her sister Lucy has taken a vow of celibacy.[21]

While Veronica blames her parents for the family's silence around sexuality, Lucy argues "es la cultura" (248). This is a very different world from Cisneros's *Mango Street* and Chávez's *Menu Girls*, in which female heterosexuality is an explicit force to be reckoned with. It is precisely because of this erasure of all female sexuality that Joanna's family attempts to produce Veronica as the "living lesbian" who seduced their innocent Joanna. Threatened by the attack on Joanna's "honor," they react first by denying that the two women had a lesbian relationship; then, when Veronica begins living openly as a lesbian, they refigure her as their daughter's seducer.

Veronica attempts to displace this narrative of "innocent girlhood," arguing for an active lesbian girlhood. For Veronica, same-sex play is a natural (physical) extension of the emotional intimacy of girlhood bonds, one that does not change the nature of that relationship, but extends it significantly.

> "Joanna and I were so close that loving each other came easily, too."
> ". . . Joanna wasn't interested in men in a sexual way. How could anything compete with what we had?"
> ". . . At first, we thought we were going through a phase, experimenting with each other before getting involved with men. We both tried dating, but we realized right away we were much more comfortable with each other." (111)

She argues against being cast as the "lesbian seducer" by stressing the mutuality of their relationship and again by attempting to show that for both girls it followed a natural progression from friendship to sexual intimacy:

"Well, no one stays innocent for long. Joanna and I started playing around when we were in grammar school. I still can't believe no one caught on." (248)

"Joanna and I used to spy on you [and your boyfriend]. Afterwards we'd go to her house and practice kissing." (264)

Both of these examples are from a conversation Veronica has with Lucy. She emphasizes the sexual precocity of her relationship with Joanna: how early they started "playing around." When she reveals that she and Joanna used to spy on Lucy, she is talking about a time before Lucy entered the convent, which took place when Veronica was thirteen. Veronica is articulating a specific model of lesbian identity, the "born lesbian" who never has voluntary sex with men. Although Lucy does not respond directly, she accepts Veronica's explanation, perhaps because she believes that homosexuality is innate and therefore not a "choice."[22] While she can accept Veronica's homosexual feelings, she cautions Veronica against claiming a lesbian identity without Joanna. To some extent, then, the ground conceded in the natural extension of particular friendship is taken back by arguing that, with the end of that girlhood friendship, lesbianism need not be embraced.[23] Implied is the idea that this lesbian adolescence must come to an end, must be replaced by adult heterosexuality.

Because of Joanna's early death, de la Peña avoids the question of betrayal of a "passionate friendship" in the sense that we have seen, albeit in less explicit form, between Esperanza and Sally and between Rocío and Eloisa in the two earlier books. Veronica is, to some extent, betrayed in adulthood when her affair with her initially heterosexual neighbor Siena ends abruptly and Siena begins sleeping with a man. The characterization of Siena is caught up in the question of coming out. Siena is explicitly criticized by the other lesbian characters in the novel for not being "out" as a lesbian, bisexual, or woman-loving woman. This is in marked contrast to their acceptance of Veronica, who is not criticized for being closeted in her ten-year relationship with Joanna, although Siena has been sexual with a woman for less than a week. This double standard is tied to the representation of the Chicano community: to be close to their families, to be within the culture, Veronica and Joanna needed to be closeted. However, the same argument is in no way held valid for Siena, an Italian American from a Catholic background no less conservative than Veronica's. Like Elizabeth Rainey in *Menu Girls*, Siena is recovering from the aftereffects of an abortion. Thus she, too, is "marked" by sexuality, but, in the new context of lesbian identity, she is also marked as untrustworthy. Her sexual desire for Veronica is invalidated by her inability to claim a lesbian identity and trivialized by the other lesbian characters. The novel privileges the "born lesbian," viewing women who have been heterosexually active with suspicion.

Ironically, Veronica herself sets aside her relationship with Joanna, just as Esperanza's and Rocío's "passionate friendships" are expected to be set aside. In this case, however, the relationship is not superseded by institutions of heterosexuality but is replaced by Veronica's new lesbian identity and lesbian relation. Joanna is relegated to the past and to the "innocence" of girlhood as the novel turns toward Veronica's mature, adult relationship with Chicana lesbian René Talamantes. The novel ends with Veronica giving a public reading from her short story collection, a "fictional recreation of Joanna" (328). As she reads, Veronica looks to René for encouragement and to the multiethnic audience at Sisterhood bookstore for affirmation. Because of its emphasis on lesbian identity, and in particular because the novel privileges identity over desire, *Margins* reinforces the division between (innocent) girlhood friendships and adult sexual relationships portrayed in both *The House on Mango Street* and *The Last of the Menu Girls*, with the significant difference that in this case adult relationships are not exclusively heterosexual.

Gulf Dreams

Emma Pérez's 1996 novel *Gulf Dreams* first appeared in short story form in the anthology *Chicana Lesbians: The Girls Our Mothers Warned Us About* (Trujillo 1991). The novel is ambitious in both range and style as it addresses socialization and sexuality in the fictional Texas Gulf town of El Pueblo. The novel has a loose chronological structure that is abruptly contested by a competing narrative of memory, which is violent, fragmented, and often cinematic in the ways in which it evokes images. The reader sees the narrator meet and fall in love with a young woman, the sister of her sister's best friend. Their relationship is extremely passionate, although, at least initially, the actual sexual activity is limited to that between the young woman and her first boyfriend, which she describes to the narrator in detail. Eventually, the two women enroll in a nearby junior college, where the young woman begins dating Pelón, a male prelaw student from the university. The two women become more intimate while their relationship is entangled with that between the young woman and Pelón and with physical and emotional violence. Although the reader is not told the details of the young woman's childhood history, Pérez makes it clear that she has been emotionally scarred by violence from those she loves. According to the narrator, the young woman thus seeks out violence along with love, first going from Pelón, who abuses her, to the narrator, who comforts her, and later verbally abusing the narrator until she too marks the young woman with bruises. The narrator then leaves Texas for California; the novel reveals little about her life there, except that she hides in anonymous sex and perhaps makes a living as a sex worker. After her departure, the young woman marries Pelón.

The narrator returns to El Pueblo some years later, after she reads a newspaper account of a gang rape in the town: Ermila, a young Chicana, is picked up and raped by five Chicanos. Pelón is the defense attorney for the offenders; he builds his case on the negative representation of Chicanos by the Anglo media—completely erasing Ermila as a Chicana as well as the violence done to her—and on the premise that, as the type of woman "who says yes," Ermila did not have the option of saying no. The narrator stays for the trial and verdict, seeing the young woman again and resuming their relationship, from which she has never truly been free. Four of the five rapists are acquitted. The fifth, the ringleader, is convicted and receives a thirty-year sentence. The narrator leaves before the appeal and returns to Los Angeles.[24]

Having given a very basic sketch of the novel, I now focus specifically on the relationship between the narrator and the young woman. The two girls are brought together when the narrator is fifteen by their sisters, who are best friends, *comadres*. In the passage that I have taken as my epigraph, Pérez introduces their relationship, contextualizing the expectations for close female friendships within this Chicano community:

> To link families with four sisters who would be friends longer than their lifetimes, through children who would bond them at baptismal rites. *Comadres*. We would become intimate friends, sharing coffee, gossip, and heartaches. We would endure the female life-cycle—adolescence, marriage, menopause, death, and even divorce, before or after menopause, before or after death.
>
> I had not come for that. I had come for her kiss. (13)

Pérez is referring here to the cultural system of *comadrazgo*. The masculine term, *compadrazgo*, refers to the relationship between the father and godfather, or the parents and godparents, of a child. The baptismal ceremony unites these people, raising their friendship to the level of kinship in recognition and mutual commitment. Thus their relationship is extended beyond the present through the lives of their children. The terms *compadre* and *comadre* are also used more informally to refer to friendship relationships that are as close as family and to specify the relationship between the parents of married children. *Compadrear*, the verb formed from the masculine noun *compadre*, means to be on familiar terms with another person. Pérez is talking specifically about the relationship between women, *comadrazgo*. The verb *comadrear*, however, has a slightly different meaning—to gossip—which she acknowledges with the phrase "sharing coffee, gossip, and heartaches" and by stressing the verbal aspect of the relationship—the telling, the sharing, the speaking. Notice that men are not essential to *comadrazgo* and that this relationship extends beyond that of the heterosexual marriage through which it is evoked. Withstanding "even divorce, before or after menopause, before or after death," *comadrazgo* emphasizes the permanence of women's relationships over the temporality of men. *Comadrazgo* itself, then, is constructed paradoxically: women are simultaneously central and marginal in each other's lives. They are central because their friendship, their intimacy, will outlast the passion, the trauma, the infidelity, or the demise of heterosexual relationships. And yet they are marginal because these friendships function as a constant prop to the heterosexual structure—maintaining and always yielding precedence to heterosexuality or, in effect, to the male.

Pérez ruptures these narratives—both that of the "female life-cycle," which is, by definition, heterosexually proscribed, and that of the "platonic intimacy" achieved by *comadrazgo*—by foregrounding the sexual desire of the narrator for the young woman: "I had not come for that. I had come for her kiss." She does not want a platonic intimacy with other heterosexual women but rather a sexual union of the flesh. Precisely because of its built-in deference to the male and to heterosexuality, the narrator attempts to avoid the pattern of *comadrazgo*: "The promise of female rituals enraged me" (15). Here it may be enlightening to think back on Esperanza's relationship to Sally, particularly in "Red Clowns," where Sally, who is forbidden to associate with boys, is allowed to go to the carnival with Esperanza. Their friendship provides the opportunity for her heterosexual rendezvous, ultimately at Esperanza's expense.

The narrator's desire is created and inspired by the young woman. Although she says "I met her in the summer of restless dreams" (11), it becomes clear that the restless dreams are brought on by their first meeting, when, with a glance, the young woman "caressed a part of me I never knew existed." For weeks after their brief meeting, the narrator is haunted by dreams of the young woman's erotic touch: "I dreamt of her fingers brushing my skin, lightly smoothing over breasts, neck, back, all that ached for her. A fifteen-year-old body ached from loneliness and desire, so unsure of the certainties her body felt" (12). The early part of the novel focuses on this lesbian desire awakened by the young woman and on the frustration of that desire both by the heterosexual limits of female friendship within the community and by the young woman's flirtatious rejection of the narrator. The desire between the two girls is tangible and even articulated, but only as mediated by the young woman's relationships with men: "That day under the shaded tree, she had spoken about a young boy. She craved his delicious, expert mouth, she said. She told me he had sucked her nipples. He was careful not to hurt her or impregnate her. Instead he licked her moistness. . . . I revered the lips that relived desire for him" (14). The young woman seduces the narrator emotionally, by verbalizing her sexual experiences. By describing her erotic activities, she gives form to what the narrator, with her more limited sexual experience, has not yet imagined that she would like to do with the young woman. Because the young woman's desire is described through her sexual behavior with the boy, the narrator's fantasies in relation to the young woman become heterosexually marked. No longer visited in her dreams by the young woman alone, instead she sees at night the scenes described under the shaded tree, sees him pleasuring the young woman in the ways she has described.

The young woman is clearly aware of the narrator's susceptibility: "She longed for someone to arouse her. Each time she dared to look directly into my eyes, she quickly averted hers. She alerted the passion, repressed it immediately" (14-15). The very structure of girlhood friendship allows the young woman to solicit the narrator's desire. Because the two girls do become "intimate friends, sharing coffee, gossip, and heartaches," the young woman can tell the narrator of her sexual activities, continuously drawing her in closer, so that she becomes both voyeur and participant in the young woman's sexual relationships: "She confessed details, delightfully. She told me how she shook with pleasure from the strokes of a ravenous tongue. I listened, opening to her seductive words, wanting more particulars to bond us intimately" (52). The narrator attempts to resist the "promise of female rituals," albeit unsuccessfully. The *comadrazgo* she sought to escape is precisely what creates and aggravates lesbian desire in this situation. Desire exists—is created—in the telling. Although she resents its inevitable frustration, the narrator cannot resist the telling: "Intimacies of the flesh achieved through words. That was our affair. Years later, I rediscovered my compulsion to consummate intimacy through dialogue— to make love with a tongue that spewed desire, that pleaded for more words, acid droplets on my skin. With her, I learned to make love to women without a touch. I craved intimate, erotic dialogue. I was addicted to words and she had spawned the addiction" (52). Ironically, then, the young woman, who is not identified as lesbian, instructs the lesbian narrator, teaching her how to make love to a woman with her tongue, literally and figuratively, by narrating eroticism. She speaks of the pleasure she receives and in doing so gains pleasure and inspires it in the narrator.

While the narrator attempts to resist this sexually heightened *comadrazgo*, she is unable to do so precisely because of the level of eroticism it contains: "She half-expected me. Took my hand, led me to her bedroom, shoved me playfully on her twin bed next to her. She spoke reasonably. She had missed me. Why had I stopped coming? Why had I stayed away? She relied on my friendship, a passionate friendship, she called it. Mute, I looked away, paralyzed, embarrassed, hurt. She played at my emotions under the guise of friendship" (17). The narrator's words bring to mind both Smith's discussion of *Sula*—which works as a lesbian novel in part "because of the passionate friendship between Sula and Nel" (Smith 1982, 165)—and Esperanza's inability to articulate fully her desire for Sally—"those boys that look at you because you're pretty. I like to be with you, Sally. You're my friend" (99). Yet for the narrator, the young woman's words are harsh, an insult, a blatant denial of her own active participation in this sexual game. However, the young woman uses the "guise of friendship" not only to incite the narrator's desire but to supplement her own heterosexual relations: "We became enraptured, entrapped, addicted to each other's eroticism. A kiss on the cheek inflamed me for hours. I witnessed her greed. Teasing reached new heights. . . . The desire to desire her—my weakness. . . . Her boyfriend grew more threatened each time I appeared. . . . She and I, trapped in social circumstances. Propriety kept us apart" (28). The boyfriend's antagonism is one of the early signs that the narrator's participation in the young woman's relationships with men is not limited to voyeurism: "After rushing to him, he would oblige her by hurting her, then she would come to me. I rescued her, then resented my duty to her. And so we played this deceitful game, angry because we didn't know how to quit" (29). In a sense, then, the narrator is the conventional *comadre*, in that she provides support for the young woman in the latter's heterosexual relationship; in addition, she acts as a sort of lesbian supplement to heterosexuality, providing a love and a level of eroticism that balances the inadequacies (for the young woman) of the heterosexual relationship and helps to maintain it.

Gulf Dreams contrasts with de la Peña's *Margins* in the way it shows female friendships to be represented within the community. Because neither Joanna nor Veronica dates or is sexual with men, both are, in the eyes of the community, sexually infantilized, which provides a screen behind which they explore their sexuality together. They are, in effect, good girls, and as Veronica wryly explains to Joanna's mother, "You have to watch those quiet ones." Ironically, their hidden lesbianism is what earns them the classification of "good girls." In the world of *Gulf Dreams*, the luxury to be a "good girl" is rather limited. Both the narrator and the young woman are introduced to sex before they are old enough to make such choices for themselves. The young woman seeks out strong men to protect her from the caresses of her stepfather, and the narrator chooses a quiet boy from Alabama, whose demands are easy to put down. But because the young woman is actively and visibly sexual, her relationship with the narrator is also more visibly marked as "queer": her first boyfriend, who has evidence enough of her heterosexuality, complains of her relationship with the narrator and finally uses it as an excuse to break up with her, saying he wants only her and "not some lezzy and a pet dog" (53). As with so many other aspects of sexuality in the novel, the young woman's heterosexual activity simultaneously masks and promotes her own "lesbianism."

Sexism and heterosexism are pernicious in the Pérez novel to a degree unseen even in *Mango Street*. Within El Pueblo, the potential for male sexual violence is omnipresent. As a two- or three-year-old child, the narrator is molested by a group of adolescent and preadolescent boys. As a nine-year-old she is sexually harassed publicly by a thirteen-year-old, to the extent that she no longer feels safe, and yet she is told to accept it, while the boy is never disciplined or even discouraged. Packs of boys roam the railroad tracks and, catching up with the narrator and her younger brother, force kisses on her, leaving her smeared with saliva. In the schoolyard, a group of boys will chase a younger girl and pull down her underwear. All of these images build up to the gang rape in El Pueblo, which becomes notable because the woman in question, Ermila, refuses to accept predatory male sexual violence and refuses to see herself as merely a tool for male sexual use. This is an atmosphere in which male sexual violence is normalized and female sexual assertion is punished with more sexual violence. Lesbian desire, while clearly present, is not only circumscribed but often violently policed. In fact, at one point, the young woman claims that her husband's domestic abuse was not a result of his personality or behavior but a consequence of her relationship with the narrator. While the narrator is justifiably suspicious of such an argument, which displaces the responsibility for the husband's violent behavior onto her, the possibility that lesbian relationships would be policed in an even more violent fashion is real enough. The possibilities for a public lesbian identity under such circumstances are severely limited. As in *Mango Street*, the text foregrounds the restrictions imposed by normative heterosexuality, as the young woman is confined to her house after her marriage, staring at the linoleum, just as Sally does after her marriage in *Mango Street*: "She stood in the middle of her kitchen, gaping at her floor, absorbed in the linoleum's stain, a muddy brown stain in the same corner of the kitchen. For years she had tried chemicals of every brand. . . . But the floor covering only looked thinner and paler and the dirty film reminded her that her world was imperfect" (47).

Unlike Veronica in *Margins*, the narrator of *Gulf Dreams* does not write herself a happy ending. Instead, she writes herself out, writes the young woman out, writes everything out of her own narrative. She writes the young woman out of the story by obfuscating how much she exists independently and how much she is merely the narrator's creation: "With phrases I create you. I create you here in text. You don't exist. I never wanted you to exist. I only wanted to invent you like this, in fragments through text where the memory of you inhabits those who read this. You have no name. To name you would limit you, fetter you from all you embody. I give you your identities. I switch them when it's convenient. I make you who I want you to be. And in all my invention, no matter how much I try, you don't have the skill to love, to love me as I am" (138-39). For the narrator, there is no ultimate resolution, no utopia to be gained in lesbian identity. The girlhood friendship, so casually glossed over in the criticism on *Mango Street* and *Menu Girls*, so easily recuperated in the narrative of an adult lesbian relationship in *Margins*, is here revealed as the most important relationship of the narrator's life, the one for which all others are pale substitutes.

Conclusion

The House on Mango Street, *The Last of the Menu Girls*, *Margins*, and *Gulf Dreams* construct images of intense emotional attachment and erotic attractions between girls and women. They contribute to the representation of Chicana lesbianism by providing images of intimacy and intensity beyond that considered appropriate for proper heterosexual girls. While such friendships are initially encouraged, especially over heterosexual relations that might result in premature sexual activity and pregnancy, the girls are expected to relinquish the primacy of these friendships as they become part of the grown-up heterosexual world. Within these fictional Chicano communities in Chicago, New Mexico, Southern California, and Texas, the female protagonists are confronted by limited options for women. Both Esperanza and Rocío leave or will leave their communities of origin so that they can make different lives for themselves. The narrator of *Gulf Dreams* also leaves her community but finds no solace in the outside world. Certainly within the Chicano communities depicted in these four works, there are no women actively claiming a Chicana lesbian identity, in spite of how they form love relationships with other females. The exception here is René Talamantes of *Margins*, who lives as a lesbian with her mother in the barrio, and whose relationship with Veronica Melendez gives the latter a sense of deep connection to her cultural heritage. Veronica makes this move to cultural identification, although it is fraught with tension with regard to her family, but prefers not to live within Chicano neighborhoods. Additionally, the Los Angeles of *Margins* is both more "multicultural" than the rural or barrio worlds in which the characters of the other three books live—thus escaping a rigid Anglo/ Chicano or Anglo/Latino dichotomy—and more permeable, so that Veronica can move to a different part of the city. She clearly has more options than the other women.

The representation of Chicano families is significant in all four of the works studied, and particularly in *Mango Street* and *Gulf Dreams*, which deal with domestic violence and sexual abuse. While all of the protagonists come from families free of abuse, they are constantly confronted by the reality that the same does not hold true for many of their friends; Esperanza and the narrator of *Gulf Dreams* are also aware that even their families are not enough to protect them from harm. These families, too, provide mixed messages about sexuality: daughters are protected but restricted; daughters are kept ignorant of sex to preserve their innocence; daughters are expected to fulfill the roles of mother and wife.

Throughout these stories, intimate girlhood friendships are predetermined to end in loss. Esperanza loses Sally, who prefers male sexual play to Esperanza's childishness. Rocío, while not rejected by Eloisa, is nevertheless disillusioned when she sees her friend enjoying lascivious male attention. Veronica loses Joanna to an automobile accident, but Joanna's death begins to take on the aspect of a natural progression, necessary in order for Veronica to live openly as a lesbian and to enjoy an "adult" relationship with René. Pérez's narrator alone does not "lose" her young woman, but she does not "keep" her either, nor can she successfully negotiate adult relationships because of the scars she carries both from childhood sexual abuse and from the emotional dynamics of her obsessive relationship with the young woman.

Mango Street, Menu Girls, and *Gulf Dreams* all show that these girls' behaviors, identities, and desires are mediated by the heteronormativity of the worlds in which they live. Love and desire are constituted in relation to heterosexuality: Esperanza knows that the way she likes Sally is different from the way boys look at Sally, even as it is different from her platonic girlhood friendships. While Eloisa does not explicitly choose a boy over Rocío, Rocío sees Eloisa's heterosexual behavior as contaminating the "brightness" of their relationship. Her perception of the inevitability of heterosexuality leads her to perceive the "brightness" of the desire between girls as that of a shooting star, intense and fleeting.

The ways in which female friendships are socially perceived and encouraged provide a space, however restrictive, for lesbian desire in these texts. The intimacy itself provides the context for lesbian desire. Because they are intimate friends, the young woman in *Gulf Dreams* will tell the narrator of her sexual pleasures, knowingly exciting the narrator, and deriving pleasure from that knowledge. On a less overtly sexual level, Esperanza can be close to Sally, hold her hairbrush, and wave to her on the tilt-a-whirl, because they are close friends. That intimacy provides a space for Esperanza's feelings of love to grow, feelings that are distinct from the male desire based on Sally's appearance. Esperanza's desire is based on Sally's self, the way she laughs, her pleasure in a carnival ride, her own desire to be loved. In *Margins* this space for lesbian desire is much more literal: their very intimacy provides Joanna and Veronica with a "good girl" image, which in turn gives them the freedom to develop a lesbian relationship. This freedom is quite material: both Veronica's and Joanna's parents are paying the rent on an apartment for their two "good girls" while they are in college.

In *Gulf Dreams*, female friendship is articulated in terms of *comadrazgo*, a friendship and commitment that is perceived as being stronger than the heterosexual marriage around which it is constituted. At the same time, the women's relationship is a supplemental component of the heterosexual marriage, providing constancy and support alongside the fluctuations of heterosexuality. Because they require deference to heterosexuality, such female friendships are undesirable to the narrator; because they provide intimacy, they are also irresistible. While Rocío consciously makes a decision to "let them go," Pérez's narrator cannot do so and instead strikes back at one of the forces that has imposed heterosexuality on her world, with a violence that equals the violence done to her.

All of these fictions represent same-sex love and desire at approximately that moment at which girls are expected to set aside female friendships in favor of heterosexual relations. Within these texts is a recognition that however privileged heterosexual desire may be, it is in no way more natural or innate than homosexual desire. Indeed, I would argue that, with one exception, these works depict a fluid and dynamic notion of female sexuality. Only in *Margins* is sexuality explicitly tied to claiming a lesbian identity. Pérez, while perhaps privileging her lesbian narrator (who has had both positive and negative relationships with men), complicates binary heterosexual/homosexual models of female sexuality through her portrayal of the young woman. Ostensibly a "heterosexual" teenager, she teaches her "lesbian" best friend about teasing, eroticism, making love through words alone, as well as the mechanics and pleasures of oral sex. The stories that *Gulf Dreams*'s narrator weaves for the young woman, of an idyllic future where she has a good husband, children, and secret male and female lovers, combine what the young woman needs socially (a good husband as equivalent to a stable family) with what she desires (children, passion, variety, and secrets).

Finally, although the lesbian content of *Mango Street* and *Menu Girls* has been ignored by literary critics, I have tried to show how that very erasure constitutes part of the representation of lesbianism. That is to say, like the social perceptions of female friendships within the four books, this very silence about the possibility of lesbianism has nevertheless provided a space for lesbian reading.

From *Signs: Journal of Women in Culture and Society* 23, no. 3 (1998): 645-682. Copyright © 1998 by The University of Chicago Press. Reprinted with permission of The University of Chicago Press.

Notes

1. See also Farwell 1993, who promotes a metaphoric usage of "lesbian," and de Lauretis, who critiques such a usage at length in "The Seductions of Lesbianism," chap. 4 of *The Practice of Love* (1994). By *utopic*, I am referring to texts that invoke the idea of lesbianism as an escape from the problems, inequalities, and power dynamics of heterosexual relationships, as if lesbian relationships would somehow be free of problems, inequalities, and power dynamics (not to mention passion). Such a romanticization of "lesbian" is curiously akin to fantasies about the convent as just such an escape. See, e.g., Alma Luz Villanueva's *Weeping Woman: La Llorona and Other Stories* (1994), particularly "El Alma/The Soul, Three" (151-56), and Denise Chávez's *The Face of an Angel* (1995). In the latter, the fantasies of the convent and lesbianism as escapes from heterosexuality are united in the figure of Sister Lizzie (439-46).

2. An excellent case in point is Becky Birtha's "Johnnieruth" (1990), in which the eponymous heroine, a fourteen-year-old African American girl, constantly resists the

gender expectations put on her by her mother and her neighborhood. While walking to church one day she sees "this lady. . . . She ain't nobody's mama—I'm sure," who is not all dressed up and on her way to church, but who (like Johnnieruth) is dressed comfortably, pleasing nobody but herself. As Johnnieruth turns to watch her walk by, the woman eyes her in recognition (73). Near the end of the story, Johnnieruth sees two women kissing "for a whole long time" (75). Again, they seem to recognize her and she them, and as she bicycles home, thinking about them kissing and then looking at her, she finds herself laughing "for no reason at all" (76).

3. I wish to reiterate that I discuss Chicana lesbian fictions within a Chicana literary context: I do not attempt either a history or a sociological study of Chicana girlhood friendships. Nor do I position these representations of Chicana girlhood friendships within a universal, and thus problematic, construction of "lesbian" and/or homosocial relations between women, which would merely inscribe Chicana lesbian fiction within a largely Anglo-American, northern European "tradition." While the characters or the texts themselves often construct Chicana sexuality against Mexicana and Anglo-American sexuality, with the former seen as more restrictive and the latter as less restrictive (see nn. 15, 21), I urge the reader to avoid a slippage from the literary to the sociological: these texts represent stories Chicanas tell about themselves and their communities that may or may not have anything to do with the material social conditions of (sexual) lives. Indeed, any sociological statement about Chicana (or Mexicana, or Anglo) sexuality per se would flatten the heterogeneous, historically embedded, and conflictive ways in which sexuality is constructed in diverse Chicana/o communities. At the same time, however, the stories themselves become part of the material social conditions, so that even while arguing against slippage I acknowledge the overlap.

4. I have deliberately chosen not to include comparable works that focus exclusively on adult friendships or adult sexual relationships, such as Estela Portillo Trambley's *Day of the Swallows* (1976), Sheila Ortiz Taylor's *Faultline* (1982), Ana Castillo's *The Mixquiahuala Letters* (1992), and Jeanne Córdova's *Kicking the Habit* (1990), to name but a few. Laura del Fuego's novel *Maravilla* (1989) could easily be included in the current study, as could short stories by Alma Luz Villanueva and Helena María Viramontes, which I hope to discuss in the future.

5. Tey Diana Rebolledo mentions de la Peña only briefly: "The 1990's has brought forth a variety of lesbian novels and other creative materials about lesbian consciousness, including *Margins* by Terri de la Peña" (1995, 199). To date, *Margins* and *Gulf Dreams* have been discussed only in book reviews. (On *Margins*, see Daly 1992; *Publishers Weekly* 1992; Robinson 1992; Wolverton 1992. On *Gulf Dreams*, see de Lauretis 1996.)

6. Rosaldo mistakenly identifies Esperanza's mother as supplying the shoes.

7. "Not a girl, not a boy, just a little baby" is one of the jump rope rhymes Nenny chants.

8. This is not to imply that wanting to be *like* Sally is wholly divorced from wanting to be *with* Sally. I develop this more in relation to Rocío in *The Last of the Menu Girls*, below.

9. "Justo y necesario" comes from the Catholic Mass in Spanish. In English, it

would be equivalent to "just, right" or "righteous and needful," although in the English-language Mass, the equivalent of "es justo y necesario" is "it is right."

10. See also María Herrera-Sobek (1987), who recognizes that Esperanza's lament "is directed not only against Sally the silent interlocutor but at the community of women." Because Herrera-Sobek is discussing "Red Clowns" without reference to the other Sally stories, she minimizes the significance of Esperanza's relationship to Sally.

11. "Sally," "What Sally Said," "The Monkey Garden," "Red Clowns," and "Linoleum Roses" appear as numbers 32, 37, 38, 39, and 40, respectively.

12. The line actually reads, "For the ones I left behind. For the ones who cannot out." Yvonne Yarbro-Bejarano, reading from the first edition, gives the last line as, "For the ones I left behind. For the ones who cannot get out" (1987, 143). One could interpret "For the ones who cannot out," which appears in the second revised edition (Arte Público, 1988), to be a printing error, with the verb accidentally omitted. However, it seems likely that such an error would have been caught in the 1991 Vintage/Random House edition. I prefer to believe that Cisneros intentionally changed the line when she revised the manuscript in 1988, leaving the gap to be bridged by the reader.

13. "Willow Came" appeared in *Nuestro* (1982), "Evening in Paris" in *Nuestro* (1981), "The Closet" in *Americas Review* (1986), and "Space Is Solid" in *Puerto del Sol* (1986).

14. Rosaldo's term for this connection is matrimony, used here as the female equivalent of *patrimony*, and thus matrilineal heritage. By choosing a term that already signifies the institution of heterosexual marriage, Rosaldo embeds a heteronormative understanding of women in general and of Rocío in particular.

15. There is an implication, however, that in Rocío's community Chicanas do not get abortions either.

16. Interestingly, Bertha, the "female" lesbian, never appears, although "Esperanza the dyke" (32) figures prominently in the ninth and eleventh sections of the story.

17. "His father was a [Seventh Day] Adventist" (my translation). That is, being from a strict religious background, he is unlikely to do such things as Rocío imagines.

18. The Los Angeles stories are "La Maya" (1989a), "Once a Friend" (1989b), "A Saturday in August" (1989c), "Tortilleras" (1989d), "Blue" (1990a), "Labrys" (1990b), "Mariposa" (1990c), "Beyond El Camino Real" (1991a), "Desert Quartet" (1991b), and "Mujeres Morenas" (1991c). Indeed, many of the characters from these stories and those from *Margins* appear in a community scene at the end of de la Peña's second novel, *Latin Satins* (1994, 250).

19. These works draw on certain essentialized notions of identity and race in their idealized depictions of Chicana/Chicana relations. This is somewhat self-consciously done, since de la Peña is working in a publishing realm in which the majority of representations are of Anglo/Anglo lesbian couples or, more infrequently, an Anglo woman with a woman of color. Indeed, a favorable but rather uninformed review of *Margins* in the *Advocate* explains that "the spectrum of lesbian literature includes so few Latina voices" because of "the dominance of the Catholic church" (Wolverton 1992, 40).

20. Closeted lesbians and bisexuals alike are represented as unhealthy partners.

21. Veronica's married (heterosexual) sister, Angela, does not appear in the novel. Like Joanna, Veronica's sister-in-law Connie died young and thus has assumed the

sexual innocence of "an angel." This sexual innocence is limited to Chicanas, for Veronica's new sister-in-law Joyce, an Anglo, is demonstrably passionate with her husband.

22. A view to which Veronica, Lucy, and indeed the Catholic Church subscribe.

23. Lucy may again be echoing the Catholic Church's judgment that while one does not choose to be a homosexual, one can—and should—refrain from acting on homosexual impulses.

24. This is the most basic outline of the novel. Structurally, there is also a second narrative, of memory, which produces abrupt images of molestation and sexually motivated violence directed against the narrator, as well as images of her turning violence against herself.

Works Cited

Bethel, Lorraine. 1976. "Conversations with Ourselves: Black Female Relationships in Toni Cade Bambara's *Gorilla, My Love* and Toni Morrison's *Sula*." Unpublished manuscript, Yale University. Quoted in Smith 1982, 166.

Birtha, Becky. 1990. "Johnnieruth." In *Breaking Ice: An Anthology of Contemporary African American Fiction*, ed. Terry McMillan, 71-76. New York: Penguin.

Butler, Judith. 1991. "Imitation and Gender Insubordination." In *Inside/Out: Lesbian Theories, Gay Theories*, ed. Diana Fuss, 13-31. New York and London: Routledge.

_____. 1993. *Bodies That Matter: On the Discursive Limits of "Sex."* New York and London: Routledge.

Castillo, Ana. 1992. *The Mixquiahuala Letters*. Tempe, Ariz.: Bilingual Press/ Editorial Bilingüe, 1986. Reprint, New York: Anchor.

Chávez, Denise. 1987. *The Last of the Menu Girls*. Houston: Arte Público.

_____. 1995. *The Face of an Angel*. New York: Warner.

Cisneros, Sandra. 1991. *The House on Mango Street*. Houston: Arte Público, 1984. Reprint, New York: Vintage.

Córdova, Jeanne. 1990. *Kicking the Habit*. Los Angeles: Multiple Dimensions.

Daly, Mary Ann. 1992. "A Study in Character." Review of *Margins*, by Terri de la Peña. *Lambda Book Report* 3 (5): 15.

de la Peña, Terri. 1989a. "La Maya." In *Intricate Passions*, ed. Tee Corinne, 1-10. Austin, Tex.: Banned Books.

_____. 1989b. "Once a Friend." In *The One You Call Sister*, ed. Paula Martinac, 49-62. San Francisco: Cleis.

_____. 1989c. "A Saturday in August." In *Finding Courage*, ed. Irene Zahava, 141-50. Freedom, Calif.: Crossing.

_____. 1989d. "Tortilleras." In *Lesbian Bedtime Stories*, ed. Terry Woodrow, 83-92. Willits, Calif.: Tough Dove.

_____. 1990a. "Blue." In *Riding Desire*, ed. Tee Corinne, 149-53. Austin, Tex.: Banned Books.

_____. 1990b. "Labrys." In *Word of Mouth*, ed. Irene Zahava, 31. Freedom, Calif.: Crossing.

_____. 1990c. "Mariposa." In *Lesbian Bedtime Stories 2*, ed. Terry Woodrow, 7-19. Willits, Calif.: Tough Dove.

_____. 1991a. "Beyond El Camino Real." In *Chicana Lesbians*, ed. Calia Trujillo, 85-94. Berkeley, Calif.: Third Woman.

_____. 1991b. "Desert Quartet." In *Lesbian Love Stories*, Vol. 2, ed. Irene Zahava, 154-61. Freedom, Calif.: Crossing.

_____. 1991c. "Mujeres Morenas." In *Lesbian Love* Stories, Vol. 2, ed. Irene Zahava, 85-93. Freedom, Calif.: Crossing.

_____. 1992. *Margins*. Seattle: Seal.

_____. 1994. *Latin Satins*. Seattle: Seal.

de Lauretis, Teresa. 1994. *The Practice of Love: Lesbian Sexuality and Perverse Desire*. Bloomington and Indianapolis: Indiana University Press.

_____. 1996. "Closing the Gulf between Us" Review of *Gulf Dreams*, by Emma Pérez. *Lesbian Review of Books* 2(4): 4.

del Fuego, Laura. 1989. *Maravilla*. Encino, Calif.: Floricanto.

Farwell, Marilyn R. 1993. "Toward a Definition of the Lesbian Literary Imagination." In *Sexual Practice, Textual Theory: Lesbian Cultural Criticism*, ed. Susan J. Wolfe and Penelope Stanley, 66-84. Cambridge, Mass., and Oxford: Blackwell. Originally published in *Signs: Journal of Women in Culture and Society* 14, no. 1 (1988), 100-118.

Harris, Bertha. 1976. "Lesbians and Literature." Paper delivered to the Modern Language Association, New York. Quoted in Smith 1982, 164.

Herrera-Sobek, María. 1987. "The Politics of Rape: Sexual Transgression in Chicana Fiction." *Americas Review* 15(3-4): 171-88.

Moraga, Cherríe, and Gloria Anzaldúa, eds. 1983. *This Bridge Called My Back: Writings by Radical Women of Color*. Watertown, Mass.: Persephone Press, 1981. Reprint, New York: Kitchen Table/Women of Color Press.

Olivares, Julián. 1987. "Sandra Cisneros's *The House on Mango Street*, and the Poetics of Space." *Americas Review* 15(3-4): 160-70.

Ortiz Taylor, Sheila. 1982. *Faultline*. Tallahassee, Fla.: Naiad.

Pérez, Emma. 1996. *Gulf Dreams*. Berkeley, Calif.: Third Woman.

Portillo Trambley, Estela. 1976. "Day of the Swallows." In *Contemporary Chicano Theater*, ed. Roberto J. Garza, 206-45. Notre Dame, Ind.: University of Notre Dame Press. Originally published in *El Grito* 4, no. 3 (1971), 4-47.

Publishers Weekly. 1992. Review of *Margins*, by Terri de la Peña. *Publishers Weekly* 239 (15): 66.

Quintana, Alvina. 1996. *Home Girls: Chicana Literary Voices*. Philadelphia: Temple University Press.

Rebolledo, Tey Diana. 1995. *Women Singing in the Snow: A Cultural Analysis of Chicana Literature*. Tucson: University of Arizona Press.

Robinson, Regan. 1992. Review of *Margins*, by Terri de la Peña. *Library Journal* 117(5): 124.

Rosaldo, Renato. 1991. "Fables of the Fallen Guy." In *Criticism in the Border-*

lands, ed. Héctor Calderón and José David Saldívar, 84-93. Durham, N.C.: Duke University Press.

Saldívar, Ramón. 1990. *Chicano Narrative: The Dialectics of Difference, the Wisconsin Project on American Writers*. Madison: University of Wisconsin Press.

Smith, Barbara. 1982. "Toward a Black Feminist Criticism." In *All the Women Are White, All the Blacks Are Men, But Some of Us Are Brave: Black Women's Studies*, ed. Gloria T. Hull, Patricia Bell Scott, and Barbara Smith, 157-75. New York: Feminist Press. Originally published in *Conditions: Two* 1, no. 2 (1977).

Trujillo, Carla, ed. 1991. *Chicana Lesbians: The Girls Our Mothers Warned Us About*. Berkeley, Calif.: Third Woman.

Villanueva, Alma Luz. 1994. *Weeping Woman: La Llorona and Other Stories*. Tempe, Ariz.: Bilingual Press/Editorial Bilingüe.

Wolverton, Terry. 1992. "Hot Reads for a Summer Night." Review of *Margins*, by Terri de la Peña. *Advocate* 604 (June 2): 40.

Yarbro-Bejarano, Yvonne. 1987. "Chicana Literature from a Chicana Feminist Perspective," *Americas Review* 15(3-4): 139-45.

Zimmerman, Bonnie. 1993a. "Perverse Reading: The Lesbian Appropriation of Literature." In *Sexual Practice, Textual Theory: Lesbian Cultural Criticism*, ed. Susan J. Wolfe and Penelope Stanley, 135-49. Cambridge, Mass., and Oxford: Blackwell. Originally published in *(En)Gendering Knowledge: Feminists in Academe*, ed. Joan E. Hartman and Ellen Messer-Davidow. Knoxville: University of Tennessee Press, 1991.

_____. 1993b. "What Has Never Been: An Overview of Lesbian Feminist Criticism." In *Sexual Practice, Textual Theory: Lesbian Cultural Criticism*, ed. Susan J. Wolfe and Penelope Stanley, 33-54. Cambridge, Mass., and Oxford: Blackwell. Originally published in *Feminist Studies* 7, no. 3 (1981), 451-75.

Of Woman Bondage:
The Eroticism of Feet in
*The House on Mango Street*_____

Michelle Scalise Sugiyama

High heels must have been a man's idea—"Their asses will look good *and* they'll be crippled!"

—Rick Overton, *Comic Strip Live*, 1991

As a literary scholar, I am embarrassed to admit that I was well into my graduate career before I thought to ask, Why does Cinderella's fate hinge upon a *shoe*, of all things? Surely it is no accident that the foot (as opposed to some other body part) features so prominently in the tale. The question came to me when I was teaching Sandra Cisneros's *The House on Mango Street*, in which female feet and shoes are strangely and strikingly bound up with romance and sexuality. The answer began to take shape during a fortuitous study break spent on what turned out to be one of those rare, rich morsels of late-night television—namely, the observation by comedian Rick Overton cited above. What started as a little piece of mind-candy developed into an intellectual smorgasbord, with entrees from folklore, ethnography, Chicano studies, feminism, and human ethology. Although the following discussion addresses Cisneros's work in particular, its scope extends far beyond literature and even folklore: Cisneros's use of the foot/shoe motif sheds light on male manipulation of female sexuality and thus on the design and operations of the human mind.

In the chapter "The Family of Little Feet," Esperanza and her friends seem excessively excited by the experience of prancing around in the cast-off high heels which have been given to them: "Do you like these shoes? Rachel says yes and Lucy says yes and yes I say these are the best shoes. We will never go back to wearing the other kind again" (41).

Why all the excitement? The answer to this question lies in the girls' budding sexuality and its concomitant power. High heels accentuate the "female"—elongating the legs, elevating and making more prominent the buttocks, and causing the hips to sway pronouncedly. When the girls slip the shoes on, they suddenly discover, "We have legs"— legs that are "good to look at, and long" (40). Almost immediately after they put the shoes on, the girls begin acting in a sexually provocative manner: Rachel teaches Esperanza and Lucy how to "cross and uncross [their] legs" (40) and the three of them begin "strutting" (41) in their high heels. They are no doubt imitating the slightly older girls in the neighborhood who have already begun to attract sexual attention and of whom Esperanza speaks in admiring and envious tones. They have yet to realize, however, that like these older girls, they too possess sexual power—they seem surprised that their mock-sexy posturing draws sexual attention: "On the avenue a boy on a home-made bicycle calls out: Ladies, lead me to heaven. But there is nobody around but us" (41).

Their resolution to "never go back to wearing the other kind" of shoe comes after they realize that the shoes make them sexually attractive to the men around them: Esperanza comments that they strut "[d]own to the corner where the men can't take their eyes off of us" (40). They also appear to sense that their strutting has an effect on women as well: "In front of the laundromat six girls with the same fat face pretend we are invisible. They are the cousins, Lucy says, and always jealous" (41).

This power to arouse men and to make women jealous initially exhilarates them—they "just keep strutting" (41), enjoying for the moment their position as the source rather than the object of power. This power begins to frighten them, however, when their bluff is called by a drunken bum who offers Rachel a dollar for a kiss.

A discussion of female power might seem out of place in a text which focuses primarily on the rigid control of women by men. However, even in a relentlessly patriarchal society, women have a power over men which only the aging process can take away: the power to sexually arouse. That the girls are at least subconsciously aware of the power the female physique has over the male libido is apparent in their deceptively innocent conversations: "You need them [hips] to dance" (49) says Lucy, to which Esperanza responds, "I don't care what kind I get. Just as long as I get hips" (51). And when Esperanza points out that you need hips to have children, Rachel cautions, "But don't have too many or your behind will spread" (50). The girls have observed this power in others and want it for themselves. In a reference to the precocious Sally, Esperanza's mother warns that "to wear black so young is dangerous" (82), but Esperanza wishes that she could wear shoes like Sally's "black ones made out of suede" (82) and wear "nylons the color of smoke" (81).

This power is ultimately a trap for the women of Mango Street, however, and this is illustrated through Cisneros's use of the shoe motif—most notably through the use of high heels. The effect that high heels have on the gait is not unlike the effect of footbinding, a practice notorious as an expression of male subjugation of women. Anyone who has ever worn high heels knows that they are uncomfortable at best and painful at worst; they slow the gait and make it virtually impossible to run. Overton inadvertently makes the connection between these distinct cultural practices quite clear in the observation that sparked this rumination: "High heels must have been a man's idea—'Their asses will look good *and* they'll be crippled!'" The responses of men to an attractive woman in high heels and to an attractive woman with bound feet are quite similar; indeed, the erotic appeal of bound feet is well documented. In her essay "The Bride-Show Custom and the Fairy-Story of Cinderella," Photeine Bourboulis cites the Chinese tale of "Miss A-pao," which features a beautiful young woman surrounded by a ring of admirers at a spring festival. The admirers' excitement intensifies as she stands up to leave, after which, Bourboulis emphasizes, the men "criticized her face and *discussed her feet*" (105). H. A. Giles, in his book *The Civilization of China*, observes that "any Chinaman will bear witness as to the seductive effect of a gaily dressed girl picking her way on tiny feet some three inches in length, her swaying movements and delightful appearance of instability, conveying a general sense of delicate grace quite beyond expression in words" (106).

Part of the appeal of bound feet is that, as Giles mentions, their growth is retarded, which dramatically decreases their length. High heels, too, cause the foot to appear smaller. Significantly, along with shoes, small feet are a recurring motif in *The House On Mango Street*. The first thing that is mentioned of Mamacita's physical appearance is her "tiny pink shoe" (76). An entire chapter is devoted to a "Family of Little Feet." And Esperanza's shame and embarrassment at having to wear *chanclas* with her new party dress is expressed as a feeling of "My feet growing bigger and bigger" and "My feet swell[ing] big and heavy like plungers" (47). On Mango Street, as in old China, female beauty is associated with foot size: because they make her feet feel large and clumsy, Esperanza feels "ugly" (47) in the *chanclas*.

An appearance of airy gracefulness is another of the appeals of bound feet mentioned by Giles: footbinding causes a woman to sway from side to side as she walks. High heels cause a similar swaying— "tee-tottering" (40) is the word Esperanza uses, which suggests the "appearance of instability" Giles refers to. No doubt the "delightful" effect this "appearance of instability" has on the male psyche is due to the actual instability caused. A crippled woman is easier to control than a woman with healthy limbs. Esperanza unconsciously senses the link between high heels and footbinding: in "My Name" she observes that she was born in "the Chinese year of the horse which is supposed to be bad luck if you're born female—but I think this is a Chinese lie because the Chinese, like the Mexicans, don't like their women strong" (10).

Footbinding was practiced, of course, for precisely this reason: to make women weak. By making women physically unstable, men were able to curtail their movement and thereby prevent their sisters, wives, and daughters from engaging in any pre- and/or extra-marital sexual activity. As Laura Betzig suggests, "sexual modesty among women, including such strict institutions as veiling, footbinding, and claustration, might function to raise the paternal confidence of their consorts" (8; see also Dickemann). "Girls are like gold, like gems," says a Chinese interviewee to Giles at the turn of the century. "They ought to stay in their own house. If their feet are not bound they go here and they go there with unfitting associates; they have no good name. They are like defective gems that are rejected" (79). A woman whose feet were bound could not walk very far or for a sustained period of time, and had to be transported from place to place via palanquin. "Chinese ladies not walk abroad like Americans," says a Chinese woman interviewed by an American journalist in 1914. "In streets they go in sedan chairs, always with chaperone." This same woman was able to walk alone only with the aid of tables and chairs (Headland, 288). Thus a foot-bound woman was virtually a home-bound woman; for all practical purposes, she was cloistered.

Interestingly, the women of Mango Street are cloistered as well. The neighborhood is populated by women leaning out of windows, women who can't come outside, women who are literally or figuratively made prisoners in their homes. Marin can't come out of her house because she has to babysit all day—"but she stands in the doorway a lot" (23-24). Rafaela, who is "getting old from leaning out the window so much, gets locked indoors because her husband is afraid Rafaela will run away since she is too beautiful to look at" (79). Sally has to go straight home after school, to a "house [she] can't come out from" (82). Minerva "has many troubles, but the big one is her husband who left and keeps leaving" (85)—confining her to the home in effect by leaving her to raise two children all by herself. In short, the men in the story control women by controlling their feet that is, by not letting them walk abroad. As Julián Olivares notes, for the women of Mango Street, the house represents "not the space of contentment but of sadness, and a dialectic of inside/outside. *The woman's place is one of domestic confinement*, not one of liberation and choice" (emphasis added, 163).

The subconscious logic behind such confinement is evident in one of the euphemisms for prostitute, *streetwalker*. A prostitute is an unchaste woman who roams the streets more or less freely. The confinement of a woman to the home can be seen as an attempt to keep her chaste. For it is not female movement per se but rather female sexuality that the men in the text are trying to control. In this way, shoes and feet ultimately come to symbolize female sexuality on Mango Street.

The association of shoes and/or feet with female sexuality is not without precedent. In an essay entitled "Psychoanalysis and Folklore," Ernest Jones discusses the obsolete custom of throwing an old shoe after departing newlyweds, which he claims is "a symbol for the (fruitful) female organ itself, an interpretation that may be supported by quoting the decidedly broad saying that used to accompany it—'May you fit her as well as my foot fits this ole shoe'" (96). In an essay on "Cinderella in China," R. D. Jameson observes that the "use of the shoe in wedding ceremonies, the sanctification of the shoe in parts of China when it is brought to the temple in a ceremony to obtain children, the worship of a shoe as a characteristic symbol of a dead bride by a mourning groom, the gift of shoes by a bride to her husband in signification of her subordination to him and the gift of shoes among Manchus by a bride to her husband's brothers who share her with the husband all lead to the suggestion that we are here dealing with a very intimate and potent symbol" (88).

This "suggestion" is underscored by the vehemence with which the men of Mango Street guard their women. Ellen McCracken argues that "the men in these stories control or appropriate female sexuality by adopting one or another form of violence as if it were their innate right" (67). The text offers numerous examples attesting to this pattern. Consider, for example, Sally. The boys at school think she is pretty, to which her father responds by telling her that "to be this beautiful is trouble" (81). He makes her come straight home from school because, according to Sally, he thinks she is "going to run away like his sisters who made the family ashamed" (92). He beats her so severely when he catches her talking to a boy that she can't go to school for several days.

Rafaela, too, is a domestic prisoner, only her jailer is her husband, who locks her in the house because he is afraid she will run off with someone else. As it turns out, Sally's father is not altogether wrong about beauty being trouble: in "The Monkey Garden," Tito and his friends steal Sally's keys and tell her "you can't get the keys back unless you kiss us" (96). Poor Sally is damned if she does and damned if she doesn't: if she kisses the boys, she risks her father finding out about it, for which she will probably be beaten; if she doesn't kiss the boys, she will lose her keys, for which she may also be beaten. Regardless of which option she chooses (i.e., giving in to their blackmail or resisting it) one can easily imagine the situation escalating to rape. Indeed, Esperanza's great-grandmother's marriage was a virtual rape; she was abducted by Esperanza's great-grandfather, who "threw a sack over her head and carried her off. Just like that, as if she were a fancy chandelier" (11). And Esperanza herself is raped in "Red Clowns." The shoe motif and the use of violence by males to control female sexuality come together in the person of Mr. Benny, whose reaction to the high-heeled girls is, to say the least, extreme: "Them are dangerous, he says. You girls too young to be wearing shoes like that. Take them shoes off before I call the cops" (41). Mr. Benny's threat to summon the police confirms that control is indeed the issue: the police are agents of patriarchal power who use force (or threatened force) to control refractory members of society.

The shoe motif enables the reader to see that the power struggle taking place in the world of Mango Street is intrasexual as well as intersexual. The attempts of the men in the story to control female sexuality can be divided into two categories: (1) those that seek to blockade female sexuality, and (2) those that seek to bombard it. In other words, the male quest to control female sexuality is rooted either in fear (that the woman will lose her chastity and thereby shame the family) or desire (to possess the woman sexually), depending on the man's relationship to the woman in question. In either case, the plight of these women is much like that of Sally in the monkey garden, where "[o]ne of the boys invented the rules" (96). Women are pawns in a male struggle for status which is defined and determined, in part, by the control of female sexuality. The link between male socioeconomic status and female sexuality is made quite explicit by Giles, who claims that the motivation behind footbinding was "the social idea that small feet are both a mark of beauty and gentility" (430). This status derives in part from the fact that the feet of slave girls were not bound:

> The large-footed has to do rough work, does not sit in a sedan chair when she goes out, walks in the street barefooted, has no red clothes, does not eat the best food. She is wetted by the rain, tanned by the sun, blown upon by the wind. If unwilling to do all the rough work of the house she is called 'gourmandizing and lazy.' Perhaps she decides to go out as a servant. She has no fame and honour. To escape all this her parents bind her feet. (Giles, 79)

Thus, the foot-bound woman increased the socioeconomic status of those to whom she belonged—first her father and later her husband, which is revealed in the statement of one of Giles's interviewees that "One of a good family does not wish to marry a woman with long feet" (79).

The women of Mango Street are used in a similar way by their husbands. The men "bind" the feet of their wives and daughters by confining them to the home. This, in theory, renders the women chaste, which in turn makes the women "persons of respectability" (Giles, 79) and saves the family from being "ashamed" (Cisneros, 92). As Olivares notes, "A woman's place may be in the home but it is a patriarchic domain" (165).

It is not paradoxical that the home-bound girls of Mango Street yearn for houses. Prisoners in houses ruled by their fathers, they seek escape in the only way they know how: by acquiring their own household to rule over—a house in which they might rule themselves. Unfortunately, the only means of acquiring a house which their rigorously patriarchal culture makes available to them is a husband. Hence, the women of Mango Street are forced into a kind of prostitution, using their sexuality to get husbands, houses, pillowcases, and plates (Cisneros, 101). They think they are escaping the bondage of their fathers but, as they realize too late, they are only exchanging "one repressive patriarchal prison for another" (McCracken, 68), leaving a "[domineering] father for a domineering husband" (Olivares, 164). A case in point is Sally, who gets married "young and not ready" in a state "where it's legal to get married before eighth grade" (101)—an obvious attempt to escape her brutally puritanical father. Sally says she is happy, but it is evident she is no better off than she was before:

> Sally says she likes being married because now she gets to buy her own things when her husband gives her money. She is happy except sometimes her husband gets angry and once he broke the door where his foot went through, though most days he is okay. Except he won't let her talk on the telephone. And he doesn't let her look out the window. And he doesn't like her friends, so nobody gets to visit her unless he is working.
>
> She sits at home because she is afraid to go outside without his permission. (101-02)

Olivares beautifully illustrates how Cisneros deromanticizes the idea of "sex and marriage as escape" through the image of the "tortilla star," Venus, which does not suggest love or romance but instead "means having to get up early, a rolling pin, and tortillas" (164).

The male definition of female beauty which results in marriages that are *de facto* prostitution and slavery is what Esperanza and her friends are becoming aware of in "The Family of Little Feet." They feel pretty when they put on the high heels, but this attractiveness results in their being propositioned by a bum, who offers Rachel a dollar for a kiss. As McCracken notes, this chapter narrates "the girls' discovery of the threatening nature of male sexual power that is frequently disguised as desirable male attention and positive validation of women, though what is, in fact, sexual reification" (67). This can be seen in "Chanclas," in which Esperanza's self-esteem is dependent upon arousing male sexual interest: "All night the boy who is a man watches me dance. He watched me dance" (48). The male definition of beauty, exemplified by high heels, is psychologically as well as physically crippling in that it requires, ultimately, submission and dependence. Compliance with this beauty standard is one of the ways in which, as María Herrera-Sobek puts it, "women are socialized into being participants in their own oppression" (173). This is perhaps best illustrated in the relationship between the tellingly named Sire and his girlfriend, "tiny and pretty" Lois, who is compared to a baby three times in the same paragraph (73). We are told not that she and Sire hold hands when they go on walks, but that she holds his hand, and that they stop periodically for him to tie her shoes. Whether or not Lois is faking this inability to tie her own shoes, the submission and dependence it results in are quite real: Esperanza tells us that "Sire *lets* Lois ride his bike around the block [emphasis added]" (implying that Lois has to ask Sire's permission) and that she "see[s] her sometimes running to the store for him" (73). The bum's solicitation of Rachel points out what is expected of women on Mango Street: that they should exchange their sexual services for economic support, and that they should not seek to earn a living in any other way. The girls ultimately reject the high heels because they don't want to be attractive on such terms. "But the truth is it is scary to look down at your foot that is no longer yours and see attached a long long leg" (40) says Esperanza. "No longer yours" suggests the ugly truth of which they are becoming aware: their bodies are not their own, but belong to their fathers, brothers, boyfriends, and husbands in succession.

Thus female beauty, self-esteem, respectability, and subjugation are conflated in the image of the crippled foot. The similarities between high heels and footbinding enable us to see, however, that it is not tiny feet *per se* but the control of female sexuality they symbolize that is the root of male pleasure here. Footbinding and high heels function, in effect, as hobbles, making it easier for men to control the sexual activity of their sisters, wives, and daughters. As Martin Daly and Margo Wilson astutely observe, due to the age-old problem of paternity uncertainty, family (i.e., male) honor is to a large degree dependent upon the chastity of its women. What we see here, then, is the male psyche making, so to speak, a virtue of necessity: signs that a woman's chastity is well-guarded (e.g., footbinding) are perceived as sexually titillating stimuli. This phenomenon is visible in a comment made by one of Giles's interviewees: "Girls are like flowers, like the willow. It is important that their feet should be short, so that they can walk beautifully, with mincing steps, swaying gracefully, thus showing that they are persons of respectability" (79). Ultimately, then, female beauty is equated with bondage. This is sadly evidenced in the character of Marin, who wants to get a job downtown not because she wants to be financially independent but because "you always get to look beautiful and get to wear nice clothes and meet someone in the subway who might marry and take you to live in a big house far away" (26).

The parallel that Cisneros draws between Cinderella and the women of Mango Street is obvious. Like Cinderella, the women of Mango Street are confined to a life of domestic drudgery. Like Cinderella, their suitability as wives is symbolically determined by their shoes and feet. Like Cinderella, they use their sexuality to acquire a husband who they think will take them far, far away where they will live happily ever after. And like Cinderella, the women of Mango Street do not see that this escape is a trap. Hence the blind, unbounded joy of Esperanza and her friends when they first put on the high heels: "Hurray! Today we are Cinderella because our feet fit!" (40). Cisneros's work does not simply re-contextualize what some might consider to be a tired myth, however. Rather, by revealing the common motive underlying cultural practices seemingly far removed from each other in both space and time, Cisneros exposes the logic beneath an otherwise puzzlingly universal symbol. In the process, she presents us with an opportunity to deepen our understanding of human nature (particularly male sexual psychology), arguably one of the highest goals a literary work can hope to achieve. I can't speak for others, of course, but I know that I will never read the Cinderella story, in any of its multifold variations, quite the same way again.

Works Cited

Betzig, Laura. "Mating and Parenting in Darwinian Perspective." *Human Reproductive Behaviour*. Eds. L. Betzig, M. Borgerhoff Mulder, and P. Turke. Cambridge: Cambridge University Press, 1988. 3-20.

Bourboulis, Photeine P. "The Bride-Show Custom and the Fairy-Story of Cinderella." *Cinderella: A Casebook*. Ed. A. Dundes. New York: Wildman Press, 1983. 98-109.

Cisneros, Sandra. *The House on Mango Street*. New York: Vintage-Random House, 1989.

Daly, Martin, and Margo Wilson. *Homicide*. New York: Aldine de Gruyter, 1988.

Dickemann, M. "Paternal Confidence and Dowry Competition: A Biocultural Analysis of Purdah." *Natural Selection and Social Behavior: Recent Research and New Theory*. Eds. R. D. Alexander and D. W. Tinkle. New York: Chiron Press, 1981. 417-38.

Dundes, Alan. *Cinderella: A Casebook*. New York: Wildman Press, 1983.

Giles, H. A. *Strange Stories from a Chinese Studio*. Vol. 1. London, 1880.

Headland, I. T. *Home Life in China*. London, 1914.

Herrera-Sobek, María. "The Politics of Rape: Sexual Transgression in Chicana Fiction." *Chicana Creativity and Criticism: Charting New Frontiers in American Literature*. Eds. M. Herrera-Sobek and H. M. Viramontes. Houston: Arte Público, 1988. 171-81.

Jameson, R. D. "Cinderella in China." *Cinderella: A Casebook*. Ed. A. Dundes. New York: Wildman Press, 1983. 71-97.

Jones, Ernest. "Psychoanalysis and Folklore." *The Study of Folklore*. Ed. A. Dundes. Englewood Cliffs: Prentice-Hall, 1965. 88-102.

McCracken, Ellen. "Sandra Cisneros' *The House on Mango Street*: Community-Oriented Introspection and the Demystification of Patriarchal Violence." *Breaking Boundaries: Latina Writing and Critical Readings*. Eds. A. Horno-Delgado, E. Ortega, N. M. Scott, and N. Saporta Sternbach. Amherst: University of Massachusetts Press, 1989. 62-71.

Olivares, Julián. "Sandra Cisneros' *The House on Mango Street*, and the Poetics of Space." *Chicana Creativity and Criticism: Charting New Frontiers in American Literature*. Eds. M. Herrera-Sobek and H. M. Viramontes. Houston: Arte Público, 1988. 160-69.

Sandra Cisneros:
Border Crossings and Beyond_____

Robin Ganz

For readers and writers of Chicana literature, the 1980s signalled the emergence of voices of power and pain which many previous decades of racism, poverty and gender marginalization had suppressed. Breaking a silence that had run long and deep, writers such as Lorna Dee Cervantes, Denise Chávez, Gloria Anzaldúa, Cherríe Moraga and Sandra Cisneros converted the unyielding forces of gender and ethnicity which had historically bound and muted them into sources of personal and stylistic strengths. Before the literary explosion of the '80s— excluded both from the mainstream and from ethnic centers of power—the Chicana had been an outsider twice over. Sandra Cisneros derived inspiration from her cultural specificity and found her voice in the dingy rooms of her house on Mango Street, on the cruel but comfortable streets of the barrio, and in the smooth and dangerous curves of borderland arroyos. In her work, she charts new literary territory, marking out a landscape that is familiar to many and unfamiliar to many more. And yet, resonating with genuineness, testifying to the ability of the human spirit to renew itself against all odds, Cisneros's voice carries across and beyond the barriers that often divide us.

Born the only sister into a family of six brothers, Sandra Cisneros "dreamed [her]self the sister in the 'Six Swans'" fairy tale. Cisneros elaborates: "She too was an only daughter in a family of six sons. The brothers had been changed into swans by an evil spell only the sister could break. Was it no coincidence my family name translated 'keeper of swans?'" (1987, 71). Cisneros was born on December 20, 1954, "the year of Rosa Parks." A year and a half later, her mother gave birth to another girl child who died in infancy, leaving Cisneros the "odd number in a set of men." That her birthplace and family home is Chicago characterizes the convergence of rootlessness and love that has shaped her family history. Her great-grandfather, whose family "boasted railroads and wealth," played the piano for the Mexican president at his mansion in Mexico City. The fortune, lost at the gambling tables, was half-cloaked in secrecy by the time her father was born. Cisneros writes: "Our ancestors, it seems, were great gamblers . . . but this is never mentioned out of politeness, although I have disinterred a few . . . for the sake of poetry." Her paternal grandfather, a military man who "survived the Mexican Revolution with a limp and a pension," had put enough aside to send Cisneros's father, Alfredo Cisneros Del Moral, to college. She writes: "Since my father had a knack for numbers, he intended to pursue an accounting career. However, he was not very interested in his books that first year, and when he failed his classes, my father ran away to the United States rather than face my *abuelito's* anger."

Alfredo Cisneros Del Moral and Cisneros's "vagabond uncle" wandered the Eastern Seaboard and spent a "naive few weeks in the South," unsure about whether they belonged in the front or the back of its Jim Crow buses and eating eggs morning and night because it was "the only English word they knew." Planning to "cut across country and head to California, because they heard there were many Mexicans there, and New York was beginning to get too cold," the brothers decided to stop in Chicago for one day to see what it was like. On that Autumn day, a chance meeting with Cisneros's mother, Elvira Cordero Anguiano, was to change the course of Alfredo's life. One day became a month and then a lifetime as love caused dreams of California to fade when Alfredo, "who liked children and wanted a large family," married Elvira and set up housekeeping, for the time being at least, in a run-down house in one of Chicago's poorest neighborhoods.

Although Elvira Cordero's family history is "blurred and broken," rooted in a town in Guanajuato whose name Cisneros doesn't know, she recognizes that her "mother's family is simple and much more humble that that of [her] father's, but in many ways more admirable." Cisneros recounts that:

My mother's father was a hard-working Indian man, big-boned and strong, with a face made of stone. His wife, my maternal grandmother, was pale and quiet. She, too, worked very hard—for her stepmother who, as my mother tells it, was very cruel to her.

And when the whirlwind of the revolution arrived, the people of the small towns were victims to the violence of war from both sides. My grandmother said, after a while you could not tell who was a *federalista* and who a *revolucionario*, both stole your chickens and raped your women. My grandfather came to the United States during this time and found work in Chicago with the railroads. All his life he would work with his hands. He saved his money and sent for his wife and her cruel relatives, and that is how my mother's family came to be here, through the railroad money my grandfather earned. (Binder 54-55)

Regretting having "thrown away his college education," and obliged to find a way to support his family, Alfredo learned upholstering from his uncle, *tío Perico* (Uncle Parrot). Cisneros relates that her "father inherited this trade as well as the nickname." Soon the Cisneros family began a compulsive circular migration between Chicago and Mexico City that became the dominating pattern of Sandra's childhood. The origin of Alfredo's obsessive need to uproot his family with almost seasonal regularity apparently lies in his relationship with his mother. Here, Cisneros describes her paternal grandmother:

She was a hysterical woman, over-sentimental, spoiled. (Come to think of it, she was not unlike myself.) She had favorites. Her best baby was my father whom she held tight to. As a result, we returned like the tides, back and forth to Mexico City. Each time we returned to Chicago, we had to find a new place to live, a new school. (Binder 55-56)

The loneliness that grew in Cisneros as a result of Alfredo's nostalgic southward journeys conjoined with other forces to shape her passion for literature and her desire to become a writer. Cisneros's feeling of aloneness intensified as the family established its own unique dynamics. In the following passage, she characterizes the alliances into which her siblings composed themselves within the frame of the family portrait:

> The six brothers soon paired themselves off. The oldest with the second-oldest, the brother beneath me with the one beneath him and the youngest two were twins, genetically as well as socially bound. These three sets of men had their own conspiracies and allegiances, leaving me odd-woman-out-forever. (1987, 69)

Each time the family returned to "yet another Chicago flat, another Chicago neighborhood, another Catholic school," Alfredo would seek out the parish priest in order to get a tuition break and "complain or boast" that he had seven sons. In her narrative recollection "Only Daughter," Cisneros writes that he meant *siete hijos*, seven children, and that she is sure that he didn't "mean anything" by that mistranslation. Yet as she heard him describe his family in this way to the Sears Roebuck employee who sold them their washing machine, to the short-order cook who served up Alfredo's ham-and-eggs breakfast, and to anyone else who would listen, Cisneros "could feel [her]self being erased and would tug [her] father's sleeve and whisper: 'Not seven sons. Six! and *one daughter*'" (256).

While Alfredo's attitudes most influenced Cisneros's incipient awareness of her feminist identity, it was Elvira who guided her intellect. A high school drop-out who "read voraciously," and "quite superseded [Alfredo] in intelligence and social awareness," Cisneros's mother was never to fulfill her intellectual promise in any material way and, sadly "limited by the restrictions of her generation," was "to be dependent on him her whole life." It would be easy to understand a tale of Elvira's bitterness about her lost opportunities to express herself but, apparently, lamentation and regret were not in her nature. Elvira capitalized on her abilities by making Cisneros the benefactor of her intellectual and literary dreams and accomplishments. Although the Cisneros family "did not have any books in the house, [Elvira] saw to it that [Sandra] had [her] first library card even before [she] knew how to read" (Binder 56).

Tracing her evolution as a lover of reading and creating poetry and prose in "Living as a Writer: Choice and Circumstance," Cisneros recounts that:

> Because of my mother, I spent my childhood afternoons in my room reading instead of in the kitchen. . . . I never had to change my little brothers' diapers, I never had to cook a meal alone, nor was I ever sent to do the laundry. Certainly I had my share of housework to do as we all did, but I don't recall it interfering with my homework or my reading habits. (68-69)

About growing up without the burden of endless housework, Cisneros said at a Chicana Poetry Conference in Santa Fe, New Mexico, in October, 1991, "I felt guilty, but not that guilty." Soon Cisneros was a prodigious reader. She writes: "Had my sister lived or had we stayed in one neighborhood long enough for a friendship to be established, I might not have needed to bury myself in books the way I did." Around the time of her early passage into the unimagined world that books opened up for her, Cisneros began to hear a voice in her head, a narrator who chronicled the routine events that made up her life:

> "I want you to go to the store and get me a loaf of bread and a gallon of milk. Bring back all the change and don't let them gyp you like they did last time." In my head my narrator would add: . . . *she said in a voice that was neither reproachful nor tender. Thus clutching the coins in her pocket, our hero was off under a sky so blue and a wind so sweet she wondered it didn't make her dizzy.* This is how I glamorized my days living in the third-floor flats and shabby neighborhoods where the best friend I was always waiting for never materialized. (1987, 70)

In 1966, Cisneros was eleven, the family somehow borrowed enough for a down payment on its first home which she describes as "an ugly little house, bright red as if holding its breath" (Binder 57). The Cisneros move into a permanent home ended their nomadic migration which had dominated Cisneros's early years. For Cisneros, the transition from the apartment on Roosevelt Road into the new house in a Puerto Rican neighborhood on the North Side called Humboldt Park also represented an important step in her development as a writer because, "it placed [her] in a neighborhood, a real one, with plenty of friends and neighbors that would evolve into the eccentric characters of *The House on Mango Street*" (57).

Cisneros composed her first poems at the age of ten, but doesn't recall writing any more poetry until her sophomore year of high school when a "bright and vivacious young woman" came to her school to teach English. A poet herself, Cisneros's teacher introduced her to the work of contemporary poets and asked her students to write about the Viet Nam War. Cisneros recounts that:

> Somewhere here, amidst the tumult of the Viet Nam War and ecological awareness, I began my first poems. They were filled with pleas for peace and saving the environment. Here and there I threw in a few catchy words like ecology and Coca-Cola. Despite all this, I continued writing and began to be known around the school as the poet. (58)

Cisneros, "too busy being a college student and falling in love," did not pick up her pen again until her junior year at Loyola University when she took a Creative Writing class. Under her teacher's tutelage she applied and was accepted into the University of Iowa's Writers' Workshop where she began to study with Donald Justice. Unfortunately, he left on sabbatical and Cisneros, feeling isolated from familiar surroundings and alienated from the workshop which "was East Coast pretentious and operated totally without mercy or kind words," floundered from one imitation to the next (61). Although Cisneros claims that the Iowa Writers' Workshop failed her, she experienced an epiphany there that she frequently designates as the moment her writing acquired a voice. What's more, in the moment of revelation in Iowa, the role which awaited her in the literary world suddenly became known to her.

It happened like this: Cisneros was enrolled in "a marvelous seminar that spring called 'Memory and the Imagination.'" The students were heatedly discussing a book from their reading list, *The Poetics of Space*, written by the French theorist Gaston Bachelard. As her classmates debated "archetypes . . . shells, with the shell as house with the house of the imagination, the attics and stairways and cellars of childhood," Cisneros felt foreign from the others, alienated and dispossessed of some communal knowledge which they shared and which she felt she would never understand. Suddenly she was homeless, having no such house in her memory. As a child she had read of such houses in books and her parents had promised her such a house, but the best they could offer was the dilapidated bungalow in an impoverished inner-city neighborhood. Sitting in that classroom, her face grew hot and she asked herself, "What [do I] know? What could I know? My classmates were from the best schools in the country. They had been bred as fine hot-house flowers. I was a yellow weed among the city's cracks." In that moment she realized that she had something to write about that her classmates had not experienced and would probably never be able to articulate with the understanding that she possessed. Cisneros recounts that, "this is how *The House on Mango Street* was born, the child-voice that was to speak all my poems for many years" (63-64).

After earning her MFA from the University of Iowa's Writers' Workshop in 1978, for the next three years Cisneros taught writing to (former) high school drop-outs at Chicago's Latino Youth Alternative High School. Since the publication of *The House on Mango Street* in 1984, she has taught creative writing as the writer in residence at many universities all over the country and given hundreds of readings. *My*

Wicked Wicked Ways, a stunning collection of poems, was released in 1987 to enthusiastic reviews. Her most recent tour de force, a collection of prose pieces entitled *Woman Hollering Creek and Other Stories*, published by Random House in April, 1991, marks her transition from the relative obscurity of the small ethnic press into the mainstream of American literary culture and, in fact, into international prominence.

In an interesting cycle, the childhood loneliness that propelled her from the "real" world into the more pleasing worlds of reading and creating books has evolved into an adult solitude that is now indispensable to her work as a writer. In a 1990 interview with Pilar Rodríguez Aranda, Cisneros joked that her relatives had long since given up questioning her about when she's going to get married. She goes on to explain that, while they seem to have grudgingly accepted her decision not to marry, they still don't understand it.

> Now instead of asking: "When are you going to get married?" they're asking: "What happened in your childhood? Who hurt you? Who did this to you?" And they don't realize . . . "Look at your own marriage, tía, look at your marriage, mother, look at your marriage, abuela, look at your marriage, tío, papa," I've never seen a model of a happy marriage, or I've never seen a marriage that is as happy as my living alone, I've never seen it! [Aranda:] *No models—like nobody . . .*
>
> I have some friends who are married and they seem to be happy, but I can't imagine myself in that kind of relationship. I really like my solitude. I don't like being lonely, but I'm not lonely. I need to be alone to work. I have very close friends and very close men in my life, but I don't want them in my house. That's the difference. . . . My writing is my child and I don't want anything to come between us. I like to know that if I come home very late from teaching—and teaching is exhausting, as exhausting as factory work, except I work more hours and get paid more—I don't want to come home to a husband. I want to come home to my books, and if I want to, I want to be alone to think. As a writer you need time to think, even if

you're not writing. . . . I wish we had little lights on our forehead like confessionals had. When someone was inside, the little light used to go red: "Ocupado." I want one like that: "Don't bother me, I'm thinking." Some men do respect. But people cannot read your mind and know that you are thinking even though you're not writing. . . . When I'm living with a man, he becomes my project. Like it or not, you find yourself doing it, then you get angry at yourself. I know that I'm difficult to live with. I like my loneness, and I think that's the way I work best. (71-72)

Sandra Cisneros's discovery of her poetic voice in Iowa was, up until that time, the single most important moment in her life as a writer and the result of that insight was both the personal accomplishment and critical success of *The House on Mango Street*. After she'd explored and mastered that territory, that is, writing from the point of view and in the voice of Esperanza (the young Sandra), moving on meant experimenting with many voices—voices as divergent and dissimilar as possible from her own. In *Woman Hollering Creek and Other Stories* she brilliantly realizes her intentions as she presents us, from one prose piece to the next, with a complex variety of voices and points of view. Her gamut of characters ranges from, for example, the disembodied spirit of Inés Zapata (Emiliano Zapata's wife), to Rudy Cantú, drag queen extraordinaire. Cisneros creates what she calls a "deluge of voices" (Campbell 6), "voices," she emphasized at the 1991 Poetry Conference in Santa Fe, "that weren't mine at all." They speak in language as rich and diverse as the expanse they embody—they are the expressions of her immediate family, of the Chicano-Riqueño community she grew up in, and the voices from her life both between and as a part of the two cultures in which she now dwells.

One particular prose piece, "Little Miracles, Kept Promises," is perhaps the most telling representation of the diversity of voices that make up *Woman Hollering Creek*. It is introduced by a prelude told in the voice of a young, working-class Chicana who, while shopping in a "religious store" for a statue or "holy picture" to give to a friend in the hospital, is told by the "crab ass" storeowner, "I can see you're not going to buy anything." When the narrator protests and says that she will, she's just thinking, he replies, "Well, if it's thinking you want, you just go across the street to the church to think—you're just wasting my time and yours thinking here." She does go across the street, and inside the church she reads the little letters of supplication that the churchgoers leave for the Virgin and other saints. A sampling follows of the twenty-three letters covering the church walls that comprise "Little Miracles, Kept Promises":

Miraculous Black Christ of Esquípulas,
Please make our grandson to be nice to us and stay away from drugs. Save him to find a job and move away from us.

Grandma y Grandfather

Harlingen

Saint Jude, patron saint of lost causes,
Help me pass my English 320, British Restoration Literature class and everything to turn out ok.

Eliberto Gonzalez

Dallas

M3r1c5145s B11ck Chr3st 4f2sq53p511s,
3 1sk y45, L4rd,w3th 1ll my h21rt p12s2 w1tch 4v2r M1nny B2n1v3d2s wh4 3s 4v2rs21s. 3 14v2 h3m 1nd 3 d4n't kn4w whit t4 d4 1b45t 1ll th3s 14v2 a1dn2ss land sh1m2 th1t f3lls m2.

B2nj1m3n T.

D21 R34 Tx (122-24)

In the case of the last letter, Benjamin T. is apparently so discomfited by his love for another man that he creates a code (a = 1, e = 2, i = 3, etc.), trusting that his faith will translate both his message and his pain:

[Miraculous Black Christ of Esquípulas,
  I ask you Lord, with all my heart please watch over Manny Benavidas
who is overseas. I love him and I don't know what to do about all this love
sadness and shame that fills me.

Benjamin T.
Del Rio TX]

One of the unexpected reasons that Cisneros's stories resonate with
such genuineness is that her indispensable source for names and other
cultural information is the San Antonio phone book. When she's
searching for just the right name for a character, she leafs through the
listings for a last name then repeats the process for a first name, thereby
coming up with a euphonious or suitable combination without appropriating anybody's real name. Cisneros also uses the Yellow Pages and
mail-order catalogues in much the same way for the names of businesses
and so forth. For inspiration, she reads the *Popul Vuh*, the Maya Bible.

About the experience of writing *Woman Hollering Creek* and giving
voice to so many different characters, Cisneros said at the Santa Fe conference, "I felt like a ventriloquist." Her advice to the writers in attendance
was to "transcribe voices of the people of a community you know," and
confided that she keeps voluminous files of snippets of dialogue or
monologue—records of conversations she hears wherever she goes.
She emphasized that she'll mix and match to suit her purpose because,
as she put it, "real life doesn't have shape. You have to snip and cut."

When Cisneros was at work on *Woman Hollering Creek*, she became so immersed in her characters that they began to penetrate her un-
conscious; once, while writing "Eyes of Zapata," she awakened in the
middle of the night, convinced for the moment that she was Inés, the
young bride of the Mexican revolutionary. Her dream conversation
with Zapata then became those characters' dialogue in her story. The
task of breaking the silence, of articulating the unpronounceable pain
of the characters that populate *Woman Hollering Creek*, was a very serious undertaking for Cisneros. She said in a recent interview: "I'm try-

ing to write the stories that haven't been written. I felt like a cartographer; I'm determined to fill a literary void" (Sager 74). The pressure intensifies for her because of her bi-culturalism and bi-lingualism: She charts not only the big city barrio back alleyways, its mean streets and the dusty arroyos of the borderland, but also offers us a window into the experience of the educated, cosmopolitan Chicano/artist, writer and academic. While she revels in her biculturalism, enjoys her life in two worlds, and as a writer she's grateful to have "twice as many words to pick from . . . two ways of looking at the world," her wide range of experience is a double-edged sword. In the Sagel interview, she revealed another side of her motivation to tell many people's stories in their own voices—the responsibility and the anxiety which that task produces: "One of the most frightening pressures I faced as I wrote this book," she says, "was the fear that I would blow it. . . . I kept asking myself, What have I taken on here? That's why I was so obsessed with getting everybody's stories out" (74).

She feels under additional pressure as the first Chicana to enter the mainstream of literary culture. Until Random House published *Woman Hollering Creek* and *The House on Mango Street* was reissued by Vintage Press, the Chicano literature that had crossed over into the mainstream remained a male domain—Gary Soto, Luis Valdez, Richard Rodriguez, Jimmy Santiago Baca and Alberto Ríos had all made the transition. Women, however, were unrepresented there until Cisneros's recent successes. On September 19, 1991, she said in a National Public Radio interview broadcast on *Morning Edition*:

I think I can't be happy if I'm the only one that's getting published by Random House when I know there are such magnificent writers—both Latinos and Latinas, both Chicanos and Chicanas—in the U.S. whose books are not published by mainstream presses or whom the mainstream isn't even aware of. And, you know, if my success means that other presses will take a second look at these writers . . . and publish them in larger numbers then our ship will come in.

While it is undeniable that Sandra Cisneros has traversed the boundary dividing the small press market and the mainstream publishing establishment, a controversy continues about her writing among the critics over the issue of genre-crossing. In her review of *Woman Hollering Creek* in the *Los Angeles Times* titled "Poetic Fiction with a Tex-Mex Tilt," Barbara Kingsolver writes that "Sandra Cisneros has added length and dialogue and a hint of plot to her poems and published them in a stunning collection called *Woman Hollering Creek*." Later on in the review she elaborates:

> It's a practical thing for poets in the United States to turn to fiction. Elsewhere, poets have the cultural status of our rock stars and the income of our romance novelists. Here, a poet is something your mother probably didn't want you to grow up to be. . . . When you read this book, don't be fooled. It's poetry. Just don't tell your mother. (3-4)

In her review in *The Nation*, Patricia Hart writes, "In her new book, *Woman Hollering Creek and Other Stories*, Cisneros breathes narrative life into her adroit, poetic descriptions, making them mature, fully formed works of fiction" (598).

We might ask then, is *Woman Hollering Creek* poetry or is it prose? Ever since the publication of *The House on Mango Street*, critics have debated the degree to which Cisneros embraces both forms simultaneously. Gary Soto addresses the mirror image of the same issue in his review of her poetry collection, *My Wicked Wicked Ways*:

> I use the term "prosaic poetry" not in disapproval, but as a descriptive phrase. Cisneros, as she illustrated in *The House on Mango Street*, is foremost a storyteller. Except for the "Rodrigo Poems," which meditate on the themes of love and deceit, and perhaps a few of the travel poems, each of the poems in this collection is a little story, distilled to a few stanzas, yet with a beginning, middle, and end. (21)

It is unlikely that critics will ever reach a definitive agreement on the matter of whether Cisneros's writing is poetic prose or prose-like poetry. I predict, however, that this question will persist throughout her literary career, continuing to arise in subsequent criticism of her work. Cisneros herself is entitled to the final word (for the time being, at least) on the subject. At a reading in Albuquerque, New Mexico, in October, 1991, she said that when she has the words to express her idea, it's a story. When she doesn't, it's a poem.

Sandra Cisneros is a relatively young writer, both chronologically and in the sense that she is a fresh voice, a new presence in the spectrum of contemporary literature. One is likely to forget her relative inexperience because of the wisdom and understanding that charge and permeate her stories and poems. From time to time I am reminded of it, however, when I come across a passage that verges on the cute—at times, whether in a poem or story, she veers dangerously toward the precious. A reviewer for *Booklist* wrote the following criticism about *The House on Mango Street*, but it could apply to her work in other instances as well:

> These vignettes of autobiographical fiction . . . written in a loose and deliberately simple style, halfway between a prose poem and the awkwardness of semiliteracy, convincingly represent the reflections of a young girl. Occasionally the method annoys by its cuteness. (281)

Far more often than it is coy or cloying however, Cisneros's work is affecting, charming and filled with the humor and the rich cultural offerings of Mexican America. Her style is as clear as water, as evinced in her unadorned syntax, her spare and elegant phrasing, and the entirely original Mexican-American inflected diction of her poetry and prose. Yet, as with the clearest water, beneath the surface, Cisneros's work is alive with complexity and depth of meaning. Cisneros's voice is the sound of many voices speaking—over the kitchen table, out on the street, across the borderlands, and through the years.

This essay first appeared in *MELUS: Journal of the Society for the Study of the Multi-Ethnic Literature of the United States*, issue 19.1 (Spring 1994), pages 19-29, and is reprinted by permission of the journal. Copyright © 1994 by *MELUS*.

Works Cited

Aranda, Pilar E. Rodríguez. "On the Solitary Fate of Being Mexican, Female, Wicked and Thirty-three: An Interview with Writer Sandra Cisneros." *The Americas Review* 18.1 (Spring 1990): 65-80.

Binder, Wolfgang, ed. "Sandra Cisneros" in *Partial Autobiographies: Interviews with Twenty Chicano Poets*. Erlangen: Verlag, Palm & Enke, 1985.

Campbell, Bebe Moore. "Crossing Borders." Rev. of *Woman Hollering Creek and Other Stories*, by Sandra Cisneros. *New York Times Book Review* 26 May 1991: 6-7.

Cisneros, Sandra. "Ghosts and Voices: Writing from Obsession." *The Americas Review* 15.1 (Spring 1987): 69-73.

_____. "Living as a Writer: Choice and Circumstance." *Revista Mujeres* 3.2 (June 1986): 68-72.

_____. "Only Daughter." *Glamour* (November 1990): 256-57.

_____. *Woman Hollering Creek and Other Stories*. New York: Random House, 1991.

Hart, Patricia. "Babes in Boyland." Rev. of *Woman Hollering Creek and Other Stories*, by Sandra Cisneros. *The Nation* 6 May 1991: 597-98.

Kingsolver, Barbara. "Poetic Fiction With a Tex-Mex Tilt." Rev. of *Woman Hollering Creek and Other Stories*, by Sandra Cisneros. *Los Angeles Times Book Review* 28 April 1991.

Rev. of *The House on Mango Street*, by Sandra Cisneros. *Booklist* 15 Oct. 1984: 281.

Sagel, Jim. "Sandra Cisneros." Interview. *Publishers Weekly* 29 March 1991: 74-75.

Soto, Gary. "Voices of Sadness and Science." Rev. of *My Wicked Wicked Ways*, by Sandra Cisneros. *The Bloomsbury Review* July/August 1988: 21.

Vitale, Tom. Interview with Sandra Cisneros. *Morning Edition*. National Public Radio. KUNM, Albuquerque. 19 Sept. 1991.

"This Bridge We Call Home":
Crossing and Bridging Spaces in
Sandra Cisneros's *The House on Mango Street*

Stella Bolaki

The representation of ethnic American subjectivity is a theme immersed in discussions of crossroads, borders and bridges. In this paper, I argue that the formation of selfhood, a central thematic concern of the *Bildungsroman* (also known as the novel of development), is defined for ethnic Americans by a constant negotiation of belonging in distinct territories, in other words by a kind of border-crossing. If in the traditional *Bildungsroman* the protagonist grows up expecting to learn 'the art of living' (cited by Rosowski, 1983, p. 49), in the ethnic American variant the protagonist becomes apprenticed to 'the art of the present' (Bhabha, 1994, p. 1), and develops 'a consciousness of the Borderlands' (Anzaldúa, 1999, p. 99). While the first phrase above suggests an organic unfolding and a harmonious integration of all aspects of the self, the other two, when used in the context of the genre, redefine traditional notions of eighteenth-century *Bildung* by turning attention away from organic integration in order to express the acute conflicts and complexity that characterises life 'on the border'.[1] Sandra Cisneros's *The House on Mango Street* (1984), a coming-of-age narrative pieced together by assembled patches like a quilt, can be read as an example of what it means for a Mexican-American female to grow up in the cultural and textual borderlands.

Although schematisations of the traditional *Bildungsroman* posit the developmental journey as a teleological movement from stage to higher stage, feminist critics have proposed an alternative geometry.[2] Susan Fraiman, for instance, envisages the female process of growing up 'not as a single path to a clear destination but as the endless negotiation of a crossroads' (1993, p. x). Gloria Anzaldúa also draws on the idea of 'The Crossroads/*La encrucijada*' (1999, p. 102), which, placed in a Mexican American or Chicano/a context, is recast as '*El camino de la mestiza*/The Mestiza Way' (1999, p. 104). In her words, the Chicana is 'caught between *los intersticios*, the spaces between the different worlds she inhabits' (Anzaldúa, 1999, p. 42). Torn between Anglo, Mexican and indigenous cultures, Chicanas face '*Una lucha de fronteras*/ A Struggle of Borders' (Anzaldúa, 1999, p. 99). The U.S.-Mexican border, to which Anzaldúa alludes in *Borderlands/La Frontera*, is not merely the geopolitical boundary, which since 1848 divides Mexico from the United States. As most border theorists agree, the idea of the border becomes even more fertile when we 'liberate it from the notion of space [or from a specific *locale*] to encompass [among others] notions of sex, class, gender, ethnicity, identity and community' (Benito and Manzanas, 2002, p. 3).

The House on Mango Street embodies and amplifies Fraiman's negotiation of crossroads and Anzaldúa's struggle of borders. The dilemma that arises here is at the centre of the traditional *Bildungsroman*, but becomes qualified with the consideration of additional factors such as gender and ethnicity, notably: How can individuality and freedom from constraint coexist with the demands of socialisation, both the larger world 'of necessity' (Moretti, 2000, p. 17) and the more intimate, though not empty of symbolic obligations, sphere of community? This tension between 'individuality' and 'normality', for Franco Moretti (2000, p. 16), puts considerable burden on ethnic American women writers, since their texts are usually judged by their ethnic communities on the basis of and according to the degree in which they fulfil their responsibilities toward them. As Sau-ling Cynthia Wong succinctly summarises their predicament:

> [V]ictimized by sexism [women] must be ready to suppress potentially damaging (to the men, that is) material; to do less is to jeopardise the united front and to prostitute one's integrity for the sake of white approval. (1992, p. 259)

In other words, any attempt by women of colour to interrogate the patriarchal structures of their local communities becomes equated with betrayal as it is considered synonymous either with an assimilationist anti-ethnic stance or with a fashionable white feminism.[3]

For ethnic women writers then, the opposition between individualism and community, or between privacy and affiliation, frequently implies another border struggle, namely between gender and ethnicity. The ways in which women of colour choose to negotiate their divided loyalties often decides, as already mentioned, whether their writing is to be dismissed as a depoliticized gesture or praised as a politicized endeavour. One could imagine that many ethnic American women writers have responded to the pseudo-dilemma 'Individualism or Community?' imposed by their male counterparts with the joke with which Slavoj Zizek opens (and entitles) one of his essays, that is, with the answer 'Yes, please!' (2000, p. 90); a refusal of choice between the two, which is accompanied by a very serious effort to articulate a synthesis of the competing values.[4] For Anzaldúa, this synthesis can take place in an ideal space, namely 'the borderlands'; 'a third element which is greater than the sum of its severed parts' (Anzaldúa, 1999, pp. 101-2) and where 'a new *mestiza* consciousness' can flourish (Anzaldúa, 1999, p. 99).[5]

I would like to suggest that *The House on Mango Street* participates in the creation of such a textual border zone through the attempt to articulate a consciousness of the Borderlands. Literary texts seem to offer an ideal site in which to explore the coexistence of conflicting principles as well as the conditions in which contradictions can be transcended and dichotomies merged. The *Bildungsroman* in particular has functioned as 'a cultural mechanism' that tests the various compromises between self and society, aiming at a proper balance between the two (Moretti, 2000, p. 9). For Moretti, what explains the continuing appeal of the genre is the fact that it has succeeded, at least in its original eighteenth-century form, in representing the fusion of such opposites as autonomy and social integration 'with a force of conviction and optimistic clarity that will never be equalled again' (2000, p. 16). The last point may be true, but this does not render the social function of the genre obsolete; its mediating and compromising project, to fuse, in other words, opposites 'into a new unity until the former is no longer distinguishable from the latter' (Moretti, 2000, p. 16) may not be convincing anymore since 'absolute cohesion and totalizing harmony' (Moretti, 2000, p. 72) do not correspond to viable ideals. Still, an attempt at integration, however contingent and precarious, should not be necessarily treated as suspect; when seen in relation to ethnic subjectivity in particular, it becomes a vital tool of survival. Indeed, by virtue of the genre's 'synthetic vocation' (Moretti, 2000, p. 17), contemporary versions of the *Bildungsroman*, could be seen as participating in the process of transcending 'unnatural' borders and boundaries through the articulation of borderlands. As I hope to show, such gestures are productive and ultimately political in that, in Bhabha's words, they can 'initiate new signs of identity and innovative sites of collaboration and contestation . . .' (1994, pp. 1-2).

Although Cisneros is not a conscious practitioner of the *Bildungsroman, The House on Mango Street* has been perceived against this conceptual horizon, in particular as a revision of a western individualistic and patriarchal genre (see Gutiérrez-Jones, 1993). Moreover, unlike other Mexican American fiction of development, which uses the geographic border as the backdrop of their protagonists' 'education', or recreates border encounters between Mexico and the United States through code switching and linguistic hybridity, *The House on Mango Street* dramatises the idea of border struggle in a more subtle way; through its basic structural principle, that is, the *vignette*.[6] The imagistic or episodic *vignette* seems a simple technique, but I would argue that its alleged lack of complexity is deceptive. Cisneros herself has described some of the sections in *The House on Mango Street* as 'lazy poems [. . .] hovering in that grey area between two genres' (1987, p. 79), and one might interpret this grey space between prose and poetry as a kind of textual borderlands. In an interview referring to *The House on Mango Street*, another statement of hers echoes the idea of fluidity associated with the *vignette* form:

I wanted to write a series of stories that you could open up at any point. You didn't have to know anything before or after and you would understand each story like a little pearl, or you could look at the whole thing like a necklace. (cited by Sanborn, 2001, p. 1345)

In *The House on Mango Street*, the compressed stories, lazy poems and vivid sketches—each with its own title—derail the progressive train of Esperanza's development by dispersing the narrative across several trajectories. The text can be thus approached not merely as a temporal continuum, which is what one would normally expect from a *Bildungsroman*, but also as a spatial configuration (Bronfen, 1999). In this spatial whole, the chapters are interchangeable and carry equal weight. At the same time, they reconstruct the narrator's process of growing up as a movement in contradictory directions by inscribing competing narratives of development (Fraiman, 1993). These rival narratives can be uncovered through a close juxtaposition of different *vignettes*. As a form, the *vignette* has soft edges that often bleed out into the surrounding area, causing 'a narrative overspill'. As a result of its fluid boundaries, then, the *vignette* can become an effective tool for establishing connections and highlighting oppositions.

A series of *vignettes* in *The House on Mango Street* underwrite the narrator's wish to escape from the confining patriarchal scripts of her community into a space of 'private enjoyment' (Sanborn, 2001, p. 1334); both into a real house and into 'the house of fiction' (Sage, 1992). This is what Esperanza, whose name means 'hope', dreams of in a section entitled 'A House of My Own':

> Not a flat. Not an apartment in back. Not a man's house. Not a daddy's. A house all my own. With my porch and my pillow, my pretty purple petunias. My books and my stories. My two shoes waiting beside the bed. Nobody to shake a stick at. Nobody's garbage to pick up after. Only a house quiet as snow, a space for myself to go, clean as paper before the poem. (Cisneros, 1992, p. 108)

This *vignette* comes before the last story of the text, and it has made a few critics suggest that Esperanza seeks 'to become more "Anglicized"' (cited by Valdés, 1993, p. 289) or that her development culminates in 'her deterritorialization from kinship, friendship, group, community, and history' (Morales, 1993, p. 231). This is the price ethnic American women presumably pay in the pursuit of a possessive individualism, or in the pursuit of Virginia Woolf's feminist dream of 'a room of one's own' (1929).

Such criticism, though not necessarily directed at Cisneros, fails to do justice to the text by treating it as univocal. As I have suggested, the text is split between competing narratives, and the individualistic *vignettes* have their communal counterparts. For instance, the above *vignette* can be juxtaposed with another in which Esperanza offers to open that very same house to 'bums', since, as the narrator confesses, she knows 'how it is to be without a house' (Cisneros, 1992, p. 87). Moreover, through an even closer attention to the text, we can see that it not only explores a conflict between the narratives of individualism and community, but also proceeds to problematize each of these narratives from within, thus challenging narrow understandings of concepts such as privacy and affiliation. For example, the narrator yearns for a private space, yet she weaves her tale of growing up with snapshots of women entrapped in houses, exploring in this way the indeterminate area between privacy and confinement. Similarly, her attitude towards the public site of the *barrio* is ambivalent. Both houses and local communities are arbitrary; like borders, they enclose people within the safety of familiar or intimate territories, but can, at the same time, become prisons. *The House on Mango Street* constantly registers this tension by mapping the protagonist's vertiginous border crossings not only from one extreme (privacy) to the other (communal affiliation), but also to several other intermediate positions.

In *Borderlands / La Frontera*, Anzaldúa imagines a way of transcending the duality that seems to be imposed by life on the border:

I am an act of kneading, of uniting and joining that not only has produced a creature of darkness and a creature of light, but also a creature that questions the definitions of light and dark and gives them new meanings. (1999, p. 103)

With this statement Anzaldúa tries to turn the experience of growing up in what initially appears to be a space of 'neither/nor' into a more inclusive and empowering position (Turner, 1967; Anzaldúa, 1999, p. 41). *The House on Mango Street* partakes in this process of uniting and joining that is also typical of the *Bildungsroman*; when seen as a whole, the text is 'a layered discursive space' (Sánchez, 1997, p. 1014), which weaves the developmental narratives of individualism and intersubjectivity *simultaneously* in its fabric. Through such a close juxtaposition, these contradictory discourses become conflated, and out of this textual collision new subject positions emerge. As Anzaldúa puts it, individualism may be 'condemned in the Mexican culture and valued in the Anglo' (1999, p. 40), but on her back the Chicana carries both the '. . . baggage from the Spanish . . . [and] the Anglo [father]' (1999, p. 104). Thus, the Chicana refuses the choice of either of the two 'opposite bank[s]' and learns to be 'on both shores [of the border] at once' (Anzaldúa, 1999, p. 100). In more technical terms, borders inevitably generate borderlands that blur boundaries by creating opportunities for cultural exchange, dialogue and 'hybridization' (Benito and Manzanas, 2002, p. 4). Though such 'third spaces' as the ones suggested by the concept of the borderlands bear 'the traces' of the positions that inform them, they are syncretic constructs which can give rise to 'a new area of negotiation of meaning and representation' (Bhabha, 1990, p. 211). Anzaldúa agrees that this is a search for a *new* consciousness, '*una cultura mestiza*', which she is determined to make 'with my own lumber, my own bricks and mortar and my own feminist architecture' (1999, p. 44).

Anzaldúa's imagery of construction is evocative of the central unifying trope in *The House on Mango Street*, that is, the house. Esperanza also builds a new space by imagining a house that moves 'toward a more whole perspective, one that includes rather than excludes' (Anzaldúa, 1999, p. 101). Neither private nor communitarian, the house she imagines belongs to 'the realm of the beyond' (Bhabha, 1994, p. 1); it is porous, an interior space, which is experienced as open; it is a creative site of introspection and at the same time a space of intimacy and connection, a refuge for the 'home girls' of the *barrio* (Quintana, 1996, p. ix) but also for all those without a roof. Thus, Esperanza's imaginary dwelling crosses customary boundaries and becomes a bridge, 'this bridge we call home' (Anzaldúa and Keating, 2002).

How does Esperanza construct this more encompassing space that fuses oppositions into a new synthesis? As Anzaldúa suggests:

[The Chicana] can be jarred out of ambivalence by an intense, and often painful, emotional event, which inverts or resolves the ambivalence. I am not sure exactly how. The work takes place underground—subconsciously. It is work that the soul performs. (1999, p. 101)

For Esperanza, as for Cisneros, it is also work that the pen performs. In 'Mango Says Goodbye Sometimes', the final *vignette* of the text, both escape from, and relocation into, the space of the community become simultaneously possible for the narrator through the means of writing: 'I put it down on paper and then the ghost does not ache so much' (Cisneros, 1992, p. 110). Like Anzaldúa, Esperanza expresses the pain, conflict and contingency that accompanies any effort at synthesis and integration. As the narrator reveals, her attempt to escape through writing is not always successful: 'I write it down and Mango says goodbye *sometimes*' (Cisneros, 1992, p. 110, my emphasis). In the same *vignette*, Esperanza reiterates her desire to leave her community only to return '[f]or the ones I left behind. For the ones who cannot out', and this promise is fulfilled at least on the level of the text since Esperanza circles back to the first words of the book: to 'what I remember most [. . .]

Mango Street, sad red house, the house I belong but do not belong to' (Cisneros, 1992, p. 110).

Esperanza's return through writing seems then to be triggered by a desire to speak for her community. Yet, as the narrator admits without remorse at the opening of this concluding *vignette*, she also 'returns' because she likes to tell stories. As Geoffrey Sanborn explains, 'Nowhere does Esperanza renounce her private enjoyment; nowhere does Cisneros suggest that she should' (2001, p. 1335). As I have suggested, individualistic and communitarian ideals not only coexist in Cisneros's text without the one erasing the other, but also cross and overlap; and it is by means of the fluid technique of the *vignette* that these imaginary acts of crossing and bridging are performed.

Like her narrator who does not wish to inherit the ready-made house of her *barrio*, Cisneros renovates 'the rented cultural space' of the *Bildungsroman* (Gutiérrez-Jones, 1993, p. 310). The fictional 'house' she builds with her Chicana and feminist architecture, in other words the textual container of these *vignettes*, accommodates within its fluid walls a multiplicity of worlds simultaneously. Nevertheless, one might ask, is this good enough for a politically self-conscious ethnic American woman writer? The *Bildungsroman* with its 'contradictory, hybrid and compromising nature' (Moretti, 2000, p. 12) does not appear to be the most suitable terrain for radical politics. Yet, just as these features are 'intrinsic to that way of [everyday] existence' refined by the traditional novel of development (Moretti, 2000, p. 12), I have shown that they are also appropriate for another mode of existence, notably what can be described as a 'constant process of revision, mediation, negotiation, and transformation dictated by life on the border' (Mermann-Jozwiak, 2000, p. 113).

In *The House on Mango Street*, Cisneros appropriates the *Bildungsroman*'s age-old function as a cultural mediator, and carves a space which becomes the meeting ground of several of the dichotomies that define ethnic female identity: the discourses of individualism and solidarity, the realms of the private and the public, and the categories of gender and ethnicity. Contesting the boundaries of the above pairs through the articulation of borderlands exposes the injustice of 'moral dilemmas', which request the curtailment of personal freedom or the sacrifice of certain allegiances in order to do service to others. Challenging the fact that the diverse loyalties of ethnic subjects are mutually exclusive is a political act that serves to multiply the sites of identification and allow people who grow up in the interstices of varying territories to claim a more inclusive and potentially empowering subject position. The outcome of this encounter in the borderlands, as exemplified in Cisneros's text (and as can be investigated in other ethnic texts), invites a comparison with a series of syncretic terms, which are constantly coined and used in critical discourse. The phrases below further reveal the increasing interest in, various applications, and political impact of in-between and third spaces. Terms among which 'interested disinterestedness' (Wong, 1993, p. 13) and 'the politics of private enjoyment' (Sanborn, 2001, p. 1334) provide a serious response, analogous to the teasing 'Yes please!', which unsettles oppositions, and deconstructs boundaries between 'Extravagance' and 'Necessity', 'individuality' and 'normality', pleasure and purpose (see n2). Thus, this blurring of boundaries also offers new dialogic models of reading literary texts, which challenge totalizing interpretive paradigms. It is for its overall contribution to the articulation of such productive border zones and bridges that *The House on Mango Street* claims a place among other 'border' novels, on the way towards 'a consciousness of the Borderlands'.

Notes

1. For the ways in which the *Bildungsroman* reflects Enlightenment ideals of a harmonious form of cultivation aimed at developing the whole person, see Martini, 1991, pp. 1-25.

2. See Howe (1930) and Buckley (1974) for an account of the narrative trajectory in the English *Bildungsroman*.

Critical Insights

3. Geoffrey Sanborn relates such responses to the tension between 'privacy and affiliation' in American literature and discusses writing as a form of private pleasure (2001, p. 1346, n1). Wong (1993) describes a similar tension between 'Necessity' and 'Extravagance' in Asian American Literature through an investigation, among other things, of writing as 'play'. Elisabeth Mermann-Jozwiak makes the distinction between postmodernism as 'an aesthetic and ahistorical practice' and 'a multicultural, political version of postmodernism' in Chicano literature (2000, p. 113). In this paper, I briefly touch upon issues of political engagement and upon the ways in which they mediate ideas of playful writing, but I have further explored the latter's relation to notions of borderlands and to the *Bildungsroman* in a more extensive chapter of my thesis, which looks at *The House on Mango Street*.

4. In Chicana fiction in particular, a second wave of women writers in the 1980s, which includes among others Sandra Cisneros, turned to oppression from within the ethnic community as opposed to merely from outside (mainstream America), thus seeking to add gender-identified perspectives to the larger Chicano cause against the racial and material conditions of oppression (Lomelí, 2002).

5. Alternative terms to Anzaldúa's 'borderlands' are Mary Louise Pratt's 'contact zones' (1992, p. 6) and Alfred Arteaga's 'border zone' (Benito and Manzanas, 2002, pp. 2-4).

6. Ana Castillo's *The Mixquiahuala Letters* (1986) is an example of a Chicana text that uses the actual Mexican-American border and the trope of border crossing (in a literal sense) in order to dramatise the protagonist's search for home. For border crossing in the sense of border writing, see Arteaga (1997). In her later work, Cisneros intersperses English with Spanish more extensively (for instance in *Woman Hollering Creek and Other Stories*, 1991). A Chicano novel of development with which *The House on Mango Street* shares a structural affinity (the use of the *vignette*) is Tomás Rivera's *. . . y no se lo tragó la tierra/. . . and the earth did not part* (1971).

Works Cited

Anzaldúa, G., 1999. *Borderlands/La Frontera: The New Mestiza*, 2nd edn. San Francisco: Aunt Lute.

Anzaldúa, G. and A. Keating (eds), 2002. *This Bridge We Call Home: Radical Visions for Transformation*. New York: Routledge.

Arteaga, A., 1997. *Chicano Poetics: Heterotexts and Hybridities*. Cambridge: Cambridge University Press.

Benito, J. and A. M. Manzanas (eds), 2002. *Literature and Ethnicity in the Cultural Borderlands*, Rodopi Perspectives on Modern Literature, 28. Amsterdam: Rodopi.

Bhabha, H., 1990. 'The Third Space', in J. Rutherford (ed.), *Identity, Community, Culture and Difference*. London: Lawrence and Wishart, pp. 207-221.

Bhabha, H., 1994. *The Location of Culture*. London: Routledge.

Bronfen, E., 1999. *Dorothy Richardson's Art of Memory: Space, Identity, Text*, trans. by V. Appelbe, Manchester: Manchester University Press.

Buckley, J. M., 1974. *Season of Youth: The Bildungsroman from Dickens to Golding*. Cambridge: Harvard University Press.

Castillo, A., 1992. *The Mixquiahuala Letters*. New York: Anchor Books.

Cisneros, S., 1987 (Spring). 'Do You Know Me? I Wrote *The House on Mango Street*', *The Americas Review*, 15(1), pp. 77-79.

Cisneros, S., 1991. *Woman Hollering Creek and Other Stories*. New York: Random House.

Cisneros, S., 1992. *The House on Mango Street*. London: Bloomsbury.

Fraiman, S., 1993. *Unbecoming Women: British Women Writers and the Novel of Development*. New York: Columbia University Press.

Gutiérrez-Jones, L. S., 1993. 'Different Voices: The Re-*Bildung* of the Barrio in Sandra Cisneros's *The House on Mango Street*', in C. J. Singley and S. E. Sweeney (eds), *Anxious Power: Reading, Writing, and Ambivalence in Narrative by Women*. Albany: State University of New York Press, pp. 295-312.

Howe, S., 1930. *Wilhelm Meister and His English Kinsmen: Apprentices to Life*. New York: Columbia University Press.

Lomelí, F. A., 2002. 'An Interpretive Assessment of Chicano Literature and Criticism', in J. Benito and A. M. Manzanas (eds), *Literature and Ethnicity in the Cultural Borderlands*, Rodopi Perspectives on Modern Literature, 28. Amsterdam: Rodopi, pp. 63-79.

Martini, F., 1991. '*Bildungsroman*—Term and Theory', in J. Hardin (ed), *Reflection and Action: Essays on the Bildungsroman*. Columbia: University of South Carolina Press, pp. 1-25.

Mermann-Jozwiak, E., 2000 (Summer). '*Gritos desde la Frontera*: Ana Castillo, Sandra Cisneros, and Postmodernism', *MELUS*, 25(2), pp. 101-118.

Morales, A., 1993. 'The Deterritorialization of Esperanza Cordero: A Paraesthetic Inquiry', in R. V. Bardeleben (ed), *Gender, Self, and Society: Proceedings of the IV International Conference on the Hispanic Cultures of the United States*. Frankfurt am Main: Lang, pp. 227-235.

Moretti, F., 2000. *The Way of the World: The Bildungsroman in European Culture*, trans. by A. Sbragia, new edn. London: Verso.

Pratt, M. L., 1992. *Imperial Eyes: Travel Writing and Transculturation*. London: Routledge.

Quintana, A. E., 1996. *Home Girls: Chicana Literary Voices*. Philadelphia: Temple University Press.

Rivera, T., 1971. *. . . y no se lo tragó la tierra/. . . and the earth did not part*. Berkeley: Quinto Sol.

Rosowski, S. J., 1983. 'The Novel of Awakening', in E. Abel, M. Hirsch and E. Langland (eds), *The Voyage In: Fictions of Female Development*. Hanover: University Press of New England, pp. 49-68.

Sage, L., 1992. *Women in the House of Fiction: Post-War Women Novelists*. London: Macmillan.

Sanborn, G., 2001. 'Keeping Her Distance: Cisneros, Dickinson, and the Politics of Private Enjoyment', *PMLA*, 116(5), pp. 1334-1348.

Sánchez, R., 1977. 'Discourses of Gender, Ethnicity and Class in Chicano Literature', in R. R. Warhol and D. Price Herndl (eds), *Feminisms: An Anthology of Literary Theory and Criticism*. Houndmills: Macmillan, pp. 1009-1022.

Turner, V., 1967. *The Forest of Symbols: Aspects of Ndembu Ritual*. Ithaca: Cornell University Press.

Valdés, M. E. de, 1993. 'The Critical Reception of Sandra Cisneros's *The House on Mango Street*', in R. V. Bardeleben (ed), *Gender, Self, and Society: Proceedings of the IV International Conference on the Hispanic Cultures of the United States*. Frankfurt am Main: Lang, pp. 287-300.

Wong, S. C., 1992. 'Autobiography as Guided Chinatown Tour? Maxine Hong Kingston's *The Woman Warrior* and the Chinese American Autobiographical Controversy', in J. R. Payne (ed), *Multicultural Autobiography: American Lives*. Knoxville: University of Tennessee Press, pp. 248-279.

Wong, S. C., 1993. *Reading Asian American Literature: From Necessity to Extravagance*. Chichester: Princeton University Press.

Woolf, V., 1929. *A Room of One's Own*. London: Hogarth Press.

Zizek, S., 2000. 'Class Struggle or Postmodernism? Yes, please!', in J. Butler, E. Laclau and S. Zizek, *Contingency, Hegemony, Universality: Contemporary Dialogues on the Left*. London: Verso, pp. 90-135.

Crossing the Borders of Genre:
Revisions of the *Bildungsroman* in
Sandra Cisneros's *The House on Mango Street*
and Jamaica Kincaid's *Annie John*_____

Maria Karafilis

The classical *Bildungsroman* refers to a specific type of novel written in a specific nation at a specific point in time (Germany in the late 18th century). It is a novel that relates the development of a (male) protagonist who matures through a process of acculturation and ultimately attains harmony with his surrounding society. Many contemporary writers and critics proclaim that the genre is dead and that the goals of such a text are naive and, in fact, impossible to achieve in postmodern societies that deny the existence of a unified self and instead affirm "an era of alienation from the society whose values in former times might have confirmed selfhood" (Braendlin 75). The frequency with which we still hear of the term *Bildungsroman*, however, and hear of such entities as the female *Bildungsroman*, the Caribbean *Bildungsroman*, and even the postmodern *Bildungsroman*, suggests that the genre is not quite dead—and that it can be lifted out of its initial context and applied productively across different historical periods, cultures, and classes.

Discussion of this particular genre continues because what we really mean, as critics, when we refuse to abandon the *Bildungsroman*, is that we are interested in how texts negotiate the development/education of their protagonists and how these protagonists negotiate themselves in a larger social context, whether it be within the dominant Anglo-American culture, a local community, ethnic group, nation, or combination of the above. As Linda Hutcheon notes, "The current poststructuralist-postmodern challenges to the coherent, autonomous subject have to be put on hold in feminist and postcolonial discourses, for both must work first to assert and affirm a denied or alienated subjectivity: those radical postmodern challenges are in many ways the luxury of the dominant order which can afford to challenge that which it securely possesses" (qtd. in Mishra and Hodge 405). The need to defer the denial of an autonomous subjectivity also applies to ethnic American literature for exactly the same reasons. Many women writers of color, both ethnic American and postcolonial, use the *Bildungsroman* precisely to "affirm and assert" the complex subjectivities of their characters and, by extension, themselves. Such writers have adopted and radically revised the classical *Bildungsroman* to suit their purposes of narrating the development of a personal identity and sense of self, and they have proven that doing so is not necessarily an impossible task even in fragmented and alienated contemporary societies.

I am particularly interested in examining this genre as part of interrogating two texts that narrate revised, nontraditional achievements of *Bildung*: that of a young Chicana growing up in a Chicago inner-city neighborhood in Sandra Cisneros's *The House on Mango Street*, and that of a young Antiguan girl growing up against the backdrop of British colonialism in Jamaica Kincaid's *Annie John*.

Transvaluating the genre across history, class lines, gender, and ethnicity, however, is a complex process, and obviously no homogeneous manner of doing so exists. But there are some fundamental questions we can ask of these texts: How do the protagonists of the modified *Bildungsroman* negotiate the different societies in which they find themselves? What constitutes "maturation" for these protagonists? What is the endpoint of their development? And also, (how) can such a character ultimately be successful?

By appropriating and modifying this traditional genre, Cisneros and Kincaid not only speak to the options, futures, and responsibilities of their young narrators, but they also comment on dominant Euro-American society by revising or even rejecting some of its values and certain aspects of its literary traditions. Thus, in a sense, Cisneros and Kincaid "colonize" this literary form and reverse traditional lines of power by controlling representation instead of passively being represented by the dominant culture. The two authors, however, do not stage an all-out war; conquest is not their objective. Rather, the ultimate goal is the realization of what Edouard Glissant terms "diversity" in national literatures and Françoise Lionnet, using Glissant's theories, discusses as "*métissage*." As Glissant explains, "a pattern of fragmented diversity . . . which is neither chaos nor sterility, means the human spirit's striving for a cross-cultural relationship, without universalist transcendence. Diversity needs the presence of peoples, no longer as objects to be swallowed up, but with the intention of creating a new relationship. Sameness requires fixed being, Diversity establishes becoming" (97-98).

We can see, through his emphasis on *becoming*, that it is quite natural to unite Glissant's notion of diversity and the genre of the *Bildungsroman*, which, more than any other genre, narrates the process of *becoming*. The traditional emphasis in the European or American *Bildungsroman* on "Sameness," "fixed being," "the fascination with the individual," and "sublimated difference" (Glissant 98) seems to suggest an incongruity or mutual exclusivity between the genre of the *Bildungsroman* and this notion of diversity. Closer examination, however, reveals that any incongruities are artificial and that a tie between these two entities (the *Bildungsroman* and Glissant's theories) is actually a very appropriate connection to make—one that is particularly fleshed out in the two novels examined here. When we apply the notion of diversity to the classical definition of the genre, we see that a dynamic, historicized conception of *Bildung* is not naive nor obsolete but actually stands up quite well.[1] As critics, we simply need to recognize that many contemporary women writers of color, such as Sandra Cisneros and Jamaica Kincaid, have shifted focus and posited that the value system to be adopted by the protagonist is not the dominant Anglo or Anglo-American society but something quite different. Bonnie Hoover Braendlin, in her article "*Bildung* in Ethnic Women Writers," maintains that the value system to be adopted is now "defined by the outsiders themselves or by their own cultures" (75).

More specifically, in *The House on Mango Street* and *Annie John*, the societies which the "outsiders" construct is one shaped by the process of *métissage*, "the simultaneous revalorization of oral traditions and reevaluation of Western concepts . . . the site of undecidability and indeterminacy" (Lionnet 4, 6). In these texts, the protagonist's ability to achieve *métissage*—in *The House on Mango Street* to reconcile her Anglo-American and Mexican cultures and, in *Annie John*, to reconcile her Anglo and Antiguan cultures—is the condition for her success and, I suggest, the condition for success in other twentieth-century *Bildungsromane* by women of color.

It is especially fruitful to pair these two particular narratives because, while they both ultimately suggest the possibility of achieving a coherent, autonomous subjectivity through the revised *Bildungsroman*, they do so in quite different ways and with one important divergence. While appropriating and revising many elements of the classical *Bildungsroman*, *The House on Mango Street* ultimately traces the satisfying development of a young woman who not only matures but also attains harmony and a greater appreciation and understanding of her surrounding society: the Chicano community represented by Mango Street. *Annie John*, however, in its revision of the genre, does not end so affirmatively.

Annie John may indeed be read as an anti-*Bildungsroman*. The novel opens with images of death instead of birth and closes with an image of evacuation and loss instead of the expected fulfillment, harmony, and absorption into a larger social body. At first glance, therefore, this novel may not seem to fit the pattern I have outlined here. I maintain, however, that *The House on Mango Street* and *Annie John* ultimately end up at the same point, even if they take different roads to get there. As we will see in the subsequent discussion of the novels, it is precisely the title character's inability in *Annie John* to recognize the importance of *métissage* and then to practice it that stunts her development and prevents her eventual achievement of *Bildung*. *Annie John*, therefore, serves as a negative example. It suggests what may happen when *métissage* is not practiced and illuminates some of the tempting, but ultimately self-destructive, means of attempting to achieve *Bildung* for young women of color.

Starting with *The House on Mango Street*, I would now like to examine several specific ways in which Cisneros and Kincaid appropriate and revise the traditional European *Bildungsroman* in order to suggest the importance of *métissage*. Three of the primary revisions Cisneros makes are her emphasis on the communal instead of the individual, her emphasis on fragmented and circular narrative patterns instead of linear movement, and her critique of American materialism and manipulation of the stereotypical "American Dream" to include those usually excluded—the poor and/or nonwhite.

One of the most explicit ways Cisneros reconciles dominant American culture and traditional Mexican culture is through her focus on the community. Several critics have examined how Cisneros supplants a focus on the "private," individual development of the protagonist by emphasizing the critical role the surrounding Chicano community plays in Esperanza's maturation. Ellen McCracken describes this shift as the rooting of Esperanza's "individual self in the broader sociopolitical reality of the Chicano community" (63).[2] Instead of striking out by herself, leaving the provinces for the city, as protagonists in traditional *Bildungsromane* do, Esperanza learns of herself and her culture in great part through her connections with other people. In many ways, the Chicano community in her Chicago barrio serves as an extended family, and Esperanza learns about herself and her complex position as a working-class Chicana in the urban United States through the stories of her neighbors. Many chapters in the novel narrate incidents in the lives of others and constitute some of the "experiences" that shape Esperanza and her maturation. Scanning the chapter titles (over half of which refer to other characters) shows this emphasis on other members of the community. We see this practice of learning from others in a chapter Cisneros places early on in the next, "My Name." From the title, it seems that the chapter will focus on Esperanza, but it does so only indirectly. What we really get in this chapter is the story of

Esperanza's great-grandmother, her namesake, a woman who was "a wild horse of a woman, so wild she wouldn't marry. Until my great-grandfather threw a sack over her head and carried her off. Just like that" (11). The experience of her great-grandmother, who "looked out the window her whole life, the way so many women sit their sadness on an elbow" (11), seems to be common for Chicanas, as we see this image of women imprisoned within the domestic sphere by husbands or fathers, confined within the frame of a window, reiterated throughout the novel. Esperanza, however, learns from these experiences, learns from the lives of her fellow Chicanas, and is able to avoid this fate in her own maturation.

The importance of community for Esperanza—of finding out where one belongs and making a space for oneself; realizing that she does indeed belong on Mango Street and to her Chicano community after all—is crucial. Cisneros demonstrates this through the image of the "four skinny trees" Esperanza looks at outside her window whenever she is "too sad and too skinny to keep keeping, when I am a tiny thing against so many bricks" (75). Cisneros directly connects these trees to Esperanza, and their physical form resembles the narrator's pre-pubescent, adolescent body: "They are the only ones who understand me. I am the only one who understands them. Four skinny trees with skinny necks and pointy elbows like mine. Four who do not belong here but are here" (74). These trees with which Esperanza identifies extol strength through interdependence and the importance of community and (human) contact. Their will is "violent" and their "ferocious" roots (ties to the land, the community) are the key to their survival: "Let one forget his reason for being, they'd all droop like tulips in a glass" (75). The presence of four trees precludes reading the image as anything other than a representation of community and its importance for ethnic Americans. Three trees could be read as signifying the Holy Trinity, two trees as representing the importance of the heterosexual marriage bond (which Cisneros repeatedly exposes as destructive to women), and one tree, of course, as symbolizing the power of the lone, self-

sufficient individual. Cisneros undermines all of these traditional sup-
ports (religion, marriage, and bourgeois independence) and leaves the
reader with a clear image of the strength and necessity of interdependence. Thus, although the text narrates the ultimate development of
one primary character, it counterbalances this liberation of the protagonist by continually reinforcing the need for community and demonstrating that it is through the recognition and appreciation of Chicano
culture and community that this human development is possible.

Sandra Cisneros also yokes the repressed and dominant traditions
through the formal elements of the text. Cisneros uses realism (she
does not write in the style of the *real maravilloso* often seen in Latino
writing of resistance); but, instead of using a straight, linear narration
to chart the chronological coming-of-age of the protagonist, she writes
her *Bildungsroman* in a fragmented, episodic form. We learn of Esperanza (and of life in the Chicano barrio) through snippets, anecdotes,
and often naively stated observations, which give the text a high degree
of orality, connecting it with the repressed oral, pre-Colombian traditions of Mexico. Thus Cisneros forces the reader to do what Esperanza
must do—to make sense of these disjointed parts and fragments and
construct them into a life, an experience, a narrative. Such construction, Esperanza tells the reader, is an action she performs constantly: "I
like to tell stories. I tell them inside my head . . . I make a story for my
life, for each step my brown shoe takes" (109).

The fragmented form of the text is especially powerful when Cisneros relates the story of Geraldo, a young man who appears at a dance
and later is killed in a hit-and-run accident. Geraldo is not mentioned in
any of the subsequent vignettes; after a few pages we never hear of him
again, just as his family "in another country" will never hear of him
again (66). The episodic narration of Cisneros's reevaluated *Bildungsroman* not only challenges the traditional, linear writing that valorizes
one particular line of progress and stifles the alternative voices and experiences that abound in Cisneros's text, but it also underscores the
transient, "insignificant" nature of the immigrant experience in domi-

nant American culture. Geraldo's tale is simply one migrant's experience in a vast, anonymous history of many.

We also see Cisneros's nonlinear writing style in the circular pattern of the text. Whereas the traditional *Bildungsroman* begins with the birth of the protagonist and proceeds chronologically until the point of maturation and assimilation into a larger society, Cisneros's novel ends virtually (but significantly not quite) where it began.[3] The first line of the text is,

> We didn't always live on Mango Street. Before that we lived on Loomis on the third floor, and before that we lived on Keeler. Before Keeler it was Paulina, and before that I can't remember. But what I remember most is moving a lot, (3)

while the closing chapter of the text reads,

> We didn't always live on Mango Street. Before that we lived on Loomis on the third floor, and before that we lived on Keeler. Before Keeler it was Paulina, but what I remember most is Mango Street, sad red house, the house I belong but do not belong to. (110)

Connecting Esperanza's pattern of repeated movement with the circular form of the text calls on the traditional trope of journeying seen in every classical *Bildungsroman* but transforms it by integrating it with the cyclical pattern found in traditional Mexican storytelling and indigenous myth. Even after the numerous displacements, Esperanza ultimately remembers Mango Street, the place where she began. Esperanza's journeying, both physical and psychological, does not cut a straight, linear path. In fact, Cisneros demonstrates that Esperanza's initial belief that she can "walk away" from her culture and her community is an illusion; she may leave temporarily (and Esperanza's friend Alicia doubts even this possibility [107]), but she must return. Her development/maturation, like her text, eventually will leave Esperanza squarely where she began: on Mango Street. This revision of the American idealization of mobility is important because instead of signifying the freedom to journey and conjuring the image of forward-moving progress, Cisneros reinforces the importance of community and returning to the neighborhood that helped to shape her as a Chicana growing up in American society.

In fact, it is a set of figures who also occupy the space between dominant American culture and traditional Mexican culture that impresses upon Esperanza the very necessity of this return to Mango Street: the three aunts, "*las comadres*" (103), who appear near the close of the work. María Elena de Valdés notes that these three "aunts," "who did not seem to be related to anything but the moon" (Cisneros 103), represent the lunar goddesses of pre-Hispanic Mexico (Tlazolteotl and Xochiquetzla), the intermediaries for all women (de Valdés 65). They also, however, resemble the fates or witches which have been a part of "Western literature from the most elevated lyric to the popular tale of marriage, birth, and the fate awaiting the hero or heroine" (de Valdés 65). It is these figures, hybrids of US and Latino literary and mythic cultures, who offer Esperanza the most important advice and guidance she receives. These women give her strategies for survival as well as knowledge of herself, and they remind her not to forget about the rest of the women in her community. The appearance of *las comadres* also signals a shift away from traditional paternal/maternal sources of guidance to a communal one. When the old women ask Esperanza to make a wish, they know she has wished to leave Mango Street. They tell her,

When you leave you must remember always to come back. . . . When you leave you must remember to come back for the others. A circle, understand? You will always be Esperanza. You will always be Mango Street. You can't erase what you know. You can't forget who you are. You must remember to come back. For the ones who cannot leave as easily as you. . . . I felt ashamed for having made such a selfish wish. (105)

The three aunts repeatedly utter Esperanza's name, calling it beautiful, "a good, good name" (104). The narrator, however, tells us at the beginning of the novel that her name is ambivalent, signifying hope in English and longing or lack in Spanish. We realize that these are precisely the two elements that Esperanza must integrate in her development: the hope and ability to break out of the cycle of poverty and oppression Chicanas often experience from both dominant American society and patriarchal Chicano society, and the memory/longing of the other women "who cannot leave as easily." Thus, when one considers only the English or only the Spanish translation of Esperanza's name, only half of the protagonist's identity is revealed. It is when the two definitions are amalgamated, incorporating both the English and Spanish meanings, that the complete, complex process of development for the protagonist becomes clear.

The third and final example of *métissage* in *The House on Mango Street* that I will examine here involves the most powerful and significant image in the text: that of the house itself. Cisneros calls on and subverts the stereotypical notion of the "American Dream": owning one's own home. She works with the idea of the traditional bourgeois home, which symbolizes individualism, isolationism, a space for exclusion, and the consolidation of the patriarchal, nuclear family, turning it into something completely different. Esperanza's alternative home, which "would be white with trees around it, a great big yard and grass growing *without a fence*" (4, my emphasis) is markedly not exclusive, allows for free access, and has room in its yard for all, which calls on the collectivity of traditional Mexican households. Later, Esperanza explicitly undermines the middle-class notion of the private home as exclusive sanctuary when she writes that she will open up her attic to passing bums, because "I won't forget who I am or where I came from . . . I know how it is to be without a house" (87). Although part of her initial desire to have a house of her own is to avoid the humiliation of pointing out to the nuns at school the run-down tenement in which she lives, by the end of the text Esperanza's motivation is something widely different and bears no relation to stereotypical American middle-class consumerism. Instead, her home will be an alternative to the male-dominated households in both American and Chicano societies. As opposed to the great number of women imprisoned in their own homes whom we see in the text, Esperanza will have the power in her abode:

> Not a flat. Not an apartment in back. Not a man's house. Not a daddy's. A house all my own. With my porch and my pillow, my pretty purple petunias. My books and my stories. My two shoes waiting by the bed. Nobody to shake a stick at. Nobody's garbage to pick up after.
>
> Only a house quiet as snow, a space for myself to go, clean as paper before the poem. (108)

Some critics have read passages such as this one, which narrate Esperanza's longing for a space for "My books and my stories. My two shoes waiting by the bed," as a desire for a house or "privatized" space that replicates the dominant culture's materialism and emphasis on bourgeois individualism.[4] I find such a reading fallacious given the profound critique of such acquisitiveness throughout the text and Cisneros's pointed revision of the "American Dream" and its materialist foundation. Rather, such passages support Doyle's reading that "Esperanza's dream of a house of her own . . . is *both solitary and communal*, a refuge for herself and others" (22, my emphasis).

Also, as the above-quoted passage from the novel suggests, an important aspect of Esperanza's development is her realization that the house she seeks is not the physical, concrete structure she desires at the beginning of the text, but a symbolic space, a metaphor for a cultural/ethnic space in which she can find fulfillment and pursue the writing that her dying aunt rightly notes, "will keep you free" (61).[5] Just as Elenita the palm reader tells her, Esperanza will have "a home in the heart" (64). The particular significance of the house "clean as paper before the poem" becomes very clear. This blank page, the act of writing, is the "space" Esperanza seeks and is a metaphoric house of her own creative imagination. And, just as the three aunts/fates tell her, even if she leaves, she must eventually return to Mango Street. When Esperanza leaves to inhabit the space of her own writing, she returns by producing the house on Mango Street, in the form of *The House on Mango Street*.

The opening up of this space, which is a potential for all women, not just Esperanza, and a space from which Esperanza will help others who "cannot leave as easily" is truly the focus of the text. Unlike most *Bildungsromane*, which focus on the development of one single protagonist and usually take the character's name as the title (like the prototypical *Bildungsroman*, Goethe's *Wilhelm Meister*), the title of this text is the house or space itself. The most significant part of Esperanza's development is the opening up of this space from which she can write and articulate her subjectivity as a Chicana growing up in inner-city Chicago.

And it is precisely Cisneros's emphasis on development in terms of "space" instead of development in terms of chronological, linear time that marks her most radical revision of the classical *Bildungsroman* and makes the modified genre so fitting to narrate the development of ethnic or postcolonial subjectivities—people who are often displaced, occupying a site between cultures, and who must strive to find a cultural space in which they can develop. Such a "space" for Chicanas, Cisneros suggests, is not in the dominant American culture nor in some type of an "authentic" traditional Mexican culture but rather a cross-cultural location of one's own creation. Perhaps Esperanza is at an advantage when dealing with the notion of *métissage*. As a Chicana, she truly represents two different cultures coming together in an egalitarian way to form a third—no hyphenation, no subordination is involved.

The crucial importance of *métissage* in achieving *Bildung* in some novels by women of color becomes especially clear when we examine our second text—Jamaica Kincaid's *Annie John*—and note the grave problems that result from a lack of such hybridization. For this reason,

Annie John serves as an illuminating countertext to *The House on Mango Street*. Although one must be careful when comparing ethnic writing and postcolonial texts, it can be done fruitfully if we consider that it is precisely the pernicious system of colonization in Antigua (the setting of *Annie John*), the usurpation of the island's actual physical geography (and the continued occupation of the space of Annie John's mind through the pervasive British influence) that hinders the protagonist's ability to achieve *Bildung* by denying her a metaphorical space (versus Esperanza's "house") in which to practice *métissage*.

As noted previously, in many ways *Annie John* reads as an anti-*Bildungsroman*. The protagonist, Annie John, describes a pre-adolescent Paradise and narrates her "fall" into womanhood and sexuality when she reaches puberty, a point at which her sweet illusions and close bond with her mother dissolve and she is left angry, jaded, and about to be indoctrinated into traditional female roles. Thus, for Annie John, growing up is not a fulfilling or satisfying realization of the ability to articulate her experience and a recognition of her place within a larger community, as it is for Esperanza, but instead involves betrayal, painful separation, and becoming "treacherous" (Kincaid 70).

For Annie John, all assumptions of power, even her own as she reaches adulthood, seem to be destructive. When Annie John matures, she becomes complicit with the colonizers by wielding her newfound power as a young woman arbitrarily and abusively:

> my mother and I both noticed that I now towered over her. . . . I acquired a strange accent . . . and some other tricks. . . . If someone behaved toward me in a way that didn't meet with my approval, without saying a word I would look at them directly with one eyebrow raised. I always got an apology. . . . If someone asked me a question, I would begin my answer with the words 'Actually' or 'As a matter of fact.' It had the effect of allowing no room for doubt. . . . My absence was felt, too. . . . Everything about me aroused envy and discontent, and that made me happy. (129)

Thus, whereas Cisneros continually displaces the narrative from Esperanza onto the community at large and suggests that the Chicano barrio is an important source of connection, knowledge, and support, in *Annie John* we have something quite different. Instead of seeking a point of contact with her community, Annie John constantly attempts to create distance and isolate herself. The community, therefore, is not a source of connection but a site of hierarchy and systems of mastery.

Gross power imbalances characterize every major relationship in which Annie John participates. The dynamics of the imbalance may shift, but the relation of dominance and submission is always extant, palpable, and painful. The best example of this is Annie John's friendship with the Red Girl. Annie John begins this relationship fancying herself the master/savior of the Red Girl but, as time progresses, she finds that a reversal has occurred. While the Red Girl may have once "followed me around worshipfully and took with great forbearance any and every abuse I heaped on her" (57), now,

> without saying a word, the Red Girl began to pinch me. She pinched hard, picking up pieces of my nonexistent flesh and twisting it around. At first I vowed not to cry, but it went on for so long the tears I could not control streamed down my face. . . . I stopped wondering why all the girls whom I had mistreated and abandoned followed me around with looks of love and adoration. (63)

By replicating in her interpersonal relationships the systems of mastery and patterns of dominance and submission that characterize the system of colonialism, and thereby foreclosing the establishment of any type of meaningful communal bonds, Annie John practices quite the opposite of Glissant's notion of diversity and precludes the possibility of utilizing the strength and support of the larger Antiguan community to foster her own maturation.

By the end of the text, Annie John ultimately is unable to channel her power as a mature, female West Indian woman living in colonial

Antigua in a productive or positive manner. Instead of reconciling the dominant and repressed cultures as Esperanza does in the space she forges for herself, Annie John practices erasure—first attempting to erase her British influences and then attempting to erase her West Indian influences. Of course, she ultimately fails at both.[6] It is precisely this inability to practice *métissage*, this insistence on constructing polarities and hierarchies instead of negotiating and reconciling multiple and often conflicting cultures and value systems, that prevents Annie John from developing some kind of coherent, autonomous subjectivity and instead leaves her horribly fragmented.

Let us first examine her attempts at erasure. In the second half of the text, during a protracted illness and delirium, Annie John suddenly gets the urge to "clean" some photographs on her nightstand. Each photograph contains some image that documents either British institutions and colonial rule or traditionally patriarchal gender roles:

> There was a picture of me in my white dress school uniform. There was a picture of me as a bridesmaid at my Aunt Mary's marriage to Monsieur Pacquet. There was a picture of my father wearing his white cricket uniform, holding a bat with one hand, the other wrapped tightly around my mother's waist. There was a picture of me in the white dress in which I had just been received into church and took Communion for the first time. (118)

After Annie John rouses from her delirium, she realizes that she erased her mother and father from the waist down in the wedding picture; erased practically everyone's faces except her own; and effaced all of herself in the confirmation picture, except for the risqué shoes she bought for the ceremony, over which she and her mother battled. It is clear that Annie John attempts to obliterate all images of British rule and has a severe anxiety about sexuality and her impending roles as a woman in patriarchal culture.[7] Of course, the desire to expunge patriarchal and colonial cultures, while it does signal a rebellious spirit, is naive and impossible. Rather, Annie John will have to negotiate such cultures and institutions.

After trying to erase things British and failing, Annie John then practices erasure of another kind and desires to leave her family, Antigua, and the West Indies to live in England. This erasure proves as ineffectual as her earlier attempt as Annie John now tries to reject her connection to West Indian culture, a tie Kincaid already has depicted as very strong through the protagonist's close relationship with her grandmother, Ma Chess, a famous obeah woman and the epitome of West Indian traditions in the text.

At the close of the novel, Annie John leaves for England to study nursing (the same type of medicine that failed to cure her during her long illness and resulted in the death of her uncle), which would force her to don a white uniform reminiscent of those she tried to erase in her "cleansing" of the photographs. The ending is also significant because, since nursing is a stereotypical occupation of the female other in Britain, it suggests how profoundly the legacy of colonialism continues to haunt the protagonist despite her desire to deny it. Annie John's insistence on erasure as a means of negotiating British and West Indian cultures causes her to become severely fragmented and feel a "hollow space inside" (144), a "hollow space" that sharply contrasts the fulfilling space of Esperanza's house.

Further, Annie John's fragmentation is not simply a postmodern fragmentation and denial of a transcendental, unified self, but a much more disturbing coming apart, a slow disintegration of oneself that results from the fact that she cannot accommodate the ambiguity and indeterminacy of being a West Indian woman in colonial Antigua. The closing image, therefore, is one of enervation, loss, and emptiness, as the protagonist leaves for the metropole, not to achieve hybridity but to repress her West Indian heritage:

> I felt I was being held down against my will. . . . I felt that someone was tearing me up into little pieces and soon I would be able to see all the little

pieces as they floated out into nothing in the deep blue sea. . . . I could hear
the waves lap-lapping around the ship. They made an unexpected sound, as
if a vessel filled with liquid had been placed on its side and now was slowly
emptying out. (144, 148)

These closing images of fragmentation and loss are of critical significance, for they challenge an interpretation of the end as a triumphant,
universalized assumption of identity read through Western/Freudian
psychoanalysis. Instead, their ambivalence prompts an examination of
the importance of the colonial backdrop of the novel, the importance of
the complex power relations and systems of authority implicit in the
colonial order, and the effects of such power relations on the protagonist as a colonized subject.[8] H. Adlai Murdoch, for example, while acknowledging the significance of the colonial relation in the text at the
beginning of his essay, does not consistently maintain this focus. This
leads him to assert that Annie John's "eventual departure from her
homeland is the outcome of her recognition of an existence which she
has outgrown and a step toward the establishment of a newer, more
valid one . . . a triumphal parade" (326, 339). Further, Murdoch reads
Annie John's delirious erasure of the photographs on her nightstand as
signifying Annie's "severing of familiar and familial ties to ensure the
survival of her new identity and independence, . . . her renouncing of
her old existence and her adoption of the new. . . . She now has succeeded in repudiating every aspect of her former life; both Antigua, the
locus of repression, and her mother, the cause of it, must be rejected in
order that this newly created self might flourish in fresh surroundings"
(338). I find such readings of Annie John's transformation problematic, not only because I am skeptical of the possibility of such a facile
substitution of an "old" identity with a "new," "valid" one, but because
the text itself questions Annie John's "successful" repudiation of her
past through the images of enervation and depletion. Further, this reading fails to explore the problematic nature of the fact that Annie John's
"fresh start" is to be at the metropole, the seat of colonial power, where

she will pursue a profession implicated in the traditional gender roles she has so ardently attempted to circumvent throughout the text. Thus, the closing chapter, "A Walk to the jetty," invites the reader to make important interconnections between Annie John's development from adolescent female to adult woman, her development as a colonized subject, and the familial and extrafamilial forces impacting this maturation.

While I would not say that hybridity is a panacea or the only effective way for ethnic or postcolonial women writers to work against dominant Euro-American systems that institutionalize racism and oppression, in some texts, particularly *The House on Mango Street*, it does offer the protagonist a means of achieving *Bildung* when the traditional means—(linear, chronological, monologic narration that ignores the importance of space for ethnic or postcolonial writers in order to valorize temporality)—would be inadequate. And, as we have seen in *Annie John*, the inability to coalesce the various fragments of one's identity can have disastrous consequences.

At this point, it is fruitful to return to the questions that initially spurred this study. After addressing the possibility and means of achieving *Bildung* for young women of color in the body of the essay, it becomes necessary to specify here, in somewhat more detail, the consequences of such development.

It is of crucial significance that we recognize that the endpoint of the maturation of characters like Esperanza and Annie John is not merely the creation of a cross-cultural space in and of itself, not merely the development of a coherent selfhood to rival the selfhood of members of the dominant culture. More importantly, it is the potential for personal and political agency that inheres in an autonomous subjectivity and is engendered by the opening of the hybridized space created through the practice of *métissage*.

Thus, to a great degree, it is Annie John's lack of *agency*, her seeming evacuation at the close of the text and the contrast between this state and her former vitality, shrewdness, and subversiveness, that make the last paragraphs of *Annie John* so poignant. In contrast, Esperanza's manipulation and negotiation of multiple cultures and ideologies offer her a remarkable agency. Esperanza uses the space opened by the process of *métissage* to mobilize herself and act as a friend, sister, defender, writer, and critic.

It is through such actions that Esperanza constitutes herself as a political agent capable of achieving and maintaining personal and political power and also demonstrates an effective means for others like her to claim a space for themselves in the world.

From *The Journal of the Midwest Modern Language Association* 31, no. 2 (Winter 1998): 63-78. Copyright © 1998 by the Midwest Modern Language Association. Reprinted with permission of the Midwest Modern Language Association.

Notes

1. James Hardin defines *Bildung* "first, as a developmental process and, second, as a collective name for the cultural and spiritual values of a specific people or social stratum in a given historical epoch and by extension the achievement of learning about that same body of knowledge and acceptance of the value system it implies" (Hardin xi).

2. In her essay, McCracken attributes a relative lack of critical and scholarly attention paid to precisely this shift in focus, which makes the text either unintelligible or unsavory to dominant ideology and institutions such as universities, publishing circles, etc. The great critical attention paid to Cisneros's work and its widespread inclusion in university course syllabi since the publication of McCracken's essay in 1989, however, attests, if not to the increased "intelligibility" of the text due to increased attention to the narrative and thematic strategies of ethnic women writers, at least to the increased receptivity of literary critics and teachers to alternatives to the bourgeois individualism permeating the literary canon and hopefully an increased self-consciousness of its existence.

3. See Jacqueline Doyle's essay, "More Room of Her Own: Sandra Cisneros's *The House on Mango Street*," for an insightful analysis of the text not as a modified *Bildungsroman*, but as a modified *Künstlerroman*, which narrates the particular development of the artist. Doyle reads the development of Esperanza as an artist as particularly significant because it is as a writer that Esperanza can "celebrate" all of the "unfulfilled talents and dreams" of the unrepresented and oppressed women in her community and "compensate for their losses" (10). This is related to the structure of the novel in that "the circular structure of the 20th-century woman's *Künstlerroman* [functions] as a way of writing 'beyond' the traditional endings available to women" (11) and thereby

offers Esperanza a means of manipulating literary traditions in order to inscribe herself into them.

4. See, for example, Pedro Gutiérrez-Revuelta, "Genéro y ideología en el libro de Sandra Cisneros: *The House on Mango Street*," and Juan Rodríguez, "*The House on Mango Street*, by Sandra Cisneros," quoted in Olivares.

5. See McCracken's essay for a reading of the motif of the house as a representation of the lack of adequate housing for many minorities under capitalism: "It is precisely the lack of housing stability that motivates the image's centrality . . . the desire for a house is not a sign of individualistic acquisitiveness but rather represents the satisfaction of a basic human need" (64). I find this analysis of the material basis of the symbol compelling and would like to add to it the metaphorical symbolism of the image which I discuss below.

6. This is not to suggest that all, or even most, postcolonial protagonists are unable to achieve *métissage* while all, or even most, ethnic American protagonists do so; this is simply the case in the two texts examined here. I do, though, posit that it often may be more difficult for the colonized subject to accomplish this due to the literal usurpation of physical space which problematizes and complicates the development of any kind of metaphorical space in which to reconcile various cultures.

7. It is important to note the conflation of colonial and sexual oppressions: it is in a picture of Annie John's father playing cricket, holding the suggestive prop of a bat, that he has a firm hold around the waist of her mother. Also, Annie John erases the representation of herself as a bridesmaid, a figure participating in the ceremony that cements a woman's assumption of traditional female roles, in the union of her aunt with a European. These representations suggest how such oppressions mutually reinforce each other and further argue for the need to analyze their corresponding systems (here, colonial and patriarchal rule) in concert instead of trying to maintain discrete categories and hierarchies.

8. Of course psychoanalytic and postcolonial readings need not be mutually exclusive, but sometimes not enough attention is paid to the effects of the colonial system on Annie John's development in psychoanalytic readings of the text, as will be seen in the example discussed below. For examples of essays that combine the two approaches very fruitfully see Donna Perry's "Initiation in Jamaica Kincaid's *Annie John*," in *Caribbean Women Writers: Essays from the First International Conference* and Moira Ferguson's reading of *Annie John* in her *Gender and Colonialism from Mary Wollstonecraft to Jamaica Kincaid*. Both essays offer nuanced readings of the novel that recognize that "familial tensions cannot be seen apart from the broader reality of racism" (Perry 252) and that Annie John is "continually negotiating contradictory positions from the center to the margins and back, sometimes occupying both spots simultaneously" (Ferguson 117).

Works Cited

Braendlin, Bonnie Hoover. "*Bildung* in Ethnic Women Writers." *Denver Quarterly* (17) 4 Winter 1984: 75-87.

Cisneros, Sandra. *The House on Mango Street*. New York: Vintage Books, 1989.

de Valdés, María Elena. "In Search of Identity in Cisneros's *The House on Mango Street*. "*Canadian Review of American Studies* (23) 1 Fall 1992: 55-72.

Doyle, Jacqueline. "More Room of Her Own: Sandra Cisneros's *The House on Mango Street*." *MELUS* (19) 4 Winter 1994: 5-35.

Ferguson, Moira. *Colonialism and Gender from Mary Wollstonecraft to Jamaica Kincaid*. New York: Columbia UP, 1993.

Glissant, Edouard. *Caribbean Discourse*. Trans. Michael Dash. Charlottesville: University of Virginia Press, 1989.

Hardin, James. *Reflection and Action*. Columbia: South Carolina UP, 1991.

Kincaid, Jamaica. *Annie John*. New York: Penguin Books, 1991.

Lionnet, Françoise. *Autobiographical Voices: Race, Gender, and Self-Portraiture*. Ithaca: Cornell University Press, 1989.

McCracken, Ellen. "Sandra Cisneros's *The House on Mango Street*: Community-Oriented Introspection and the Demystification of Patriarchal Violence." In *Breaking Boundaries: Latina Writing and Critical Readings*. Ed. Asunción Horno-Delgado et al. Amherst: Massachusetts UP, 1989. 62-71.

Mishra, Vijay, and Bob Hodge. "What is Post(-)Colonialism?" *Textual Practice* (5) 3, 1991: 399-414.

Murdoch, H. Adlai. "Severing the (M)other Connection: The Representation of Cultural Identity in Jamaica Kincaid's *Annie John*." *Callaloo* (13) 2 Spring 1990: 325-40.

Olivares, Julián. "Sandra Cisneros' *The House on Mango Street*, and the Poetics of Space." *Chicana Creativity and Criticism: Charting New Frontiers in American Literature*. Eds. María Herrera-Sobek and Helena María Viramontes. Houston: Arte Público Press, 1988: 160-70.

Perry, Donna. "Initiation in Jamaica Kincaid's *Annie John*." *Caribbean Women Writers: Essays from the First International Conference*. Ed. Selwyn R. Cudjoe. Wellesley: Calaloux Publications, 1990: 245-53.

The House on Mango Street:
A Space of Her Own

Annie O. Eysturoy

> By writing I put order in the world, give it a handle so I can grasp it. I write to record what others erase when I speak, to rewrite the stories others have miswritten about me, about you. To discover myself, to preserve myself, to make myself, to achieve self-autonomy.
>
> —Gloria Anzaldúa

The House on Mango Street (1985) by Sandra Cisneros is probably the best-known Chicana novel to date. The winner of the American Book Award in 1985, it has received more critical attention than any other Chicana novel. Set in a contemporary Latino neighborhood of a big American city, *The House on Mango Street* is composed of forty-four interrelated stories narrated by Esperanza, the female "I" and central consciousness of the novel.[1] In each story Esperanza narrates her own perception of her sociocultural context, that is, the barrio, its people, its conditions of life, and how she is inextricably connected to that context, an engagement with her immediate surroundings that brings about a gradual coming into consciousness about her own identity as a woman and as a Chicana. Sandra Cisneros gives voice to the ordinary experiences of a young Chicana by letting Esperanza tell her own coming-of-age story, thus articulating the subjective experiences of the female "I" who resists entrapment within sociocultural norms and expectations. The narrating "I" stands in a dialectic relationship to her sociocultural context, and it is through the very act of constructing and telling her own story that Esperanza resolves the contradictions that inform her life. Her *Bildungs* process is thus closely linked to her development as an artist in the process of discovering, synthesizing, and narrating her experiences within the community of Mango Street, a development that turns *The House on Mango Street* into what we may call "a portrait of the artist as a young woman," that is, a *Künst-*

lerroman. It is through the process of telling her stories that Esperanza discovers the power of her own creativity, that "language is a way of becoming" (Seator, 32), a way of imagining herself beyond the confinements of the status quo, a way of imagining a different ending to her own *Bildungs* story. Collectively these stories reveal a female *Bildungs* process that moves from rejection of prescribed roles to the recognition of creativity as a path toward a self-defined identity.

* * *

As the title indicates, both "the house" and "Mango Street" are central symbols throughout the novel. Mango Street and the house Esperanza lives in constitute her world, the world she has to come to grips with as she grows up. It is her response to this particular environment, the interplay between psychological and social forces, that determines the direction of her *Bildungs* process. It is through her dialectical relationship to the house—in other words, the private sphere, the family, the collective memory—as well as to Mango Street—that is, the social sphere, the larger Hispanic community—that the narrating "I" comes to an understanding of her own individual self. Esperanza's world on Mango Street is a world unto its own, an Hispanic barrio of a large American city, yet unspecified in respect to its exact geographical and historical setting, a symbolic "microcosm for the larger world" (Gonzales-Berry and Rebolledo, 114) that lends a universal quality to this Chicana *Bildungsroman*.

It is significant that the initial word in this Chicana quest novel is "We": "We didn't always live on Mango Street" (7). Esperanza recalls her family history of moving from one dilapidated house to another until they finally move into their own house on Mango Street, yet the house is not what the family had hoped for: "The house on Mango Street is ours. . . . But even so, it's not the house we'd thought we'd get" (7). Esperanza's sense of self is here firmly lodged within the collective identity of her family. It is, however, in this initial story, homonymous with the novel itself, that the narrating "I" becomes aware of her own subjective perceptions as she begins to differentiate between family dreams and social realities and becomes conscious of her parents' inability to fulfill their promises of the perfect house. "They always told us that one day we would move into a house, a real house" (7). The "real house" Esperanza expected would be "like the houses on TV":

> Our house would be white with trees around it, a great big yard and grass growing without a fence. This was the house Papa talked about when he held a lottery ticket and this was the house Mama dreamed up in the stories she told us before we went to bed.
>
> But the house on Mango Street is not the way she told it at all. (8)

The house is just the opposite of what she had been told would be their house one day, a fact that stands in direct opposition to the words of her parents. This contrast between expectation and reality awakens her awareness of herself as a social being and provokes her own interpretations of the significance the house holds in her life.

Esperanza sees the house on Mango Street as a symbol of poverty that she associates with the humiliation she has felt in the past, living in similar places:

> Where do you live? she said.
> There, I said, pointing up to the third floor.
> You live *there*?
> *There.* I had to look to where she pointed—the third, the paint peeling, wooden bars Papa had nailed on the windows so we wouldn't fall out.
> You live *there*? The way she said it made me feel like nothing. *There.* I lived *there*. I nodded. (8-9)

In another situation a teacher prejudicially assumes that Esperanza, because she is Chicana, lives in a building that "even the raggedy men are ashamed to go into" (43), thus automatically identifying her with the poverty and degradation the house represents. Made to feel ashamed of living in houses other people show obvious contempt for, thus ashamed of "her entire social and subject position" (Saldívar, 1990, 182), Esperanza sees the house as a symbol of the shame that threatens her own self-perception. To Esperanza the house on Mango Street is an emblem of the oppressive socioeconomic situation that circumscribes her life and is the source of her feelings of alienation. It is this alienation that becomes a catalyst for her desire to distance herself from this "sad red house" (101) she does not want to belong to.

This psychological rejection of the house on Mango Street is further underscored by her own description of the house as narrow and confining, where even the windows appear to be "holding their breath" (8), a description that shows an almost claustrophobic reaction to her parents' house. According to Cirlot, breathing is a process whereby one assimilates spiritual power. Esperanza's perception of the house as not breathing is indicative of the spiritual suffocation the house represents. This depiction of the house is, as Julián Olivares points out, "a metonymical description and presentation of the self" (162), a self that feels constrained as well as ashamed when identified with a house that represents only confinement and therefore knows that she needs another house, one that would liberate her from the oppression of her present situation:

I knew then I had to have a house. A real house. One I could point to. But this isn't it. The house on Mango Street isn't it. For the time being, Mama said. Temporary, said Papa. But I know how these things go. (9)

The last phrase, "But I know . . . ," indicates the emerging consciousness of the protagonist, that her passage from childhood innocence to knowledge has begun, a development that marks the beginning of her *Bildungs* process. Through her own interpretative agency she now knows that she cannot rely on what her parents tell her and that they will not be able to provide her with the house that she needs. Although at this point she imagines a "real house" to be something like the Dick and Jane reader's version of an American home, the importance of the house lies not so much in its physical features as in its symbolic value in a sociocultural context. Her desire for a house is, as Ellen McCracken points out, "not a sign of individualistic acquisitiveness" (64); she wants a house she can "point to," that is, one she can point to as hers without feeling "like nothing" (9), one that does not destroy her sense of self, clearly connecting the house with her own self-perception. By rejecting the house of her parents she rejects a structure that threatens her sense of self and takes the first step toward claiming her right to self-definition.

In this initial story, "The House on Mango Street," the image of the house serves a twofold symbolic function: it is a symbol of the socio-economic condition in which Esperanza finds herself and its alienating effect on her, and more importantly in the context of the novel, as a symbol of human consciousness. Her search for a new house, that is, her search for a viable self, becomes a leitmotif throughout the novel. It is significant that in the course of the story the initial "we," Esperanza's sense of herself being part of the collective identity of her family, gives way to the subjective "I" who begins to analyze her neighborhood on Mango Street.

Like the house, Mango Street is the physical and psychological marker of an oppressive socioeconomic situation that makes Espe-ranza conscious of her own status in a socioeconomic hierarchy: "The neighborhood is getting bad," she says, and this is why people have to move "a little farther away every time people like us keep moving in" (15). Much as with the house, a negative analogy is established be-tween Esperanza and her barrio; she lives there and therefore the neighborhood is "getting bad," the narrating "I" again being defined by her external, socioeconomic circumstances:

Those who don't know any better come into our neighborhood scared. They think we're dangerous. They think we will attack them with shiny knives. They are stupid people who are lost and got here by mistake. (29)

The implications of being defined by a poor, deteriorating neighborhood and prejudicial stereotypes make Esperanza conscious of the particular socioeconomic conditions that circumscribe her life and trap her in a marginalized world of "too much sadness and not enough sky" (33).

Despite the cumulative threat the house and Mango Street present to her sense of self, however, she begins to imagine herself beyond Mango Street, determined to "make the best of it" (33). Estranged by the social implications of living in this environment, Esperanza disavows her relationship to Mango Street—"I don't ever want to come from here" (99)—identifying herself with the only piece of nature present in the barrio, four trees "who do not belong here but are here":

> Their strength is secret. . . . When I am a tiny thing against so many bricks, then it is I look at trees. When there is nothing left to look at on this street. Four who grew despite concrete. Four who reach and do not forget to reach. (71)

This identification with a small piece of nature in this urban environment exemplifies the primacy of nature in female development, when the adolescent feels "a sense of oneness with cosmos" (Pratt, 1981, 17) as an alternative to her alienation from an oppressive environment. In her longing to escape her present circumstances, Esperanza sees the trees as role models for her own liberation: they grow "despite concrete," thus symbolizing Esperanza's own struggle to grow in a hostile environment, her desire to reach beyond the concrete, beyond class and race boundaries, for self-definition.

Esperanza's process of individuation is thus initiated by her resolution to escape the confinements of her socioeconomic condition represented by the house and by Mango Street, and she does this by seeking refuge in her own imagination:

I like to tell stories. I tell them inside my head. . . . I make a story for my life, for each step my brown shoe takes. I say, "And so she trudged up the wooden stairs, her sad brown shoes taking her to the house she never liked." I like to tell stories. I am going to tell you a story about a girl who didn't want to belong. (101)

It is through the process of making "a story for my life," that is, the imaginative re-creation of her own experiences and interactions with her environment, that the narrating "I" begins her search for meaning and a new way of being in the world. Through the act of participating, interpreting, and narrating her life, she gradually comes to an understanding of herself and her relationship to the community on Mango Street.

Esperanza makes a clear link between language and identity when she turns to the act of narrating her experiences on Mango Street from her own experiential perspective as a strategy to escape social oppression and the threat this oppression presents to her own budding sense of self. Naming her own experiences is a way of defining and validating these experiences as well as her own perspectives. It is, at the same time, an affirmation of her own being that is grounded in language, in a new naming of self and her sociocultural reality. In this process of constructing herself as a subject through language, she begins to analyze the significance of her name, Esperanza, as a marker of her own identity. Her attempt to decode the meaning of her name becomes an attempt to come to terms with her bicultural identity:

In English my name means hope. In Spanish it means . . . sadness, it means waiting. . . . It is the Mexican records my father plays on Sunday mornings when he is shaving, songs like sobbing. . . . At school they say my name funny as if the syllables were made out of tin and hurt the roof of your mouth. But in Spanish my name is made out of a softer something like silver. (12, 13)

To Esperanza her name embodies contradictory meanings—hope or sadness and waiting—much as the very pronunciation of her name changes with language and cultural context. Her name is thus a sign of a complex bicultural context that requires her to negotiate among opposing cultural meanings to come to terms with her own self.

This multiplicity of meanings that intersect in her name is further underscored by the female legacy the name Esperanza carries in the family. Named after her Mexican great-grandmother, Esperanza is linked through her name to her cultural past and to her identity as a woman within a particular sociocultural context. The grandmother, a recurring character in Chicana literature, often figures as the embodiment of Chicano cultural heritage: "For the most part *abuelitas* form a complex of female figures who are nurturing, comforting, and stable. They are linked symbolically and spatially to the house and home, and are often associated with an idealized cultural space" (Rebolledo, 1987, 150). In the story Esperanza has inherited about her great-grandmother, however, her *bisabuelita* does not inhabit such an idealized cultural space:

> My great-grandmother. I would've liked to have known her, a wild horse of a woman, so wild she wouldn't marry until my great-grandfather threw a sack over her head and carried her off. Just like that, as if she were a fancy chandelier. That's the way he did it. And the story goes she never forgave him. She looked out the window all her life, the way so many women sit their sadness on an elbow. (12)

This story of her namesake, of a strong and rebellious woman who nevertheless had to succumb to patriarchal coercion and control, makes Esperanza conscious of the position women in general hold within her own cultural framework, that the fact that "Mexicans don't like their women strong" (12) kept her great-grandmother from being "all the things she wanted to be" (12). Esperanza links her great-grandmother's fate, her confinement, her sadness and lost hope, with her own name, that is, her self, making her name tantamount to her culture's definitions of gender roles, definitions she can only reject: "Esperanza. I have inherited her name, but I don't want to inherit her place by the window" (12). She thus makes a clear distinction between the wild great-grandmother she would have liked to have known, her cultural foremother, and the sociocultural system that subdued her. By accepting her name, but refusing to accept a heritage of female confinement, Esperanza carries on a metonymic legacy of rebellion against patriarchal definitions of female selfhood.

In the process of analyzing the significance of the conflicting cultural connotations that intersect in her name—hope, sadness, rebellion, confinement—Esperanza becomes conscious of a complex, and, to her, confusing cultural framework that calls forth some ambivalence in respect to her own cultural heritage. This ambivalence is suggestive of a complicated relationship between ethnic heritage and female quest for a self-defined identity. If one's name is, as Mary Dearborn argues, "inextricable from identity" (93), then Esperanza's name carries some cultural implications that threaten her identity as a woman. She does not, as Renato Rosaldo points out, "stand in one place, looking straight ahead, and shout, 'Yo soy Esperanza'" (163), as that would mean, among other things, embracing patriarchal values and patriarchal definitions of herself. Rather, her ruminations on the cultural implications of her name lead her to wish for a new naming of herself. "I would like to baptize myself under a new name, a name more like the real me, the one nobody sees. . . . Something like Zeze the X will do" (13). Her choice of name, Zeze the X, indicates that what she wants is a name that carries no contradicting cultural connotations; it is, culturally speaking, a "hollow" name she would have to invest with meaning and identity, and unlike her name "Esperanza," it is not "culturally embedded in a dominating, male-centered ideology" (Olivares, 163). Much as she wants a new house, one she can point to, so she wants to give herself a new name that is more attuned to herself, "the one nobody sees." This desire is indicative of her refusal to be externally defined either by her house, by her socioeconomic circumstances, or by her name, that is, by traditional patriarchal values, in her quest for a self-defined identity.

In her exploration of the "real" Esperanza, the emerging female self "nobody sees" (13), the narrating "I" becomes increasingly aware of her own emerging sexuality. Her biological transformation marks a crucial point in Esperanza's self-development, as it is then that she begins to note not only her own sexual difference but also its implications for her as a woman.

The first notions of the changes her body is undergoing fill her with expectancy: "Everything is holding its breath inside me. Everything is waiting to explode like Christmas. I want to be all new and shiny" (71); she feels like "a new Buick with the keys in the ignition. Ready to take you where?" (47). This last question is crucial, indicating Esperanza's own awareness of the importance of sexuality in her own development and to her future self, as it is exactly through the control of female sexuality that women are socialized into accepting culturally prescribed roles of wives and mothers. The threat sexuality presents to the female self appears within the context of play when Esperanza and her friends, dressed in "magic high heels," are confronted with men who "can't take their eyes" off them and a "bum man" who says, "come closer. I can't see very well. Come closer. Please. . . . If I give you a dollar will you kiss me?" (39). This scene, with the shoes as symbols of female sexuality and the man's attempt to lure her closer, is a Chicana version of "Little Red Riding Hood," the fairy tale about "the curbing and regulation of sexual drives . . . that has always been used as a warning to children, particularly girls, a symbol and embodiment of what might happen if they are disobedient and careless. She epitomizes the good girl gone wrong" (Zipes, 1). Esperanza's confrontation with the "bum man" becomes an implicit demonstration of the danger sexuality, in a patriarchal context, presents to her own sense of self.

Through her interactions with Sally, Esperanza becomes increasingly aware that her friend already adheres to prescribed feminine behavior and has "her own game" (89), which, as it turns out, is not "her own game" but a male game into which she enters:

> One of the boys invented the rules. One of Tito's friends said you can't get the keys back unless you kiss us and Sally pretended to be mad at first but she said yes. It was that simple. . . . Something wanted to say no when I watched Sally going into the garden with Tito's buddies all grinning. . . . So what, she said. (89)

The socializing and conditioning effect of games is clearly evident in this episode where, pretending to be playing, the boys imitate patriarchal power by setting the rules of the game, and Sally, imitating what she thinks are female means of gaining male approval, passively acquiesces to sexual control. Whereas Esperanza intuits that "something wasn't right" (89), that the boys are violating Sally's natural right over her own body, Sally, having internalized male definitions of her sexuality, sees her own actions as a sign of being a grown-up woman.

In the role she has assumed as the streetwise, grown-up woman, Sally becomes Esperanza's guide to what to her are the secrets of womanhood—how to put on make-up, how to dress—with the implication that Sally also becomes the transmitter of cultural values in respect to how girls are supposed to relate to boys. The initial presentiment, however, that something is wrong in the way the adolescent boys interact with Sally is confirmed when Esperanza, left alone by Sally and her boyfriend in an amusement park, is confronted with male power and sexually attacked by a group of boys. To Esperanza the reality of this brutal sexual initiation stands in sharp contrast to what she has been told about sexual relationships: "Sally, you lied. It wasn't what you said at all. What he did. Where he touched me. I didn't want it, Sally. The way they said it, the way it's supposed to be, all the storybooks and movies, why did you lie to me?" (93).

This last question is central to Esperanza's sexual initiation, as it shows that she feels violated, not only physically by the boys, but also psychologically by a framework of omnipresent cultural myths that shroud the reality of patriarchal violence in idealistic romance. Her disillusionment with the reality of sexual encounters is thus aggravated by her bewilderment as to why "they"—Sally, other women, mass media—have lied to her and left her vulnerable to male sexual advances and domination. As Herrera-Sobek points out, Esperanza's diatribe is directed particularly against the community of women who participate in a "conspiracy of silence": "The protagonist discovers a conspiracy of two forms of silence: silence in not denouncing the 'real' facts of life about sex and its negative aspects in violent sexual encounters, and complicity in embroidering a fairy-tale-like mist around sex" (1988, 178). Thus Esperanza expresses her sense of alienation and betrayal:

> Why did you leave me all alone? I waited my whole life. You're a liar. They all lied. All the books and magazines, everything that told it wrong. Only his dirty fingernails against my skin, only his sour smell again. . . . He wouldn't let me go. He said, I love you, I love you, Spanish girl. (94)

Realizing that cultural stories do not tell the whole story, Esperanza condemns this cultural conspiracy around sexuality which—as the depreciatory epithet "Spanish girl" indicates—makes her particularly vulnerable. Esperanza's sexual initiation is thus an initiation into knowledge about herself as a sexual subject who has been manipulated by a framework of cultural myths. By telling her own version of her sexual initiation, however, Esperanza creates a text that stands in direct opposition to the cultural texts, the storybooks, magazines, and movies "that told it wrong," thus refusing to participate in the conspiracy of silence which co-opts women into partaking in their own oppression.

In her attempt to deconstruct sociocultural lies by telling the truth, Esperanza turns her narrative attention to the women on Mango Street. Realizing that their fate can be hers, she begins to examine their lives in order to come to an understanding of her own relationship to the sociocultural world of the barrio. Perceived from Esperanza's female perspective, this environment takes on distinct characteristics, in that she, in her evolving consciousness about herself as a woman, becomes increasingly aware of the contradictions between her emerging female self and the circumstances that inform women's lives on Mango Street. It is through a continuous tension between herself and her environment and through her interaction with the women in the barrio, that she becomes aware of the true nature of patriarchal ideology and her own position as a woman within her particular sociocultural context.

In her adolescent search for role models, Esperanza observes the lives of the women in the neighborhood in order to get some clues to her own future life as a woman. In narrating the stories about these women, Esperanza constructs an image of the women around her that is predominantly one of entrapment and constraint. Women are behind windows, entrapped in their own houses, entrapped in the circumstances that determine their lives as women in a poor Latino barrio. There is Mamacita, who "doesn't come out because she is afraid to speak English" (74); and Rosa Vargas, "who is tired all the time from buttoning and bottling and babying, and who cries every day for the man who left without even leaving a dollar . . . or a note explaining how come" (30); and Minerva, who

is only a little bit older than me but already she has two kids and a husband who left . . . and keeps leaving. . . . He comes back and sends a big rock through the window. Then he is sorry and she opens the door again. Next week she comes over black and blue and asks what can she do? . . . Her mother raised her kids alone and it looks like her daughters will go that way too. (80)

The women portrayed here exemplify the triple oppression poor Latino women on Mango Street have to face in their daily lives and how "women's marginality leads to economic and social dependence on the male" (Herrera-Sobek, 1988, 175); unable to break the cycle of poverty or their dependency on men, the daughters are often doomed to repeat the fate of their mothers.

A common denominator uniting almost all the different women Esperanza portrays is, not only their entrapment in oppressive sociocultural circumstances, but their internalization of a definition of self that is determined by phallocentric cultural values. They are thus not only confined within their own houses, but also confined by their own minds, by the conditioned limitations of their own self-perception. Their lives and actions, dominated by fathers and husbands, are physically and psychologically entrapped within oppressive patriarchal structures, and they can envision themselves only in the seemingly inescapable roles of future wives and mothers. Rafaela, for instance, who "gets locked indoors because her husband is afraid she will run away since she is too beautiful to look at . . . leans out the window . . . and dreams her hair is like Rapunzel's" (76), dreams of being liberated from her prison, but as in the fairy tale, by a man. And so Rafaela dreams of going dancing where "always there is someone offering sweeter drinks, someone promising to keep them on a silver string" (76); dreaming of being released of her present imprisonment, she can only dream of walking into another. This dependency on a man to liberate you from the oppressive circumstances of your present life also conditions Marin's dreams of the future, of

> a real job downtown because that's where the best jobs are, since you always get to look beautiful and get to wear nice clothes and can meet someone on the subway who might marry and take you to live in a big house far away. (27)

Like Esperanza, Marin wants to escape from Mango Street, but unlike Esperanza she envisions marriage as the only possible way of getting away.

It is, however, in her attempt to understand her friend Sally that the narrating "I" begins to see why girls repeat the fate of their marginalized mothers and become caught in a cycle of patriarchal violence and control. Esperanza wants to be beautiful like Sally, dress like Sally, whose father thinks that "to be this beautiful is trouble" (77) and whom the whole world expects "to make a mistake" (79). Yet by narrating Sally's story, she begins to understand that to be Sally also means to end up confined within patriarchal prisons like most of the women on Mango Street.

Sally, who becomes different when she has to go home, cannot leave her house because of her father: "He hits me . . . with his hands just like a dog . . . like if I was an animal. He thinks I'm going to run away like his sisters who made the family ashamed. Just because I'm a daughter" (85). Constant scars on her skin are signs of her father's continuous violent attempts to control her sexuality and force her into adhering to his patriarchal definition of womanhood. This violent drama culminates one day when "he just went crazy, he just forgot he was her father between the buckle and the belt" (85). Making connections between female behavior and patriarchal violence, Esperanza begins to understand why Sally, like Minerva and all the other women on Mango Street, went "that way too" (80) and exchanged her father's prison for that of a husband, believing, like Rafaela, in someone promising to give her "sweeter drinks," to keep her on "a silver string" (76):

> Sally got married like we knew she would, young and not ready but married just the same. . . . She has her husband and her house now, her pillowcases and her plates. She says she is in love, but I think she did it to escape. Sally says she likes being married because now she gets to buy her own things when her husband gives her money. . . . Except he won't let her talk on the telephone. And he doesn't let her look out the window. . . . She sits at home because she is afraid to go out without his permission. (96)

Confined physically and psychologically to her house, Sally is trapped in an existence that is completely circumscribed and controlled by her husband; aware of no other alternatives, she leads a life that reflects a recurrent pattern in patriarchal cultural myths, one in which "women do not grow up. They simply change masters—from a beastly father to a fatherly beast" (Rose, 223). Narrating Sally's story, Esperanza comes to understand that, by marrying, Sally remains under the control of a man, and that the house she inhabits, rather than being a liberating space, is a stifling confinement in which Sally is trapped, "looking at walls, the linoleum roses on the floor, the ceiling smooth as a wedding cake" (95). She is, in effect, trapped between the myth and the reality of women's lives.

Sally's house stands as an antithesis to the house Esperanza dreams of inhabiting one day; it is also a far cry from Gaston Bachelard's image of a house as "felicitous space" (xxxv), or Tomás Rivera's definition of *la casa* as a "constant refuge" (1979, 22) from a hostile world. In Bachelard's reveries, a house is "the non-I that protects the I" (5), "a roomy home" where a family can live "in security and comfort" (30), where one shivers "merely from well-being" (31). He deems this experience of the house as a "material paradise" (7) to be so universal that it can be used as "a tool for analysis of the human soul" (xxxvii). It is obvious that this image of the house has its roots in Bachelard's own comfortable background and that his reveries on the house are circumscribed by a male-centered middle-class ideology. His "nostalgic and privileged utopia" (Olivares, 160) is based on experiences that differ dramatically from those of women like Sally and Esperanza.

There is a marked economic and cultural difference between Bachelard's concept of the house as "material paradise" and Tomás Rivera's concept of la casa as a "constant refuge" (1979, 22) from a hostile environment. In his article "Fiesta of the Living," Rivera presents *la casa*, *el barrio*, and *la lucha* as constant and essential elements in the struggle for cultural survival in a hostile environment. To Rivera, *la casa* is the center of cultural continuity, a safe haven where ethnic pride and family solidarity are perpetuated. Central to this concept of *la casa* is also the image of the much eulogized *madre abnegada*, who sacrifices herself for her family. This concept of the traditional family may perpetuate ethnic integrity and mitigate the blows of oppression, but for the Chicana it may also be the very concept that perpetuates her own oppression. Despite their differences, both Bachelard and Rivera see the house as a protective sphere, "the non-I that protects the I," a concept that does not always apply to women, as it is often within the very confines of the home that violence is visited upon her. To Sally, the house is neither a "material paradise" nor a "constant refuge"; in order to escape the physical violence in her father's house, she marries, only to realize that she has exchanged one prison for another.

Esperanza comes to realize, in examining the lives of the women on Mango Street, that a woman's house is often a confining patriarchal domain rather than the house of liberation she imagines for herself. Having arrived at this realization, Esperanza begins to resist the social conditioning that leads women on the path to marriage:

> My mother says when I get older my dusty hair will settle and my blouse will learn to stay clean, but I have decided not to grow up tame like the others who lay their necks on the threshold waiting for the ball and chain. I have begun my own quiet war. Simple. Sure. I am one who leaves the table like a man, without putting back the chair or picking up the plate. (82)

Esperanza's refusal to adhere to social expectations of female behavior goes far beyond the mere action itself, as it is a symbolic refusal to "grow up tame," to accept a prescribed female destiny. Esperanza's action has been interpreted as a "somewhat adolescent gesture" that is likely "to increase the work for another woman in Esperanza's household" (McCracken, 72) and as an attempt "to increase her own power by starting out to be as rude as men" (Alarcón, 1989, 100), yet her refusal to do so-called female chores marks an important step toward breaking the cycle of female self-sacrifice. With her self-defining assertions, "I have decided not to grow up tame . . . , I am one who leaves the table," Esperanza claims control over her own *Bildungs* process by envisioning a role for herself that stands in direct opposition to the sociocultural roles and expectations imposed on women by a male-defined culture. In her own "quiet war," Espeanza begins to assert a self-defined destiny by "daring to be selfish" (Huf, 157), by daring to kill the "angel in the house" (Woolf, 1942, 236), so that she can inhabit her own liberating space, a house of her own making:

> Not a flat. Not an apartment in the back. Not a man's house. Not a daddy's. A house all my own. With my porch and pillow, my pretty purple petunias. My books and my stories. My two shoes waiting besides the bed. Nobody to shake a stick at. Nobody's garbage to pick up after. Only a house as quiet as snow, a space for myself to go, clean as paper before the poem. (100)

Her initial wish for an illusive "real house," one she can point to, is thus in the course of her narrative transformed into a more defined desire for a place that transcends the mere physical living quarters to mean a life of her own creation. She wants not only a house but also a life that is unconfined by either a father or a husband or prescriptive social expectations, a nonpatriarchal space in which she can create herself and a self-defined destiny.

In the process of her exploration of her sociocultural context, of discovering, synthesizing, and narrating her own experiences within the community on Mango Street, Esperanza has come to understand that the "real house" she has been searching for is an unconfining creative space. Telling her own story, the narrating "I" participates in the process of her own self-formation, while she at the same time creates a poetic space that stands as an alternative to the confining conditions on Mango Street: "I like to tell stories. . . . I put it down on paper and then the ghost does not ache so much. I write it down and Mango Street says goodbye sometimes. She does not hold me with both arms. She sets me free" (101). This sense of liberation through the creative act of writing and narrating her own stories is predicted early on by a dying aunt who encourages Esperanza to write: "'That's nice. That's very good,' she said in her tired voice. 'You just remember to keep writing, Esperanza.

You must keep writing. It will keep you free,' and I said, 'yes,' but at that time I didn't know what she meant" (56). Attention here turns to the narrating "I," who, through the creative reconstruction of this encounter, comes to understand that in writing about her experiences she has come to inhabit a liberating poetic space of her own.

Esperanza's vision of creativity as a form of liberation takes on social and cultural dimensions, as it becomes clear that *The House on Mango Street* is the narrator/author's textual return to Mango Street. The narrating "I," initially ashamed of her entire "social and subject position" (Saldívar, 1990, 182), is driven throughout the narrative process by the desire to escape not only her great-grandmother's "place by the window," but also the confinement of her socioeconomic circumstances on Mango Street. Yet in the course of telling her stories she comes to recognize the significance of Mango Street in her life, that it forms an inextricable part of her own self.

In the course of her *Bildung*, Esperanza encounters several guides, each of whom connects her with her cultural context in vital ways and provides important messages about the uniqueness of her own identity. There is her mother who "could've been somebody" (83) if it had not been for the shame of being poor: "Shame is a bad thing, you know. It keeps you down. You want to know why I quit school? Because I didn't have nice clothes. No clothes, but I had brains" (84). That the feeling of shame can entrap one in the very situation one wants to escape becomes a crucial lesson for Esperanza, who, throughout the narrative, has expressed being ashamed of her position on Mango Street. Her friend Alicia, furthermore, insists that Mango Street, the very place Esperanza wants to escape, forms an integral part of Esperanza's identity: "Like it or not you are Mango Street and one day you will come back" (99). This emphasis on her connection to Mango Street is reiterated by three *comadres*, three indigenous guides—reminiscent of the three Fates in Greek mythology who govern human destiny—who tell her that she is "special," that she will "go far" (97), but also that she must not forget that she comes from Mango Street:

Esperanza . . . a good, good name.

When you leave you must remember always to come back, she said. . . .
When you leave you must remember to come back for the others. A circle,
understand? You will always be Esperanza. You will always be Mango
Street. You can't erase what you know: You can't forget who you are. You
must remember to come back. For the ones who cannot leave as easily as
you.

Yes, yes, I said a little confused.

I didn't understand everything they had told me. (98)

Once more the attention turns to the narrating "I" who, through the creative reconstruction of her life on Mango Street, has come to understand that she will always be Esperanza. She will always be a Chicana, and Mango Street will always form a part of her identity. The *comadres* predict a different destiny for Esperanza, yet remind her at the same time that her origins, her cultural and socioeconomic roots, form an important part of her future self. When Esperanza in the end envisions her own departure from Mango Street, it is with the intention of returning, of creating *Esperanza* for those she leaves behind:

One day I will pack my bags of books and paper. One day I will say goodbye to Mango. I am too strong for her to keep me here forever. One day I
will go away.

Friends and neighbors will say, What happened to that Esperanza?
Where did she go with all those books and paper? Why did she march so far
away? They will not know that I have gone away to come back. For the
ones I left behind. For the ones who cannot get out. (102)

By the end of her *Bildungs* experience, Esperanza has thus gained an awareness of herself as a potential writer who ventures into the larger world with a firm sense of who she is, where she comes from, and where she is going.

* * *

The House on Mango Street is a narrative of self-discovery in which Esperanza narrates her own quest for a house, a life of her own making. Through the act of narrating, the Chicana protagonist becomes the conscious subject of her own *Bildungs* story. She is a female *Bildungsheld* who dismantles "the cultural text as she grows up in resistance to it" (J. Frye, 109), resisting cultural norms that demand that women "grow down rather than up" (Pratt, 1981, 168). In the process she creates a text that subverts the traditional female quest story of the "thwarted or impossible journey" (Heller, 14) that inevitably leads to sociocultural entrapment of the female hero. Narrating her own *Bildungs* story, the narrating "I" engages in the subversive act of replacing the cultural text with her own. This aspect of the narrative lends a poetic dimension to this Chicana quest story: Esperanza's search for a "real" house is at the same time a quest for self-expression, for a liberating self-creation that dismantles traditional male-defined myths and texts that have locked the Chicana into confining stereotypes.

When Esperanza at the end of her self-discovering narrative envisions the "real" house she has been searching for, she defines it as "not a man's house. Not a daddy's. A house all my own. . . . A house quiet as snow, a space for myself to go, clean as paper before the poem" (100). This connection between the house and the text—her house is a poem yet to be written—turns her rejection of a "man's house" into a rejection of what Gilbert and Gubar have termed "patriarchal poetics" (72); her escape from the house of the fathers is an escape from male texts. Her own quest for a "real" house is thus a quest for a new Chicana text, one that names her own experiences and represents her as a Chicana in all her subjective complexity, one that does not make her "feel like nothing."

This use of the house as a metaphor for a new Chicana poetic space is further underscored by Espeanza's image of her own house as a place of ethnic consciousness and with room for outsiders: "One day I'll own my own house, but I won't forget who I am or where I came from. Passing bums will ask, Can I come in? I'll offer them the attic, ask them to stay, because I know how it is to be without a house" (81). Espeanza's house/text, the poem that is yet to be written, is thus going to include the traditional outsiders, the sociocultural "others," who have been excluded from inhabiting houses/texts of their own. And in fact, many of these "others" inhabit the finished text, *The House on Mango Street*, as for example Geraldo, who did not have a last name, who was "just another *brazer* who didn't speak English. Just another wetback. You know the kind. The ones who always look ashamed" (63). By making room for the story of a *mojado* in her text, Espeanza gives poetic space to one of the many outsiders who otherwise sink into oblivion, nameless and forgotten.

The House on Mango Street is a text that houses outsiders, where those who look ashamed because they do not have houses/texts of their own can feel at home. It is a concern that may stem from Cisneros's own feelings of textual exclusion. In a biographical essay, Sandra Cisneros recalls her encounter with Gaston Bachelard's *The Poetics of Space* in college. She did not understand Bachelard's reveries on the house of the imagination, yet everyone else was quite comfortable with this book, and that made her feel "foreign from the others, out of place, different" (63):

> They seemed to have some communal knowledge which I did not have, did not understand—and then I realized that the metaphor of the *house* was totally wrong for me, that it did not draw from any archetype in my imagination, in my past culture. Suddenly I was homeless. There were no attics, and cellars, and crannies. I had no such house in my memories. (63)

Cisneros's feelings of homelessness in Bachelard's text stem from her inability to relate to a concept of the house that is based on a male-centered, middle-class ideology that is foreign to her. Bachelard's "felicitous space" finds no echo in Cisneros's imagination, and the house of her childhood was not the "material paradise" (7) that Bachelard seems to presume is a universal given. *The House on Mango Street* is thus a countertext to Bachelard's *The Poetics of Space*, a Chicana poetics of space that houses images which reverberate in the Chicana imagination. With *The House on Mango Street*, Cisneros has created a text that, unlike Bachelard's text, can house the imagination of the textual outsider.

Much in keeping with Esperanza's promise to return for the women she leaves behind, "the ones who cannot get out" (102), *The House on Mango Street* stands as a symbolic return to the women in a Latino barrio. Not only is this Chicana *Bildungsroman* dedicated "A las Mujeres/ To the Women," but the narrative itself centers on the community of women on Mango Street who form part of Esperanza's *Bildungs* process. Elsewhere Sandra Cisneros argues that "the world of thousands of silent women . . . needs to be, must be recorded so that their stories can finally be heard" (76). Through the narrator/protagonist, Esperanza, Sandra Cisneros gives voice to a Chicana *Bildungsheld* who tells her own story, who in the process of constructing herself as a subject "dares to confront lies and to deconstruct myths" (Gonzales-Berry, 14) about la Chicana. Esperanza grows up, not down, and gains in the process a clear understanding of her social, cultural, and sexual identity as a Chicana. Through her role as a writer, as a teller of stories, however, her *Bildung* is not merely individual, but takes on communal significance, as she, with the text, is reaching back to the women on Mango Street so that her own liberating self-creation may in turn become a symbolic *Bildungs* experience for those "who cannot get out":

Marin, under the streetlight, dancing by herself, is singing the same song somewhere. I know. Is waiting for a car to stop, a star to fall, someone to change her life. Anybody. (28)

The communal significance of Esperanza's *Bildung* is further underscored by the fact that, while her primary concern is for the women who cannot escape marginalization, the text goes beyond an exclusive portrayal of the oppression of Chicanas to name and give voice to other outsiders in the community. *The House on Mango Street* thus exemplifies how Esperanza's *Bildung* involves an understanding of her own relationship to the entire Chicano community and that such understanding is essential to a true Chicana *Bildungs* process.

Note

1. There is a wide discrepancy among critics about how to define the narrative structure, the genre, of *The House on Mango Street*. I have chosen to define its narrative structure as interrelated stories that in their entirety form a novel, a *Bildungsroman*. For a discussion on the question of genre in *The House on Mango Street* see "Género e ideología en el libro de Sandra Cisneros: *The House on Mango Street*" by Pedro Gutiérrez-Revuelta.

Works Cited

Alarcón, Norma. "Chicana Writers and Critics in a Social Context: Towards a Contemporary Bibliography." *Third Woman* 4 (1989): 169-78.

_____. "The Sardonic Powers of the Erotic in the Work of Ana Castillo". In *Breaking Boundaries: Latina Writing and Critical Readings*, edited by Asunción Horno-Delgado, Eliana Ortega, Nina M. Scott, and Nancy Saporta Sternbach, 94-107. Amherst: University of Massachusetts Press, 1989.

Bachelard, Gaston. *The Poetics of Space*. Boston: Beacon Press, 1994.

Cisneros, Sandra. *The House on Mango Street*. Houston, Tex.: Arte Público Press, 1985.

Dearborn, Mary V. *Pocahontas's Daughters: Gender and Ethnicity in American Culture*. New York: Oxford University Press, 1986.

Frye, Joanne S. *Living Stories, Telling Lives: Women and the Novel in Contemporary Experience*. Ann Arbor: The University of Michigan Press, 1986.

Gilbert, Sandra M., and Susan Gubar. *The Madwoman in the Attic: The Woman Writer and the Nineteenth-Century Literary Imagination*. New Haven, Conn.: Yale University Press, 1979.

Gonzales-Berry, Erlinda. "Unveiling Athena: Women in the Chicano Novel." Unpublished manuscript.

_____, and Tey Diana Rebolledo. "Growing Up Chicano: Tomás Rivera and Sandra Cisneros." *Revista Chicano-Riqueña* 13, no. 3/4 (1985): 109-19.

Gutiérrez-Revuelto, Pedro. "Género e ideología en el libro de Sandra Cisneros: The House on Mango Street." *Crítica* 1, no. 3 (Fall 1986): 48-59.

Heller, Dana A. *The Feminization of Quest-Romance: Radical Departures.* Austin: University of Texas Press, 1990.

Herrera-Sobek, María. "The Politics of Rape: Sexual Transgression in Chicana Fiction." In *Chicana Creativity: Charting New Frontiers in American Literature*, edited by María Herrera-Sobek and Helena María Viramontes, 171-81. Houston, Tex.: Arte Público Press, 1988.

Huf, Linda. *A Portrait of the Artist as a Young Woman: The Writer as Heroine in American Literature.* New York: Frederick Ungar, 1983.

McCracken, Ellen. "Sandra Cisneros' The House on Mango Street: Community-Oriented Introspection and the Demystification of Patriarchal Violence." In *Breaking Boundaries: Latina Writing and Critical Readings*, edited by Asunción Horno-Delgado, Eliana Oretega, Nina M. Scott, and Nancy Saporta Sternbach, 62-71. Amherst: University of Massachusetts Press, 1989.

Olivares, Julián. "Sandra Cisneros' *The House on Mango Street*, and the Poetics of Space." In *Chicana Creativity: Charting New Frontiers in American Literature*, edited by María Herrera-Sobek and Helena María Viramontes, 160-70. Houston, Tex.: Arte Público Press, 1988.

Pratt, Annis. *Archetypal Patterns to Women's Fiction.* Bloomington: Indiana University Press, 1981.

Rebolledo, Tey Diana. "Tradition and Mythology: Signatures of Landscape in Chicana Literature." In *The Desert Is No Lady: Southwestern Landscapes in Women's Writing and Art*, edited by Vera Norwood and Janice Monk, 96-124. New Haven: Yale University Press, 1987.

_____. "Abuelitas: Mythology and Integration in Chicana Literature." In *Woman of Her Word: Hispanic Women Write*, edited by Evangelina Vigil, 148-58. Houston, Tex.: Arte Público Press, 1987.

_____. "Hispanic Women Writers of the Southwest: Tradition and Innovation." In *Old Southwest/New Southwest: Essays on a Region and Its Literature*, edited by Judy N. Lensink, 49-61. Tucson, Ariz.: Bilingual Press, 1987.

Rivera, Tomás. "Chicano Literature: Fiesta of the Living." In *The Identification and Analysis of Chicano Literature*, edited by Francisco Jiménez, 19-36. New York: Bilingual Press/Editorial Bilingüe, 1979.

Rose, Ellen Cronan. "Through the Looking Glass: When Women Tell Fairy Tales," In *The Voyage In: Fictions of Female Development*, edited by Elizabeth Abel, Marianne Hirsch, and Elizabeth Langland, 209-27. Hanover & London: University Press of New England, 1983.

Saldívar, Ramón. "Ideologies of the Self: Chicano Autobiography." *Diacritics* 15, no. 3 (Fall 1985): 25-34.

_____. "The Dialectics of Subjectivity: Gender and Difference in Isabella Ríos, Sandra Cisneros, and Cherríe Moraga." In *Chicano Narrative: The Dialectics of Difference*, 171-99. Madison: University of Wisconsin Press, 1990.

Woolf, Virginia. *A Room of One's Own*. New York: Harcourt Brace Jovanovich, 1929.

_____. "Professions for Women," *The Death of the Moth and Other Essays*, 226-38. New York: Harcourt Brace, 1942.

Zipes, Jack. *The Trials and Tribulations of Little Red Riding Hood*. South Hadley, Mass.: Berger and Garvey, 1983.

Coming of Age in the Curriculum:
The House on Mango Street and *Bless Me, Ultima* as Representative Texts_____

Delia Poey

Since the late 1960s, there has been a growing current of debate within the humanities surrounding the canon. This current has had visible effects on the curriculum as evidenced by the institutionalization and growth of programs in areas such as Black Studies, Women's Studies, Chicano Studies, Latino Studies, and so on. Recently, there has been a trend within traditional programs, such as English, involving curriculum revisions resulting in departments not only offering more courses emphasizing works by minority writers but actually requiring students to complete a minimum of course work centering on issues of gender, race, and class. While these changes have been interpreted as too radical and accused of "political correctness" by conservative factions, others have described them as superficial, implemented for the purpose of stabilizing institutions in the face of growing dissent and militancy from disenfranchised groups.[1]

These curricular debates have tended to center around the term *multiculturalism*. There exists a great body of work arguing the term's definitions, parameters, pedagogical practices, and political implications. This ongoing debate has even moved from the usual academic settings of departmental meetings, professional journals, and books published by university presses to candidate speeches, mass media, and mainstream publishers. Take, for example, Pat Buchanan's speech during the 1992 Republican National Convention, which employed military rhetoric to rally support in fighting the "culture wars" being waged against "American" values and traditions—a war "over the hearts and minds of the American people." Specific attacks on curricular reform have also appeared in book form. These books have been marketed for a mainstream audience that is not necessarily academic. Titles such as *Cultural Literacy: What Every American Needs to Know*

(Houghton Mifflin, 1987) by E. D. Hirsch, *Tenured Radicals: How Politics Has Corrupted Higher Education* (Harper Collins, 1990) by Roger Kimball, and *The Closing of the American Mind* (Simon and Schuster, 1987) by Allan Bloom received media attention, reflecting a broader public anxiety regarding contested definitions of history, art, and culture in an American (U.S.) context.[2]

These reactions to curricular debates and revisions can be described as a backlash against a perceived erosion of a common ground in the construction, representation, and reproduction of knowledge within institutions of higher learning. In denouncing multiculturalism as politically motivated, the voices of the backlash re-edify the Eurocentric, white, male, and middle-class values. This position proposes the white, male, middle-class perspective as the apolitical, naturalized norm.[3] We take these arguments seriously, given their prominence in discourses both within and outside of academe. First, we must examine how multiculturalism is being defined. Then we must look at how and to what extent it has been implemented in curricular reform, and finally question the legitimacy of Bloom, Kimball, and Hirsch's worries, regardless of whether or not we share their political positions as defenders of the canon.

Because definitive and fully inclusive answers to these questions are well beyond the scope of a single chapter, or a single volume for that matter, this study focuses on the circulation of two texts: *Bless Me, Ultima* by Rudolfo Anaya and *The House on Mango Street* by Sandra Cisneros. Both have become "representative" of Chicano and Latina/o literature. This chapter attempts to plot the position of these texts in the multicultural matrix using as coordinates key factors in their reception. These factors are here identified as *degree of intelligibility*, which corresponds to a given text's approachability through existing paradigms and methodologies, and relative flexibility for incorporation through *manageable difference*. In other words, this chapter examines how and to what extent these two texts are incorporated as additives to the already established canonical tradition and looks at the logic behind their promotion as documented, legal trespassers into the academic landscape.

Peter McLaren identifies four forms of multiculturalism: conservative, liberal, left-liberal, and critical. The first, conservative multiculturalism, is defined by its drive to construct a common culture, using the term *diversity* "to cover up the ideology of assimilation that undergirds its position. In this view, ethnic groups are reduced to 'add-ons' to the dominant culture. Before you can be 'added on' to the dominant United States culture you must first adopt a consensual view of culture and learn to accept the essentially Euro-American patriarchal norms of the 'host' country" (McLaren 49). This particular form of multiculturalism is also linked to the process Renato Rosaldo has described as "cultural stripping." This entails that individuals shed or strip their former cultures in order to become "transparent" American citizens (Rosaldo, *Culture*).

A second form of multiculturalism, as described by McLaren, is the liberal approach or definition. This form is closely identified with "universalistic humanism in which legitimating norms which govern the substance of citizenship are identified most strongly with Anglo-American cultural-political communities" (McLaren 51). The third form, left-liberal multiculturalism, differs from both conservative and liberal forms in its emphasis on difference. However, "work within this perspective [has] a tendency to essentialize cultural differences . . . and ignore the historical and cultural 'situatedness' of difference" (McLaren 52).

Critical multiculturalism rejects the conservative and liberal forms on the grounds that they stress sameness. That is, they focus on the ways that "we are all the same after all." Critical multiculturalism, however, also takes issue with the left-liberal emphasis on difference. Both the highlighting of sameness and the highlighting of difference present the same problem. According to McLaren, both of these emphases suffer from "essentialist logic: in both, individual identities are presumed to be autonomous, self-contained and self-directed" (McLaren 53).

In place of this, critical perspectives situate representations of race, class, and gender in contexts of social struggle where meaning is constructed and deconstructed in specific histories and power relations. Critical multiculturalism does not simply emphasize "textual play or metaphoric displacement as a form of resistance (as in the case of left-liberal multiculturalism)" but rather moves beyond it to interrogate "the construction of difference and identity in relation to a radical politics" (McLaren 53).

Locating the reception of these two representative texts on Mc-Laren's graph points to a shifting plotting point between conservative and liberal quadrants, with an occasional bow toward a left-liberal position, but only as this third form conforms, to the requisites of conservative and liberal forms. What is generally lacking from the use of these texts as representative in pedagogical and critical practices is an emphasis "positioned against the neo-imperial romance with monoglot ethnicity grounded in a shared or 'common' experience of 'America' that is associated with conservative and liberal strands of multiculturalism" (McLaren 53). That is, conservative and liberal strands of multiculturalism do not challenge the melting pot paradigm, and these tend to be the approaches used in working with these texts.

Referring to *Bless Me, Ultima* and *The House on Mango Street* as representative texts does not carry the implication that they encompass sole and complete representation of Chicano or Latino literary expression. The term *representative* is here used as reflective of existing institutional practices that overwhelmingly include one or both of these texts to the exclusion of others. These texts become representative, then, by often being the only Latina/o works assigned in a relatively broad spectrum of courses. For example, one or both are frequently the only Latina/o texts included or excerpted on Multicultural Literature and Contemporary American Literature syllabi.[4]

That these texts and their respective authors share striking similarities may be a first step in explaining their reception, yet even these similarities cannot fully account for their selection over others. For example, both Anaya and Cisneros have strong ties to universities. Anaya holds a Ph.D. and retired as professor emeritus after thirty years of service at the University of New Mexico. Cisneros is a graduate of the Iowa Creative Writing Program, where she wrote and workshopped *The House on Mango Street* as a student. While there is no doubt that both these writers' relationships with academia inform their work, this cannot account for their works' relative prominence within that context, since most Latina/o authors share similar connections. Alberto Ríos, Helena María Viramontes, Tomás Rivera, Ana Castillo, Judith Ortiz Cofer, Rolando Hinojosa, to name a few, are all examples of writers connected with institutions of higher learning. In fact, we would be hard pressed to name a handful who would be excluded from this list. Although some have argued that this is a situation specific to Chicanos and Latinos, it is probably more a reflection of the institutionalization of writing in general in the United States.[5]

Marketing forces yield similarly ambivalent results in terms of their explanatory potential since both works were initially published by small presses–*Bless Me, Ultima* was published with Tonatiuh and *Mango Street* was originally published with Arte Público—with limited distribution and resources. Nor can we credit the authors themselves as promoting these works as representative texts. Cisneros actively resists the label, as evidenced by her refusal to allow publication of excerpts from *Mango Street* in the *Norton Anthology of American Literature* as a protest against the editors' exclusion of other Latina and Latino voices. Anaya is similarly involved in broadening rather than narrowing literary representation. He has worked as an editor, providing publication access to less-recognized authors as well as establishing and funding "La Casita," which provides writers—particularly Chicanas and Chicanos—with room and board while completing creative projects.

Having ruled out or severely restricted the roles of institutionalization through ties with the university literary establishment, marketing and publishing forces, and self-promotion on the parts of the authors, let us return to the set of factors previously hypothesized as bearing relevance to these texts becoming established as representative. The first of these, intelligibility, is here defined as the degree to which a given text is accessible to a given community of readers based on that community's prior knowledge and expectations deployed in making meaning and assigning value. Critical work on speech act theory and reader response informs this term as well as its application in this chapter to the reception of *Bless Me, Ultima* and *The House on Mango Street.*[6]

As the discipline of linguistics has demonstrated, all units of language are necessarily incomplete or open. No utterance or written text is free of ambiguity. In the case of the written text, undecidability is further complicated in that body language or physical expressions are absent as contextual clues, and clarification on the part of the speaker is simply not an option. The negotiation of meaning, then, is removed from the speaking or writing subject and transferred to the text, so that interaction is contextualized through the reader's prior experience and knowledge of other written texts. Intelligibility, then, hinges on the extent to which a reader is able to make use of this prior knowledge or, to use Jonathan Culler's terminology, to perform "reading competence."[7]

In this regard, both of the texts under consideration can be argued to conform to a high degree of intelligibility in terms of both language and content. Most notably, they both fall into the category of the bildungsroman, or coming-of-age novel. This particular genre, deeply rooted in the conventions and formulas of a patriarchal and individualistic tradition, draws both of these texts into a specific intertextual framework. Culler's "competent reader" can then plug into this familiar framework and fill in the interstitial spaces that Anaya's and Cisneros's bicultural works make fluid and unstable. In other words, the reader possesses a thematic map of the bildungsroman, drawn to specifications embedded in a predominantly white, male system of cultural values and artistry. The reader, then, is competent to navigate these "other" texts with a diminished level of frustration. Anaya's novel is particularly well suited for grafting onto the bildungsroman cartography, while Cisneros's book (given the protagonist's gender as well as its structure as a story cycle) is more flexibly aligned with the form.

The term *bildungsroman* is applied here as it has been defined and used in English literary studies, as opposed to its somewhat different and more specific application in Germanic studies.[8] Jerome Buckley's appropriation of the term as the novel of youth or apprenticeship, a definition expanded and detailed by Randolph Shaffner, is used here as the model of the bildungsroman as it has been understood in relation to an English language tradition.

According to this model, the protagonist moves through various stages of maturity, encountering tests that lead to a fulfillment of potential and the formation of a self capable of reconciling the individual with a larger social order. *Bless Me, Ultima* follows this master plot closely, even while simultaneously articulating a Chicano mythopoetics with strong ties to indigenous New Mexico culture and cosmologies.

The novel opens with the protagonist, Antonio, first learning about Ultima, la Grande, leaving the *llano* and coming to live with his family on the outskirts of town. This marks the beginning of his apprenticeship, in the most literal sense, as Ultima's assistant. The tests that compose his progressive initiation into both Ultima's magic and the larger society include his witnessing the violence of a man shot and killed, his becoming the focal point of the struggle between the destructive magic of the *brujas* and Ultima's power, and his encounter with the Giant Carp—an important turning point in the boy's coming to spiritual understanding.

In addition to adhering to the master plot of the bildungsroman, *Bless Me, Ultima* also fulfills the set of presuppositions that Shaffner identifies as corollaries of the genre:

1. The idea that living is an art which the apprentice may learn.
2. The belief that a young person can become adept in the art of life and become a master.
3. The key notion of choice.
4. The prerequisite of potential for development into a master.
5. An affirmative attitude toward life as a whole. (Shaffner 18)

While the novel bears out all of these presuppositions, it does so within historical, societal, and economic parameters. In the world of the novel, the privileged reality is the one constructed by and through the immediate community. This reality does not deny the existence of a larger society, nor the differential locations of power—as in the passages relating to the racism encountered at school. Value, rather, is placed first and foremost in the context of the Chicano community—its order, values, and internal cohesion.

Within these parameters, Antonio struggles with a multiplicity of choices. For example, at his birth Antonio's maternal family, the Lunas, desire to have the child follow their traditions of farming: "And to show their hope they rubbed the dark earth of the river valley on the baby's forehead, and they surrounded the bed with the fruits of their harvest so the small room smelled of fresh green chile and corn, ripe apples and peaches, pumpkins and green beans" (Anaya 6).

In conflict with this is the paternal family, the Márez, and their wish to make him a vaquero: "And they smashed the fruits and vegetables that surrounded the bed and replaced them with a saddle, horse blankets, bottles of whiskey, a new rope, bridles, chaps, and an old guitar. And they rubbed the stain of earth from the baby's forehead because man was not to be tied to the earth but free upon it" (Anaya 6). Further complicating the child's choices is his mother's wish that he become a priest. Settling the raging argument, Ultima intercedes. "I pulled this baby into the light of life, so I will bury the afterbirth and the cord that once linked him to eternity. Only I will know his destiny" (Anaya 7).

That Antonio's future is predestined by Ultima does not, in the logic of the novel, occlude his ability to make choices. Because Ultima keeps his destiny literally buried, Antonio's coming of age and fulfillment of that destiny is still regulated by the interplay between his will and his growing spiritual consciousness. The "key concept of choice" is present in the novel, as are the other presuppositions of the bildungsroman identified by Shaffner. This ability to be grafted onto the genre's master plot allows the reader to make meaning of the spaces in the novel that display marked differences.

According to Reed Way Dasenbrock, writing in the *PMLA*, "one could say, adapting the language of Paul Grice, that there is implicit in any act of reading a maxim of intelligibility, which is that readers—like speakers and listeners—will work to make texts as intelligible as possible. Assuming that a work makes sense and has significance, the reader will try to find that sense and significance even when they are not readily apparent" (Dasenbrock 14). This commentary bears relevance to the reception of representative texts in two ways. First, it assumes that readers will work toward making meaning, but only to a point. Second, it assumes that a reader has decided at some point, perhaps prior to reading the text, that the work "makes sense and has significance." This second assumption is problematic when we are dealing with noncanonical texts. *Sense* and *significance*, in this context, are highly contested terms. Because we cannot take for granted that the reader has made this determination, we can assume that the reader will work toward making meaning in a more limited way since she/he is more uncertain about the potential payoff for the effort.

This point becomes clearer as Dasenbrock further states that "this principle can be abused, but a skillful writer will make the reader work hard only at those moments where the work is meaningful. . . . Only by doing that work, by striving to understand a different mode of expression, are we brought up against the fact of cultural difference. If everything is translated into our terms and made readily intelligible, then our cultural categories will be reinforced, not challenged" (Dasenbrock 14).

These lines, which on the surface seem to be arguing for the pedagogical and cultural "value" of multicultural texts, contain some disturbing implications. For example, there is a differentiation between the "skillful" and the "unskillful" writer based on the degree to which the text produced requires "work" on the part of the reader—work here is defined as the negotiation of meaning when confronted with difference from hegemonic norms. Dasenbrock praises the "skillful" writer who requires the reader to work hard, but in a limited way: "only at those moments where the work is meaningful." The assumption here is that we can with confidence identify these "moments," as well as discount other "moments" in the text presumed to lack meaningfulness.

What we can begin to decipher about Dasenbrock's perspective on multiculturalism is that it falls under what Goldberg calls "weak multiculturalism." Goldberg's term, which encompasses McLaren's conservative and liberal forms, is defined as consisting of "a strong set of common, universally endorsed, centrist values to which everyone— every reasonable person irrespective of the divisions of race, class, and gender—can agree. These universal principles are combined with a pluralism of ethnic insight and self-determination provided no particularistically promoted claim is inconsistent with the core values" (Goldberg 16).

Thus far, this chapter has argued that Anaya's *Bless Me Ultima* has become a representative text based on its high degree of intelligibility in regard to form (the novel) and content (adherence to the master plot of the bildungsroman). Yet, according to Dasenbrock's taxonomy of intelligibility, this novel is "much more difficult" than other multicultural texts due to its "aggressively bilingual mode of presentation" (Gingerich 215-16 quoted in Dasenbrock 15). He argues that, "though the novel is in English, it includes a substantial amount of Spanish, for which there is very little covert or overt translation" (Dasenbrock 15).

According to Dasenbrock, this use of code switching could be a barrier to intelligibility. Yet, Dasenbrock argues, in *Bless Me, Ultima* it is used strategically to convey a bilingual reality in which not everyone understands everything all of the time. The older generation is monolingual in Spanish and the Anglo teachers are monolingual in English. Only the children who have attended school are bilingual. This is partly correct, yet the text's use of Spanish is much more limited than the "reality" Dasenbrock argues it reflects. Translations, for example, are supplied in both covert and overt fashion.

The following lines typify the text's use of both overt and covert translation: "'It would be a great honor to provide a home for la Grande,' my mother murmured. My mother called Ultima la Grande out of respect. It meant the woman was old and wise" (Anaya 4). Note that Antonio's mother's dialogue is in English, although it is understood that she is speaking in Spanish. More subtly, the translation of "la Grande" is in fact provided. What the novel does do, which can be interpreted as "aggressive use of bilingualism," is not italicize Spanish words. By not signaling the appearance of these words, the text catches the reader off guard and causes moments of disruption in the reading process. Even so, the tension brought on by the surprise appearance of a "foreign" word is quickly dissipated as the reader regains confidence through direct or contextualized translation.

Even Dasenbrock's brief summary of the novel signals his dominant culture-centric approach. The brevity of the description, "a novel about a young Hispanic growing up in bilingual New Mexico in the 1940s" (Dasenbrock 15), is understandable, particularly since the article also discusses three other texts, yet even in its brevity it exemplifies a number of problems in multicultural critical practices. The most obvious of these is the use of the term *Hispanic*, which has a controversial history as a term brought into circulation by the U.S. Census Bureau to homogenize differences among groups such as Puerto Ricans, Chicanos, and Cuban Americans. The term is also offensive to many Chicanos because of its emphasis on Peninsular culture.[9] This lumping together of various distinct groups with specific cultures, histories, and modes of expression also blurs important racial and class-based distinctions within groups.[10] Such generalization is particularly dangerous in the case of a writer such as Anaya who writes from a specific location as a

New Mexico Chicano mestizo, with special emphasis on his indigenous heritage.

Secondly, Dasenbrock's "young Hispanic" lacks gender, and although the protagonist's gender is unmarked (not female), it certainly is significant, as will become obvious when we compare *Bless Me, Ultima* to *Mango Street*. These crucial oversights become even more disturbing in light of the fact that the article appeared in the *PMLA*, which is indicative of the lack of participation of multiculturalists with a more critical bent on editorial boards at elite publications. Not surprisingly, this was the first article on Latina/o literature published in the *PMLA*.[11] Furthermore, it is not dedicated solely to a Latina/o text, but to the broad label of multiculturalism.

Herein lies the danger of blanket terms such as *multiculturalism*. Through normative institutional practices, the term allows for a recognition of "difference," yet because the term itself is overdetermined, it provides opportunities for exploitative uses of marginalized texts. These uses can function as strategies of containment, which on the one hand acknowledge the cultural specificity of texts such as *Bless Me, Ultima* and *Mango Street* but regulate their oppositional or transformational potentialities by requiring "manageable differences" as conditional to acceptance.

In these two texts, the fact that they are both narrated through the voices of children is exemplary of manageable difference, whereby misinformation and stereotypes can be re-edified. These two texts in and of themselves do not engage in stereotypic representations, yet because they have become representative, their portrayals of characters and community life are easily generalized. The child narrator in particular facilitates problematic readings of Chicanas and Chicanos as childlike, which undercuts anxiety regarding the policing of minority individuals and communities. In other words, these two texts, read outside of a fuller context of inclusion that would provide opportunities for recognition of diversity within diversity, foster an illusion of communities that are not only nonthreatening to the dominant society, but

also by association with the child narrator, less knowing, less experienced, and less empowered than the adult reader.

Sandra Cisneros's *Mango Street* can, like Anaya's novel, be classified as a bildungsroman, but due to gender, and to some extent form, it
imposes itself on the cartography of the genre more resistantly, push-
ing and stretching boundaries in all directions. The gender difference
in the bildungsroman, most critics agree, turns on the concept of
choice, and "even the broadest definitions of the bildungsroman pre-
suppose a range of social options available only to men" (Abel et al. 7).

While the male protagonist of the genre undergoes a process of education to become a "master," for the female protagonist an education as
to her function and role in society leads her in the opposite direction,
toward subservience. And, as Annis Pratt points out, whereas in rites
of passage, adolescent males undergo tests in valor and strength, younger girls are given "tests in submission" (Pratt, A. 14). Thus gender
problematization is built in to the *Bildung* the moment it is undertaken
by a female protagonist. That in Cisneros's book this protagonist is a
working-class Chicana further interrogates the presuppositions of the
genre's universal tenets.

Yet, even as a revision of the genre, *Mango Street* offers a veneer of
familiarity in its association with coming-of-age books. As in other
works of the genre, the protagonist of Cisneros's book, Esperanza, undergoes a process of individuation, constructing a self in relation to and
in opposition from others. In connection to this process of individuation, and a requisite of the bildungsroman, is the protagonist's physical
removal from family and community in the form of a departure. In the
conventional bildungsroman, the completion of a formal education
prompts the protagonist's leaving home. There is a promise of this in
the final vignette of *The House on Mango Street*: "one day I will say
goodbye to Mango. I am too strong for her to keep me here forever"
(Cisneros 101). But for Esperanza, leaving Mango Street in the process
of individuation is neither the beginning of her apprenticeship nor the
goal. Rather, the departure is seen as a step toward the return, toward

reconnection or attachment: "They will not know I have gone away to come back for the ones I left behind. For the ones who cannot out" (Cisneros 102).

This going away to return, or seeking distance as a step toward reunion and public responsibility, is reflective of an alternative Chicano tradition of the bildungsroman exemplified by writers such as Tomás Rivera in his classic work . . . *y no se lo tragó la tierra* [*And the Earth Did Not Devour Him*]. This alternative tradition, informed by the ideology of the Chicano Movement and the emergence of a new group identity, worked toward a "decentering of individualism" (Calderón 112) through both content and experimentation in form. This experimentation has led to the widespread use of the short story cycle, a form characterized by Renato Rosaldo as "the novel's 'poor relation'" (Rosaldo, "Fables" 88) and by Héctor Calderón as "prenovelistic" (Calderón 100).[12]

Mango Street's structure as a short story cycle enables the text to "poach" elements from the bildungsroman (Gutiérrez-Jones 310) while participating in a counterhegemonic discursive tradition that works to subvert the ideology of individualism. As a critique of the novel and the social, economic, patriarchal structures that gave rise to the novel and that the genre in turn reproduces, the short story cycle relies on oral narrative traditions, matriarchal heritage, and community-centered values. Unfortunately, because this is a relatively obscure form, story cycles are often read *as if* they were novels. This leads to a disregard for the construction of meaning through form.

In the case of *Mango Street*, this disregard has led to some conflicted readings of the text. Feminist critics, for example, familiar with arguments of relationships between gender and genre have questioned the possibilities of the female bildungsroman. Feminist readings of the text have been carried out which argue the text's relation to more traditional forms of the genre. Yet, as important as establishing this text in a feminist context may be, it is also imperative to locate it within a Chicano critique of the genre through the story cycle.

As feminist critics have noted, "isolate individualism is an illusion. It is also the privilege of power. A white man has the luxury of forgetting his skin color and sex. He can think of himself as an 'individual.' Women and minorities, reminded at every turn in the great cultural hall of mirrors of their sex or color, have no such luxury" (Friedman 39). Esther Labovitz has argued that because the sanctioned social role of women has in the past precluded the search for or the existence of an individual self, there was no possibility of a female counterpart to *Bildung* prior to societal changes in the twentieth century. She goes on to argue that the evolution of the genre parallels the male *Bildung* as "cultural and social structures appeared to support women's struggle for independence" (Labovitz 70).

While this may hold true, at least to some degree, for white, middle-class women, it is questionable to assume it could be applied to women of color or, more generally, women marginalized on the basis of race, ethnicity, sexual orientation, or class (Gutiérrez-Jones 299). What Labovitz's evolutionary model is lacking is an interrogation of the construction of the autonomous individual and the desirability of the adoption of such a construct by marginalized women.

Regenia Gagnier, in a review essay of women's autobiographies in the 1980s, looks at several texts including Gloria Anzaldúa's *Border-lands/La Frontera* and Cisneros's *Mango Street* in relation to the ideology of individualism and the exceptionalization of the artist. While Gagnier does engage in a critique of the political implications such an ideology carries when adopted by women of color, she reads Cisneros and Anzaldúa as reproducing that ideology in their respective texts (Gagnier 140). As it is argued in chapter 4, such a reading is fostered through a displacement of these texts from their respective contexts and intertextual play with other discourses and traditions.[13] Gagnier, for example, does not acknowledge the structural subtext of *Mango Street* and in fact misidentifies it as an autobiography.

Mango Street negates the ideology of individualism in several ways, the most notable being that even as the narrator remains constant, the text is composed of forty-six vignettes describing and expressing the interiority of a wide spectrum of characters who make up the Mango Street neighborhood. For example, there is Mamacita for whom "home is a house in a photograph" (Cisneros 77). There is Geraldo No Last Name, whose life Esperanza, in spite of never meeting him and learning of him from someone else, can nevertheless imagine and explain: "They never saw the kitchenettes. They never knew about the two room flats and sleeping rooms he rented, the weekly money orders sent home, the currency exchanges. How could they?" (Cisneros 66). And there is Marin who dances under the streetlight, "waiting for a car to stop, a star to fall, someone to change her life" (Cisneros 27).

In the traditional bildungsroman, attention remains focused exclusively on the protagonist, while *Mango Street* disperses the spotlight to include the community as inseparable from the protagonist's identity. As the three sisters tell Esperanza: "You will always be Esperanza. You will always be Mango Street" (Cisneros 105).

Unlike the protagonist of the traditional bildungsroman, Esperanza does not travel during the course of the book, nor does the text end with an escape. This is significant in that her psychic movement from childhood to adolescence to adulthood takes place within the geographic and cultural boundaries of her community. Her individuation is undertaken, like Antonio's in *Bless Me, Ultima*, in a community-centered context, a marked difference from the master plot of the genre in which the protagonist physically travels outward. This community centeredness demonstrates a point of negotiation of the conflict, for the Latina/o author working within the bildungsroman tradition, between the valorization of the individual inherent in the genre and its incompatibility with the political and cultural implications that valorization carries for minority intellectuals.

Generalized readings of these two texts that connect them solely to the familiar mapping of the novel, and more specifically to the bildungsroman with its assumption and valorization of the autonomous individual, reduce reader frustration at moments of difference, be it content based as in Anaya's text, or structural difference as in Cisneros's. This diminished frustration leads to a higher degree of intelligibility, and the assigning of a higher status for these two texts, relative to that of other Latina/o texts. By isolating these texts from their discursive and historical contexts, they can also function as mirrors of the hegemonic and confirmations of stereotypic representations. Thus, it is not the texts themselves that are problematic, since they do engage in layered critiques and propose their own aesthetics. Rather, it is their acceptance as representative that is troubling, given that they do provide opportunities for easy incorporation, which erases their transformative possibilities.

From *Latino American Literature in the Classroom: The Politics of Transformation* (2002), pp. 79-92. Copyright © 2002 by the University Press of Florida. Reprinted courtesy of the University Press of Florida.

Notes

1. For a fuller discussion of minorities and minority studies in institutions of higher learning, see Rosaura Sánchez's article "Ethnicity, Ideology and Academia."

2. There has been an equally if not more vocal response to this backlash, yet most of these responses have been published within the traditional channels of scholarship. See, for example, Mary Louise Pratt, "Humanities for the Future: Reflections on the Western Culture Debate at Stanford," John Guillory, "Canon, Syllabus, List," Michael Geyer, "Multiculturalism and the Politics of General Education," and Henry Louis Gates Jr., *Loose Canons*. A specific response to Hirsch's *Cultural Literacy* and Bloom's *The Closing of the American Mind* is Graywolf Press's *Multicultural Literacy: Opening the American Mind*.

3. A succinct example of the backlash's anxiety regarding the dangers of multiculturalism is Kimball's summation of the implications of multiculturalism as an attack on what Matthew Arnold described as our common legacy, descending largely from the Greeks and the Bible which "preserves us from chaos and barbarism."

4. Anaya's novel is also frequently included in Native American Literature courses, and Cisneros's book is also frequently used in Women's Literature syllabi.

5. Chicano critic Hector Calderón argues that, given the fact that most Chicano writers work from within educational institutions, we cannot deny "how institutionally Western our literature is." Yet, he points out, this does not erase or neutralize their cultural productions' oppositional potential.

6. For a fuller understanding and explanation of speech act theory see J. L. Austin and Paul Grice. For an explanation and discussion of reader response see Stanley Fish. Mary Louise Pratt's article, "Interpretive Strategies/Strategic Interpretations: On Anglo-American Reader Response Criticism," also offers a solid summary as well as a critique of reader response theory.

7. The term *reading competence*, as it is used here, is taken from Jonathan Culler's article "Prolegomena to a Theory of Reading" (1980).

8. Jeffrey L. Sammons, in his essay, "The Bildungsroman for Nonspecialists: An Attempt at Clarification," argues the genre's Germanness and points out misappropriations of the term in English Studies, including the work of Jerome Buckley.

9. The term *Latino* is more accepted as a blanket term, if we must have one, since it implies a strategic political alliance. For a fuller discussion of the problematic nature of labels and labeling terms as well as their history, see Suzanne Oboler's *Ethnic Labels, Latino Lives*.

10. Carlos Muñoz Jr., in his study *Youth, Identity, Power*, has argued that the term *Hispanic* in the mid-1970s became associated with a "politics on white ethnic identity" by emphasizing "whiteness" through European descent (Spain) and erasing racial and interracial identities (African, Asian, indigenous) in the Americas, specifically denying Mexican American/Chicano ties to Mexico.

11. Since the publication of Dasenbrock's article, the *PMLA* has published two other articles on Latina/o texts: one on Richard Rodríguez's *Hunger of Memory*, and another on Piri Thomas's *Down These Mean Streets*.

12. Calderón describes the short story cycle as "prenovelistic" in that it bears parallels to Cervantes's work during the late sixteenth and early seventeenth centuries in terms of societal forces influencing production as well as audience. He argues that the form is a critique of the novel by its return to alternative structures used and developed prior to the novel's becoming "the bourgeois literary monument it is today" (Calderón 100).

13. For contextualized readings of *The House on Mango Street* in relation to a Chicano formative tradition in the short story cycle, see Erlinda Gonzales-Berry and Tey Diana Rebolledo's article "Growing up Chicano: Tomás Rivera and Sandra Cisneros" and Renato Rosaldo's "Fables of the Fallen Guy."

Works Cited

Abel, Elizabeth, Marianne Hirsch, and Elizabeth Langland, eds. *The Voyage In: Fictions of Female Development*. Hanover, N.H.: University Press of New England, 1983. 1-27.

Anaya, Rudolfo. *Bless Me, Ultima*. Berkeley: Tonatiuh, 1972.

Anzaldúa, Gloria. *Borderlands/La Frontera: The New Mestiza*. San Francisco: Spinster/Aunt Lute, 1987.

Austin, J. L. *How to Do Things with Words*. New York: Oxford University Press, 1965.

Bloom, Allan. *The Closing of the American Mind.* New York: Simon and Schuster, 1987.

Calderón, Héctor. "The Novel and the Community of Readers: Reading Tomás Rivera's *y no se lo tragó la tierra.*" *Criticism in the Borderlands: Studies in Chicano Literature, Culture, and Ideology.* Ed. Héctor Calderón and José David Saldívar. Durham: Duke University Press, 1991. 97-113.

Cisneros, Sandra. *The House on Mango Street.* Houston: Arte Público, 1986.

Culler, Jonathan. "Prolegomena to a Theory of Reading." *The Reader in the Text: Essays on Audience and Interpretations.* Ed. Susan R. Suleiman and Inge Crosman. Princeton: Princeton University Press, 1980. 46-66.

Dasenbrock, Reed Way. "Intelligibility and Meaningfulness in Multicultural Literature in English." *PMLA* 102.1 (1987): 10-19.

Fish, Stanley. *Is There a Text in This Class?* Cambridge: Harvard University Press, 1980.

Friedman, Susan Stanford. "Women's Autobiographical Selves: Theory and Practice." *The Primitive Self: Theory and Practice of Women's Autobiography.* Ed. Shari Benstock. Chapel Hill: University of North Carolina Press, 1988. 34-62.

Gagnier, Regenia. "Feminist Autobiography in the 1980s." *Feminist Studies* 17.1 (1991): 135-48.

Gates, Henry Louis, Jr. *Loose Canons: Notes on the Culture Wars.* Oxford: Oxford University Press, 1992.

Geyer, Michael. "Multiculturalism and the Politics of General Education." *Critical Inquiry* (1993): 499-533.

Goldberg, David Theo. "Multicultural Conditions." *Multiculturalism: A Critical Reader.* Ed. David Theo Goldberg. Cambridge: Blackwell, 1994. 1-44.

Gonzales-Berry, Erlinda, and Tey Diana Rebolledo. "Growing up Chicano: Tomás Rivera and Sandra Cisneros." *International Studies in Honor of Tomás Rivera.* Ed. Julián Oliváres. Houston: Arte Público, 1986. 109-20.

Grice, Paul. "Logic and Conversation." *Speech Acts: Syntax and Semantics.* Ed. Peter Cole and Jerry L. Morgan. New York: Academic, 1975. 41-58.

Guillory, John. "Canon, Syllabus, List: A Note on the Pedagogic Imaginary." *Transition* 52 (1991): 36-54.

Gutiérrez-Jones, Leslie. "Different Voices: The Re-*Bildung* of the Barrio in Sandra Cisneros' *The House on Mango Street.*" *Anxious Power: Reading, Writing, and Ambivalence in Narrative by Women.* Ed. Carol J. Singley and Susan Elizabeth Sweeney. Albany: State University of New York Press, 1993. 295-312.

Hirsch, E. D., Jr. *Cultural Literacy: What Every American Needs to Know.* Boston: Houghton Mifflin, 1987.

Kimball, Roger. *Tenured Radicals: How Politics Has Corrupted Higher Education.* New York: HarperCollins, 1990.

Labovitz, Esther Kleinbord. *The Myth of the Heroine: The Female Bildungsroman in the Twentieth Century.* New York: Peter Lang, 1986.

McLaren, Peter. "White Terror and Oppositional Agency: Toward a Critical Multiculturalism." *Multiculturalism: A Critical Reader.* Ed. David Theo Goldberg. Cambridge: Blackwell, 1994. 45-74.

Muñoz, Carlos, Jr. *Youth, Identity, Power*. London: Verso, 1989.

Oboler, Suzanne. *Ethnic Labels, Latino Lives: Identity and the Politics of (Re)Presentation in the United States*. Minneapolis: University of Minnesota Press, 1995.

Pratt, Annis. *Archetypal Patterns in Women's Fiction*. Bloomington: Indiana University Press, 1981.

Pratt, Mary Louise. "Humanities for the Future: Reflections on the Western Culture Debate at Stanford." *South Atlantic Quarterly* 89.1 (1990): 7-25.

_____. "Interpretive Strategies/Strategic Interpretations: On Anglo-American Reader Response Criticism." *Boundary 2* 11.1-2 (1982): 201-31.

Rivera, Tomás. *. . . y no se lo tragó la tierra*. Berkeley: Quinto Sol, 1971.

Rodríguez, Richard. *Hunger of Memory: The Education of Richard Rodríguez*. Boston: D. R. Godine, 1981.

Rosaldo, Renato. *Culture and Truth: The Remaking of Social Analysis*. Boston: Beacon, 1989.

_____. "Fables of the Fallen Guy." *Criticism in the Borderlands: Studies in Chicano Literature, Culture, and Ideology*. Ed. Héctor Calderón and José David Saldívar. Durham: Duke University Press, 1991. 84-93.

Sammons, Jeffrey L. "The Bildungsroman for Nonspecialists: An Attempt at a Clarification." *Reflection and Action: Essays on the Bildungsroman*. Ed. James Hardin. Columbia: University of South Carolina Press, 1991. 26-45.

Sánchez, Rosaura. "Ethnicity, Ideology and Academia." *The Americas Review* 15.1 (1987): 80-88.

Shaffner, Randolph P. *The Apprenticeship Novel: A Study of the "Bildungsroman" as a Regulative Type in Western Literature with a Focus on Three Classic Representatives by Goethe, Maugham, and Mann*. New York: Peter Lang, 1984.

Simonson, Rick, and Scott Walker, eds. *Multicultural Literacy: Opening the American Mind*. Saint Paul, Minn.: Graywolf, 1988.

Thomas, Piri. *Down These Mean Streets*. New York: Vintage Books, 1975.

Homeplaces and Spaces of Their Own_____
Maria Antònia Oliver-Rotger

How do we create spaces not only for our private selves but also for our collective selves? Spaces where we can together admit our dreams and fears, using our emotions as resources for discovery? [. . .] How do we create space for ourselves to be ourselves, our multiple Latina, Hispana, Mexicana, Chicana selves?

—Pat Mora, *Nepantla* (1993)

The concept of "homeplace" as described by bell hooks has gendered connotations that perpetuate the association of women with the domestic realm. This African American critic sustains that, in the minds of young people in the black community, "houses belonged to women. They were their special domain, not as property, but as places where all that truly mattered in life took place—the warmth and comfort of shelter, the feeding of our bodies, the nurturing of our souls" (hooks 41). In the particular context of hooks' collectivity, the role of women was not merely to serve others; they constructed "a safe place where black people could affirm one another and by so doing heal many of the wounds inflicted by racist domination" (42). The home may have been a space of oppression, but it was also a place where solace, comfort, self-esteem, and refuge from adverse public spaces could be found.

Like hooks, Chicana writers have paid a strong tribute to the willing and conscious (not natural) self-sacrifice of women for the benefit of others. The *abuelita*'s house in Viramontes' "The Moths" is an example of this particular representation of the home as a haven from a hostile world. The home is identified with women's capacity to give and identify with the suffering of others, a capacity that Sara Ruddick has termed "maternal thinking." Ruddick sustains that "maternal thinking" can be transformed into a revolutionary discourse that is not tied to the biological conditioning of being a woman. When such thinking embraces self-assertion and the will to have a public voice, it becomes a challenge to a social order that relegates the nurturing and caretaking aspects of life to the private, domestic sphere. It is therefore a challenge to the traditional division between public and private, masculine and feminine spaces.

The reconciliation of personal liberation and collective commitment has been articulated by Viramontes and Cisneros through reinvented spatial images that challenge these divisions by highlighting the interdependence of communal and individual freedom, of material and psychological needs. Independence and creativity are conflated with political commitment and collective enfranchisement in what Terry Eagleton terms an "aesthetics of materialist ethics" (*The Ideology* 413). In a more fanciful exploration of family history Pat Mora's latest *House of Houses* (1997) creates an imaginary homeplace in the desert of the American cultural mainstream. This collective autobiography or "family memoir," as she has preferred to call it, asserts the psychological value of place, community, family, history, and tradition for the construction of a future based on mutual respect, sustenance, and solace in a country that is not quite one's home.

1. "Summoning Home All Those Who Stray": Sandra Cisneros and Helena Viramontes

For many women of Mexican descent the home or the house as Bachelard understands it—"a space of protected intimacy," an archetypal image of the individual imagination, the center of our dreams, and the germ of our inner happiness, introversion, and creativity— rarely corresponds to its actual material experience. However, in the most optimistic writings of Chicanas like Cisneros and Viramontes, the evocation of spaces of intimacy is tied to a sense of individual freedom that is inextricable from collective needs. Thus, the poetics of space of these writers is necessarily an ethical poetics that embraces issues of social and gender equity.

In *The Ideology of the Aesthetic* (1990) Terry Eagleton argues that the fact the discourse on the aesthetic has usually tended to exclude the routine aspects of life, the everyday, the banal, and the material, ensues from the separation of the realms of the ethical, the political, and the aesthetic aspects of human life within the modern bourgeois state. Eagleton's main argument is that the conventional widespread notion of the aesthetic is tied to modern notions of autonomy, self-referentiality, and subjectivity that have developed within the European middle-class bourgeoisie. The concept of the aesthetic has disparate implications. On the one hand, it provides the middle class with the model of subjectivity that is necessary for its material operations. On the other, it underscores the independent nature of human thought, sensitivity, and action that will turn against bourgeois capitalist ideology. The symptom of modernity, Eagleton says, is that "[e]verything should now become aesthetic" (368). Morality, truth, that which satisfies the mind, have now become a matter of style, pleasure, and intuition (368). Culture and art are autonomous objects through which human beings have sublimated certain necessities and desires. Self-fulfillment is understood by modern ethical thought as a personal matter rather than a political one, so that aesthetics, as conceived by modernity, engages the relationship between the particular and the universal by beginning with self-identity and individual desire (413). Thus, the domestic realm, occupied by women, and the spaces occupied by the downcast and the poor cannot enter traditional concepts of the aesthetic unless they are disembodied or idealized representations of an essence.

The American critic Jean Franco has pointed to the patriarchal bias of this notion of the aesthetic and the concept of subjectivity on which it is based. The private, Franco says, is the space of freedom and intimacy that is necessary for creativity and intellectual thought to develop, a space that men have enjoyed more often than women. Yet, she observes it is also in that very intimacy of the private space that one confronts death, mortality, and the possibility of dissolution. Thus, she argues, the union with an ideal feminine is the means by which many male artists have compensated their own fear of death ("Going Public" 74-76). The gender bias of Bachelard's phenomenological approach to space corroborates Franco's contention. The idea of home as a "space of protected intimacy" grounds itself upon a romanticization of women's work in the home, upon the idea of "la maternité de la maison" (*La poétique* 57). According to Bachelard's idealized vision, women's care-taking activity ties the present with the past, wakes up the dormant furniture, creates an inner balance out of everything that is inside the house. The inside of a maternal house is an idealized haven from outside deadly forces. Men, on the contrary, can only build houses from the outside (*La poétique* 74).

While traditional aesthetics assumes that the relationship between the particular and the universal prioritizes self-identity, privacy, comfort, and independence, the "aesthetics of materialist ethics" proposed by Eagleton assumes that the individual is one whose desire is always inseparable from the desire of others. The universal is thus reached through this implication with others, which brings to the fore *public*, *political*, and *material* questions of justice as well as debates about which desires should be curtailed and which should be fulfilled: "[T]he incessant process of arguing all this belongs to the public sphere, in which all individuals must have equal participatory rights whatever their distinguishing particularities of work, gender, race, interests, and so on" (*The Ideology* 414). This critic's reflections on the political, material value of aesthetics are certainly in accord with Lefebvre's desire to establish a dialectics between lived spaces and conceived or imagined spaces.

Patricia Waugh has cogently argued that the aesthetic tendencies of many contemporary women writers resist classification within the established literary categories of realism, modernism, or postmodernism because their works are not complicit with the notion of the uniform, coherent, autonomous self that grounds modern views of aesthetics. In *Feminine Fictions: Revisiting the Postmodern* (1989), Waugh contends that these fictions propose a self that, in spite of its fragmentation, acknowledges the need for connectedness and relationship with others. The work of many contemporary Chicana writers certainly opposes both the unified subject of rationalism and the schizophrenic postmodern subject through what we could call a *politics of the local*. Although influenced by a post-structuralist conception of the subject, the self that Chicana writers are speaking about has not emerged out of a merely escapist, or formalist signifying game. Rather, it springs out of the specific social, cultural, and political tensions of actual borderland spaces or locations such as the home, the neighborhood, the fields, and/or the body.

In Cisneros' *The House on Mango Street* (1985) the voice of Esperanza craves for a family house "that would be ours for always," "a real house. One I could point to" (*Mango Street* 7-9). Esperanza is once told by a fortune-teller that she will develop "a home in the heart," a remark that, on that occasion, she does not quite understand. In "Bums in the Attic" Esperanza, tired of "looking at what [her family] can't have" (81), recalls her refusal to go on her family's Sunday trips to the rich neighborhood where her father works. As we have seen in Chapter 3, in Cisneros' work social differences translate into spatial images that correlate the geographical separation between rich and poor neighborhoods and the detachment between the material and the intellectual or spiritual realm. Esperanza herself comments on this correlation: "People who live on hills sleep so close to the stars they forget those of us who live too much on earth. They don't look down at all except to be content to live on hills. They have nothing to do with last week's garbage or fear of rats" (*Mango Street* 81). Towards the end of Cisneros' work, a more mature and independent Esperanza longs for a house that is only hers: "Not a flat. Not an apartment in the back. Not a man's house. Not a daddy's" (*Mango Street* 100). The young woman's desire for an intimate, comfortable space of her own is a pre-condition for artistic creation and imagination. Echoing both Woolf and Bachelard, Cisneros has her character say: "Only a house quiet as snow, a space for myself to go, clean as paper before the poem" (*Mango Street* 100).

The middle-class, feminist, aesthetic implications of Esperanza's words are ineludible, but they have to be considered in relation to her incipient collective social consciousness. Her freedom as a woman and as an artist together with the social reality of those "who live too much on earth" will be the constitutive elements of her aesthetics: "One day I'll own my own house, but I won't forget who I am or where I came from. Passing bums will ask, Can I come in? I'll offer them the attic, ask them to stay, because I know how it is to be without a house" (81). The "attic" is here particularly relevant as an alternative spatial image, an expression of intellectual, artistic, and political commitment. For Bachelard, the attic, symbolizing rationality and clear thinking, is the space of quiet and pleasurable solitude; one never wishes to descend from the attic (Bachelard 41). As Cisneros has stated in an unpublished interview with the author of this volume, the attic has similar connotations for her.

The "attic," however, has multiple connotations in different cultural contexts. For middle-class women, the attic is, as Debra Castillo puts it, "a forerunner of Woolf's room and also its analogous representations in those other rooms where women have been confined by custom and tradition: the kitchen, the bedroom" (7). The Spanish meaning of the word in its adjectival form in Spanish means, as Castillo points out, "Attic (from Athens), and therefore signifies 'elegant'" (8). Someone who has Attic taste is elegant and has the economic security to cultivate it (Castillo 8). Yet, in Spanish, the *ático* designates the place under the roof that is occupied by the servant or the maid in the houses of the middle and upper middle class in many Latin American countries (Castillo 8). The title of Sandra Gilbert's and Susan Gubar's well-known *The Madwoman in the Attic* (1984) refers to the mad woman in Charlotte Brontë's *Jane Eyre* (1847) as a metaphor for women's repressed desire to write and express themselves. This desire would be accomplished thanks to the feminist movement, and at the expense of other women "who live too close to the earth"—the working-class servants, maids, nannies—and also at the expense of the *criolla*, who is in-between two classes, two cultures, and two value systems. As Jean Rhys' novel *Wide Sargasso Sea* (1966) shows, the *real* madwoman in the attic is a *criolla*, a Jamaican lady whose life-story the Caribbean author committed herself to writing. In Rhys' novel the rage and derangement of Antoinette, the "madwoman," are shown to stem from her double oppression as a colonized subject and as a woman who wants to participate in the middle-class ideology of the colonizer.

In Cisneros' story the "attic" may be seen as referring to the space inhabited by the middle-class feminist writer of working-class origin who is mad (angry) and whom many people inside and outside her community may consider to be mad (crazy). It is also the space the speaker wants to share with the bums, the working class that Cisneros commits herself to sheltering in the house of her writing. As a descendant of working-class Mexican immigrants, Cisneros is not a *criolla* but a *mestiza* (in Anzaldúa's sense of the word). She stands in-between working-class Mexicans whom she descends from and the American middle class she belongs to now. Unlike other female writers, she does not hide the existence of the marginalized. Castillo says that "it is hard to imagine an Attic attic" (8), but in Cisneros' writing the house or "room of one's own," symbolizing the Attic taste (aesthetics as well as economic and intellectual freedom), converges with the other attic (the attic of the poor and the underclass).

Cisneros' story entitled "Little Miracles, Kept Promises" in the volume *Woman Hollering Creek* is perhaps one of the most representative examples of this writer's borderlands consciousness, a broad vision of community and culture that embraces the interests of men, women, children, the poor, and the homosexual. Inspired by the popular votive Catholic traditions of the *milagro* and the *ofrenda*, Cisneros' piece addresses the most quotidian concerns of people of Mexican American descent.[1] The story recasts these votive traditions by reproducing the texts of the prayers and dedications that accompany the offerings. A conflation of voices from the Mexico-Texas border, the story becomes a religious *heterotopia* that is both a manifestation of local culture and folklore as well as a reference to a variety of interrelated social spaces and issues.

In these prayers and petitions Cisneros discloses multiple female and male subject positions according to the age, generation, gender, sexuality, origin, and social background of her protagonists. A family thanks the *Santo Niño de Atocha* for having helped their son quit drinking and abusing his wife and children; a couple asks *San Martín* to make their daughter "see some sense" and understand her parents are too poor for her to go to school and that her "place is in the home helping us out" (*Woman Hollering* 117). A woman asks to be set free from men, to be left alone like she was before; another woman, who is often abused by her husband, prays to be forgiven for not loving her husband anymore and to be taught to love him back; another one still prays for a decent man "who is not a pain in the *nalgas*": A "man, man," "someone who is not ashamed to be seen cooking or cleaning or looking after himself" (*Woman Hollering* 117). A young girl asks the virgin for help to lose weight so as not to end up "dressing saints." The more resigned women pray that their husbands and sons will change their ways.

Some prayers illustrate the social maladjustment of Mexicans in the U.S. Immigrants for whom "there is no one else [they] can turn to in this country" ask the saints for decent jobs, or for the pay that never comes and must be sent to Mexico to the kids and in-laws (120). The parents and grandparents of a young man pray that he will stay away from drink and drugs; a student prays to pass the British Restoration literature class. There are also other prayers for the arrival of the disability check, for the income tax "to pay los bites," for a winning lottery ticket (*Woman Hollering* 122). Cisneros also records the health problems of Mexican Americans, ranging from the pimples of a teenager, through a woman's hemorrhage after an operation, to the cancer treatment of a two-year-old. Finally, the story also addresses the question of the discrimination of homosexuals by the Church through a coded prayer full of shame and sadness in which a young man asks the Black Christ of Esquípulas to watch over the man he is in love with.

Significantly, the last and longest of these petitions is Rosario's, Cisneros' *mestiza* character who learns to make the positive elements of her familial heritage compatible with the liberating aspects of American culture and values. Rosario rejects the traditional Mexican roles of mother and wife and resents the sneering comments of her relatives about her artistic ambitions. She scorns the figure of the *Virgencita de Guadalupe* which she associates with her mother's and grandmother's subservience: "Couldn't look at you without blaming you for all the pain my mother and her mother and all our mothers' mothers have put up with in the name of God" (*Woman Hollering* 127). Unable to look at the *Virgencita* without being reminded of women's inaction in her culture, she conjures up an entirely different Guadalupe: "I wanted you bare-breasted, snakes in your hands. I wanted you leaping and somersaulting the backs of bulls. I wanted you swallowing raw hearts and rattling volcanic ash" (127).

Cisneros' rebellious protagonist might well find a visual representation of her Guadalupe in Yolanda López's drawing *Portrait of the Artist as the Virgin of Guadalupe* (1978): Stepping into material history and out of the halo of saintliness that keeps her immobile, the Guadalupe represented in López's work is an athletic figure dressed in modern sporting clothes who looks forward as she runs over the red, white and blue wings of an angel (probably a figurative representation of U.S. patriarchy). She is holding a snake, the Aztec symbol of power. In representing herself as Guadalupe, López not only brings the religious idol closer to the reality of contemporary women; she also rescues Guadalupe from the position of immobility and "silent suffering" to highlight other attributes of Mexican women such as activity, impetus, and capacity for regeneration. In Yolanda López's painting, Guadalupe is the new mediating, Chicana-feminist subject of the future who brings together modernity, the icons of a pre-Columbian cultural background, Catholicism, and the survival skills passed on to her by her female ancestors.

In a similar vein, the female protagonist of "Little Miracles" finally grasps the strength and invigorating potential of Guadalupe as a crucial collective emblem within the history of the *mestizo/a* Mexican people and the history of Mexican American people's struggle for rights. This power, she concludes, is perhaps no different from the power and strength that her female relatives have harbored with their patience, their endurance, and their sympathy for others:

> That you could have the power to rally a people when a country was born, and again during civil war, and during a farmworkers' strike in California made me think maybe there is power in my mother's patience, strength in my grandmother's endurance [. . .]. The power of understanding someone else's pain. And understanding is the beginning of healing. (*Woman Hollering* 128)

Once she acknowledges this power, she ceases to be ashamed of her origins and claims her female ancestors back in a final gesture of thankfulness that materializes in her offering of a *milagro* to a Guadalupe that, like the figure in López's painting, is a personal re-appropriation. In particular, Cisneros' persona views Guadalupe as a representation of the ecumenicity of female power that she recognizes in all religious icons, "all at once the Buddha, the Tao, the true Messiah, Yahweh, Allah, the Heart of the Sky, the heart of the Earth, the Lord of the Near and Far, the Spirit, the Light, the Universe [. . .]" (128): "Mighty Guadalupana Coatlaxopeuh Tonantzín. What 'little miracle' could I pin here? Braid of hair in its place and know that I thank you" (129).

Following the line of the female liberation plot adopted by Cisneros in some of her stories and in *The House on Mango Street*, in her latest work Helena Viramontes has left behind the harsh tone that characterized her first productions. The narratives I tackle here have adopted a more lyrical though no less critical tone about the conditions of Mexican Americans in the U.S. With her story "The Jumping Bean" (1992) and her novel *Under the Feet of Jesus* (1995) she has demonstrated her capacity for reconciling the poetics of oppression with the poetics of liberation. "The Jumping Bean" introduces a shift in the treatment of male characters and an optimistic note about the possibility of dignified and caring human relations that was far from present in most of her previous stories. In this story about a working-class Mexican family living in L.A., Viramontes focuses mainly on the figure of the father and on the figure of his eldest daughter, who, like Cisneros' Esperanza, is a potential organic intellectual. The story is partially told from the perspective of the youngest girl in the family, a peripheral observer of the main events. Viramontes' sympathetic characterization of the male character differs from her usually prototypical representation of Mexican American men as authoritarian, oppressive, and despotic. As the author has said, this story was written as a tribute to her father, and as an effort to "understand why this man was the way he was, the origin of all the rage that he took out on his family" (Christoph 10). The conflict between the self-assertive eldest female child of the family and the hard-working father that this story deals with is no doubt one more of Viramontes' critical assertions about patriarchal relations within the family. However, "jumping bean," the mocking nickname used by the resentful construction workers to refer to the father, is a reference to his strength, resilience, and determination in spite of the inhibiting social environment of U.S. society. The insect is also a metaphor for the whole family's struggle, their endless fight against their social confinement, and, more particularly, for the eldest daughter's desire to break free of the constraints of her social and family environment. The narrative alternates episodes that focus respectively on the figures of the father and the eldest child. It reaches its climax in a scene where the father has to choose between asserting his patriarchal authority over his daughter, or accepting the validity of her arguments and the possibility of her liberation.

With this realistic depiction of a male Mexican immigrant worker inspired by her own relationship with her father, Viramontes undermines the stereotype of the Mexican worker, the "spic," usually thought to be lazy and untrustworthy. The joke played on the father by his workmates ("what's the difference between a spic and a drunk?"

["Jumping" 104]), reflects the social prejudice affecting Mexican workers. The joke's punch line ("a drunk will sober up, but a spic will always be a spic" ["Jumping" 104]) hints at the widespread prejudice in the United States that people of Latin American origin are undependable and incapable of moving up in the social scale; hence, their permanent inferior status. This joke is Viramontes' commentary on the ways in which popular culture is instrumental in the perpetuation of certain stereotypes and social prejudices based on racial categories. However, her partially omniscient narrator also comments on the "peripheral vision" and "standards" that produce such stereotypes. In fact, the story shows they are more grounded in social panic and resentment at newcomers than in actual facts. Significantly, the father cannot grasp the racist implications of the joke and feels "possessed by [questions like this that] he does not understand" and that his eldest daughter has to clarify for him ("Jumping" 109).

The battered mother of the story is an example of the long-suffering working-class Mexican woman. Yet the eldest daughter poses a challenge to the endless pain of this woman and the social discrimination of Mexicans in the United States by refusing to be silent and seeking her way out of social depression through education. After nine weeks of school nonattendance due to her mother's illness, the "truant officer," an "official looking gringo" comes to fetch her. Echoing the official discourse ("You need to be learning," "You'll end up like some old lady in the shoe" ["Jumping" 106]), he takes for granted Mexican immigrants' equal opportunities of social mobility. In a house crammed with nine children, the only space of one's own in the house is the toilet, and it is there that the youngest sister finds Maria de la Luz trying to read a book. As the name indicates, Maria de la Luz is a character full of hope, a woman for whom liberation is a possibility.

"The Jumping Bean" anticipates Viramontes' less tragic look upon women's lives that has culminated in her novel *Under the Feet of Jesus* (1995). The final confrontation between father and daughter over the freeing of the caterpillar inside the bean is Viramontes' symbolic juxtaposition of two forces that should not be at odds with one another. As long as the father places his authority above the spirit of social resistance championed by his daughter and embodied by the bean, he becomes a potential threat to his own daughter's liberation. The necessary, though not yet fully possible reconciliation between father and daughter, between women's individual liberation and the liberation of the collectivity, is perhaps the most important message of the story. Emerging with surprising force at the end of the narrative, the silent, observant youngest sister is a redemptive center who does not yet speak for herself but who, by swallowing the bean over which the antagonism between father and daughter has arisen, transforms this family confrontation into positive energy. The character's symbolic action, leading to the happy note on which the story ends, may be interpreted as the writer's faith in a better future in which the home will be a homeplace where women's freedom will be part and parcel of the whole community's well-being.

Under the Feet of Jesus (1995), the first novel written by Helena Viramontes, illustrates the complexity of social tensions in the lives of migrant workers. This novel has inherited some of the aspects of the other *local* migrant worker Chicano narratives like Tomás Rivera's . . . *y no se lo tragó la tierra* (1970) and Miguel Méndez's *Peregrinos de Aztlán* (1973). Its setting, the luxuriant, fertile landscape of golden California, cannot but remind us of that other migrant story told by John Steinbeck in *The Grapes of Wrath* (1939).

The setting and ideological ground of this novel are contemporary U.S. border politics and agribusiness. Viramontes addresses current *global* socio-economic issues such as the creation of a Mexican transnational labor force in the U.S. and their *local* repercussions: the militarization of the U.S.-Mexico border, the indiscriminate raids on Mexican immigrants, sickness from pesticide poisoning, and the exploitation of *pizcadores* by agri-business. In dedicating her novel to César Chávez and her parents, Viramontes creates a continuum between the present where the novel is set—the end of the twentieth century—the campesino revolt of 1962 led by the United Farm Workers Association (UFWA) founded by Chávez, and the story of her own parents, who worked as cotton pickers in the fields of Arizona. Other issues alluded to in her novel are the abolition of affirmative action and the harsh laws against the legal and illegal immigrants' rights to the welfare services of health care and education in the state of California, enacted after the approval of propositions 187 and 209, respectively.[2]

Viramontes' novel gives us a particular gendered version of the plight of Mexican immigrants by focusing on a female character. The narrative structure transgresses the convention of the uniform perspective of the *Bildungsroman* heroine. As various feminist critiques of the nineteenth-century feminine *Bildungsroman* have shown, this genre usually ended in marriage or in death, reproducing what Patricia Waugh terms a "'consensus' aesthetics".[3] This aesthetics was based on the received notion that the consciousness of the female protagonist was motivated by interiority, morality, sentiment, and sensitivity (28). Through the combination of the *Bildungsroman* and the migrant novel, Viramontes reworks the pattern of the feminine romance plot, and breaks the rigid boundary between the private and the public spheres that grounds the realist romance novel. Nor can the novel be classified within the "women's novels" of liberation that became popular in the 1970s. Intent on giving an alternative "feminine" perspective and on reversing existing stereotypes of womanhood, works such as Erica Jong's *Fear of Flying* (1974) reacted against the realist romance plot, privileged women's sensuality, and resisted the novelistic convention of marriage as the only way out for the heroine.

Rosalind Coward has observed that in so far as the novels of liberation give a description of women's development exclusively around sexual matters, they cannot offer an effective resistance to the patriarchal discourse that has strictly defined women's inferiority on the basis of their sexual difference. Using Foucault's argument that speaking about sex may also be a way of establishing, controlling, and classifying the subject and the body, Coward argues that these novels reproduce an ideology that has always viewed women in relation to their sexual experience. This ideology sustains that a woman comes to know herself only in so far as she deals with her sexual life, which entails that woman has access to knowledge, but not to power. Viramontes' novel incorporates some of the elements of the "novel of liberation" plot such as the awakening to love and sexuality of a strong-willed female character, but, due to the writer's borderlands Chicana feminist politics, it considers factors other than sexual awakening and romance as essential for women's self-development.

In *Under the Feet of Jesus* (1995) Viramontes has used a technique very similar to that used by Rivera and Méndez in their migrant novels. She has juxtaposed a variety of male and female voices: the female protagonist, Estrella; the strong, long-suffering mother abandoned by her husband; Perfecto, the surrogate head of the family, a battered old man with an unspoken history, tired of the hard life in the U.S., and dreaming of his return to an idealized Mexico; and Alejo, an illegal worker who has migrated to the U.S. enticed by promises of the American dream. The third-person omniscient narrator refrains from passing moral judgement on the characters, its ambiguous position being that of both master and slave: a master in that he represents the *pizcadores*; a slave in that he becomes involved in their experiences and looks at the world through their eyes. In this novel the problem of the gulf between the intellectual and the working class is transcoded in the omniscience through which Viramontes has chosen to tell her story (Franco, "Going Public" 69). Through this fictional account, she becomes both an interpreter and a transmitter of the lives and concerns of the marginal workers who are usually concealed by everyday official "public" discourse, but she does so through the literary discourse of the privileged.

The novel articulates the faith in the instrumental power of language that this writer has expressed in her testimonial essay "Nopalitos" (1989). Estrella craves knowledge and is eager to decipher "the diagonal lines written in chalk on the blackboard," but is frustrated to see that the teachers are more concerned with her dirty fingernails (*Under* the Feet 24). Teachers use a language with her that hurts "like rusted nails piercing the heels of her bare feet" (25). Eventually, she establishes a mental link between the practical use of language and the box of tools of the old man Perfecto. Learning the names of those tools is connected to the learning of their function, their use, and therefore, to power:

> The curves and tails of the tools made no sense and the shapes were as foreign and meaningless to her as chalky lines on the blackboard [. . .]. Tools to build, bury, tear down, rearrange and repair, a box of reasons [Perfecto's] hands took pride in. She lifted the pry bar in her hand, felt the coolness of iron and power of function, weighed the significance it awarded her, and soon she came to understand how essential it was to know these things. That was when she began to read. (26)

Thus far, Estrella has not owned books, except for the catechism chapbook given to her by her grandmother, which she had read and reread. She also reads over and over the words in newspapers thrown in trash cans, words publicizing an ironically inaccessible, aseptic world of consumerism whose existence depends on people like her: "*Clorox makes linens more than white . . . It makes them sanitary, too! Swanson's TV Dinners, closest to Mom's Cooking. Coppertone—Fastest Tan Under the Sun with Maximum Sunburn Protection*" (*Under the Feet* 31). The commercial advertisements of cleanliness and a healthy tan contrast with Estrella's constant exposure to pesticides and polluted water and with her sunburnt skin from whole days of work in the fields.

Viramontes has said the role of the writer should be akin to that of the subversive activist. The task of those who write from such a position is to clear away the "abstract" from words and bring them down to the "material."[4] Like the acclaimed Chicano writer Tomás Rivera, in *Under the Feet of Jesus* Viramontes comments on the blinding, mystifying power of language and representation.[5] Estrella becomes aware of deceptive cultural representations of Californian agricultural work and its social context. Through this character, Viramontes ironizes on the ideals of Californian agrarian landscape as plentiful and almost pastoral. Indeed, the picture of the woman and her rural surroundings on the box of raisins that Estrella sees in the market is a stylized depiction of landscape giving, as cultural geographer Jonathan Smith puts it, a "sense of completion, of stability, of permanence" (78). According to Smith, representations of landscape, especially those associated to memory and retrospection, often rise above time and circumstance: "It is the sense of transcendence provided by the metaphorical elevation of memory that landscape, treated as scenery, unwittingly reproduces and recalls. It is this partial escape from the temporal flux which landscape, treated as scenery, unfailingly represents as an occurrence" (Smith 79). Luminous, golden scenes produce the illusion of stepping out of history. Landscapes seem to surpass the process by which they were created.

Probably inspired by the work of Chicana artist Ester Hernández, *Sun Mad Raisins* (1982), Viramontes unsettles the idealization of the Californian landscape and the rural worker through an ironic contrast between representation and material reality. Vexed by the sentimentalized, disembodied image of the field worker in the picture, Estrella points at the disjuncture between such a representation and the harsh conditions under which she herself has to work:

Carrying the full basket to the paper was not like the picture on the red raisin boxes Estrella saw in the market, not like the woman wearing a fluffy bonnet, holding out the grapes with her smiling, ruby lips, the sun a flat orange behind her. The sun was white and it made Estrella's eyes sting like an onion, and the baskets of grapes resisted her muscles [. . .]. The woman with the red bonnet did not know this. Her knees did not sink in the hot white soil [. . .]. The woman's bonnet would be as useless as Estrella's own straw hat under a white sun so mighty, it toasted the green grapes to black raisins. (*Under the Feet* 49-50)

The representation of the woman with the red bonnet as a non-corporeal, aesthetized object, perfectly integrated with a non-aggressive, idyllic nature, conveys a romanticized vision of field work that bears no relationship whatsoever to the material, socio-economic issues that affect migrant workers like Estrella.

The title of the novel, *Under the Feet of Jesus*, is another direct reference to Viramontes' secular, materialist thought, as well as to the abstracting, deceiving reassurance of spiritual values, beliefs, and myths that are not connected with immediate locations and experiences. Estrella's pragmatic connection of talk with action needs to be contrasted to the superstition and blind faith in religion of Gumencindo, Perfecto, and Estrella's own mother. The statue of Jesus under which Estrella's mother keeps the immigration papers is, on the one hand, a representation of Petra's religious faith as her particular form of resistance and strength. On the other, a figuration of the disenfranchised immigrants' oppression under an economic system and a Catholic discourse of resignation that keeps them down. Towards the end of the novel, Petra's crumbling faith and energy are symbolized by the fall of the statue of Jesus from its usual place, its head breaking from his neck, his eyes staring up at her "like pools of dark ominous water" (*Under the Feet* 167):

> How could she possibly think to protect her children if such a little clawing insect [the scorpion] could inspire a whole midnight of fear? [. . .]. That was all she had: papers and sticks and broken faith and Perfecto, and at this moment all of this seemed as weightless against the massive darkness, as the head she held. (*Under the Feet* 168-69)

In the climactic scene of the novel, Estrella's friend, Alejo, poisoned by a chemical spray on the fields, is faced with the barriers of an American health care service that is too expensive for them to afford. Estrella finally realizes that she, her friend, and her family are part both of the cosmic life cycle as well as of the human capital and energy that produces growth, riches, and surplus value:

She remembered the tar pits. Energy money, the fossilized bones of energy matter. How bones made oil and oil made gasoline. The oil was made from their bones, and it was their bones that kept the nurse's car from not halting on some highway, kept her on her way to Daisyfield to pick up her boys at six. It was their bones that kept the air conditioning in the cars humming, that kept them moving on the long dotted line of the map. Their bones. Why couldn't the nurse see that? Estrella had figured it out: the nurse owed *them* as much as they owed her. (*Under the Feet* 148)

In anger and desperation, she grabs the crowbar, one of Perfecto's tools, and slams it on the pictures of the children of the white perfumed nurse that has charged them more than they can afford for a vague diagnosis. Thus, Estrella symbolically opposes the secure, private institutional domain that protects the leisurely life and economic well-being of the nurse and her family and that excludes people like her and her family from decent social service. At this point, confused by the discovery of the violence she is capable of inflicting, she comes to grips with her strength and resisting power: "They make you that way, she sighed with resignation. She tried to understand what happened herself. You talk and talk and talk to them and they ignore you. But you pick up a crowbar and break the pictures of their children, and all of a sudden they listen real fast" (*Under the Feet* 151).

Estrella is suddenly split into two selves. One is the resigned woman relying on religious and superstitious faith she has been brought up to become; the other, a practical, strong, fierce woman that will fight for herself and her people's rights: "One was a silent phantom who obediently marked a circle with a stick around the bungalow as the mother had requested, while the other held the crowbar and the money" (*Under the Feet* 150). This internal split between the active and the passive self is the first stage towards an awareness of the importance of social struggle within this character's *Bildung*. Indeed, the attainment of individuality and self-worth in the social context depicted by the novel involves breaking away from the circle of silence and anonymity to become a subject committed to the advancement of workers' rights in the U.S. In this sense, Viramontes' message is in step with the message of other Californian Chicana artists, such as the dramatist Cherríe Moraga and the visual artist Yolanda López.

In *Under the Feet of Jesus*, the barn symbolizes the triumph of the socially active self over the "silent phantom." Evoked throughout the novel as Estrella's wide place of intimacy, this powerful spatial image becomes a cool place away from the sun and the fields where she comes to terms with her love for Alejo, and where she takes refuge from the world outside. No doubt, Viramontes purposefully draws on this quintessential symbol of American rural life: an unerring sign of fertility and one of the many metaphors embraced by the "master symbol of the garden [. . .] expressing fecundity, growth, increase, and blissful labor in the earth, all centering about the idealized frontier farmer armed with that supreme agrarian weapon, the sacred plow" (Smith, *Virgin Land* 123). The barn is an essential structure in the long-lived myth of the "agricultural paradise" or the Myth of the Garden. The myth offered a representation of the simple, honest lifestyle of the common yeoman, and it was linked to equality, democracy, and freedom in nineteenth-century America (124). Henry Nash Smith mentions that this myth gained paradoxical relevance in the mid and late nineteenth century, after the passing of the Homestead Bill in 1862 and the occupation of large extensions of Southwestern land by an elite of monopolists. It served to "[mask] poverty and industrial strife with the pleasing suggestion that a beneficent nature stronger than any human agency, the ancient resource of Americans, the power that had made the country rich and great, would solve the new problems of industrialism" (205-206).

The barn is appropriated and renarrativized by Viramontes and endowed with very different connotations in the context of postmodern industrialized agriculture and migrant Mexican labor. Besides figuring Estrella's discovery of love and sexual desire, the "cathedral-like building" symbolizes Estrella's new faith in the unity and struggle of the Mexican American community in the U.S., a hope momentarily threatened by Perfecto's plans to tear the barn down and make enough money to return to Mexico. It is not fortuitous that Viramontes sets the last scene of her migrant story in the barn, which also acquires symbolic connotations at the end of John Steinbeck's classic migrant novel *The Grapes of Wrath* (1939) and, in a more mock-ironic tone, at the end of Flannery O'Connor's short story "Good Country People" (1955).

The feminist leanings of Viramontes and her political commitment alter considerably the traditional connotations of this place, which, in Steinbeck's novel, stands as a symbol of fertility, as well as of women's practical sense, strength, and resources in the face of extreme desperation. In O'Connor's story it is the scene of a mocking satire of the naive notion that "country people" are essentially good. In *Under the Feet of Jesus* the barn brings together the female protagonist's awakening to love and sexuality with a resisting political awareness of the perversity of America's social and economic system. Taking into account Viramontes' association of words with tools in the novel, the barn, the place where these tools are stored, is also a call for words, a testament to the writer's faith in their limited but still necessary power for an effective collective action.

The final scene of the novel, describing Estrella's slow and arduous climbing to the roof of this apparently private refuge, stands as a figurative representation of the return of her particularity to a universality that is by no means abstract. Estrella's climbing to the top of the barn is, as Bachelard would want to put it, a poetic image of her own quiet privacy. Yet, Estrella's thoughts in this moment of privacy lay bare the connection between her own needs and the needs of others. According to Eagleton's proposal of an aesthetics of materialist ethics in *The Ideology of the Aesthetic* (1990), the purpose of universality is "that the unique particularities of individuals may be respected and fulfilled" (414). Estrella remains as "immobile as an angel on the verge of faith," and "[l]ike the chiming bells of the great cathedrals" believes "her heart powerful enough to summon home all those who strayed" (*Under the Feet* 176). The space of the barn, significantly associated to a cathedral, a public building, figures Estrella's new "religion" of social commitment and a space of political legitimacy for Mexican Americans as rightful citizens working American soil and producing economic benefits. The barn evokes a "public homeplace," that is, a comfortable space for a collective self who understands itself in relation to the commitment to others within the ideal American ethos of democracy represented by the agrarian space. By re-appropriating this essentially American rural space and re-inhabiting it, the young Mexican American female character transforms it into a space of gendered and collective resistance devoid of the exclusion and inequality concealed in the past by the Myth of the Garden. Like Cisneros, Viramontes proposes an aesthetics of materialist ethics through a poetics of space. This aesthetics presumes that the fundamental American ideals of intimacy, privacy, and freedom depend on others being free as well, on the individual's committed engagement with the universal right of human beings to be acknowledged as autonomous and different subjects.

2. Pat Mora's *House of Houses* and the Dream of a Homeplace with No Boundaries

Gaston Bachelard has described the house as "a space of protected intimacy," the germ of secure happiness (33-34), the space where the immemorial and the past are evoked, and continuity with the past is assured (36-37). The implicit ideas of this description are nostalgia, stasis, stability, and protection from the adverse forces of movement, history, and the passage of time. This view of space harbors the danger of conveying a coherent, non-contradictory sense of identity, a romantic and reactionary appeal to one's origins or one's tradition. bell hooks and Doreen Massey have both drawn attention to the fact that the nostalgia for a place and a culture is of no use unless it fosters the creation of something new. The appeal to local places has to be exploited for the invigorating transformation of the present (hooks 147, Massey 140).

As hooks says, one must learn to see beauty in the culture, traditions, and spaces of one's ancestors as a collective "life-giving" endeavor that renews the spirit and enhances the well-being of all. When beauty is constructed collectively it becomes regenerating and uplifting (104-105).

hooks' faith in the beauty of the communal spirit for the reinvention of the future ties in with Pat Mora's views that "[r]eturning to the source means [. . .] not to restore the past or to worship it as a false idol, but to build an authentic future" (*Nepantla* 18). The pride in one's heritage, language, and tradition should lead to the appreciation of cultural differences in facing up to contemporary internationalizing and globalizing forces. The preservation of cultural heritages goes hand in hand with the defense of basic human rights, both of which should be seen as central to democracy (*Nepantla* 19).

According to Mora, we have to understand global citizenship as the appreciation of and respect for the varied cultural heritages on the planet. Contrary to those who think the exploration of difference leads to balkanization, Mora argues that the diverse perspectives within a community have to be accepted, and that the recovery of a cultural past is a source of inspiration, tolerance, and psychological well-being (*Nepantla* 21-23). Her discourse is local, but by no means chauvinist or fetishist. Mora's proposal of a notion of culture that is not exclusively based on consumption and commodification is inclusive rather than exclusive. Culture should not be vindicated as a means to assert the superiority of some over others, but to include, make known, make visible the cultures of the poor, the so far excluded, regional cultures, and folk cultures (*Nepantla* 26-32). The conservation of one's cultural heritage is, as Mora puts it, one more commitment to social change and the survival of the oppressed, for ethnicity has a psychological value as a strategy of subsistence: "Pride in cultural identity, in the set of learned and shared language, symbols, and meanings, needs to be fostered not because of nostalgia or romanticism, but because it is essential to our survival" (*Nepantla* 35-36).

Mora's experience as a third-generation immigrant in an environment where references to her past and heritage were not accessible increased her curiosity for her family's past and her awareness that the reasons for her Western Eurocentric education were to be found in the univocal, chauvinistic way of understanding America:

> I had grown up in an environment that did not value, and often hated, my cultural heritage. Those in positions of power, the audible voices of political, educational, cultural, and economic leaders, tried, some still try, to ignore or suppress—dark skin, the Spanish language, expressiveness [. . .]. Now some of us realize that America is a continent not a country. (41)

In step with Gloria Anzaldúa, Mora acknowledges the strength of being able to draw from two cultural heritages, of being an inhabitant of the border, or as she prefers to call it, "Nepantla", the land in the middle. Although Mora refuses to construct a collective identity that is "frozen into nostalgia" (*Nepantla* 42), she insists that the retrieval of the past is "historically sound, politically expedient, psychologically healthy, linguistically necessary, morally essential" (*Nepantla* 46). Echoing the essay of the African American poet Audre Lorde "Poetry Is Not a Luxury," Mora sustains that she does not merely write for pleasure but to provide a necessary nourishing sustenance for the spirit (*Nepantla* 50). She has also said that as a writer she cannot bring resolution to conflicts, but occasional joy (Rebolledo, "Pat Mora" 138).

Her task as writer is, she argues, akin to that of the Mexican *curandera*, whose art is based on the verbal traditions of the present and the past. Like the *curandera*'s craft, much of the writing of Chicanas comes from an informal training of listening to oral stories and collective, popular wisdom (*Nepantla* 127). While *curanderas* heal physical wounds, Chicanas heal psychological, historical wounds "by providing opportunities to remember the past, to share and ease bitterness, to describe what has been viewed as unworthy of description, to cure by incantations and rhythms" (*Nepantla* 131). To be a border woman, Mora states, is to come from a tangled reality of conflict.

The border, she says in an interview with Tey Diana Rebolledo, is present in her writings as a constant shifting back and forth, as the effort to find accommodation in a space where conflict is magnified, and where resolution is not even believable (138). The very physical and geographical U.S.-Mexico border where she has lived is a "glare of truth," a place of "stern honesty" that constantly reminds her of the differences between those who live comfortable lives and those who do not (*Nepantla* 14). The border is, nonetheless, a place of hope as well, for it is there that one confronts a new culture and the possibility of gradual change in the cultural landscape of the U.S. (*Nepantla* 144-145).

The desert of El Paso, the Texan town where she was born, and the Mexican heritage of her parents and relatives have been very present in Mora's poems and prose writings. She has written with a strong sense of audience, trying to capture the interest of the people from the region she usually writes about. Yet, she has also admitted she would be deluding herself if she thought herself to be writing for a single Chicano audience (Rebolledo, "Pat Mora" 132-133). Her community, she says in *Nepantla*, "is not only my ethnic community but also all like-minded souls seeking a more equitable world" (*Nepantla* 147). Mora's localist focus on a cultivated garden in *House of Houses* (1997) is used to establish a parallel between human diversity and natural diversity, a parallel that is also articulated in her book of essays *Nepantla*.

In the first lines of this collective autobiography Mora explicitly alludes to Gaston Bachelard's *The Poetics of Space* (1957). The image of the house as a place of "protected intimacy," a direct and explicit allusion to Bachelard's work, discloses the speaker's aim to reconstruct fragmented memories and stories and put them together through writing. In Mora's imaginary house, "time loses its power" as it does in the individual memories of a happy childhood and past that Bachelard also traces back to the family house (*La poétique* 4).

As the very title of her work, the book cover to the first edition, and the epigraph to the first section of the book suggest—"As the rose is the flower of flowers, so this is, the house of houses" (*House* 1)—this house is a singular place in a singular landscape, both of them highly valued in the speaking persona's imagination as the settings of her family memories.

Similarly to Texas writer Norma Cantú in her "autobioethnography" *Canícula* (1995), Mora includes fourteen family pictures in the first pages of the book to add verisimilitude to her story. Displaying a desire to recover what is past, to revive old stories and lives, both the captioned pictures and the autobiographical text have the referential power of a family album.

Mora's text gives content to the pictures and complements what they do not or cannot tell. The main purpose of Mora's family memoir is therefore to revive community and family life through the gradual imaginary and literary re-construction of a house, its garden and the surrounding landscape. The words of her relatives and the speaker's own words will create "My Word-house," as she says in her poem "Foreign Spooks" (*Nepantla* 3). Like *Canícula*, this memoir evolves mainly around the world of women. The maternal world, garden, and home, central to the protagonist, are constantly alluded to through references to food, herbs and remedies, flower smells, folklore, women's suffering, solidarity, and comforting power.

All through the narrative, there is a deep attachment to landscapes, especially to the desert, as part of the world the narrative voice tries to reconstruct. As Mora puts it, landscapes "leave their imprint" on the self (*House* 25) and, as Jonathan Smith observes, they "are believed to possess a reality surpassing that of the process by which they were created" (81):

> The power of geography, how the landscape imprints itself; and when we can't see the world that is home to us whether mountains, desert or beaches, we yearn to see the shapes and vistas that live in our interior; after a rain to smell the plants and trees whose names or shapes we know; to hear bird whistles or wind thumps, rhythms that comfort us like a heartbeat comforts a child; a vague preconscious memory. (*House* 25-26)

However, the terms of Mora's landscape creation go beyond aesthetics and styling and do not "lift us out of the dreariness of necessity" (quoted in Smith 81). In *House of Houses* Mora's poetics fluctuate between two complementary poles: the desire for familial and communal unity, represented by the domestic space, and the reality of a fragmented, disperse and muted past and history that the speaker tries to reconstruct. In an unpublished interview with the author of this study, the writer acknowledges her own ethnocentrism, which like many Chicana writers she has claimed as a strategy for spiritual survival. Thus, the house, the garden, the fountain, and the desert are fundamental symbols for the assertion of ethnicity and sense of place, signs "of life in an arid land" (*House* 3). The desert, which for Mora means freedom and personal growth (Rebolledo, "Pat Mora" 137), is here also a symbol of the thirst for knowledge of a Mexican American woman for whom the border has been a geographical as well as a psychological, emotional, and social division. The culture and history of Mexican American families have been split just as the land has been divided into countries and states (*House* 3).

For Mora's speaking subject, the adobe house hovering "near the Rio Grande between El Paso and Santa Fe" (*House* 4) is a house of paradox and change. Unique and special as this imaginary house may be, it cannot be a closed space. As the narrator says and most of the works analyzed in this study have confirmed, "walls, like doors and locks can be confining" (*House* 12). But the house is a necessary, strengthening, and liberating presence if one conceives it as an open space, "if I have the physical and emotional space to enter and exit at will" (*House* 12). Following Bachelard's *Poetics of Space*, the house is here a primary archetype through which the speaker may discover her own voice and the voices of those who were "often silent when they left these walls, reticent to reveal themselves" (*House* 12). The narrator is "after stories" from those old voices and bodies who can still remember. The feminine collective autobiographical subject has created a nearly ideal literary heterotopia where the living and the dead, the present and past coexist thanks to her recuperation of stories, anecdotes, sayings, recipes, and traditions. Indeed, Mora's speaker's imagined house, charged with private and collective memory, allows her to live the past as a dream or reverie without making claims to historical accuracy.

This house of the imagination has emerged from an effort to create "a world we can call our own" (7), a collective space, but also from an effort to find private, personal comfort and solace. From the very beginning of this work, her speaking persona confesses that she retreats to this place to salvage what can be empowering about it. The ghosts of her ancestors whom she summons and who speak to us directly, describe their movements from one home to another in the face of adversities such as the Mexican Revolution or times of economic hardship, the traumatic family separations or the abandoning of cherished places. This imagined house of houses is a familial space located between El Paso (Texas, on the border with New Mexico and Mexico) and Santa Fe (New Mexico), a building constructed out of the disparate life-stories of nearly five generations across a wide U.S.-Mexico border.

In a humorous, lighthearted manner, this family memoir also shows the disparate ideologies across generations and genders. The staunch *Porfirista* leanings of Mora's maternal aunt contrast with the more romanticized and politically critical view of Mexican history of the younger generation of Mexican immigrants, who have romanticized the figures of Emiliano Zapata and Pancho Villa as heroes who "took from the rich" (*House* 30). Yet, as Denise Chávez's image of the dark closet in *The Last of the Menu Girls* (1986) suggests, memory provides an incomplete version of the story and cannot salvage questions that remain in the dark, unanswered: Why do women speak so much about others, about family lives and so little about what they feel, about themselves? Why do they always adapt without a frown to their new and often hostile surroundings? Why don't they ever talk about their sorrows? Why is the discovery of emotion in men's words surprising for the speaker?

The stories of Mora's family *dreamhouse* are told in a scattered, non-sequential manner, thus imitating the also disperse workings of memory and the imagination. Joining all these stories and anecdotes is the motif of a common space in the narrator and compiler's imagination. Made up of thirteen chapters, twelve of which are entitled after the months of the year, the structure gives coherence to this collective autobiography and evokes the circularity of time. Mora does not organize her work following a linear temporal sequence, but rather in a cyclic structure that evokes the rhythms of nature affecting all living creatures; both have, as Mora puts it, "[their] moods, [their] storms, [their] seasons" (*House* 45). The title of each chapter contains popular Spanish sayings related to each month of the year *Enero friolero*, *Febrero loco, Marzo airoso*—or to the nature and the seasons—*Huerta sin agua, cuerpo sin alma*. This temporal division into the yearly seasonal cycles also ties in with the Mesoamerican understanding of life and death as part of a natural cyclic process. In a particular recasting of the popular Mexican Catholic tradition of the Day of the Dead (All Souls Day), *el día de los muertos*, the speaker finds the imagery to celebrate her desired union with the dead and the continuity of her family's Mexican American history.

In Mora's family chronicle the union of the living and the dead often expressed by Mesoamerican peoples through floral images (Gutiérrez-Spencer 31) merges with the Spanish Catholic tradition of flower arrangement in temples and shrines. The poetic and sensual allusion to the cultivated plants and flowers that pervade *House* and that contrast with the wilderness of the desert are in tune with the homely microcosm, the domesticated oasis that Mora wants to create in a hostile environment. Women like aunt Carmen love gardening and taking care of plants and flowers that are foreign to the local vegetation of the desert and are rather more typical of Spain: roses, geraniums, begonia, and bougainvillea.

Mora goes beyond the use of local metaphors that associate women with nature and mother earth as fertile and passive, or as debased and animalistic (Ortner 67-87). In this work, as in one of her poems included in her volume *Borders* (1986), Mora pays homage to the strength and survival skills of women:

> Desert women know
> about survival.
> Fierce heat and cold
> have burned and thickened
> our skin. Like cactus
> we've learned to hoard,
> to sprout deep roots,
> to seem asleep, yet wake
> at the scent of softness
> in the air, to hide
> pain and loss by silence,
> no branches wail
> or whisper our sad songs
> safe behind our thorns.
>
> Don't be deceived.
> When we bloom, we stun.
>   (80)

The desert, which has inspired Mora's homage to women in this poem, is also used as a symbol of women's endurance and power in *House of Houses*. The women depicted in *House*—Mora's aunt Lobo, her mother, her maternal and paternal grandmothers—are strong women who devote their lives to others, who are not sure about their love for their husbands, but who persevere in bringing warmth to the "cold house" in the U.S. (*Nepantla* 67). They pave the way and struggle for the future generations of daughters and granddaughters. Thus, the distinctive plants and flowers are, on the one hand, references to a different landscape and a different culture that is not part of the desert;

and on the other, figurations of female healing and nurturing powers, spirituality, and comfort. Women's connection to the earth and to the soil through the cultivation of gardens evokes the creation of a sense of place and a herbal culture that survives against the years. Plants have many practical uses: "[P]lants, humans' first medicines, through ritual and religion intertwine with our lives," the speaker says and "become sources of food, shelter, warmth, weapons, clothing, dyes, cosmetics, wine" (*House* 8):

> For gum trouble, people chew wild pieplant, *canaigre*. If our eyes are red, Mamá washes them carefully with *manzanilla*. And, of course, we drink the teas I make for you–*hierbabuena y gordo lobo, romero* for rheumatism. Plenty of honey and lemon for a cough. (*House* 73)

Women's Catholic prayers are also connected to flowers, in particular the rose: The rosary "originally connoted an enclosed rose garden," and flower perfumes are said to have been offerings to heavenly beings (*House* 249). The preservation of Catholic traditions needs to be traced back to the cultural life inherited by Mexican women from Spanish beliefs. As the research of cultural geographer Raquel Rubio-Goldsmith demonstrates, gardens cultivated by Mexican women of the northern desert (*norteñas*) during and after the Anglo American invasion of Mexico are symbolic constructions sustaining these women's "visions of a Spanish paradise" they had inherited. These gardens also allowed *norteñas* to face the material hardship of the desert frontier. As she puts it, "I use the gardens of the *norteñas* to understand the ways these women merged their symbolic (psychological and spiritual) worlds and the material conditions of their everyday lives" (*House* 276). Influenced by Spanish customs, positivist ideas of Indian inferiority and the harsh life in the desert, *norteñas* expressed their cultural identity as superior Spanish, civilized Christians through walled gardens that would protect them against barbarism and the desert (*House* 276-277).

While references to Indian tribes are not present in Mora's chronicle, the connections between the tiny, sanctuary-like gardens described by Rubio-Goldsmith and the imaginary garden of *House of Houses* are evident. Like most of Mora's female ancestors, these Mexican women were part of a great number of refugees who started their lives anew in the United States. Just like these *norteña* gardens, Mora's garden is situated in the former northern deserts of Mexico. Furthermore, in both *norteñas'* and Mora's familial garden Catholicism is inflected with indigenous spiritual traditions such as the Day of the Dead, which were considered pagan in American Catholic parishes (Rubio-Goldsmith 284). Mora's narrator shows the interdependence of sensuality and spiritual comfort, thus following the Mesoamerican belief that the dead sustain life by manifesting themselves in nature (Gutiérrez-Spencer 31). The Catholic ideology of a spiritual, dematerialized afterlife acquires a radically different meaning when merged with the notion that the dead nurture the living with their almost physical presence in nature:

[T]here's something eerie or maybe appealing—all that Catholic dust-to-dust stuff—about digging ourselves into earth, loosening the soil and burying some of our essence, or breath, even if we are alive becoming part of the compost. (*House* 68)

The dead are lured back by what they love, sweet temptations [. . .]. The Egyptians, like the Maya and Aztecs, believed that nourishment needs to be provided to ensure life after death, supplies placed in the tomb, the house of eternity. (*House* 257)

In terms of the poetics of space, Mora's *House of Houses* is a personal refashioning of the pre-Columbian Aztec concept of poetic writing, "flower and song," reflected in the title of the first collection of poems of the Californian poet Alurista, *Floricanto en Aztlán* (1976). As Laura Gutiérrez-Spencer and Jorge Klor de Alva have stated in their respective essays, the metaphoric association between flower and song has been well ingrained in Chicano poetry since the late 1960s (29, 20). The title of Alurista's poetic collection is an invocation of the power of nature's vitality as the poet's source of inspiration and resistance against oppressive social forces. In Mora's *House of Houses*, the connection between flower and song (the senses and writing) underlies the construction of a house full of pleasurable sensory and cultural experiences that revitalize the speaker as they are being told; a happy, open, nurturing house, where there is room for the stories of a family in-between cultures and countries. Like the medicinal, ornamental, healing use her female ancestors gave to flowers and plants, the narrator merges sensory delight with sustaining homely remedies and recipes, spirituality with the regenerating function of bringing the dead back to life, of recovering a polyvalent past for the spiritual regeneration of the future.

Much as the garden in Mora's imaginary house in the desert is a kind of sanctuary or shrine against hostile outside forces, it is however no paradise. The speaker describes her female ancestors' harsh experience of poverty, war, the crossing of borders, and the endurance of authoritarian husbands. As Mora has said in her poems, "[t]he desert is no lady" (*Chants* 8), "[d]esert women know about survival" (*Borders* 80). Women like her mother and her maternal aunt Lobo know what it is to lose a home under the occupation of American homesteaders (*House* 200). These women have little to do with the role model of the glamorous, decorative, sensual, and enigmatic woman of Mexican and American mainstream society. Nor have these women's lives embodied the ideal of romantic love that continues to be part of many U.S. and Mexican women's fantasies (*Nepantla* 60-61); they are austere, self-denying, and life-giving.

The writer has stated that she was always close to her mother's side of the family, and in particular to two old women—women who took care of her and her siblings when they were sick, mothering them as they would mother their own children: her maternal aunt and her grandmother. In *House of Houses* the personality and the power of these two women are described with images of struggle, though not of violence. At the time of the revolution, the broom becomes a "savage weapon" in the hands of her maternal aunt Lobo, a domestic symbol of her desire to get rid of dirt, disorder, and corruption (*House* 35). Her paternal grandmother, who has no useful weapons in the eyes of the soldiers, acts like "the law," "like a General" when it is time to abandon their home in Chihuahua and leave for Juárez and then El Paso. These women, however, talk more about others than about themselves. Lobo, "the mother who never marries," tells stories about the outside world but never about her own feelings: "I wonder about what she loved, what she feared. How she spent her days? Who were the men she noticed, hoped would ask her to dance, or hold her hand or whisper in her ear. 'But tell me about you, Lobo'" (29). Lobo is said to have worked all her life, but never to have owned a house or a car, as all her money goes to her nephews and her sisters.

The female narrative voice constructs her imaginary *dreamhouse* and garden out of the life-stories of the dead and living, male and female members of a scattered family. The narrating "I" has, to use Doris Sommer's words, a lateral, metonymic relation with the collectivity whose stories she has compiled, recorded, and transmitted. Some of these stories are complementary to official versions of history. Border conflicts of discrimination against people of Mexican descent are brought up with the story of uncle Lalo, whose family house is despised by a schoolmate as a place where one can only "exist," but not "live" (*House* 219). Lalo's white skin masks his Mexicanness, but his surname gives it away. When applying for enlistment in the Civilian Conservation Corps, he is told to change his name "Delgado" to an Anglo-sounding name. His devotion to his recently deceased father and his duty as an eldest son to bear his name, prevent Lalo from doing so. Lalo recounts various instances in which his white skin makes his identity as a Hispanic or Latino questionable to immigration authorities and local institutions (*House* 221). The book is also an homage to men like Mora's maternal grandfather, who saved his whole family in the dangerous crossing of the Rio Grande during the revolution, and who was forced to sell his property in Juárez for a low price to the Anglo hands supporting the Villistas (*House* 29). The man most revered and endearingly portrayed is the speaker's father. As a child, he saved his grandmother from death, started to work at the age of ten delivering newspapers, and was fired during the depression for being "Mexican" (*House* 85-87). After a life of hard work and faced with the competition of larger optical companies, her father has to witness the failure of his optical business. The family reluctantly abandons their house in El Paso and migrates to Santa Monica (California) in search of a better future. Sad memories of the speaker's father's last days of suffering from a degenerative disease, intermingle with memories of his authoritarian manners and harsh discipline with his wife and children, as well as with recollections of his lessons to his first female child on how to take care of herself when in danger. In the family of ancestors the writer brings together, men are also very fond of gardening: Mora's father's favorite flower is the rose, which he himself cultivates; *abuelo* Gregorio prays to *Santa Clara* and *Santa Rosa* who both planted gardens; uncle Lalo keeps a compost heap in his garden.

A way of recording familial and individual stories and memories is through the smell of flowers and plants that evoke them. Mora records the smell of her maternal and paternal ancestors' fear after having crossed the "river of sorrows" and the Texas desert during and after the Mexican Revolution: "[H]ard, sandy mesas; fossils who murmur the time of great waters; hawks and snakes; yucca and agave; roots and branches thorny for survival; the smell of fear, fear of dryness and fangs, human fangs and coilings" (*House* 45). Flowers and plants bring back the smell of illness, of the sustenance of homely recipes, and of remedies to ease the homesickness. The smell of the relief felt after summer in the desert during walks down the river, "the rain [. . .] cleaning the air that tastes the lavender of blooming sage" (*House* 223).

Like the garden, Mora's inherited imagined adobe house of the desert "blooms" as a sacred place, and becomes what Foucault terms a "happy heterotopia," where all the family secrets, stories, sayings, refrains, and riddles come together. A place that is constantly transformed by time and generations, where time does not matter because it "never stops building up" (Foucault, "Of Other Spaces" 26). The Latin sentence in *Natural History* reproduced by the narrator's father—as the rose is the flower of flowers, so this is the house of houses (*"Ut rosa flos florum, sic est domus ista domorum"* [4])—points at the uniqueness of the flower and the house, but also at their connection to other related flowers, houses, and gardens. This single garden is therefore a personal myth with singular gender and cultural connotations created out of memories of cultivated gardens in the speaker's family. It is not a sign of conquest in the mode of Nash Smith's Myth of the Garden, although it certainly *is* an imaginary re-appropriation of space and a very moving account of the interdependence between people and, more specifically, women and nature. Both "private and communal; a space of labor and frustration, also of meditation, solace, hope, and sensory delights" (*House* 8), it symbolizes, like the Persian garden, "the smallest parcel of the world" and "the totality of the world" (Foucault, "Of Other Spaces" 26). Like the Mexican *chinampa* (floating garden), this is a sacred garden, a haven, or an oasis where local and foreign vegetation come together: mezcal, sage, camomile, flowers whose names have religious connotations (*Flor de San Juan, Flor de Santa Rita, Manto de la Virgen*), thyme, roses (the symbol of the beloved, the Virgin Mary, and the speaker's father's favorite flower), orange trees, daffodils, berries, cactus, *canaigre, manzanilla, hierbabuena, gordo lobo*, and *romero*. Remembered as a refuge for children to imagine fantastic stories about "the little people" (*House* 237), this is also a place to cultivate the senses for a female narrator whose husband lives too much "in [his] head" (*House* 236-7).

Rather than adjusting to circumstances as many of her female ancestors did, Mora's autobiographical persona creates a space of her own from the traditions and stories she has inherited. Instead of transforming herself to suit social demands as many women have done (*Nep-*

antla 69), the narrator transforms place according to personal and collective needs. In a culture where women have been socialized to please, the strength and stubbornness she has inherited from her ancestors, have helped her to claim and achieve her own narrative imaginative space (*Nepantla* 71). Like many other contemporary women writers, Mora has relished in private space, in the spacious room where she can "get away from people" in order to write about herself through her relationship to others (Rebolledo, "Pat Mora" 137). Viramontes and Cisneros have combined this very same vindication of private space for personal development and creativity with an aesthetics of materialist ethics that interweaves individual, social, and communal concerns. In *House of Houses* Mora has demonstrated a less social, more spiritual, sensual, and intimate conception of subjectivity—though no less positive, resisting, and uplifting.

My analysis of Mora's *House of Houses* has aimed to underscore that the creation of a metaphoric communal and familial space can be psychologically positive and culturally invigorating even if it involves an ethnocentric stance for the sake of recovery, not of exclusion. This fictional collective autobiography may certainly be read as a reaction to the homogenizing forces of postmodernity, a conscious effort to preserve imprecise, fragmented though vivid and poignant memories of a dispersed family, as well as a creative endeavor to reclaim spaces that were once Mexican and traditions that still prevail. As the narrative voice says and Mora herself asserts in an interview with this author, the imaginary adobe house between Santa Fe and El Paso is a metaphor of complex dualities: human frailty and strength, privacy and collectivity, dispossession and recovery, dislocation and imaginative relocation. Those who inhabit it are "fragile yet sturdy; a paradox like the house that's green yet in the desert, visible yet private, unique yet organic, old yet new, open yet closed, imagined yet real, a retreat, private yet communal" (*House* 289). Although *House of Houses* undoubtedly shows an awareness that geopolitics and ideology shape human lives, Mora is more concerned with affirming that "the universe is more than matter"

(*House* 263), that a multiple, collective spirit, culture, and history still breathe and can be recovered through writing.

From *Battlegrounds and Crossroads: Social and Imaginary Space in Writings by Chicanas* (2003), pp. 291-331. Copyright © 2003 by Rodopi. Reprinted with permission of Rodopi.

Notes

1. The *milagro* or *exvoto* is a painted picture or silver reproduction of the miracle a saint has performed. It includes parts of the body, animals or people that have been healed by the saint. The *ofrenda* is any offering, including the above *milagros*, placed by the figures of the saints to thank them for their help or to demonstrate devotion.

2. Proposition 187 was a ballot initiative of the Californian group SOS (Save Our State) to fight illegal immigration. Endorsed by Republican Governor Pete Wilson and passed in 1994, this proposition denied illegal immigrants and their families' welfare, health care, and public education. At that time, 7 percent of the population of California was illegal. Although some minor modifications have been made, this proposition is still operative in California. The gains of bilingual education and affirmative action programs in higher and junior colleges were threatened in the mid-nineties. Proposition 209, which put an end to affirmative action in admission policies at the University of California, was supported by California voters in 1996.

3. I am referring to Rachel Blau DuPlessis' above-mentioned *Writing Beyond the Ending* (1985), Nancy Armstrong's *Desire and Domestic Fiction* (1987), Rosalind Coward's "The True Story of How I Became My Own Person" (1989) and Patricia Waugh's *Feminine Fictions* (1989).

4. She mentioned this in an unpublished presentation titled "Being the Border: A Train of Thought, Imaginative Training" delivered at the International Conference of Chicano Literature, held in Granada (Spain) in 1998.

5. The title of Rivera's novel, . . . *y no se lo tragó la tierra*, refers to the main character's fear that he might be swallowed by the earth if he questions the existence of God. This character's resistance to oppression depends to a great extent on his defiance of Catholic stoicism and of the idea of an omnipotent divine will.

Works Cited

Alurista. *Floricanto en Aztlán*. Los Angeles: Chicano Studies Center, University of California, 1971.

Anzaldúa, Gloria. *Borderlands: La Frontera*. San Francisco: Spinsters/Aunt Lute, 1987.

_____, ed. *Making Face, Making Soul*. San Francisco: Ann Hale Foundation, 1990.

_____. *Interviews/Entrevistas/Gloria Anzaldúa*. Ed. AnaLouise Keating. New York and London: Routledge, 2000.

Armstrong, Nancy. *Deseo y ficción doméstica* [*Desire and Domestic Fiction*]. Valencia: Ediciones Cátedra, 1987.

Bachelard, Gaston. *La poétique de l'espace* [*The Poetics of Space*]. Paris: Quadrige/PUF, 1957.

Belsey, Catherine, and Jane Moore, eds. *The Feminist Reader*. Cambridge MA and Oxford UK: Blackwell, 1989.

Brodzki, Bella, and Celeste Schenck, eds. *Life/Lines: Theorizing Women's Autobiography*. Ithaca: Cornell UP, 1988.

Cantú, Norma Elia. *Canícula: Snapshots of a Girlhood en la Frontera*. Albuquerque: U of Mexico P, 1995.

Castillo, Debra. *Talking Back: Toward a Latin American Feminist Criticism*. Ithaca and London: Cornell UP, 1992.

Chávez, Denise. *The Last of the Menu Girls*. Houston: Arte Público Press, 1986.

Christoph, Nancy. "An Interview with Helena María Viramontes." *Baneke: A Latino Review of Arts and Literature* 3 (1995): 10-11.

Cisneros, Sandra. *The House on Mango Street*. Houston: Arte Público Press, 1985.

_____. *Woman Hollering Creek and Other Stories*. New York: Vintage, 1991.

Coward, Rosalind. "The True Story of How I Became My Own Person." In Belsey and Moore: 35-48.

Duncan, James, and David Ley, eds. *Place/Culture/Representation*. London and New York: Routledge, 1993.

DuPlessis, Rachel Blau. *Writing Beyond the Ending: Narrative Strategies of Twentieth-Century Women Writers*. Bloomington IN: Indiana UP, 1985.

Eagleton, Terry. *The Ideology of the Aesthetic*. Oxford: Basil Blackwell, 1990.

Foucault, Michel. "Of Other Spaces." 1984. *Diacritics* 16 (1986): 22-23.

Franco, Jean. "Going Public: Reinhabiting the Private." In Yúdice, Franco, and Flores: 65-83.

Gilbert, Sandra M., and Susan Gubar. *The Madwoman in the Attic: The Woman Writer and the Twentieth-Century Literary Imagination*. New Haven and London: Yale UP, 1984.

Gutiérrez-Spencer, Laura. "The Desert Blooms. Flowered Songs by Pat Mora." *Bilingual Review* 20 (1995): 28-36.

Hardy Aiken, Susan, Ann Brigham, Sallie A. Marton, Penny Waterstone, eds. *Making Worlds: Metaphor and Materiality in the Production of Feminist Texts*. Tucson: U of Arizona P, 1997.

hooks, bell. *Yearning. Race, Gender, and Cultural Politics*. Boston: South End Press, 1990.

Klor de Alva, Jorge. "California Chicano Literature and Pre-Columbian Motifs: Foil and Fetish." *Confluencia* 1 (1986): 18-26.

Lorde, Audre. *Sister Outsider: Essays and Speeches by Audre Lorde*. Freedom CA: The Crossing Press, 1984.

_____. *Zami: A New Spelling of My Name: A Biomythography by Audre Lorde*. Freedom CA: The Crossing Press, 1982.

Massey, Doreen. *Space, Place, and Gender*. Minneapolis: U of Minnesota P, 1994.

Méndez, Miguel. *Peregrinos de Aztlán*. Berkeley: Editorial Justa, 1974.

Mora, Pat. *Borders*. Houston: Arte Público Press, 1986.

_____. *Chants*. Houston: Arte Público Press, 1985.

_____. *Nepantla: Essays from the Land in the Middle*. Albuquerque: U of New Mexico P, 1993.

_____. *House of Houses*. Boston: Beacon Press, 1997.

O'Connor, Flannery. *A Good Man is Hard to Find*. New York: Harcourt & Brace Company, 1955.

Ortner, Sherry. "Is Female to Male as Nature is to Culture?" *Women, Culture, and Society*. Eds. Michelle Zimbalist Rosaldo and Louise Lamphère. Stanford: Stanford UP, 1984. 67-87.

Rebolledo, Tey Diana. "Pat Mora. Interview by Tey Diana Rebolledo." *This Is about Vision: Interviews with Southwestern Writers*. Ed. William Balassi. Albuquerque: U of New Mexico P, 1990. 129-139.

Rhys, Jean. *Wide Sargasso Sea*. 1966. New York and London: W.W. Norton & Company, 1982.

Rivera, Tomás. *. . . y no se lo tragó la tierra*. Arte Público Press, 1987.

Rubio-Goldsmith, Raquel. "Civilization, Barbarism, and Norteña Gardens." In Hardy Aiken et al.: 274-287.

Ruddick, Sara. *Maternal Thinking: Towards a Politics of Peace*. Boston: Beacon Press, 1989.

Smith, Henry Nash. *Virgin Land: The American West as Symbol and Myth*. Cambridge MA: Harvard UP, 1950.

Smith, Jonathan. "The Lie that Blinds: Destabilizing the Text of Landscape." In Duncan and Ley: 78-92.

Sommer, Doris. "'Not Just a Personal Story': Women's *Testimonios* and the Plural Self." In Brodzki and Schenk: 107-130.

Steinbeck, John. *The Grapes of Wrath*. 1939. New York: Bantam Books, 1966.

Viramontes, Helena. "Being the Border: A Train of Thought, Imaginative Training." *International Conference on Chicano Literature*. Universidad de Granada, 1998.

_____. "The Jumping Bean." *Chicana (W)rites on Word and Film*. Eds. María Herrera-Sobek and Helena María Viramontes. Berkeley: Third Woman Press, 1992. 101-114.

_____. "'Nopalitos': The Making of Fiction." *Breaking Boundaries: Latina Writing and Critical Readings*. Ed. Asunción Horno-Delgado et al. Amherst: U of Massachusetts P, 1989. 33-38.

_____. *Under the Feet of Jesus*. New York: Dutton, 1995.

Waugh, Patricia. *Feminine Fictions: Revisiting the Postmodern*. London: Routledge, 1989.

Yúdice, George, Jean Franco, and Juan Flores, eds. *On Edge: The Crisis of Contemporary Latin-American Culture*. Minneapolis: U of Minnesota P, 1996.

More Room of Her Own:
Sandra Cisneros's *The House on Mango Street*_____

Jacqueline Doyle

"Books continue each other," Virginia Woolf told an audience of young women some sixty years ago, "in spite of our habit of judging them separately" (*Room* 84). Books such as Ellen Moers's *Literary Women*, Elaine Showalter's *A Literature of Their Own*, Patricia Meyer Spacks's *The Female Imagination*, Tillie Olsen's *Silences*, and Alice Walker's *In Search of Our Mothers' Gardens* continue Virginia Woolf's own book, *A Room of One's Own*, extending her fertile meditations on the effects of economic deprivation on women's literature, and her pioneering efforts to reconstruct a female literary tradition. Tillie Olsen has uncovered a rich vein of writing by American working class women, and has offered poignant personal testimony to the obstacles to writing posed by gender and class. Alice Walker has explored the silences created by gender and race in America: "What did it mean for a black woman to be an artist in our grandmothers' time? In our great-grandmothers' day? It is a question with an answer cruel enough to stop the blood" (233).

While feminists following Woolf's advice to "think back through our mothers" have expanded the literary canon in the past two decades, too many have ignored the questions of race, ethnicity, and class in women's literature. Adrienne Rich laments the "white solipsism" of white feminists—"not the consciously held *belief* that one race is inherently superior to all others, but a tunnel-vision which simply does not see nonwhite experience or existence as precious or significant" ("Disloyal" 306). Barbara Smith, Alice Walker, and Toni Morrison have angrily denounced the canon implicit in early studies of women's literature such as Moers's and Spacks's.[1] To Spacks's tepid defense that she preferred to dwell on authors depicting "familiar experience" and a "familiar cultural setting" (5), Walker counters: "Why only these? Because they are white, and middle class, and because to

Spacks, female imagination is only that—a limitation that even white women must find restrictive" (372).

Confined by what Rich criticizes as the "faceless, raceless, classless category of 'all women'"[2] ("Notes" 13) women of color in the United States have all too often felt themselves compelled to choose between ethnicity and womanhood. Mitsuye Yamada speaks for many when she observes: "I have thought of myself as a feminist first, but my ethnicity cannot be separated from my feminism" (73). Sonia Saldívar-Hull writes of the damaging "color blindness" and "ideological erasure" of contemporary white feminist "sisterhood" (204). Yvonne Yarbro-Bejarano points out that while a Chicana feminist perspective shares "with the feminist perspective an analysis of questions of gender and sexuality, there are important differences between a Chicana perspective and the mainstream feminist one with regard to issues of race, culture and class" (140). Many women of color reject the monolithic notion of a "woman's voice." If Woolf in *A Room of One's Own* brought Shakespeare's silenced sister to life, María C. Lugones and Elizabeth V. Spelman point to new silences within contemporary feminist discourse itself: "Indeed, many Hispanas, Black women, Jewish women—to name a few groups—have felt it an invitation to silence rather than speech to be requested—if they are requested at all—to speak about being women (with the plain wrapper—as if there were one) in distinction from speaking about being Hispana, Black, Jewish, working-class, etc., women" (574). Sandra Cisneros recalls sitting in a University of Iowa seminar at the age of twenty-two and suddenly realizing that she was "different from everybody" there:

It wasn't as if I didn't know who I was. I knew I was a Mexican woman. But, I didn't think it had anything to do with why I felt so much imbalance in my life, whereas it had everything to do with it! My race, my gender, and my class! And it didn't make sense until that moment, sitting in that seminar. That's when I decided I would write about something my classmates couldn't write about. (Aranda 65)

Cisneros's *The House on Mango Street*, dedicated in two languages "A las Mujeres/To the Women," both continues Woolf's meditations and alters the legacy of *A Room of One's Own* in important ways. Her series of vignettes is about the maturing of a young Chicana and the development of a writer; it is about the women she grows up with; it is also about a sense of community, culture, and place. Esperanza, the young protagonist, yearns for "a space for myself to go, clean as paper before the poem," and for a house of her own:

Not a flat. Not an apartment in back. Not a man's house. Not a daddy's. A house all my own. With my porch and my pillow, my pretty purple petunias. My books and my stories. My two shoes waiting beside the bed. Nobody to shake a stick at. Nobody's garbage to pick up after. (*House* 108)

Instead she shares a bedroom with her sister Nenny, in a house marked by constriction and absence: "windows so small you'd think they were holding their breath," a front door "so swollen you have to push hard to get in," "no front yard," and a small garage out back "for the car we don't own yet" (4).

The dilapidated series of apartments and houses Esperanza inhabits with her mother, father, sister, and two brothers—particularly their dwelling on Mango Street—represents her poverty, but also the richness of her subject matter. "Like it or not you are Mango Street," her friend Alicia tells her, "and one day you'll come back too" (107). "You must remember to come back," the three aged sisters tell her, "for the ones who cannot leave as easily as you" (105). *A Room of One's Own* would seem to allow Esperanza this subject, even to encourage it. "All these infinitely obscure lives remain to be recorded," as Woolf told her young female audience. Pondering the shopgirl behind the counter, she commented, "I would as soon have her true history as the hundred and fiftieth life of Napoleon" (*Room* 93-94). But Woolf's class and ethnic biases might also deter Esperanza from achieving her own literary voice.

Cisneros's *The House on Mango Street* covertly transforms the

---

terms of Woolf's vision, making room in the female literary tradition for a young working-class Chicana who "like[s] to tell stories": "I make a story for my life," Esperanza tells us, "for each step my brown shoe takes. I say, 'And so she trudged up the wooden stairs, her sad brown shoes taking her to the house she never liked'" (109). If Esperanza's name means "too many letters," means "sadness" in the life she knows in Spanish, it translates as "hope" in English (10). Thinking back through her mothers and their comadres and across through her sisters, she builds her house from the unfulfilled hopes and dreams around her. "I could've been somebody, you know?" sighs her mother (90). Edna's Ruthie next door "could have been [many things] if she wanted to," muses Esperanza, but instead she got married to a husband nobody ever sees (68). Esperanza inherited her name from her great-grandmother, a "wild horse of a [young] woman" who, tamed by marriage, spent her days confined in her husband's house. "She looked out the window all her life," says Esperanza: "I wonder if she made the best with what she got or was she sorry because she couldn't be all the things she wanted to be. Esperanza. I have inherited her name, but I don't want to inherit her place by the window" (11). As Esperanza revises and lays claim to her matrilineal inheritance, so Cisneros in *Mango Street* offers a rich reconsideration of the contemporary feminist inheritance as well.

1

No one has yet written *A Room of One's Own* for writers, other than women, still marginal in literature. Nor do any bibliographies exist for writers whose origins and circumstances are marginal. Class remains the greatest unexamined factor.

(Tillie Olsen *Silences* 146)

Woolf famously concluded *A Room of One's Own* with her hopes for the resurrection of Shakespeare's voiceless sister. "She lives in you and in me," Woolf told her young female listeners, "and in many other women who are not here tonight, for they are washing up the dishes and putting the children to bed" (117).[3] Woolf's all-inclusive vision of sisterhood, however, barely admits the possibility of actual artistic expression among those women "not here tonight"—particularly those marginalized by race, ethnicity, and class. The five hundred pounds a year that afford her first-person narrator the freedom and independence to write are a legacy from her aunt (37-38). While Woolf expresses the hope that young women of the future will actually be "capable of earning over five hundred a year," and suggests that they limit child-bearing to "twos and threes" rather than "tens and twelves" (117), she seems to overlook the obstacles to creative freedom that a job and motherhood might pose even for the woman privileged with an income and a room of her own. She sees little future for women without those privileges.

Arguing the necessity of economic security for artistic production, Woolf asserts that "genius like Shakespeare's is not born among laboring, uneducated, servile people. . . . It is not born today among the working classes" (50). When she numbers among the advantages of "being a woman" the fact that "one can pass even a very fine negress without wishing to make an Englishwoman of her," she excludes women of color both from her audience and from her implicit definition of "being a woman" (52).[4] Similarly, when she observes that "genius of a sort must have existed among women as it must have existed among the working classes" (50), she implicitly addresses a community of women in the middle and upper classes, and thereby excludes working-class women. Tillie Olsen's wry footnote to this passage some years later reads: "Half of the working classes are women" (*Silences* 11n). And Alice Walker invites us to recast Woolf's sentence to read: "Yet genius of a sort must have existed among slaves as it must have existed among the wives and daughters of sharecroppers" (239).

In *Silences*, Olsen supplements Woolf's well-known comments on the "Angel in the House" in "Professions for Women" with her working-class equivalent: *"another angel . . . the essential angel,* with whom Virginia Woolf (and most women writers, still in the privileged class) did not have to contend—the angel who must assume the physical responsibilities for daily living, for the maintenance of life" (34). So "lowly as to be invisible," the essential angel makes no appearance in *A Room of One's Own.* If Woolf nods to those women "not here tonight, for they are washing up the dishes and putting the children to bed" (117), Adrienne Rich draws our attention to "women whom she left out of the picture altogether—women who are washing other people's dishes and caring for other people's children, not to mention women who went on the streets last night in order to feed their children" ("When We Dead" 38).

In a tribute to the "essential angel" of her own childhood, Cisneros has acknowledged the importance of Woolf's belief that a room of one's own is a necessary precondition for writing. Allowing her room of her own, Cisneros's mother enabled her daughter to create: "I'm here," Cisneros explained to an audience of young writers, "because my mother let me stay in my room reading and studying, perhaps because she didn't want me to inherit her sadness and her rolling pin" ("Notes" 75). In "Living as a Writer," Cisneros again stresses that she has "always had a room of [her] own": "As Virginia Woolf has said, a woman writer needs money, leisure, and a room of her own" (71). Elsewhere Cisneros indirectly questions the class bias of Woolf's perspective, however, when she discusses her early "dream of becoming a writer" and the inspiration of Emily Dickinson as a female literary precedent for her poetry. "What I didn't realize about Emily Dickinson," Cisneros told a junior high audience, "was that she had a few essentials going for her":[5]

1) an education, 2) a room of her own in a house of her own that she shared with her sister Lavinia, and 3) money inherited along with the house after her father died. She even had a maid, an Irish housekeeper who did, I suspect, most of the household chores. . . . I wonder if Emily Dickinson's Irish

housekeeper wrote poetry or if she ever had the secret desire to study and be anything besides a housekeeper. ("Notes" 75)

As Woolf speculated on Shakespeare's hypothetical, silenced sister, Cisneros speculates on Dickinson's housekeeper, comparing her to her own mother, "who could sing a Puccini opera, cook a dinner for nine with only five dollars, who could draw and tell stories and who probably would've enjoyed a college education" if she could have managed one ("Notes" 75). In *The House on Mango Street*, Esperanza's mother tells her that she herself should never have quit school (91). "Study hard," she tells her daughter, stirring the oatmeal, "Look at my comadres. She means Izaura whose husband left and Yolanda whose husband is dead. Got to take care all your own, she says shaking her head" (91).

Woolf stressed the importance of a female tradition for the woman writer: "we think back through our mothers if we are women" (*A Room* 79). For both Alice Walker and Sandra Cisneros, these mothers include women outside the "tradition" as it is conventionally understood, women who, perhaps anonymously, "handed on the creative spark, the seed of the flower they themselves never hoped to see; or . . . a sealed letter they could not plainly read" (Walker 240). Esperanza's mother— her encouragement, but also what she has not written, not expressed— is central to the community of female relationships informing her daughter's development as an artist. Esperanza's tribute to her mother, "A Smart Cookie," opens: "I could've been somebody, you know? my mother says and sighs." Her list of talents—"She can speak two languages. She can sing an opera. She knows how to fix a T.V."—is framed by her confinement in a city whose subway system she has never mastered, and extended in a list of unfulfilled desires: "Someday she would like to go to the ballet. Someday she would like to see a play" (*House* 90). *The House on Mango Street* strikingly enacts what Rachel Blau DuPlessis sees as a "specific biographical drama that has entered and shaped *Künstlerromane* by women": "Such a narrative is engaged with a maternal figure and . . . is often compensatory for her losses. . . . The daughter becomes an artist to extend, reveal, and elaborate her mother's often thwarted talents" (93). Esperanza's mother points to the girl's godmothers (her own *comadres*, or, literally translated, "comothers," powerful family figures in Chicano culture) as examples of the necessity "to take care all your own" (91). In the extended filiations of her ethnic community Esperanza finds a network of maternal figures. She writes to celebrate all of their unfulfilled talents and dreams and to compensate for their losses.

Cisneros loosely structures her series of prose pieces as a *Künstlerroman*, whereby the final piece circles back to the opening.[6] Esperanza's closing statement, "I like to tell stories. I am going to tell you a story about a girl who didn't want to belong," is followed by a repetition of the opening lines of the book that she is now able to write (109, 3). The paired sections opening and closing the book strongly evoke Esperanza's maternal muse. While the opening chapter describes their ramshackle series of third-floor flats and the unsatisfactory house on Mango Street where Esperanza has no room of her own, her mother's body in the second chapter provides all of the security and warmth and "room" that the small girl desires:

> But my mother's hair, my mother's hair, . . . sweet to put your nose into when she is holding you, holding you and you feel safe, is the warm smell of bread before you bake it, is the smell when she makes a little room for you on her side of the bed still warm with her skin, and you sleep near her, the rain outside falling and Papa snoring. The snoring, the rain, and Mama's hair that smells like bread. (6-7)

The two closing sketches, "A House of My Own" and "Mango Says Goodbye Sometimes," describe the grown Esperanza's ideal house of her own where she can create, "a space for myself to go, clean as paper before the poem" (100), and also her new relation to Mango Street and her origins. The house on Mango Street becomes an overtly maternal figure who collaborates in her freedom and creativity: "I write it down and Mango says goodbye sometimes. She does not hold me with both arms. She sets me free" (110).

DuPlessis sees the circular structure of the twentieth-century woman's *Künstlerroman* as a way of writing "beyond" the traditional endings available to women, what Woolf in *A Room of One's Own* called "breaking the sequence" of conventional plot (*A Room* 85, 95). "In these works," DuPlessis writes, "the female artist is given a way of looping back and reenacting childhood ties, to achieve not the culturally approved ending in heterosexual romance, but rather the reparenting necessary to her second birth as an artist" (94). The "maternal muse" and "reparenting motifs," DuPlessis suggests, are among the "strategies that erode, transpose, and reject narratives of heterosexual love and romantic thralldom" (94). Esperanza contrasts fairy tale romances with the lives of the women around her as she develops a new narrative form to tell their stories and give shape to her own vocation. "You must keep writing," her aunt tells her, "It will keep you free" (61).

2

There will be narratives of female lives only when women no longer live their lives isolated in the houses and the stories of men.

(Carolyn G. Heilbrun *Writing a Woman's Life* 47)

In *A Room of One's Own*, Woolf looked ahead to the woman in the future who would write a different sort of "novel," "some new vehicle, not necessarily in verse, for the poetry in her" (80). She anticipated that women writers would need to break the sentence and to break the sequence, "the expected order," in order to develop forms "adapted to the [woman's] body" and expressive of women's lives (85, 95, 81). Women's books, she suggested, would possibly "be shorter, more concentrated, than those of men" (81), and would undoubtedly deal with new subjects (86-96). *The House on Mango Street* fulfills many of Woolf's prophecies, most obviously in its brevity and generic instability. Cisneros herself has called her stories "a cross between poetry and fiction,"[7] which she wanted her readers to be able to read both in and out of sequence: "I wanted to write a collection which could be read at any random point without having any knowledge of what came before or after. Or, that could be read in a series to tell one big story. I wanted stories like poems, compact and lyrical and ending with a reverberation" ("Do You Know Me?" 78).

Woolf specified gender and class as the two subject areas yet to be explored. The female writer of the future need no longer depict women exclusively in relation to men; she would be free to explore "relationships between women," particularly friendships, "those unrecorded gestures, those unsaid or half-said words, which form themselves, no more palpably than the shadows of moths on the ceiling, when women are alone, unlit by the capricious and coloured light of the other sex" (*A Room* 86, 88). Further, Woolf wrote, "she will not need to limit herself any longer to the respectable houses of the upper middle classes" (92). In lectures Cisneros has explained that her subject emerged in a "defensive and rebellious" reaction to her white middle-class fellow graduate students at the University of Iowa Writers' Workshop: "My intent was simply to chronicle, to write about something my classmates couldn't" ("Do You Know Me?" 78).

Poverty was the "ghost" she attempted to escape before she found her subject, Cisneros told an audience of young writers ("Ghosts" 72). "As a poor person growing up in a society where the class norm was superimposed on a t.v. screen, I couldn't understand why our home wasn't all green lawn and white wood like the ones in 'Leave It to Beaver' or 'Father Knows Best'" (72). The metaphor of the house emerged, Cisneros said, in a heated graduate seminar discussion of Gaston Bachelard's *Poetics of Space*: "What did I know except third-floor flats. Surely my classmates knew nothing about that. That's precisely what I chose to write: about third-floor flats, and fear of rats, and drunk husbands sending rocks through windows, anything as far from the poetic as possible" (73).

Julián Olivares argues that Bachelard's book delineates a "poetics of space" that is particularly the provenance of the privileged upper-class white male, "probably never having to do 'female' housework and probably never having been confined to the house for reason of his sex." Bachelard's reveries of "felicitous space," he contends, evoke "images of a house that a woman might not have, especially an impoverished woman raised in a ghetto" (160). Olivares overlooks a number of feminist writers, however, who have explored the special relation of women to houses and rooms, the traditional realm of their "separate sphere."[8] In *A Room of One's Own* Woolf described the creative power exerted by women in the drawing-room or nursery, "the centre of some different order and system of life" (90):

> One goes into a room—but the resources of the English language would be much put to the stretch, and whole flights of words would need to wing their way illegitimately into existence before a woman could say what happens when she goes into a room. . . . One has only to go into any room in any street for the whole of that extremely complex force of femininity to fly in one's face. How should it be otherwise? For women have sat indoors all these millions of years, so that by this time the very walls are permeated by their creative force, which has, indeed, so overcharged the capacity of bricks and mortar that it must needs harness itself to pens and brushes and business and politics. But this creative power differs greatly from the creative power of men. (91)

While it might be argued that Woolf's privileged experience of domestic space more closely approximates an upper-class white Englishman's than a contemporary woman of color's in the United States, Toni Morrison has also commented on the peculiar "intimacy" of a woman's sense of place, "a woman's strong sense of being in a room, a place, or in a house." "Sometimes my relationship to things in a house would be a little different from, say my brother's or my father's or my sons'," she told Robert Stepto in an interview, "I clean them and I move them and I do very intimate things 'in place': I am sort of rooted in it, so that writing about being in a room looking out, or being in a world looking out, or living in a small definite place, is probably very common among most women anyway" (Stepto 213).[9]

The domestic realm arouses a variety of responses in contemporary women writers. Tillie Olsen has most vividly described the difficulty of making space in a woman's daily life for writing: "habits of years—response to others, distractibility, responsibility for daily matters—stay with you, mark you, become you" (39). Esperanza boldly proclaims her intention to break these habits early: "I have begun my own quiet war. Simple. Sure. I am one who leaves the table like a man, without putting back the chair or picking up the plate" (*House* 89).[10] Gender roles, as well as class, condition Esperanza's response to women's confinement to the household. Olivares is largely correct in his central premise that "Cisneros . . . inverts Bachelard's pronouncement on the poetics of space; for Cisneros the inside, the here, can be confinement and a source of anguish and alienation" (161). In story after story of the women in her community, Esperanza recognizes that a room—if not of one's own—can be stifling.

Her own grandmother, unhappily married, "looked out the window all her life, the way so many women sit their sadness on an elbow" (11). Because Rafaela is beautiful, her husband locks her indoors on Tuesday nights while he plays dominoes; Rafaela is "still young," Esperanza explains, "but getting old from leaning out the window so much" (79). Louie's cousin Marin "can't come out—gotta baby-sit with Louie's sisters—but she stands in the doorway a lot" (23-24). "We never see Marin until her aunt comes home from work," Esperanza tells us, "and even then she can only stay out front" (27). Across the street on the third floor, Mamacita, who speaks no English, "sits all day by the window and plays the Spanish radio shows and sings all the homesick songs about her country" (77). Sally's father keeps her inside and beats her when he thinks of his sisters who ran away. Later Sally's husband won't let her talk on the phone or even look out the window:

> She sits at home because she is afraid to go outside without his permission. She looks at all the things they own: the towels and the toaster, the alarm clock and the drapes. She likes looking at the walls, at how neatly their corners meet, the linoleum roses on the floor, the ceiling smooth as wedding cake. (102)

"There Was an Old Woman She Had So Many Children She Didn't Know What to Do" suggests the Mother Goose character who lived in a shoe; "Rosa Vargas' kids are too many and too much" and even the neighborhood has given up trying to help (29). Throughout Esperanza's narrative shoes intersect with the theme of dwellings as images of constricting femininity.[11] The enormously fat Mamacita with her tiny feet arrives in the United States with "a dozen boxes of satin high heels" and then never leaves her room again, perhaps because she's fat, perhaps because she doesn't speak English, perhaps because she can't climb the three flights of stairs (77). Sire ties his girlfriend Lois's shoes as Esperanza concludes that Lois doesn't know how. "Mama says those kind of girls, those girls are the ones that go into alleys. Lois who can't tie her shoes. Where does he take her?" (73). In "The Family of Little Feet," Esperanza and her girlfriends Lucy and Rachel spend a day teetering on high heels, sampling adult femininity. "It's Rachel who learns to walk the best all strutted in those magic high heels. She teaches us to cross and uncross our legs, and to run like a double-dutch rope, and how to walk down to the corner so that the shoes talk back to you with every step." The men on the corner "can't take their eyes off" them. The grocer tells them they're "too young to be wearing shoes like that," the shoes are "dangerous" and he's going to "call the cops." A bum accosts Rachel and offers her a dollar for a kiss. "Tired of being beautiful," the girls abandon the shoes and never wear them again (40-42).

Gender identity in "The Family of Little Feet" becomes an arbitrary cultural construct assumed like a pair of shoes.[12] "The boys and girls live in separate worlds," as Esperanza explains to us (11), yet it is possible to act like a male by refusing household chores, or to act like a female by wobbling helplessly on high heels. Even "scientific facts" marking gender difference, such as women's hips, become part of the cultural production of gender identity as the girls speculate on their functions:

> They're good for holding a baby when you're cooking, Rachel says turning the jump rope a little quicker. She has no imagination.
>
> You need them to dance, says Lucy.
>
> If you don't get them you may turn into a man. Nenny says this and she believes it. She is this way because of her age.
>
> That's right, I add before Lucy or Rachel can make fun of her. She is stupid alright, but she *is* my sister.
>
> But most important, hips are scientific, I say repeating what Alicia already told me. It's the bones that let you know which skeleton was a man's when it was a man and which a woman's. (47)

Like the high heels, hips require practice. "You gotta know how to walk with hips," Esperanza explains, "practice you know—like if half of you wanted to go one way and the other half the other" (50). As their jump rope game progresses, what separates Nenny from the three older girls is not the immaturity of her hips, but her inability to improvise new rhymes on hips as they swing the rope. "Not that old song, I say. You gotta use your own song. Make it up, you know? But she doesn't get it or won't. It's hard to say which. The rope turning, turning, turning" (50).

By improvising their own songs, Esperanza and her friends "write beyond the ending" of the cultural scripts confining the women around them,[13] rejecting "that old song" that Nenny repeats, or the "same story" that Minerva tells, every time she takes her husband back (50,

85). Esperanza observes that the "stories the boys tell in the coatroom" about her friend Sally are "not true," and also that Sally herself has perpetuated lies from the "storybooks and movies": "Sally, you lied. It wasn't what you said at all. . . . The way they said it, the way it's supposed to be, all the storybooks and movies, why did you lie to me?" (99). Just as the relationship between the two girls is more central to Cisneros's loosely structured plot than any heterosexual bonds, so Esperanza seems to feel Sally's betrayal more keenly than the rape she suffers while she waits for Sally at the carnival. "Sally Sally a hundred times," she says, hoping her friend will "make him stop" (100). And later she repeats over and over, "You're a liar. They all lied. All the books and magazines, everything that told it wrong. Only his dirty fingernails against my skin, only his sour smell again. The moon that watched" (100). When she cries, "I waited my whole life" (100), Esperanza bitterly evokes the "romance" of deflowering as well as the eternity she waited for Sally to rescue her.

Woolf suggested that twentieth-century women writers would be free to explore relationships between women, who in the past had "not only [been] seen by the other sex, but seen only in relation to the other sex" (*A Room* 86). The friendship between Esperanza and Sally in *Mango Street* recalls Clarissa's bond with another Sally in Woolf's experimental novel *Mrs. Dalloway*. Esperanza's Sally, like Clarissa's bohemian friend, represents danger and adventure: "Sally is the girl with eyes like Egypt and nylons the color of smoke" (*House* 81). While Clarissa's Sally is undone by the relatively benign institutions of bourgeois marriage and motherhood, Esperanza's Sally endures physical abuse from her father, the cruel gossip of the boys in the coatroom, and an unhappy marriage before she reaches eighth grade. When Sally ignores Esperanza's attempt to "save" her from Tito and his friends, who significantly will return her keys only if she kisses each of them, the grief-stricken Esperanza loses the Edenic innocence of her girlhood: "I looked at my feet in their white socks and ugly round shoes. They seemed far away. They didn't seem to be my feet anymore. And the

garden that had been such a good place to play didn't seem mine either" (98).[14] Esperanza's "monkey garden," choked with weeds and
abandoned cars, would seem "far away" from the flower-filled British
terrace of Woolf's novel, where Clarissa and Sally's kiss was rudely in-
terrupted by Clarissa's suitor Peter and the intrusive cultural expectations of adult heterosexuality (*Mrs. Dalloway* 52-53).[15] Yet within their
disparate socioeconomic settings, both narratives self-consciously resist the closure of the conventional romance or marriage plot, which
DuPlessis defines as "the use of conjugal love as a telos and of the developing heterosexual love relation as a major . . . element in organiz-
ing the narrative action" (200n22).

Tensions between Esperanza's new narratives and "all the books
and magazines, everything that told it wrong" are most evident in her
use of fairy tales as counterpoints to women's lives in the barrio.
Locked in her room, Rafaela "dreams her hair is like Rapunzel's" and
yearns to be rescued (79). Marin moons in the doorway under the
streetlamp, hoping the boys will see her: "Is waiting for a car to stop, a
star to fall, someone to change her life" (27). When they receive the
gift of the discarded shoes, Esperanza and her friends shout, "Hurray!
Today we are Cinderella because our feet fit exactly" (40). Their encounters with men as they strut in their glass slippers escalate in danger
until they flee from the drunken "bum man," a leering Prince Charming whose kiss they refuse.[16]

Princes are conspicuously absent or threatening in almost all of
Esperanza's stories. Rosa Vargas's husband "left without even leaving
a dollar for bologna or a note explaining how come" (29). Minerva's
"mother raised her kids alone and it looks like her daughters will go
that way too" (84). Edna's daughter Ruthie sleeps on a couch in her living room and "says she's just visiting and next weekend her husband's
gonna come back to take her home. But the weekends come and go and
Ruthie stays" (69). Esperanza's godmothers's husbands left or died
(91). Minerva's husband, who "left and keeps leaving," throws a rock
through the window when she "finally" puts him out. "Then he is sorry

and she opens the door again. Same story. Next week she comes over black and blue and asks what can she do? Minerva. I don't know which way she'll go. There is nothing *I* can do" (85). When Sally marries a marshmallow salesman out of state, she tells Esperanza she is in love, but Esperanza thinks "she did it to escape" her father's beatings. Trapped in her room with its linoleum roses and "ceiling smooth as wedding cake," Sally is imprisoned by the very prince who was to rescue her (102).

Most of the women yearn for different endings. Minerva secretly writes poems on "little pieces of paper that she folds over and over and holds in her hands a long time, little pieces of paper that smell like a dime" (84). On Tuesday nights Rafaela lowers a shopping bag on a clothesline from her locked room so that the children can send up coconut and papaya juice, "and wishes there were sweeter drinks, not bitter like an empty room, but sweet—sweet like the island, like the dance hall down the street where women much older than her throw green eyes easily like dice and open homes with keys" (80). Yet if Rafaela desires her own key, she continues to dream of what DuPlessis terms "romantic thralldom" (66-67), the same stories that locked her in her room: "And always there is someone offering sweeter drinks, someone promising to keep them on a silver string" (80). Marin also yearns for the silver string—a job downtown, where you "get to wear nice clothes and can meet someone in the subway who might marry you and take you to live in a big house far away" (26). Esperanza's little sister Nenny insists "she won't wait her whole life for a husband to come and get her," nor does she want to leave the house like Minerva's sister by having a baby: "She wants things all her own," Esperanza says, "to pick and choose. Nenny has pretty eyes and it's easy to talk that way if you are pretty" (88). Esperanza, whose hair "never obeys barrettes or bands" (6), tells us that she is the "ugly daughter," "the one nobody comes for" (82). She dreams of being a movie screen *femme fatale*, "beautiful and cruel": "Her power is her own. She will not give it away" (89). She has decided, she tells us, "not to grow up tame like the others" (88).

Indifferent to the prince's glass slipper, Esperanza seeks to develop an autonomous identity. She and Lucy and Rachel decisively abandon their high heels after a day of playing grownup princesses at the ball. In a related episode, Esperanza, dressed in new clothes for her cousin's baptism, is ashamed to dance because of her old and scuffed brown and white saddle shoes. Her feet "grow bigger and bigger" as she declines invitations to dance until her uncle pulls her onto the dance floor:

> My feet swell big and heavy like plungers, but I drag them across the linoleum floor straight center where Uncle wants to show off the new dance we learned. And Uncle spins me and my skinny arms bend the way he taught me and my mother watches and my little cousins watch and the boy who is my cousin by first communion watches and everyone says, wow, who are those two who dance like in the movies, until I forget that I am wearing only ordinary shoes, brown and white, the kind my mother buys each year for school. (47)

Esperanza reconciles herself to "ordinary shoes" as she will later reconcile herself to Mango Street. In both cases this reconciliation entails a new freedom, to dance, to imagine a house of her own with her "two shoes waiting beside the bed," a house "quiet as snow," "clean as paper before the poem" (108). The blank page allows her the freedom to imagine new scripts for women's lives. "You can never have too much sky," she tells us (33).

Woolf's Mary Beton in *A Room of One's Own* explained that her aunt's legacy of five hundred pounds a year "unveiled the sky" to her, "substituted for the large and imposing figure of a gentleman, which Milton recommended for my perpetual adoration, a view of the open sky" (39). Esperanza's first vision of a house with a room of one's own is inspired by her passionate sorrow for Sally, her wish that Sally could escape the life she leads on Mango Street:

Sally, do you sometimes wish you didn't have to go home? Do you wish your feet would one day keep walking and take you far away from Mango Street, far away and maybe your feet would stop in front of a house, a nice one with flowers and big windows and steps for you to climb up two by two upstairs where a room is waiting for you. And if you opened the little window latch and gave it a shove, the windows would swing open, all the sky would come in. (82-83)

In an environment where "there is too much sadness and not enough sky" (33), Esperanza's dream is collective and redemptive: to liberate the women around her from the tyrannies of male houses and male plots.

3

One day I will pack my bags of books and paper. One day I will say goodbye to Mango. I am too strong for her to keep me here forever. One day I will go away.

Friends and neighbors will say, What happened to that Esperanza? Where did she go with all those books and paper? Why did she march so far away?

They will not know I have gone away to come back. For the ones I left behind. For the ones who cannot out.

(Sandra Cisneros The House on Mango Street 110)

Pondering the doors shut by the male custodian of the library, Woolf in 1928 "thought how unpleasant it is to be locked out; and . . . how it is worse perhaps to be locked in" (*A Room* 24). To be confined within male structures might be as great a disadvantage to the female artist as to be outside them. To achieve the "freedom and fullness of expression" Woolf considered necessary to art, women must design new spaces appropriate to their dreams and needs. "A book is not made of sentences laid end to end," wrote Woolf, "but of sentences built . . . into arcades or domes. And this shape too has been made by men out of their own needs for their own uses" (80).

As Esperanza shapes her narrative, images of constricting, infelicitous space are balanced by powerful feminine images of what Bachelard terms "felicitous space." Their third-floor flat on Loomis above the boarded-up laundromat, which they had to leave "quick" when the water pipes broke, is an early source of shame to Esperanza, when the nun from her school says "'You live *there*?' . . . You live *there*? The way she said it made me feel like nothing" (5). The series of third-floor flats, on Loomis, and before that on Keeler, and before that on Paulina, more flats than Esperanza can remember, would not seem to exemplify Bachelard's intuition that "life begins well, it begins enclosed, protected, all warm in the bosom of the house" (7). What Esperanza "remember[s] most is moving a lot" (3). "I never had a house," she complains to Alicia on Mango Street, ". . . only one I dream of" (107). Yet the "maternal features of the house" that Bachelard describes are literally exemplified in the felicitous peace of Esperanza's mother's body, "when she makes a little room for you on her side of the bed still warm with her skin, and you sleep near her," "when she is holding you, holding you and you feel safe" (6). Within this shelter, the small girl can begin to dream.

The overcrowded house on Mango Street, with its "swollen" door, "crumbling" bricks, and "windows so small you'd think they were holding their breath," is "not the house we'd thought we'd get," Esperanza complains, "not the way they told it at all" (3-4). Yet Mango Street becomes an integral part of herself, the source of her art and her freedom. *Las comadres*, the three magical sisters, tell Esperanza: "When you leave you must remember to come back for the others. A circle, understand? You will always be Esperanza. You will always be Mango Street. You can't erase what you know: You can't forget who you are" (105). If Mango Street is "not the way they told it at all," then Esperanza's developing resolve is to re-member herself through a new telling that will not erase realities, and to begin by circling back to "what I remember most . . . Mango Street, sad red house, the house I belong but do not belong to" (110). Bachelard suggests that circular structures "help us to collect ourselves, permit us to confer an initial constitution on ourselves," and advises that "by remembering 'houses' and 'rooms,' we learn to 'abide' within ourselves" (234, xxxiii). Esperanza's negotiation with her origins is more ambivalent and less nostalgic than Bachelard's, but remembering Mango Street is nevertheless intimately connected to the formation of her identity as a woman, an adult member of her community, and a writer.

Through Mango Street, Esperanza is able to explore the tensions between belonging and not belonging. Hers is a story, she tells us, "about a girl who didn't want to belong" (109). In "My Name" she confides her rebellious desire to "baptize myself under a new name, a name more like the real me, the one nobody sees. Esperanza as Lisandra or Maritza or Zeze the X. Yes. Something like Zeze the X will do" (11). Her successive baptisms, like the names for the shape-shifting clouds in "And Some More," keep Esperanza's identity fluid. Yet she also acknowledges that the name Esperanza belongs to her, a legacy from her great-grandmother, a "wild horse of a woman." "I have inherited her name," Esperanza tells us, "but I don't want to inherit her place by the window" (11). When Alicia tells her that "like it or not" she is Mango Street and will come back, she replies:

> Not me. Not until somebody makes it better.
> Who's going to do it? The mayor?
> And the thought of the mayor coming to Mango Street makes me laugh out loud.
> Who's going to do it? Not the mayor. (107)

Through naming herself and her community, Esperanza returns both to accept and to alter her inheritance. Her most conspicuous alliances when she constitutes herself as speaking subject are ethnic and local. The "we" she speaks of is Hispanic, herself and her barrio neighbors.[17] "Those who don't know any better come into our neighborhood scared," she says of outsiders:

But we aren't afraid. We know the guy with the crooked eye is Davey the Baby's brother, and the tall one next to him in the straw brim, that's Rosa's Eddie V. and the big one that looks like a dumb grown man, he's Fat Boy, though he's not fat anymore nor a boy. (28)

Names and stories create an intimate realm of safety in Esperanza's early stories. "All brown all around we are safe" (29). In "And Some More," a litany of names punctuates the girls' conversation: Rachel's cousin who's "got three last names and, let me see, two first names. One in English and one in Spanish. . . . Phyllis, Ted, Alfredo and Julie. . . . Jose and Dagoberto, Alicia, Raul, Edna, Alma and Rickey . . ." (35-36). Musing on the Eskimos's thirty names for snow, Esperanza and her friends supply over fifty-two names of the people around them, drawing their magic circle to a close with the communal declaration of their own names: "Rachel, Lucy, Esperanza, and Nenny" (38).

Yet as Rachel, Lucy, Esperanza, and Nenny grow, this sense of community shifts. The dangers that threaten them come from without but also within their own neighborhood, even within their own households. Men's names appear far less frequently in the latter part of Esperanza's narrative, where women's names and the bonds between women predominate. Alicia is "young and smart and studies for the first time at the university," but her father defines her reality and her "place" when he insists that she is "just imagining" the mice in the kitchen and that "anyway, a woman's place is sleeping so she can wake up early with the tortilla star" (31). Rafaela's husband locks her in. Sally becomes a "different Sally" when she hurries "straight home after school," where her father beats her "just because [she's] a daughter" (82, 92). Minerva's husband leaves her "black and blue" (85), and though she "cries" and "prays" and "writes poems on little pieces of paper" she remains trapped in the "same story," the same cycle of violence. Esperanza and her girlfriends successfully flee the bum who wants to kiss them, but already Rachel, "young and dizzy," is tempted by the "sweet things" he says and the dollar in his pocket, and "who can blame her" (41). Later Esperanza endures the unwanted kiss of the "older Oriental man" at her first job, and the brutal sexual assault at the fair where she waits in vain by the grotesque red clowns for Sally.[18] "Why did you leave me all alone?" (100). Sally's escape from the violence of her father's household leads to a new form of confinement and a husband who sometimes "gets angry and once he broke the door where his foot went through, though most days he is okay" (101). Impatient with writers who "make our barrios look like Sesame Street," Cisneros told an interviewer that "poor neighborhoods lose their charm after dark. . . . I was writing about it in the most real sense that I know, as a person walking those neighborhoods with a vagina" (Aranda 69).

Esperanza's dream of a house of her own—"Not a man's house. Not a daddy's." (108)—is both solitary and communal, a refuge for herself and for others. In *Felicitous Space*, Judith Fryer dwells on the spaces women inhabit, as well as those they imagine:

> It is not only, then, as Virginia Woolf suggested, that women have had no space to themselves, not only that they have been forbidden spaces reserved for men. Trapped, as she has been at home, a home that in America has been "not her retreat, but her battleground . . . her arena, her boundary, her sphere . . . [with] no other for her activities," woman has been unable to move. She has been denied, in our culture, the possibility of dialectical movement between private spaces and open spaces. But let us not forget the room of one's own. . . . (50)

In Cisneros's reconstruction of Woolf's "room of one's own," Esperanza's "house of my own" simultaneously represents an escape from the barrio, a rejection of the domestic drudgery of "home" ("Nobody's garbage to pick up after" [108]), a solitary space for her creativity, and a communal expression of women's lives. Like her name, her dream of a house is a legacy from her family. "Our house would be white with trees around it," Esperanza explains in the opening chapter, "a great big yard and grass growing without a fence. This was the house Papa talked about when he held a lottery ticket and this was the house Mama dreamed up in the stories she told us before we went to bed" (4). The older Esperanza stops listening to her mother's stories of the house when she begins to develop her own (86). As she gazes longingly at the houses on the hill, "the ones with the gardens where Papa works," she vows that she'll allow space for bums in the attic when she owns her own house (86). The house becomes as well an imaginary dwelling— the "home in the heart," "house made of heart" prophesied by the witch woman Elenita (64)—as Esperanza's sympathy for Sally animates her vision of a house "with plenty of blue sky," providing shelter for laughter and imagination: "And you could laugh, Sally. You could go to sleep and wake up and never have to think who likes and doesn't like you. You could close your eyes and you wouldn't have to worry what people said because you never belonged here anyway and nobody could make you sad and nobody would think you're strange because you like to dream and dream" (83). Finally the house for Esperanza becomes a creative refuge, "quiet as snow, a space for myself to go, clean as paper before the poem" (108). Many women in the community help her to arrive there: Edna's Ruthie, who listens when she recites "The Walrus and the Carpenter"; Elenita, who tells her fortune; her Aunt Lupe, who listens to her read library books and her first poems; Minerva, who trades poems with her; the three sisters, who offer her prophecies; and her mother, who encourages her to study.

Esperanza dreams of release and of reunion. She will leave Mango Street, "the house I belong but do not belong to" (110), but, she tells us, "I won't forget who I am or where I came from" (87). Traditionally the *Künstlerroman* closes with a departure. Joyce's Stephen Dedalus in *Portrait of the Artist as a Young Man* leaves the poverty and numbing provinciality of Dublin behind him, ready to "fly" the "nets" of "nationality, language, religion" in order to devote himself to art (203). But Esperanza will go away "to come back": "For the ones I left behind. For the ones who cannot out" (102). Her book, dedicated "*A las Mujeres*/To the Women," will tell not only the story of her own artistic development but the stories of the many women around her. "You must remember to come back," Lucy and Rachel's mysterious aunt tells her, "for the ones who cannot leave as easily as you" (98).

4

First world feminist criticism is struggling to avoid repeating the same imperializing moves that we claim to protest. We must leave home, as it were, since our homes are often sites of racism, sexism, and other damaging social practices. Where we come to locate ourselves in terms of our specific histories and differences must be a place with room for what can be salvaged from the past and what can be made new.

(Caren Kaplan "Deterritorializations: The Rewriting of Home
and Exile in Western Feminist Discourse" 194-95)

In *A Room of One's Own* Woolf suggested that the female writer is always "an inheritor as well as an originator" (113). Her own legacy has crossed color and class lines in the feminist community. Michèle Barrett, writing from a Marxist-feminist perspective, applauds Woolf's fruitful and still largely unexplored insight in *A Room of One's Own* that "the conditions under which men and women produce literature are materially different" (103). Tillie Olsen uses *A Room* to meditate on the silences of women more marginal than Shakespeare's sister, exploring not only gender as one of the "traditional silencers of humanity," but also "class—economic circumstances—and color" (24).[19] *A Room of One's Own* serves explicitly as the foundation for Alice Walker's reconstruction of her African American mothers' and grandmothers' creative achievements in "In Search of Our Mothers' Gardens."[20] Elsewhere Walker numbers Tillie Olsen and Virginia Woolf among the artistic models indispensable to her development (14). Amy Ling stresses "how much we share as a community of women and how often our commonalities cross cultural and racial barriers": "Reading Barolini, like reading Alice Walker's 'In Search of our Mothers' Gardens' and *The Color Purple*, Audre Lorde's poems and essays, and Virginia Woolf's *A Room of One's Own* is like finding sisters I didn't know I had" (154).

While some women of color have expressed radical alienation from the privileged position of "our reputed foresister Virginia Woolf," others read Woolf through Olsen's class perspective.[21] "Ideally," the Chicana writer Helena María Viramontes comments, "it would be bliss to manipulate the economic conditions of our lives and thus free our minds, our hands, to write. But there is no denying that this is a privilege limited to a certain sex, race, and class. The only bad thing about privilege, Virginia Woolf wrote (I'm paraphrasing from Tillie Olsen) was that not every one could have it" (34). Viramontes and Cherríe Moraga have acknowledged the inspiration of contemporary African American women writers for their own writing.[22] Cisneros's "house of my own"—"Not a daddy's. A house all my own. With my porch and my pillow, my pretty purple petunias" (100)—may have been inspired not only by Woolf's "room of one's own" but also by a similarly complex crossing of Emily Dickinson's dwelling "in Possibility – / A fairer House than Prose –," Alice Walker's maternal gardens and "Revolutionary Petunias," and Audre Lorde's landmark statement "The Master's Tools Will Never Dismantle the Master's House."[23]

Jane Marcus has designated Virginia Woolf "the mother of us all" (Meese 91), who invited her feminist successors to become "co-conspirators against culture," and who envisioned "untying the mother tongue, freeing language from bondage to the fathers and returning it to women and the working classes" ("Thinking Back" 83, 73). Yet Woolf's relation to women of the working classes is frequently problematic. In 1930, when she was invited to write an introduction to a collection of papers by working women, Woolf found much of interest in "these voices . . . beginning only now to emerge from silence into half-articulate speech." But she also asserted emphatically, "It is not from the ranks of working-class women that the next great poet or novelist will be drawn" ("Memories" 148, 147). Woolf and many of her contemporary defenders seem all too often to imagine speaking from a privileged position for the obscure, the silenced, and the oppressed. In "Still Practice, A / Wrested Alphabet," Marcus elaborates her well-known metaphor of Woolf as the swallow Procne voicing the tongue-less Philomel's text:

> The voice of the nightingale, the voice of the shuttle weaving its story of oppression, is the voice which cries for freedom; an appropriate voice for women of color and lesbians, it speaks from the place of imprisonment as political resistance. The voice of the swallow, however, Procne's voice, is the voice of the reader, the translator, the middle-class feminist speaking for her sisters: in a sense, the voice which demands justice. The socialist feminist critic's voice is a voice of revenge, collaboration, defiance, and solidarity with her oppressed sister's struggle. She chooses to attend to her sister's story or even to explicate its absence, as Virginia Woolf told the story of Shakespeare's sister. (215-16)

While Procne may support and even empower her sister, Marcus neglects to address the possibility that Procne may fail to attend to her sister's story, may even herself silence Philomel in the process of explicating her story's "absence."

Certainly much of the anger and frustration voiced by the women of color in collections such as *This Bridge Called My Back* and *Making Face, Making Soul* derives from the easy assumption of power among white middle-class feminists, who seem either to ignore their presence or to usurp their voices. "What I mind is the pseudo-liberal ones who suffer from the white women's burden," Gloria Anzaldúa writes: "She attempts to talk for us—what a presumption! This act is a rape of our tongue and our acquiescence is a complicity to that rape. We women of color have to stop being modern medusas—throats cut, silenced into a mere hissing" ("La Prieta" 206). Chandra Mohanty firmly concludes her discussion of the position of "third world women" within Western feminist discourses with the directive: "It is time to move beyond the Marx who found it possible to say: They cannot represent themselves; they must be represented" (354). Countless Philomels have not lost their tongues. If she is truly to achieve "collaboration" and "solidarity" through her song, Procne needs to imagine more harmonious alternatives to her solo performance. Adrienne Rich and Audre Lorde are among the growing number of feminists voicing the urgent necessity for dialogue between groups divided by race, ethnicity, class, and sexual preference within the feminist movement.[24] While the editors of *This Bridge Called My Back* uncovered radical "separation" in their effort to forge a "connection" with white women, the aim of their anthology was nevertheless to "create a definition that expands what 'feminist' means to us" (*This Bridge* 61, xxiii).

By engaging *A Room of One's Own* in *The House on Mango Street*, Cisneros opens a dialogue. Preserving Woolf's feminist architecture, she enlarges and even reconstructs Woolf's room to make space for her own voice and concerns. "I like to tell stories," her protagonist announces simply. "I put it down on paper and then the ghost does not ache so much" (101). Woolf predicted that the female writer would remain conscious of "the experience of the mass . . . behind the single voice" and of "the common life which is the real life and not . . . the little separate lives which we live as individuals" (69, 117). The female writer would enjoy a greater anonymity than the male writer, who was unhappily prone to erect an "I" that overshadowed his subject (*A Room* 52, 115, 103-105). Esperanza, who often speaks as "we," and sometimes is not present at all in her stories, achieves a collective as well as an individual voice. In vignettes such as "What Sally Said" and "A Smart Cookie," she is primarily a listener, aware, as Woolf was, of the "accumulation of unrecorded life" on Mango Street (*A Room* 93). In "Geraldo No Last Name" we hear "what he told" Marin, the "story" that Marin told "again and again. Once to the hospital and twice to the police." And the story that no one told: "Only Marin can't explain why it mattered, the hours and hours, for somebody she didn't even know.

The hospital emergency room" (65-66). Yvonne Yarbro-Bejarano has suggested that an impulse toward a "collective subject" is characteristic of the Chicana writer, who finds "the power, the permission, the authority to tell stories about herself and other Chicanas . . . from her cultural, racial/ethnic and linguistic community" (141).

Free to tell stories, Esperanza—hope—will speak for herself and her people, in her own voice, from a vividly imagined house of her own. "One day I'll own my own house," she assures us, "but I won't forget who I am or where I came from" (81). She will speak in two tongues, English and Spanish, from inside and outside the barrio. She will speak for the nameless: for "Geraldo No Last Name"—"just another wetback" who died in the emergency room before anyone could identify him.

> His name was Geraldo. And his home is in another country. The ones he left behind are far away. They will wonder. Shrug. Remember. Geraldo. He went north . . . we never heard from him again. (63)

She will speak for the speechless: for Mamacita, who "doesn't come out because she is afraid to speak English" (74), and whose son grows away from her in America.

> And then to break her heart forever, the baby boy who has begun to talk, starts to sing the Pepsi commercial he heard on T.V.
>
> No speak English, she says to the child who is singing in the language that sounds like tin. No speak English, no speak English, and bubbles into tears. No, no, no as if she can't believe her ears. (75)

She will speak for all the women shut in their rooms: for Rafaela, "who is still young but getting old from leaning out the window so much" (76), for Sally, who "sits at home because she is afraid to go outside without [her husband's] permission" (95), for her great-grandmother Esperanza, who "looked out the window all her life" (12).

She will speak for the banished: for Louie's other cousin, who gave all the kids a ride in his yellow Cadillac before the cops took him off in handcuffs (25-26), for Marin, whose employers will send her back to Puerto Rico.

> Marin, under the streetlight, dancing by herself, is singing the same song somewhere. I know. Is waiting for a car to stop, a star to fall, someone to change her life. (28)

She will speak for the dead: for her Aunt Lupe (54-57), for Geraldo, for her great-grandmother, for Lucy and Rachel's baby sister (96), for Angel Vargas, "who learned to fly and dropped from the sky like a sugar donut, just like a falling star, and exploded down to earth without even an 'Oh'" (31).

She will speak for herself: "I have decided not to grow up tame like the others who lay their necks on the threshold waiting for the ball and chain" (82). Instead, like the four trees "who grew despite concrete," "four who reach and do not forget to reach" (71), Esperanza survives to reach for her own freedom and to release the stories of those around her. "There are so few of us writing about the powerless," Cisneros said in a lecture, "and that world, the world of thousands of silent women, women like my mama and Emily Dickinson's housekeeper, needs to be, must be recorded so that their stories can finally be heard" ("Notes" 76).

This essay first appeared in *MELUS: Journal of the Society for the Study of the Multi-Ethnic Literature of the United States*, issue 19.4 (Winter 1994), pages 5-35, and is reprinted by permission of the journal. Copyright © 1994 by *MELUS*.

Notes

I am grateful to Professor C. Lok Chua for his encouragement, to Professors Stephen D. Gutierrez, Reuben M. Sánchez, and Lynda Koolish for their helpful readings of earlier versions of this essay, and to too many of my students at CSU, Fresno, to list here—most particularly Josephine Vasquez, who launched my rethinking of *A Room of One's Own*. Thanks are also due to CSU, Fresno, for providing generous support in the form of an Affirmative Action Faculty Development Award and a Summer Research Award. A shorter version of this paper was presented in May 1993 at the University of California, Berkeley, at the Seventh Annual Conference of MELUS.

1. See Smith 160-62, Walker 371-79, and Tate interview with Morrison 121. Lillian Robinson also professes herself "disheartened" by the "increasingly hegemonic, essentialist tendencies in feminist scholarship and criticism," arguing forcefully for the total reevaluation of women's literature that an open canon would entail: ". . . the difference of gender is not the only one that subsists among writers or the people they write about. It may not always be the major one. Women differ from one another by race, by ethnicity, by sexual orientation, and by class. Each of these contributes its historic specificity to social conditions and to the destiny and consciousness of individual women. Moreover, these differences are not simply or even primarily individual attributes. They are social definitions, based on the existence and the interaction of groups of people and of historical forces. As scholarship—itself primarily or secondarily feminist—reveals the existence of a black female tradition or a working-class women's literature, it is insufficient simply to tack these works onto the existing canon, even the emerging women's canon. Once again, every generalization about women's writing that was derived from surveying only relatively privileged white writers is called into question by looking at writers who are not middle class and white" ("Feminist Criticism" 148, 146). See also Robinson, "Canon Fathers and Myth Universe"; Judith Kegan Gardiner, Elly Bulkin, Rena Grasso Patterson, and Annette Kolodny, "An Interchange on Feminist Criticism"; the writings by women of color collected in *This Bridge Called My Back*, edited by Cherríe Moraga and Gloria Anzaldúa, and *Making Face, Making Soul/Haciendo Caras*, edited by Gloria Anzaldúa; and Audre Lorde's collection of essays *Sister Outsider*, particularly "The Master's Tools Will Never Dismantle the Master's House" (also included in *This Bridge Called My Back*), "Age, Race, Class and Sex: Women Redefining Difference," "The Uses of Anger: Women Responding to Racism," and "Eye to Eye: Black Women, Hatred, and Anger."

2. See also essays by María C. Lugones and Elizabeth V. Spelman, Caren Kaplan, Cora Kaplan, and Chandra Mohanty. Mohanty writes: "What is problematical, then, about this kind of use of 'women' as a group, as a stable category of analysis, is that it assumes an ahistorical, universal unity between women based on a generalized notion of their subordination. Instead of analytically demonstrating the production of women as socioeconomic political groups within particular local contexts, this move limits the definition of the female subject to gender identity, completely bypassing social class and ethnic identities. What characterizes women as a group is their gender (sociologically not necessarily biologically defined) over and above everything else, indicating a monolithic notion of sexual difference. Because women are thus constituted as a coherent group, sexual difference becomes coterminous with female subordination, and power is automatically defined in binary terms: people who have it (read: men), and people who do not (read: women). Men exploit, women are exploited. As suggested above, such simplistic formulations are both reductive and ineffectual in designing

strategies to combat oppressions. All they do is reinforce binary divisions between men and women" (344).

3. Jane Marcus leans heavily on this line in her defense of Woolf as a "socialist feminist"; see particularly "Still Practice, A / Wrested Alphabet" (235-36), and her discussion of the "romantic socialist vision of the charwoman" in "Daughters of Anger" (298-99). See also Lillian S. Robinson's "Who's Afraid of a Room of One's Own?" for a class-based critique of *A Room* and specifically of Woolf's stirring peroration (146).

4. I am indebted to Mary Lou Emery's discussion of this passage in her unpublished conference paper. "The sentence quoted above," Emery writes, "not only makes use of the no longer acceptable term 'negress,' but it constitutes its subject—'woman' and 'one'—as exclusively white. The subject of the sentence excludes black women from the category 'woman' and presumes to judge them as 'very fine' in the same breath that it criticizes masculine imperialist habits of thought. My point here is not to smash the idol (feminism's 'great mother and sister') Virginia Woolf but, borrowing a term from Julia Kristeva, to demassify it in an exploration of the ways 'western feminist' writings constitute colonized and working-class women as outside of the subject 'woman.'" See also Mary Eagleton's discussion of this passage in "Women and Literary Production" (42) and Michèle Barrett's thoughtful deconstruction of a similar passage in her own earlier work "Ethnocentrism" (35).

5. Tillie Olsen makes similar observations on Emily Dickinson's privileges in her essay "Silences" (*Silences* 17).

6. This form evolved gradually. Cisneros describes piecing the book together like a patchwork quilt ("Do You Know Me?" 79). In an interview, she explained that originally she did not even conceive of Esperanza as a writer: "When I started the series she was not going to be a writer. The book started out as simply memories. Later on—it took me seven years—as I was gaining my class, gender and racial consciousness, the book changed, the direction changed. I didn't intend for her to be a writer, but I had gotten her into this dilemma, and I didn't know how to get her out. . . . So the only way that I could make her escape the trap of the barrio was to make her an artist" (Aranda 69).

7. Cisneros, who published two volumes of poetry before *The House on Mango Street*, in fact sees many of these sketches as unrealized poems: "If several of the stories read like poems it's because some of them originally had been poems. Either poems redone as a story ('The Three Sisters') or a story constructed from the debris of an unfinished or unsuccessful poem ('Beautiful and Cruel' and 'A House of My Own')" ("Do You Know Me?" 79). Elsewhere she has referred to these prose pieces as "vignettes" ("The softly insistent voice of a poet," *Austin American Statesman*, March 11, 1986, qtd. in Olivares 161).

8. See Judith Fryer's *Felicitous Space* for a particularly rich and imaginative meditation on women's interconnections with "the spaces they inhabit, break free from, transform" (xiii). In Nancy Mairs's memoir *Remembering the Bone House*—directly inspired by Catherine Clément, Hélène Cixous, and Bachelard's *Poetics of Space*—female embodiment unfolds in a series of domestic and erotic spaces (7).

9. Bachelard himself dwells on the phenomenology of "women's construction of the house through daily polishing," though he is perhaps more excited about the sacramental potential of housework than most housewives might be: "Through housewifely

care a house recovers not so much its originality as its origin. And what a great life it would be if, every morning, every object in the house could be made anew by our hands, could 'issue' from our hands" (69).

10. In *My Wicked Wicked Ways*, Cisneros prefaces her title section with a line chosen from Maxine Hong Kingston's *The Woman Warrior*: "Isn't a bad girl almost like a boy?" The narrator in *The Woman Warrior* also flouts the female roles prescribed for her by deliberately spilling soup, breaking dishes, neglecting her grooming, and affecting an unattractive limp.

11. "Perhaps women were once so dangerous that they had to have their feet bound," Maxine Hong Kingston writes in *The Woman Warrior* (23). Cisneros uses a line from *The Woman Warrior* as an epigraph to a section in *My Wicked Wicked Ways*; in *The House on Mango Street* Esperanza explains that "the Chinese, like the Mexicans, don't like their women strong" (12).

12. See Sandra Gilbert ("Costumes of the Mind") for an illuminating discussion of costumes and the creation of sexual identity in female modernist texts such as Woolf's *Orlando*.

13. The term "writing beyond the ending" is from Rachel Blau DuPlessis, who writes: "When women as a social group question, and have the economic, political and legal power to sustain and return to questions of marriage law, divorce, the 'couverte' status, and their access to vocation, then the relation of narrative middles to resolutions will destabilize culturally, and novelists will begin to 'write beyond' the romantic ending" (4). DuPlessis explores a variety of strategies that undermine the romance plot, itself "a trope for the sex gender system as a whole": "Writing beyond the ending means the transgressive invention of narrative strategies, strategies that express critical dissent from dominant narrative. These tactics, among them reparenting, woman-to-woman and brother-to-sister bonds, and forms of the communal protagonist, take issue with the mainstays of the social and ideological organization of gender, as these appear in fiction" (5).

14. The Biblical resonance of Esperanza's loss of innocence in the monkey garden is underlined when the children spread the rumor "that the monkey garden had been there before anything" (96). Though Esperanza is the one who wants to "save" Sally from kissing the older boys, she is left feeling "ashamed" and displaced from her former Edenic child's play. The substitution of two young women—Esperanza and Sally—for Adam and Eve parallels the shift in narrative focus from the heterosexual romance plot to a female-centered *Künstlerroman*. Elizabeth Ordóñez has suggested three modes of discourse common to recent works by ethnic women writers that all seem clearly relevant to *Mango Street*: 1. "disruption of genre"; 2. "the power to displace 'the central patriarchal text,' that is, the Bible"; and 3. "the invention—either through inversion or compensation—of alternate mythical and even historical accounts of women" ("Narrative Texts" 19).

15. Possibly Cisneros also acknowledges Woolf's feminist agenda in *Mrs. Dalloway* when she adds solitude to a "room of one's own" as necessary for the creation of art: "And I'm here because I didn't marry my first boyfriend, that pest who never gave me any time alone, something crucial to every writer—'aloneness' breeds art" ("Notes" 75). Clarissa Dalloway rejects Peter's marriage suit on similar premises.

16. Erlinda Gonzales-Berry and Tey Diana Rebolledo also see echoes of "Little Red Riding Hood" in this scene, as the bum, like the wolf, asks the girls to come closer and closer (116). Gonzales-Berry and Rebolledo argue persuasively that Cisneros plays these fairy tales against a new model of the female *Bildungsroman* whereby the heroine is allowed the mythic quest and achievement of the traditional male hero.

17. María C. Lugones and Elizabeth V. Spelman explore "the differences among women and how these differences are silenced" through a dialogue. The Hispana in the dialogue reflects on the different contexts in which she uses the word "we." In the paper, "when I say 'we,' I am referring to Hispanas," she writes; "you" refers to "the white/Anglo women that I address." However, she adds, "'we' and 'you' do not capture my relation to other non-white women," and in a footnote she meditates on her general use of "we" outside of the paper: "I must note that when I think this 'we,' I think it in Spanish—and in Spanish this 'we' is gendered, 'nosotras.' I also use 'nosotros' lovingly and with ease and in it I include all members of 'La raza cosmica' (Spanish-speaking people of the Americas, la gente de colores: people of many colors). In the US, I use 'we' contextually with varying degrees of discomfort: 'we' in the house, 'we' in the department, 'we' in the classroom, 'we' in the meeting. The discomfort springs from the sense of community in the 'we' and the varying degrees of lack of community in the context in which the 'we' is used" ("Have We Got a Theory" 575). Although *The House on Mango Street* is clearly a feminist text, Esperanza does not use "we" to refer to women; instead "we" refers to herself and her family, herself and her childhood girlfriends, and herself and her neighborhood ethnic community ("brown all around").

18. Esperanza's "first job" is at the Peter Pan Photofinishers, where she paradoxically must appear grown up by pretending to be older than she is, and where the older man's kiss "on the mouth" damages her innocence. Both her violations come from men outside of her culture. For useful discussions of the rape in "Red Clowns" and violence against women in *Mango Street*, see María Herrera-Sobek, Ellen McCracken, and Ramón Saldívar.

19. See Elizabeth Meese's discussion of Olsen's reshaping of Woolf's vision. Meese documents "almost forty appearances by Virginia Woolf" in Olsen's *Silences* (110).

20. Walker quotes repeatedly from *A Room of One's Own* in this landmark essay. Her bracketed substitutions in Woolf's prose revise Woolf's perspective to incorporate black women's experiences in often startling ways; however, she is clearly inspired by Woolf's essay. Elsewhere she mentions that she has taught Woolf and Kate Chopin in her course on black women writers, "because they were women and wrote, as the black women did, on the condition of humankind from the perspective of women" ("From an Interview" 260).

21. The phrase is from Trinh T. Minh-ha (246). See also Gloria Anzaldúa ("Speaking in Tongues" 170), and Nellie Wong, who writes: "You are angered by the arrogance of some articles that would tell you that Virginia Woolf is your spiritual mother, your possible role model, for the work you have to do: to write. And why are you angered except for the fact that she was white and privileged, yet so ill that she walked into the sea" (178). Toril Moi offers a somewhat useful discussion of Woolf's controversial position in contemporary white feminist theory in "Who's Afraid of Virginia Woolf?," though she is conspicuously uninterested in women writers of color.

22. "Once I discovered the Black women writers—Walker, Morrison, Brooks, Shange, again to name a few," Viramontes writes, "womanism as a subject matter seemed sanctioned, illuminating, innovative, honest, the best in recent fiction that I've seen in a long time" ("'Nopalitos'" 37). In an interview, Moraga remarked, "I feel that I am a part of a movement of women of color writers. I feel that I have gotten a lot of inspiration from Black women writers in this country" (Umpierre 66).

23. See Walker's discussion of the title poem in *Revolutionary Petunias* in "From an Interview" (266-69). Lorde's influential essay appears in both *Sister Outsider* and *This Bridge Called My Back*. Cisneros credits Emily Dickinson, her "favorite American poet," with giving her "inspiration and hope all the years in high school and the first two in college when I was too busy being in love to write" ("Notes" 74, 75). She prefaces the four sections of *My Wicked Wicked Ways* with epigraphs from Emily Dickinson, Gwendolyn Brooks, Maxine Hong Kingston, and the Portuguese feminist text *The Three Marias*. These choices seem deliberately to suggest the national, international, class, and ethnic range of her feminist alliances.

24. See particularly Rich's "Disloyal to Civilization," the essays in Lorde's *Sister Outsider*, which also includes an "interview" dialogue between Lorde and Rich, and the essays in *Making Face, Making Soul/Haciendo Caras*, ed. Gloria Anzaldúa. Richard Ohmann has recently written of the challenges involved in all "alliance politics." Reflecting on his role as a white male who "work[s] in women's studies," he points out, "What we do there ['in feminism'] with our experience, our competence, and our gender and class confidence, is a matter to be negotiated through caution, flexibility, improvisation, listening, and often doubtless through a strategic fade into the wallpaper. But I don't see drawing back from the knowledge that feminism is our fight, too. So is racial equality, so is gay liberation, so is antiimperialism. I see the difficulties of our participation in these struggles as parallel to those of our joining in women's liberation, and in consequence I see alliance politics as our challenge and aim" ("In, With" 187).

Works Cited

Anzaldúa, Gloria. "La Prieta." In Cherríe Moraga and Gloria Anzaldúa. 198-209.

_____, ed. *Making Face, Making Soul/Haciendo Caras: Creative and Critical Perspectives by Feminists of Color.* San Francisco: Aunt Lute, 1990.

_____. "Speaking in Tongues: A Letter to Third World Feminists." Cherríe Moraga and Gloria Anzaldúa, 165-74.

Aranda, Pilar E. Rodríguez. "On the Solitary Fate of Being Mexican, Female, Wicked and Thirty-three: An Interview with Writer Sandra Cisneros." *The Americas Review* 18 (Spring 1990): 64-80.

Bachelard, Gaston. *The Poetics of Space.* 1958. Trans. María Jolas. Boston: Beacon P, 1969.

Barrett, Michèle. "Ideology and the Cultural Production of Gender." *Women's Oppression Today: Problems in Marxist Feminist Analysis.* London: New Left, 1980.

Barrett, Michèle, and Mary McIntosh. "Ethnocentrism and Socialist-Feminist Theory." *Feminist Review* 20 (June 1985): 23-47.

Cisneros, Sandra. "Do You Know Me?: I Wrote *The House on Mango Street.*" *The Americas Review* 15 (Spring 1987): 77-79.

_____. "Ghosts and Voices: Writing from Obsession." *The Americas Review* 15 (Spring 1987): 69-73.

_____. *The House on Mango Street.* 1984. New York: Vintage, 1988.

_____. "Living as a Writer: Choice and Circumstance." *Revista Mujeres* 3 (June 1986): 68-72.

_____. *My Wicked Wicked Ways.* Bloomington: Third Woman P, 1987.

_____. "Notes to a Young(er) Writer." *The Americas Review* 15 (Spring 1987): 74-76.

DuPlessis, Rachel Blau. *Writing Beyond the Ending: Narrative Strategies of Twentieth-Century Women Writers.* Bloomington: Indiana U P, 1985.

Eagleton, Mary. "Women and Literary Production." *Feminist Literary Theory: A Reader.* Ed. Mary Eagleton. New York: Basil Blackwell, 1986.

Emery, Mary Lou. "The Voice of Witlessness: Displacing the Other/Demassifying an Idol." Women's Studies Conference, "Women's Bodies/Women's Voice: The Power of Difference." University of Iowa, April 14-16, 1988.

Fryer, Judith. *Felicitous Space: The Imaginative Structures of Edith Wharton and Willa Cather.* Chapel Hill: U of North Carolina P, 1986.

Gardiner, Judith Kegan, Elly Bulkin, Rena Grasso Patterson, and Annette Kolodny. "An Interchange on Feminist Criticism: On 'Dancing Through the Minefield.'" *Feminist Studies* 8 (Fall 1982): 629-75.

Gilbert, Sandra M. "Costumes of the Mind: Transvestism as Metaphor in Modern Literature." *Writing and Sexual Difference.* Ed. Elizabeth Abel. Chicago: U of Chicago P, 1982. 193-219.

Gonzales-Berry, Erlinda, and Tey Diana Rebolledo. "Growing Up Chicano: Tomás Rivera and Sandra Cisneros." *Revista Chicano-Riqueña* 13 (Fall-Winter 1985): 109-19.

Heilbrun, Carolyn G. *Writing a Woman's Life.* New York: Ballantine, 1988.

Herrera-Sobek, María. "The Politics of Rape: Sexual Transgression in Chicana Fiction." *The Americas Review* 15 (Fall-Winter 1987): 171-81.

Joyce, James. *A Portrait of the Artist as a Young Man.* 1916. New York: Penguin, 1976.

Kaplan, Caren. "Deterritorializations: The Rewriting of Home and Exile in Western Feminist Discourse." *Cultural Critique* 6 (Spring 1987): 187-98.

Kaplan, Cora. "Pandora's Box: Subjectivity, Class and Sexuality in Socialist Feminist Criticism." *Sea Changes: Essays on Culture and Feminism.* London: Verso, 1980. 147-76.

Kingston, Maxine Hong. *The Woman Warrior: Memoirs of a Girlhood Among Ghosts.* New York: Vintage, 1977.

Ling, Amy. "I'm Here: An Asian American Woman's Response." *New Literary History* 19 (Autumn 1987): 151-60.

Lorde, Audre. *Sister Outsider.* Freedom: Crossing P, 1984.

Lugones, María C., and Elizabeth V. Spelman. "Have We Got a Theory For You! Feminist Theory, Cultural Imperialism and the Demand for 'The Woman's Voice.'" *Women's Studies International Forum* 6 (1983): 573-81.

Mairs, Nancy. *Remembering the Bone House: An Erotics of Place and Space*. New York: Harper and Row, 1989.

Marcus, Jane. "Daughters of Anger/Material Girls: Con/Textualizing Feminist Criticism." *Women's Studies* 15 (1988): 281-308.

_____. *Art and Anger: Reading Like a Woman*. Columbus: Miami U and Ohio State U P, 1988.

McCracken, Ellen. "Sandra Cisneros' *The House on Mango Street*: Community-Oriented Introspection and the Demystification of Patriarchal Violence." *Breaking Boundaries: Latina Writing and Critical Readings*. Ed. Asunción Horno-Delgado, Eliana Ortega, Nina M. Scott, and Nancy Saporta Sternbach. Amherst: U of Massachusetts P, 1989. 62-71.

Meese, Elizabeth A. "Deconstructing the Sexual Politic: Virginia Woolf and Tillie Olsen." *Crossing the Double-Cross: The Practice of Feminist Criticism*. Chapel Hill: U of North Carolina P, 1986. 89-113.

Moers, Ellen. *Literary Women*. New York: Doubleday, 1976.

Mohanty, Chandra Talpade. "Under Western Eyes: Feminist Scholarship and Colonial Discourses." *boundary* 2.12-13 (Spring-Fall 1984): 333-58.

Moi, Toril. "Who's Afraid of Virginia Woolf?" *Sexual/Textual Politics: Feminist Literary Theory*. New York: Methuen, 1985. 1-18.

Moraga, Cherríe, and Gloria Anzaldúa, eds. *This Bridge Called My Back: Writings by Radical Women of Color*. Watertown: Persephone P, 1981.

Ohmann, Richard. "In, With." *Men in Feminism*. Ed. Alice Jardine and Paul Smith. New York: Methuen, 1987. 182-88.

Olivares, Julián. "Sandra Cisneros' *The House on Mango Street*, and the Poetics of Space." *The Americas Review* 15 (Fall-Winter 1987): 160-70.

Olsen, Tillie. *Silences*. New York: Delacorte/Seymour Lawrence, 1978.

Ordóñez, Elizabeth. "Narrative Texts by Ethnic Women: Rereading the Past, Reshaping the Future." *MELUS* 9 (Winter 1982): 19-28.

Rich, Adrienne. "Disloyal to Civilization: Feminism, Racism, Gynephobia." *On Lies, Secrets, and Silence: Selected Prose 1966-1978*. New York: W.W. Norton, 1979. 275-310.

_____. "Notes Towards a Politics of Location." *Women, Feminist Identity, and Society in the 1980s*. Ed. Myriam Diaz-Diocaretz and Iris M. Zavala. Philadelphia: John Benjamins, 1985. 7-22.

_____. "When We Dead Awaken: Writing as Re-Vision." *On Lies, Secrets, and Silence: Selected Prose 1966-1978*. New York: W.W. Norton, 1979. 33-49.

Robinson, Lillian S. "Canon Fathers and Myth Universe." *New Literary History* 19 (Autumn 1987): 23-35.

_____. "Feminist Criticism: How Do We Know When We've Won?" *Feminist Issues in Literary Scholarship*. Ed. Shari Benstock. Bloomington: Indiana U P, 1987. 141-49.

_____. "Who's Afraid of a Room of One's Own?" *Sex, Class, and Culture*. Bloomington: Indiana U P, 1978. 97-149.

Saldívar, Ramón. *Chicano Narrative: The Dialectics of Difference*. Madison: U of Wisconsin P, 1990.

Saldívar-Hull, Sonia. "Feminism on the Border: From Gender Politics to Geopolitics." *Criticism in the Borderlands: Studies in Chicano Literature, Culture, and Ideology*. Eds. Héctor Calderón and José David Saldívar. Durham: Duke U P, 1991. 203-20.

Showalter, Elaine. *A Literature of Their Own*. Princeton, NJ: Princeton U P, 1977.

Smith, Barbara. "Toward a Black Feminist Criticism." *But Some of Us Are Brave*. Ed. Gloria T. Hull, Patricia Bell Scott, and Barbara Smith. Old Westbury: Feminist P, 1982. 157-75.

Spacks, Patricia Meyer. *The Female Imagination*. New York: Avon, 1975.

Stepto, Robert. "'Intimate Things in Place': A Conversation with Toni Morrison." *Chant of Saints: A Gathering of Afro-American Literature, Art, and Scholarship*. Urbana: U of Illinois P, 1979. 213-29.

Tate, Claudia. "Interview with Toni Morrison." *Black Women Writers at Work*. Ed. Claudia Tate. New York: Continuum, 1983. 117-31.

Trinh T. Minh-ha. "Commitment from the Mirror-Writing Box." *Making Face, Making Soul/Haciendo Caras: Creative and Critical Perspectives by Feminists of Color*. Ed. Gloria Anzaldúa. San Francisco: Aunt Lute, 1990. 245-55.

Umpierre, Luz María. "With Cherríe Moraga." *The Americas Review* 14 (Summer 1986): 54-67.

Viramontes, Helena María. "'Nopalitos': The Making of Fiction." *Breaking Boundaries: Latina Writing and Critical Readings*. Ed. Asunción Horno Delgado, Eliana Ortega, Nina M. Scott, and Nancy Saporta Sternbach. Amherst: U of Massachusetts P, 1989. 33-38.

Walker, Alice. *In Search of Our Mothers' Gardens*. New York: Harcourt Brace Jovanovich, 1983.

Wong, Nellie. "In Search of the Self as Hero: Confetti of Voices on New Year's Night—A Letter to Myself." *This Bridge Called My Back: Writings by Radical Women of Color*. Ed. Cherríe Moraga and Gloria Anzaldúa. Watertown: Persephone P, 1981. 177-81.

Woolf, Virginia. "Memories of a Working Women's Guild." *Collected Essays*. Vol. 4. New York: Harcourt Brace, 1967.

_____. *Mrs. Dalloway*. 1925. New York: Harvest, Harcourt Brace Jovanovich, 1953.

_____. "Professions for Women." *Collected Essays*. Vol. 2. New York: Harcourt Brace, 1967. 284-89.

_____. *A Room of One's Own*. 1929. New York: Harcourt Brace Jovanovich, 1957.

Yamada, Mitsuye. "Asian Pacific American Women and Feminism." Cherríe Moraga and Gloria Anzaldúa. 71-75.

Yarbro-Bejarano, Yvonne. "Chicana Literature from a Chicana Feminist Perspective." *The Americas Review* 15 (Fall-Winter 1987): 139-45.

Nature Despoiled and Artificial:
Sandra Cisneros's *The House on Mango Street*_____

James R. Giles

Sandra Cisneros's *The House on Mango Street* is, in form, the most innovative text discussed in this book; Cisneros so deliberately blurs traditional literary definitions that critics disagree about whether her text should be seen as an experimental novel or a unique kind of auto-biography. María Elena de Valdés has offered a compromise position on this question, describing it as "a fictional autobiography of the nar-rator and central character Esperanza Cordero"; de Valdés defines "fic-tional autobiography" as "a postmodern form of fiction stitching to-gether a series of lyrical pieces, 'lazy poems' Cisneros calls them . . . into the narrativity of self-invention through writing."[1] De Valdés's ap-proach is perceptive in more than one way. In its stress upon the act of writing as essential to first constructing and then asserting identity *The House on Mango Street* recalls texts by other women and minority American writers. For instance, in Maxine Hong Kingston's *The Woman Warrior* (1976), the narrator "Maxine" appropriates her mother's leg-acy of "talk story" to (re)invent a personal and family history, often providing multiple accounts of undocumented events. When this pro-cess of reinvention is complete, "Maxine," who of course has much in common with Maxine Hong Kingston, can defy her dominating mother and assert her independence. Cisneros's paralleling of writing with identity also calls to mind Henry Louis Gates's analysis of the central-ity of the "talking book" in African American literature.[2]

The innovative form of *The House on Mango Street* is reminiscent of two earlier narratives, Jean Toomer's *Cane* (1923) and Tomás Rivera's . . . *y no se lo tragó la tierra* (. . . and the earth did not swallow him) (1971). In the former, Toomer dispenses with most of the tradi-tions of the novel (a developed plot, recurrent characters, and consis-tent setting), while exploring through lyrical stories, sketches, and po-ems the nature of African American identity. Lacking a clear narrative center, *Cane*'s thematic focus is on communal, rather than individual, identity. Not only because of its subject matter, Rivera's text seems even more obviously to anticipate *The House on Mango Street*. Rivera's . . . *y no se lo tragó la tierra* tells, in fragmentary and lyrical form, of the individual and then the cultural awakening of a young Chicano boy, the son of exploited laborers who live in Texas but travel each year to the Midwest for work. In delineating the emerging awareness of her urban female protagonist, Cisneros echoes Rivera's pattern of growth from a limiting personal to a liberating communal consciousness.

Cisneros's setting is Chicago's Chicano community, and, in keeping with its other innovative aspects, it represents a merger of Sidney H. Bremer's two categories of Chicago novels, the "standard Chicago novel," informed primarily by economic issues and a vision of technology as a dehumanizing force, and the "residential" novel, texts written by women that depict the city as a predominantly supportive environment: "As an epitome of woman's place, home was not coterminous with a physical house, as cultural critic Elizabeth Janeway . . . has explained. For these Chicago [residential] writers, however, the family house was central, implicated in civic and cultural, as well as personal and domestic, activities. . . . For [them], the family house was a domestic microcosm for—not a bulwark against—the city itself."[3]

It is crucial to point out that in *The House on Mango Street* Cisneros, unlike the earlier Chicago novelists in either of Bremer's two categories, is writing from the perspective of an exploited ethnic group. She thus could not, even if she had wanted to, view Chicago as affirmatively as Edith Franklin Wyatt, Clara Laughlin, Elia W. Peattie, and Willa Cather did. In addition, she can hardly treat the concept of ethnicity with the detachment of a middle-class writer. For Cisneros, ethnic identity is not an abstraction, but a defining aspect of her identity. Like Wyatt, Laughlin, Peattie, and Cather, a woman, she shares their sense of the centrality of "house" and "home," but, unlike them, she can only yearn for a supportive physical and emotional environment. Certainly, the house of the title does not provide anything like that.

The volume's first four sentences emphasize the transient life that Esperanza, the young narrator, and her family have led: "We didn't always live on Mango Street. Before that we lived on Loomis on the third floor, and before that we lived on Keeler. Before Keeler it was Paulina, and before that I can't remember. But what I remember most is moving a lot."[4] Recalling an incident in which "a nun from [her] school" had expressed contemptuous disbelief upon seeing the family's third-floor dwelling on Loomis Street, Esperanza describes her dream of someday having "[a] real house. [O]ne I could point to," but emphasizes that "[t]he house on Mango Street isn't it" (p. 5).

The "real house" of which Esperanza dreams functions in the novel both as a concrete place of refuge and as a metaphor for her repressed, but emerging, identity. The strong sense of self that Esperanza does ultimately succeed in constructing is firmly anchored in gender, class, and culture. Julián Olivares quotes Cisneros as acknowledging two quite different sources for *The House on Mango Street*: "She states that the nostalgia for the perfect house was impressed on her at an early age from reading many times Virginia Lee Burton's *The Little House*. . . . In a class discussion [at the Iowa Writers' Workshop] of Gaston Bachelard's *The Poetics of Space*, she came to this realization: 'the metaphor of a house, a *house, a house*, it hit me. What did I know except third-floor flats? Surely my classmates know nothing about that.'"

Burton's *The Little House* is a children's book that tells the story of a house that is built in the country where it is happy until the city grows up around it and it is left to deteriorate; the little house, which is referred to as "she," is rescued from destruction only when the granddaughter of the original inhabitant notices it and has it moved back to the countryside. It is essentially urban sprawl and technology (cars and subways) that almost submerge the little house. The text assumes that urban life is unnatural:

> [P]retty soon there was an elevated train
> going back and forth above the Little House.
> The air was filled with dust and smoke,
> and the noise was so loud
> that it shook the Little House.
> Now she couldn't tell when Spring came,
> or Summer or Fall, or Winter.
> It all seemed about the same.[5]

It is possible to move the house back to the country because, despite the urban decay that surrounds it, it remains strong. Returned to the countryside, the little house is again content:

> Never again would she be curious about the city . . .
> Never again would she want to live there . . .
> The stars twinkled above her . . .
> A new moon was coming up . . .
> It was Spring . . .
> and all was quiet and peaceful in the country.
>
> (p. 40)

Thus, in Burton's book, the country is associated with life and the natural in the double sense of containing "nature" and being a human norm, while the city is viewed as being connected with death and the unnatural, an alien imposition upon the norm of nature. A not dissimilar pastoralism underlies *The House on Mango Street*.

In her essay, Olivares argues convincingly that Cisneros "reverses" Bachelard's privileged, male view of a house as "an image of 'felicitous space . . . the house shelters the daydreaming, the house protects the dreamer, the house allows one to dream in peace. . . . A house constitutes a body of images that give mankind proofs or illusions of stability.'" As an "impoverished woman raised in a ghetto," Cisneros can hardly share Bachelard's concept of a house as a "felicitous space."[6] In the world of Mango Street, women have little time or opportunity for "daydreaming," and "stability" is a dream, not a reality. For her and for Esperanza, a house as the embodiment of a secure home is in itself a dream; she only yearns for what the early-twentieth-century Chicago residential novelists could assume.

For much of her novel, Cisneros's text depicts the Chicago barrio as a terrain made dangerous and literally unnatural by poverty and violence. As in John Rechy's *The Miraculous Day of Amalia Gómez*, violence in it is the immediate legacy of class and racial oppression and of a valorization of machismo. Thus, women and female children become the perennial recipients of physical and emotional abuse. Unlike several of the novel's female characters, Esperanza is largely spared such abuse within her immediate family but encounters it virtually everywhere else. In *The House on Mango Street*, the female is thoroughly commodified, reduced to a possession without rights or voice. In fact, the struggle to claim a female voice lies at the thematic heart of the text.

As a part of her struggle for self-definition, Esperanza even desires to escape her given name and what she feels are its negative connotations: "In English my name means hope. In Spanish it means too many letters. It means sadness, it means waiting. It is like the number nine. A muddy color. It is the Mexican records my father plays on Sunday mornings when he is shaving, songs like sobbing" (p. 10). This passage is illustrative of the imaginative approach to symbolism that characterizes Cisneros's text. The traditional positive connotation of the name "Esperanza" is acknowledged, but only in order that it can be challenged; as a female of Mexican American descent living in an economically deprived neighborhood that is surrounded and controlled by a male- and Anglo-dominated society, she indeed has few reasons to feel hopeful. Outside the barrio, her name sounds foreign; it does seem to have "too many letters." The passive side of hoping is, of course, waiting, and most of the female characters in the novel are depicted as waiting, often literally, for someone to rescue them from the hopelessness in which they are trapped.

Here Cisneros's language becomes lyrical and elusive in ways that recall *Cane* and *. . . y no se lo tragó la tierra*. One can feel more easily than analyze the associations of "Esperanza" with "the number nine" and "a muddy color." Esperanza is perhaps saying that, in the eyes of a racist Anglo society, her skin color is associated with images of dirt and secrecy. At any rate, the young narrator wishes to rename and thereby recreate herself: "I would like to baptize myself under a new name, a name more like the real me, the one nobody sees. Esperanza as Lisandra or Maritza or Zeze the X. Yes. Something like Zeze the X will do" (p. 11). Obviously, she has been influenced by American popular culture—"Zeze the X" sounds like the name of a male "superhero" and especially recalls Zorro, "the Mexican Robin Hood" who was given to cutting the letter "Z" with his sword on walls and curtains. The desire to be "Zeze the X" is in part, of course, an amusing indication of Esperanza's adolescence; but, more important, it indicates her early rejection of passivity, of "waiting." Finally, she will not expect a male to rescue her, but, with the help of some adult female role models, will save herself, essentially by narrating her "story."

It takes Esperanza a while to discover such positive models. She perceives instead repeated violence against innocent young women. There is Sally whose father, frightened by her beauty, attempts to imprison her in their apartment: "Her father says to be this beautiful is trouble. They are very strict in his religion. They are not supposed to dance. He remembers his sisters and is sad. Then she can't go out. Sally, I mean" (p. 81). Sally, who longs desperately for love, is usually pictured as literally "leaning" against her open window or against cars driven by young men. She becomes the very embodiment of the "waiting" against which Esperanza rebels.

Enraged in part by his daughter's innocence, Sally's father regularly and savagely abuses her. Still, Sally attempts to protect him, explaining her bruises at school by saying "she fell": "That's where all the blue places come from. That's why her skin is always scarred" (p. 92). Inevitably, the father "one day . . . catches her talking to a boy" and "just went crazy, he just forgot he was her father between the buckle and the belt" (p. 93). Not surprisingly, Sally soon runs away to get married, and, again as one might have expected, her husband, a "marshmallow salesman," proves to be abusive. In fact, her situation after her marriage is, if anything, even more desperate than it was before: "[her husband] won't let her talk on the telephone. And he doesn't let her look out the window. And he doesn't like her friends, so nobody gets to visit her unless he is working" (pp. 101-2). Now she is denied even the consolation of "leaning" out of the window. The fate of Sally illustrates the fallacy of "waiting" for the female in Cisneros's text, which emphasizes that repression and violence are the bitter fruits of such passivity. The poverty and despair of the barrio produce an unnatural environment in which men forget that they are fathers and husbands or lovers. In *The House on Mango Street*, women are possessions to be zealously guarded except during those occasions when they are proudly exhibited.

The character who is most clearly Esperanza's double, the representative of what might have happened to her, is Minerva. The short segment focusing on her is significantly entitled "Minerva Writes Poems," and its opening sentence encapsulates the young woman's desperate situation: "Minerva is only a little bit older than [Esperanza] but already she has two kids and a husband who left" (p. 84). Like the narrator, she attempts to rescue her endangered sense of self by writing poetry, seeking through language to create evidence of an identity separate from her husband and children. But her attempt is doomed—she, unlike Esperanza, will be unable to create a lasting text. The hopelessness of her situation is intensified by the fact that her husband has not truly "left"; rather he leaves repeatedly only to return. Finally, Minerva resolves to lock him out of her house and her life forever, but sadly and inevitably relents when he once again returns.

The sketch ends with a brief paragraph that utilizes internal rhyme and borrows the lyrics of an American popular song to convey the hopelessness and the triteness of the young woman's fate: "Next day she comes over black and blue and asks what can she do? Minerva. I don't know which way she'll go. There's nothing I can do" (p. 85). Interestingly, the song lyric echoed here asks, "What *did* I do/ to be so black and blue?" Belatedly, Minerva is starting to comprehend the economic and cultural determinism in which she is trapped. The text has established the "way she'll go" or more precisely the fact that she has nowhere to go. Esperanza begins to realize that, while she is helpless to save her friend, she can and indeed must save herself through language, by writing, and that she must not allow herself to become trapped like Minerva in circumstances that would make this impossible.

It should be said that parental and spousal abuse are not the only forms that violence takes in the novel. The brutal urban environment assaults innocence in other forms as well. In one of the most powerful segments, called "Geraldo No Last Name," it appears in the guise of brutal accident and this time the central victim is male. The Geraldo of the title is a young man who is not really known by the community of Mango Street; another of Esperanza's friends, Marin, meets him at a dance and is with him when he is fatally injured in a hit-and-run accident. She then waits at the hospital while he lies dying in the emergency room. Racial prejudice and economic injustice contribute to the anonymity of Geraldo's death: "Nobody but an intern working all alone. And maybe if the surgeon would've come, maybe if he hadn't lost so much blood, if the surgeon had only come, they would know who to notify and where" (p. 66). Cisneros is calling attention in this sketch to the financial "cutbacks" that have plagued most urban public hospitals, including Chicago's, over the past decade. She is also emphasizing that, to the dominant Anglo society, the death of an unknown young Chicano man is of no significance:

> They never saw the kitchenettes. They never knew about the two-room flats and sleeping rooms he rented, the weekly money orders sent home, the currency exchange. How could they?

His name was Geraldo. And his home is in another country. The ones he left behind are far away, will wonder, shrug, remember. Geraldo—he went north . . . we never heard from him again. (p. 66)

It is in these two brief paragraphs that Cisneros's prose most directly communicates the poetic anger at senseless and unnecessary suffering that one finds in Tomás Rivera.

In *The House on Mango Street*, poverty and violence threaten to reduce everyone to anonymity; it is therefore essential that one find models of survival wherever possible in such a dangerous and unnatural world. Perhaps the text's most symbolically important sketch describes four unlikely such models. In "Four Skinny Trees," Esperanza describes her attachment to some trees planted by the city with the apparent intention of creating the illusion of a patch of benevolent nature within the concrete harshness of the urban streets. She insists that she communicates with the trees ("They are the only ones who understand me. I am the only one who understands them" [p. 74]). She and the "skinny trees with skinny necks and pointy elbows" are alike, she believes, and, in crucial ways, they are.

As do the trees, Esperanza represents innocence, hope, and affirmation artificially grafted onto a landscape of despair. Like the trees, she is not a "natural" outgrowth of the concrete city, but, also like them, she is ultimately strengthened by the challenge of survival: "Their strength is secret. They send ferocious roots beneath the ground. They grow up and they grow down and grab the earth beneath their hairy toes and bite the sky with violent teeth and never quit their anger. This is how they keep" (p. 74). The trees, while initially a gift of city officials to the barrio, survive by sending their roots beneath, and thus outside, the city. The earth in which they secure themselves has, of course, existed infinitely longer, and is thus more natural, than the steel and concrete that have arbitrarily been imposed on it. Like *Suttree*, *The House on Mango Street* provides a clear illustration of Arnold L. Goldsmith's ideas about the importance of nature in urban fictions.

In "Four Skinny Trees," the affirmative self that Esperanza finally creates is, to a large extent, rooted in normally negative emotions. She too learns that she must never "quit [her] anger." In this approach, "Four Skinny Trees" recalls a poem by the Harlem Renaissance writer Claude McKay. In "The White City," McKay's African American narrator asserts that white hatred has unwittingly shaped his identity:

> Deep in the secret chambers of my heart
> I muse my life-long hate, and without flinch
> I bear it nobly as I live my part.
> My being would be a skeleton, a shell,
> If this dark Passion that fills my every mood,
> And makes my heaven in the white world's hell,
> Did not forever feed me vital blood.[7]

There is, of course, a difference between "anger" and "hate"; still, "Four Skinny Trees" and "The White City" develop similar ideas. McKay's sonnet and Cisneros's "lazy poem" emphasize the necessity of passionate resistance to oppression, in fact, of using that resistance as the cornerstone of self-awareness rather than allowing one's identity to be destroyed. The overriding message of both texts is the same: to survive, one must embrace emotions that resist oppression.

"Four Skinny Trees" concludes by stressing the importance of sheer survival: "Four who grew despite concrete. Four who reach and do not forget to reach. Four whose only reason is to be and be" (p. 75). Esperanza will soon understand that "to be" means to write, to record one's personal triumph over violence and injustice. The four trees are artificially imposed on a landscape that is itself unnatural, just as the sketch and all of *The House on Mango Street*, and indeed all works of art, are artifacts, constructs representing transcendence of the human condition. Like other marginalized writers, Cisneros and McKay pursue triumph over the ridiculous brutality of socioeconomic repression as well as over the ultimate absurdity of death.

In addition to the four seemingly fragile but deceptively strong trees, the novel describes another endangered outpost of nature in the city. "The Monkey Garden," a retelling of the archetypal garden of Eden story, describes an abandoned garden that Esperanza and her friends convert into a playground after its former owners move away. In keeping with the sketch's emphasis on lost innocence, it is narrated from the perspective of the still childlike Esperanza struggling to resist the ominous advent of adulthood. The garden got its name from an actual monkey, a pet of the people who once lived there. Esperanza and the other children inevitably remember the monkey and not the people and ascribe to the animal a very human capacity for decisive action: "The monkey doesn't live there anymore. The monkey moved— to Kentucky—and took his people with him" (p. 94). Significantly, the move described here constitutes a reversal of a familiar pattern, economically desperate people being drawn to Chicago and other northern urban centers from the South by the hope of finding work. In much of "The Monkey Garden," the reader's expectations are reversed.

Sexuality in this sketch, as well as in much of the novel, is tied strongly to violence and represents therefore a threat to the safety of female characters; "The Monkey Garden" describes, in fact, Esperanza's doomed attempt to deny her own emerging sexuality. What should be a life-affirming force is transformed by poverty and the threat of male violence into something destructive and unnatural. The dominant imagery of the sketch echoes more than one classic analysis of American literature, most obviously Leo Marx's *The Machine and the Garden: Technology and the Pastoral in America* (1964). Nature in the children's adopted playground is simultaneously luxuriant and decayed: "There were sunflowers as big as flowers on Mars and thick cockscombs bleeding the deep red fringe of theater curtains. There were dizzy bees and bow-tied fruit flies turning somersaults and humming in the air. Sweet sweet peach trees. . . . There were big green apples hard as knees. And everywhere the sleepy smell of rotting wood, damp earth and dusty hollyhocks thick and perfumy like the blue-blond hair of the dead" (pp. 94-95).

Death in the monkey garden is not solely a process of natural decay and regeneration. Human beings have infringed upon the garden in pernicious and decidedly unnatural ways; Marx's machine, or more precisely its vestiges, is present here: "Dead cars appeared overnight like mushrooms. First one and then another and then a pale blue pickup with the front windshield missing. Before you knew it, the monkey garden became filled with sleepy cars" (p. 95). The description of the dead cars appearing "overnight like mushrooms" works on at least three metaphoric levels. First, the abandoned cars are, like some mushrooms, poisonous and have polluted what was once a pristine landscape. Moreover, they quickly become so numerous as to seem the garden's natural vegetation. Finally, the rusting automobiles are emblematic of a polluting and uncaring capitalism that makes life in the barrio almost impossible.

Appropriately, it is Sally who inspires the advent of sexuality into the garden and the foreground of Esperanza's awareness. When Sally permits a group of young boys to follow her there for a kiss, Esperanza is outraged and attempts to "rescue" her older friend and evict the boys from her child's sanctuary. She is dismayed when Sally tells her to go away, that she does not want to be rescued: "And then I don't know why but I had to run away. I had to hide myself at the other end of the garden, in the jungle part, under a tree that wouldn't mind if I lay down and cried a long time" (p. 97). Just as she did with the monkey, Esperanza is attributing a power of agency to the tree that it cannot, of course, possess. She desires to preserve the bond with nature she has always felt, and, in order to do so, she tries to retreat to the innocence of her childhood.

In its perversion of sexuality into brutal oppression of the female and in its destructive pollution of the environment, the adult world has virtually destroyed any possibility of redemption through nature. In the context of the implicit Garden of Eden symbolism in "The Monkey

Garden," the tree beneath which Esperanza seeks shelter can hardly offer lasting sanctuary; it is a "tree of knowledge" for Esperanza, a complex trope signifying loss of innocence and new as well as old dangers in her environment. The sketch ends with a succinct statement of the corruption of the monkey garden as a viable sanctuary for her: "And the garden that had been such a good place to play didn't seem mine either" (p. 98). The lasting and defining image of nature for Esperanza must be the artificially created one, "the four skinny trees."

Significantly, "Red Clowns," the sketch that immediately follows "The Monkey Garden," describes Esperanza's own sexual initiation and, once again, Sally is the instigating force in the incident. To convey the fear and sheer ugliness that overwhelms the young narrator, Cisneros turns to language and imagery derived from literary and popular Gothicism. In describing the setting, she echoes the bizarre unreality that characterizes Edgar Allan Poe stories such as "The Masque of the Red Death" and "The Cask of Amontillado." Sally has taken Esperanza to a carnival only to desert her when a "big boy" asks her to follow him; as she leaves she instructs her younger companion to wait for her "by the red clowns." There is a tradition of popular "horror films" and television programs that incorporate clowns as ominous, psychopathic characters, and it is natural that this tradition would inform a contemporary American initiation novel. In these cultural artifacts, garish costume as emblem of grotesque disguise is a recurrent motif: the criminal hides his deadly persona inside a costume of gaiety.

At any rate, Esperanza is herself assaulted by a group of boys, and the language describing this ugly incident effectively conveys the terror and unreality of the experience, as well as the young narrator's disillusionment with the images of sexual romance that she has derived from American popular culture: "They all lied. All the books and magazines, everything that told it wrong. Only his dirty fingernails against my skin, only his sour smell again. The moon that watched. The tilt-a-whirl. The red clowns laughing their thick-tongue laugh" (p. 100). The reference to the tilt-a-whirl metaphorically communicates that Esperanza's life has been turned upside down and that long-established perspectives of her position in the world have been perverted and thus no longer offer comfort and assurance. The boy who initiates the assault of the narrator twice calls her "Spanish girl," signaling that he has bought into the cultural stereotype of Hispanic women as sexually promiscuous, as possessing a capacity for erotic pleasure of which their Anglo counterparts are incapable.

Interestingly, the text leaves ambiguous the ethnic identity of the boy himself, communicating perhaps the widespread American acceptance of this dehumanizing view of the Hispanic woman. The strong possibility exists, of course, that he and his companions are themselves Chicanos and are expressing the machismo of the barrio. Certainly, women are reduced to sexual objects throughout Cisneros's text.

Nevertheless Esperanza comes to accept an obligation to speak for her community. In fact, Cisneros emphasizes the role of the marginalized writer as spokesperson for a community that is otherwise deprived of voice; while Esperanza for most of the novel yearns to escape Mango Street, she gradually learns that such escape is both impossible and irresponsible. While poverty and violence may threaten her personally, she discovers that by surviving them she has become inextricably bound to her environment. The process of Esperanza's coming to understand this is the focus of the four sketches that conclude the text. In "The Three Sisters," she attends a funeral for the infant sister of her friends Lucy and Rachel. Afterward, she is approached by three women whom she has never seen before and who quickly communicate to her that they possess the gift of prophecy:

"Tomorrow it will rain."
"Yes, tomorrow," they said.
"How do you know?" I asked.
"We know." (p. 104)

Echoing such other legends as that of the Hispanic rain god, the three rather eccentric sisters are contemporary incarnations of "the three fates" of classical mythology and they proceed to tell Esperanza of her future and to convey to her her responsibilities to the community: "When you leave you must remember to come back for the others. A circle, understand? You will always be Esperanza. You will always be Mango Street. You can't erase what you know. You can't forget who you are. . . . You must remember to come back. For the ones who cannot leave as easily as you" (p. 105). The words of the sisters are essential to the sense of self that the young narrator ultimately constructs. She will soon understand that, while she will leave Mango Street physically, she cannot and should not want to forget what she experienced there. In her consciousness and in her spirit, she can no more escape Mango Street than she can stop being Esperanza and, indeed, she has been fated to become the voice, the "hope" of those who will remain trapped there.

Earlier in the text, she had learned never to "quit her anger" and, now, she is beginning to realize how to convert that anger into the affirmation of writing, of art. This prophetic sketch concludes by emphasizing the supernatural identity of the three sisters—they seem to vanish almost before Esperanza's very eyes, and she never sees them again. In the next sketch, she is shown to be still resisting their message, but a friend named Alicia reinforces it and in fact clarifies its implications:

> [Alicia:] Like it or not you are Mango Street, and one day you'll come back too.
>
> [Esperanza:] Not me. Not until somebody makes it better.
>
> [Alicia:] Who's going to do it? The mayor?
>
> And the thought of the mayor coming to Mango Street makes me laugh out loud.
>
> Who's going to do it? Not the mayor. (p. 107)

Like the three sisters, Alicia is assuming that Esperanza will succeed in leaving Mango Street physically; but, also like the three older women, she is communicating the truth that memory cannot escape experience. She is also telling her friend why the marginalized writer has no choice but to speak for her community. Politicians as agents of an exploitative capitalism have turned their backs on the community; thus artists must give voice to the concerns of its inhabitants. Of necessity, this voice will often be one of outrage, of anger. Cisneros thus confronts directly the issue of social protest and its importance in minority writing; while accepting such protest as an inescapable obligation, her text demonstrates that it is not antithetical to lyricism or to individuality. Like McKay, she proves that poetry can express "dark" passions.

The volume's penultimate sketch, "A House of My Own," echoes and thereby pays tribute to Virginia Woolf. In two brief paragraphs, the second consisting of only one sentence, Esperanza repeats her desire to live in her own place. The novel's feminist perspective, which is often merely implicit in the text, is stated overtly here: "Not a flat. Not an apartment in back. Not a man's house. Not a daddy's. A house all my own" (p. 108). The complex metaphoric significance of the dreamed-of house, as opposed to the house on Mango Street, is succinctly expressed in the sketch's concluding sentence: "Only a house quiet as snow, a space for myself to go, clear as paper before the poem" (p. 108). The imagined house is expressed as a physical dwelling, but, more important, as the private space in which to create a work that will realize Esperanza's emerging self. Thus, the "house of [her] own" is not the house on Mango Street, but it is *The House on Mango Street*. With the help of the three sisters and of Alicia, Esperanza has created a hopeful identity that affirms her race, her class, her gender, and her individuality. The space that was the paper before the poem is a metaphor for the space she needed to construct a text and a self.

The novel's concluding sketch, "Mango Says Goodbye Sometimes," effectively ties together the major strands in the three that precede it. It opens with a short, but important assertion by Esperanza: "I like to tell stories" (p. 109). In fact, Cisneros's text can be appreciated in the context of Walter Benjamin's distinctions between the roles of the storyteller and the novelist. In his influential essay "The Storyteller," Benjamin says that, in the twentieth century, storytelling as the legacy of oral cultures is dying, that it has been superseded by the novel, the narrative form of print cultures. Storytelling, he says, has traditionally been a communal function in which usually anonymous voices shape tales for the practical and moral enrichment of others. In contrast, the modern novel is the product of an isolated artist with no immediate ties to any community: "The storyteller takes what he tells from experience—his own or that reported by others. And he in turn makes it the experience of those who are listening to the tale. The novelist has isolated himself The birthplace of the novel is the solitary individual, who is no longer able to express himself by giving examples of his most important concerns, is himself uncounseled, and cannot counsel others."[8]

For much of Cisneros's text, events seem to be conspiring to disqualify Esperanza from being, in Benjamin's sense, a storyteller. She has not isolated herself, but she, as a woman in a marginalized culture, is initially isolated, as indicated in her desire to escape Mango Street. But the counsel that she receives from the three sisters, Alicia, and others gives birth in her to an understanding of communal responsibility that finds expression in her stories. "Mango Says Goodbye Sometimes"—and thus *The House on Mango Street*—ends with Esperanza asserting again that she will leave the community of her childhood because "I am too strong" to stay there, but this time significantly qualifying her assertion: "Friends and neighbors will say, What happened to that Esperanza? Where did she go with all those books and paper? Why did she march so far away? They will not know I have gone away to come back. For the ones I left behind. For the ones who cannot out" (p. 110).

Writing the stories of her personal struggle certainly, but also of the struggles of those around her, will be a form of liberating dialogue for her. She will construct an identity through words that evolve from her developing sense of an individual and a communal self. Even before the four concluding sketches, the essence of this realization has been expressed. In "Born Bad," Esperanza reads her poems to a dying aunt, who warns her against abandoning her writing because it will "keep [her] free" (p. 61). While not yet understanding what her aunt means, she senses its importance. In the ultimately serious, but still amusing, "Bums in the Attic," she vows not to become like the wealthy Anglos with expensive homes in the hills whose gardens her father tends: "People who live on hills sleep so close to the stars they forget those of us who live too much on earth" (p. 86). In the house that she will someday have, she will not forget the economically oppressed, vowing to turn its attic into a shelter for hobos: "Some days after dinner, guests and I will sit in front of a fire. Floorboards will squeak upstairs. The attic grumble. Rats? they'll ask. Bums, I'll say, and I'll be happy" (p. 87). The attic of Esperanza's imagined house will be a refuge for passing bums just as Cisneros's text voices the aspirations of oppressed Chicana women.

The House on Mango Street is narrated by a strong young woman who, by clinging to the image of the "four skinny trees" and by heeding the advice of some wise female counselors expresses, transcends, and even redeems the poverty and violence of her environment. Though her innocence is violated, her faith in her community and in her art is not destroyed. By substituting her "lazy poems" for the traditional narrative techniques of the novelist and by affirming the importance of individuality and community, Cisneros effectively merges Benjamin's "storyteller" and "novelist" prototypes. Esperanza will neither be bound by Mango Street nor abandon it for an existence "close to the stars" and removed from her people.

From *Violence in the Contemporary American Novel: An End to Innocence* (2000), pp. 70-83. Copyright © 2000 by the University of South Carolina Press. Reprinted with permission of the University of South Carolina Press.

Notes

1. María Elena de Valdés, "In Search of Identity in Cisneros's *The House on Mango Street*," *Canadian Review of American Studies* 23 (Fall 1992): 68-69.

2. Especially as developed in Gates's *The Signifying Monkey* (New York: Oxford University Press, 1988).

3. Sidney H. Bremer, *Urban Intersections: Meetings of Life and Literature in United States Cities* (Urbana: University of Illinois Press, 1992), pp. 97-98.

4. Sandra Cisneros, *The House on Mango Street* (New York: Random House Vintage, 1991, p. 3; subsequent references to this work are cited parenthetically in the text.

5. Virginia Lee Burton, *The Little House* (Boston: Houghton Mifflin, 1942), p. 25; all subsequent references to this work are to this edition and are cited in the text. I am indebted to my student Kathi Strong for introducing me to Burton's text.

6. Julián Olivares, "Sandra Cisneros' *The House on Mango Street*, and the Poetics of Space," *Americas Review* 15 (Fall-Winter 1987): 160; all subsequent references to this article are cited parenthetically in the text.

7. Claude McKay, "The White City," in *Selected Poems of Claude McKay* (New York: Bookman Associates, 1953), p. 74.

8. Walter Benjamin, "The Storyteller: Reflections on the Works of Nikolai Leskov," in *Illuminations: Essays and Reflections*, ed. Hannah Arendt (New York: Schocken Books, 1969), p. 87.

Remembering Always to Come Back:
The Child's Wished-For Escape and the Adult's Self-Empowered Return in Sandra Cisneros's *House on Mango Street*_____

Reuben Sánchez

In an essay on "home" and "homelessness" in children's literature, Virginia L. Wolf suggests that one distinction between literature for children and literature for adults may be that the former tends to embrace myth while the latter tends to embrace reality: "Whereas much adult literature laments our homelessness and reflects the fragmentation or loss of myth, most children's literature celebrates home and affirms belief in myth" (54). In doing so, however, children's literature might very well offer an unrealistic view of the world: "Even though I celebrate all those wonderful mythic houses in children's literature as an invaluable legacy of comfort, I worry that they deny too much of reality. Certainly, if children are to reach their potential and make their contribution to humanity, they must eventually move beyond a perception of the world as they desire it to be and accept it as it is—enormously destructive, turbulent, and chaotic as well as creative and peaceful" (66). Though children find myth attractive, they might nonetheless acquire a distorted "perception of reality" should the book emphasize myth—or if myth and reality are irreconcilable. Wolf's distinctions between myth and reality and between literature for children and literature for adults are crucial to scholars who wish to fashion a hermeneutics of discourse concerning children's literature. But as one might expect, the practice of literary interpretation could render such distinctions problematic in certain texts.

The foremost proponent of archetypal criticism, Northrop Frye, describes the structure of the monomyth in historical terms as a movement in Western literature from primitive myth to modern irony, a schema that does much to subordinate myth to irony. Frye's rigorous schema has since been critiqued by historicists, structuralists, post-structuralists, and feminists, but there nonetheless remains a tendency in literary studies to view myth as the opposite of reality. Such a tendency might limit the appeal, perhaps the usefulness, of texts that are said to be mythic. For the purposes of this essay, however, I should like to consider myth in the sense that Joseph Campbell defines it in *The Hero with a Thousand Faces*: "It would not be too much to say that myth is the secret opening through which the inexhaustible energies of the cosmos pour into human cultural manifestation. Religions, philosophies, arts, the social forms of primitive and historic man, prime discoveries in science and technology, the very dreams that blister sleep, boil up from the basic, magic ring of myth" (3). Campbell's definition blurs the distinction between myth and irony, which allows us to recognize how and why myth moves us and is useful to us, adults and children alike. Through story telling the writer's perception of the world is manifested. We might think of myth, therefore, as cultural story telling, a way by which the writer who belongs to and identifies with a particular community explains why the world is the way it is, from the point of view of that particular community. The writer either validates a myth, or modifies a myth without rejecting it, or rejects a myth and creates a new myth based on his or her own experience. In *The House on Mango Street*, Sandra Cisneros participates in the third type of story telling by combining myth (home) and irony (homelessness) in her depiction of life in the barrio as seen through the eyes of a girl.

Cisneros addresses the theme of home versus homelessness in a series of forty-four vignettes—some as short as a few paragraphs, others as long as four or five pages—written in a language that is easily accessible and in a style that is sophisticated in its presentation of voice and theme. There is no single narrative strand, though the vignettes are loosely connected to each other in that they concern a brief period in which Esperanza, the book's protagonist, lives on Mango Street. We are never told her age, but she seems to be about ten or eleven years old. She wishes to find a house of her own:

Not a flat. Not an apartment in back. Not a man's house. Not a daddy's. A house all my own. With my porch and my pillow, my pretty purple petunias. My books and my stories. My two shoes waiting beside the bed. Nobody to shake a stick at. Nobody's garbage to pick up after.

Only a house quiet as snow, a space for myself to go, clean as paper before the poem. (108)

This type of story telling incorporates both extremes—home contrasted with homelessness, the ideal house contrasted with the realistic, harsh surroundings—into a larger myth concerning the child's perception of her world and her rejection of the patriarchal myth that would prevent her from finding a house of her own. To free her protagonist of one myth, Cisneros must create another myth.

Esperanza recognizes the reality of her own homelessness, for she points out that until they move into the house on Mango Street her family has lived in several different houses; on Mango Street she continues to wish for her ideal house, a wish that initiates and concludes the narrative, the narrative thus ending with a type of return, a tradition in children's literature. There is closure to the narrative in the repetition of a specific passage at the end of *The House on Mango Street*. At the beginning Esperanza states, "We didn't always live on Mango Street. Before that we lived on Loomis on the third floor, and before that we lived on Keeler. Before Keeler it was Paulina, and before that I can't remember. But what I remember most is moving a lot" (3). Near the end she reiterates, "We didn't always live on Mango Street. Before that we lived on Loomis on the third floor, and before that we lived on Keeler. Before Keeler it was Paulina, but what I remember most is Mango Street, sad red house, the house I belong but do not belong to" (109-110). What Esperanza adds to the second passage evinces her discovery that although what she remembers *initially* is moving often, what she remembers *finally* is Mango Street. The addition to the second passage suggests that there has been a change in Esperanza from the beginning to the end of her story telling, where her concern is with a particular neighborhood and a particular house, to which she vows she will return.

The closure resulting from the narrative circling back on itself by means of repetition can also be described as an example of Freud's *fort da* idea, *fort* meaning "gone away" and *da* meaning "here."[1] Once the reading process has been completed, the reader recognizes how and why the beginning and the end depend upon one another. As Terry Eagleton points out: "*Fort* has meaning only in relation to *da*" (186). Although repetition suggests closure, the narrative, in fact, is not self-enclosed; rather, it is open-ended and encourages the reader to consider what will become of Esperanza after the book has ended.

Margaret Higonnet has suggested that in "its ideological functions of social control" children's literature is an "imperialist form," but that the form is artistic as well as ideological (37-38). Because children's literature is often characterized by repetition and a firm sense of closure, even predictability in that closure, any deviation from that form results in a narrative fragment or rupture—an artistic deviation that involves the child reader in the process of giving meaning to the text. Higonnet describes two types of fragments: the *mosaic* is a gap within the story, which the child reader must fill in; the *sherd* is a gap at the end of the story, which compels the child reader to supply an ending for the (incomplete) story after the narrative itself has concluded. Higonnet argues, "A somewhat older audience permits an author to use the sherdlike fragment not only to evoke threatening subjects but to provoke the reader's conscious activity. The most interesting type of fragment, then, may be that which deliberately propels the reader into responsibility for the *unwritten* narrative conclusion" (49). The sherdlike fragment applies to the ending of *The House on Mango Street*. Although the book has closure, it is also open-ended in that it does not tell us whether Esperanza finds her ideal house. Essential to the didactic quality of the text, however, is the lesson that if Esperanza does indeed escape Mango Street, and we cannot help but believe she will, she must return "for the others." In her depiction of the reality of homelessness and the myth of home, Cisneros shows how and why dialectic—home-lessness/home, irony/myth, escape/return—influences Esperanza's growing awareness of who she is and what her ideal house means to her. But the unique fort da quality of the narrative leaves the outcome of that search for the ideal house unresolved for the child/adult reader.

By the end of the narrative, Esperanza recognizes that she must someday "return" to Mango Street empowered as a writer. Cisneros was raised in Chicago and, like Esperanza, in her writing returns to the barrio. Although Cisneros is writing fiction, there are nonetheless parallels between Cisneros and Esperanza. In her autobiographical essay "Ghosts and Voices: Writing from Obsession," Cisneros tells that hers was a large family (six brothers and her parents) living in small apartments, the family traveling often between Chicago and Mexico (69). Like her protagonist (who also comes from a large family—three brothers, a sister, and parents), Cisneros has learned to write about "the ones who cannot out" (110), which implies a tie not only between narrator Esperanza and the characters within the fictional narrative but also between writer Cisneros and the readers of the text. In writing about Esperanza's childhood, Cisneros, as Aidan Chambers would say, writes "on behalf of adolescence" (199). Chambers argues that writers who reject "the adult exploitation of youth" instead write "on behalf of a state of life that still lives inside you, even though you are past the age when it is the socially evident and psychologically pertinent expression of your existence" (199).

The return of the writer—Esperanza and Cisneros—to her childhood is symbolized by the mythic image of the circle, a symbol both of the circular journey she as a writer must take when remembering and writing about her childhood, and of the circle that binds "las Mujeres/the Women," to whom the book is dedicated, *within* and *outside* the narrative. The child's wished-for escape and the adult's self-empowered return comprise the fort da quality of a narrative that is, in its sherdlike conclusion, incomplete.

In the vignette "The Three Sisters," which comes near the end of the book, Esperanza is instructed about what leaving and returning means. At the wake of a child, "Lucy and Rachel's sister," Esperanza meets "las comadres," three old women whom she finds very mysterious. The Spanish word *comadre* is a term that mother and godmother use to refer to each other; it could also be the term women friends who are not related use to address each other. But the word possesses other connotations as well. In New Mexico, for example, La Comadre Sebastiana (or Doña Sebastiana, as she is also known) is the skeletal image of Death seated on *la carreta de la Muerte* (the death cart) in Penitente processions. Penitentes (penitents) are a lay brotherhood of Roman Catholics who observe rituals associated with the passion of Christ. Since the image of La Comadre Sebastiana seems exclusive to New Mexico, Cisneros may not have this specific image in mind in her presentation of las comadres. Yet, the aura of death surrounds these three women; one might say that, like La Comadre Sebastiana, the three sisters are intended to remind us of death:

> They came with the wind that blows in August, thin as a spider web and barely noticed. Three who did not seem to be related to anything but the moon. One with laughter like tin and one with eyes of a cat and one with hands like porcelain. The aunts, the three sisters, *las comadres*, they said.
>
> The baby died. Lucy and Rachel's sister. One night a dog cried, and the next day a yellow bird flew in through an open window. Before the week was over, the baby's fever was worse. Then Jesus came and took the baby with him far away. That's what their mother said. (103)

The vignette is about death, but it is also about life. It concerns the beginning—or, in mythic terms, the birth—of Esperanza's recognition of what it will mean to return to her past.

The three sisters sense that Esperanza wants to leave Mango Street, wants to leave the barrio. "When you leave you must remember always to come back," one of las comadres tells her. But la comadre emphasizes that there is more to it than simply coming back:

When you leave you must remember to come back for the others. A circle, understand? You will always be Esperanza. You will always be Mango Street. You can't erase what you know. You can't forget who you are.

Then I didn't know what to say. It was as if she could read my mind, as if she knew what I had wished for, and I felt ashamed for having made such a selfish wish.

You must remember to come back. For the ones who cannot leave as easily as you. You will remember? She asked as if she was telling me. Yes, yes, I said a little confused. (105)

The thrice-repeated injunction to come back for the others emphasizes for the child the lesson to be learned, but it also focuses the reader's attention on the central issues in *The House on Mango Street*: why Esperanza must leave, and how and why she must return. Esperanza feels "ashamed for having made such a selfish wish," although the injunction does not imply that her wish to escape Mango Street is selfish. Rather, la comadre instructs Esperanza to "return," instructs her to "remember." The return will not necessarily be literal but rather symbolic, described as a circle. As of yet Esperanza is "a little confused," but the implications of this injunction will soon be clear to her.

In "Alicia & I Talking on Edna's Steps," the vignette following "The Three Sisters," Alicia repeats la comadre's injunction to Esperanza, though more emphatically: "Like it or not you are Mango Street, and one day you'll come back too" (107). Esperanza is identified with, is bound to, her neighborhood. Indeed, she *is* Mango Street, as the young woman (Alicia) and the old woman (la comadre) point out to her. Esperanza finds little if any comfort in the recognition that she is bound to Mango Street. Nor can she find comfort in the prospect of returning. She declares that she will not return, "Not until somebody makes it better." "Who's going to do it?" asks Alicia. "The mayor?" (107). The very thought of the mayor making it better seems funny to Esperanza. She must learn that *she* will have to make it better—by remembering her past and writing about it.

Esperanza learns that she must not leave simply to find a house on a hill in another part of town. She must "remember to come back for the others," and thereby come back for herself. The path she will take as writer is circular: Leaving to come back to leave again, and so on.

* * *

Lissa Paul suggests that the restriction of the child or the woman to the home is a common theme in literature, but that the significance of that restriction is only now being recognized: "Because women and children generally have to stay at home without the affairs of state to worry about, their stories tend to focus on the contents of their traps, the minute and mundane features of everyday life around which their lives revolve: household effects, food, clothes, sewing, interior decorating, and nuances of social relationships. These homely details have been redeemed by feminist critics . . . as having interest; as being as worthy for critical attention as descriptions of battles or card games or beer drinking" (151). By focusing on such details and recognizing their significance for the protagonist, feminist critics articulate the "physical, economic, and linguistic entrapment" in which the heroine finds herself. Paul argues that whereas the hero traditionally relies upon *forza* (violence) in his quest, the "survival tactic" the heroine traditionally relies upon to free herself is *froda* (fraud): "Though deceit is the traditional tactic of the heroine, it is most visible in the tactics of defenceless child protagonists in children's literature" (154). This survival tactic is one way that the "difference" or "otherness" can be seen between the male and the female, the adult and the child. That difference is also being recognized as relevant to all readers: "The quickening of academic interest in women's and children's literature testifies that something in their stories is in touch with the temper of our time. Trickster stories express a contemporary reality; powerlessness is no longer a condition experienced primarily by women, children and other oppressed people. It is a condition we all recognize" (153). Powerlessness is of course Esperanza's condition, and she is in danger of remaining powerless. Showing why the female is powerless enables Cisneros to offer a way by which her protagonist may empower herself. Esperanza learns that she can empower herself through "books and paper"—a form of "deceit" in that books and paper enable her to "subvert" the "physical, economic and linguistic traps in women's and children's literature" (Paul 155).

Why Esperanza wishes to escape Mango Street and how and why she must return are the issues Cisneros addresses by means of the home versus homelessness theme. In doing so, she has created a narrative account of "a condition we all recognize"—a narrative, further, accessible to both the adult reader and the child reader. Esperanza wants to escape Mango Street, wants a house of her own, but unlike her male counterparts in other works she does not escape to the pastoral world. Chicanas usually choose to write about female characters in urban settings, whereas Chicanos usually choose to write about male characters in pastoral settings or in either pastoral or urban settings (sometimes moving freely between both settings). Although the choice of setting may not strictly depend upon gender, there does seem to be a tendency among Chicanos to allow their male characters the freedom to move about in the city or in the country or both, whereas there seems to be a tendency among Chicanas to restrict their female characters to movement within the neighborhood, or the house.

The pastoral traditionally concerns the urban poet's praise of nature and the simple life of the shepherd, in contrast with the complicated life of the city dweller. Though seemingly unaffected by the problems typically found in the city, the pastoral is not always and simply utopian, for there are conflicts the protagonist must face. In American literature one might even consider why the writer uses a particular version of the pastoral as a setting: uncontrolled nature (forests, rivers, plains), or controlled nature (fields, pastures, gardens, orchards). These two versions of the pastoral are found in, for example, Rudolfo Anaya's *Bless Me, Ultima*, where the young protagonist Antonio is torn between the *llano* (the plain, representing his father's side of the family) and *Las Pasturas* (the pastures, representing his mother's side of the family). Although his family lives outside the small town, the town is nonetheless a significant factor in that it represents sources of conflict for Antonio.

Often, the male protagonist's movement from the urban to the pastoral may serve only as a momentary escape from the harshness of the urban, the protagonist eventually returning to face his troubles in the city. Or the pastoral itself may be threatening to the protagonist. In works by Chicanos, the pastoral is apropos as well to the search for the mythical Aztlan, the search for what Aztlan symbolizes.[2]

The Chicana's concern with "place"—a house, or a room of one's own—is a reaction against the patriarchal myth that denies the Chicana a place of her own. Whereas the Chicano is free to journey through the mountains or the cities, the Chicana's movement has often been restricted by the Chicana writers themselves.[3] The reality the Chicana addresses, then, is the reality of her restriction to the urban setting—particularly the house or the room. That setting is Esperanza's past and her present in *The House on Mango Street*; she recognizes that it might very well be her future as well.

Instead of wishing to escape to the pastoral, Esperanza wants her house to be in another part of town:

> One day I'll own my own house, but I won't forget who I am or where I came from. Passing bums will ask, Can I come in? I'll offer them the attic, ask them to stay, because I know how it is to be without a house.
>
> Some days after dinner, guests and I will sit in front of a fire. Floorboards will squeak upstairs. The attic grumble.
>
> Rats? they'll ask.
>
> Bums, I'll say, and I'll be happy. (87)

Her vision of an escape is to a house on a hill, far away from Mango Street but still in the city. Some of the visitors she will receive will not be from the utopian world of the pastoral but from the realistic world of the barrio. The passage is a poignant and gently humorous reminder of the significance of the home versus homelessness theme in this book.

Yet, the passage has also drawn criticism. Ramón Saldívar states, for example: "Incapable of imagining a house without rats in the attic, and naively accepting the derogatory epithet 'bums' for all street people, the child innocently combines the features of a cognac advertisement with a scene from a shelter for the homeless" (184). Saldívar might be distinguishing between Esperanza's naivete and Cisneros's maturity, might not be criticizing Cisneros per se. Although a concern with the protagonist's naivete might be relevant to children's literature, Saldívar's concern seems more ideological than literary. In many children's books the young protagonist seems naive, but can also seem sophisticated for her years. Recall Alice, Dorothy, Bobbie (Roberta from *The Railway Children*), Jo March, Mary Lennox, Meg Murray, Lucy Pevensie, and a host of princesses from fairy tales.

Esperanza's use of the word *bums* is derogatory only from the adult reader's perspective—perhaps an example of "the adult exploitation of youth." The negative implication of the word is not indicative of Esperanza's attitude toward the homeless. That is, if she "naively" uses a derogatory term, she certainly does not have a derogatory attitude toward the homeless. (On the other hand, her use of the term "Bum man" in the vignette "The Family of Little Feet" is intended to be derogatory because of the sexual threat the man poses to Rachel and to the others.) Esperanza declares that she will give the homeless shelter and will care for them because she identifies with their plight: "I know how it is to be without a house." If they are homeless, she implies, then so is she. The word *bums* should perhaps be understood more properly in its specific context in the story and by means of criteria appropriate to the literary text.

A much harsher view of Esperanza—and, by extension, Cisneros—is expressed by Juan Rodríguez in his review of *The House on Mango*

Street. Like Saldívar, Rodríguez faults Esperanza for wanting a particular type of house: "That Esperanza chooses to leave Mango St., chooses to move away from her social/cultural base to become more 'Anglicized,' more individualistic; that she chooses to move from the real to the fantasy plane of the world as the only means of accepting and surviving the limited and limiting social conditions of her barrio becomes problematic to the more serious reader" (quoted in Olivares 168). The literary value of *The House on Mango Street* is thus suspect for Rodríguez, but his conclusions seem based on whether Cisneros espouses a particular political ideology. Rodríguez does not recognize that Cisneros's text is political *and* serious in that she writes about oppression (political, economic, sexual) and the way her protagonist might free herself from that oppression. Her politics just do not happen to be his politics. Of the significant distinctions to be made between Chicano narrative and Chicana narrative, one might thus distinguish in terms of politics. The intention, however, should be to understand as fully and clearly as possible both the politics and the manner in which the politics is presented. Even Saldívar's critique of Esperanza's politically incorrect use of the word *bums*—Esperanza's politics, if you will—does little to clarify this distinction, since his overall treatment of Chicana narratives is rather brief (one twenty-eight-page chapter, six pages of which are devoted to Cisneros's book) in comparison to his overall treatment of Chicano narratives (six chapters).

Conclusions that the word *bums* is derogatory and indicative of Esperanza's naivete and that Esperanza's desire to escape her environment shows that she (with Cisneros) lacks political commitment serve as examples of what can happen when one does not evaluate a literary text on its own terms and on the terms appropriate to the genre, when one complains instead of analyzes. If we prefer complaint to analysis, we may miss the significant points made in the vignette "Bums in the Attic": Esperanza will not give up her dream; she will not forget "those who cannot out"; she will not forget who she is; she will find a house of her own.

The dangers critics like Saldívar and Rodríguez risk when they evaluate the work of a writer like Cisneros are similar to the dangers adults risk when they attempt to evaluate children's literature according to criteria they may bring with them from their work in other genres or other disciplines. The criteria by which one evaluates literature for children is often, and perhaps unavoidably, at least in part the same criteria by which one evaluates literature for adults. "Whatever the topic to be studied," Margaret Meek argues,

> in literature, as elsewhere, we inherit the theories of our predecessors, willy nilly: and in making our own we are bound to represent not only their earlier methods of inquiry, but also the pattern of associated constructs already existent in our own minds. Thus, I cannot speculate about children's literature without incorporating the tissues of ideas that inform my everyday thinking about literature, children, reading, writing, language, linguistics, politics, ideology, sociology, history, education, sex, psychology, art, or a combination of some or all of these, to say nothing of joy or sadness, pleasure or pain. This is a lengthy way of saying that those who would theorize do so initially about themselves. (166-167)

We cannot, therefore, help but evaluate children's literature according to what we have learned from our predecessors and according to our personal tastes. Yet as Meek reminds us: "In the past 20 years, we have outgrown the need to establish children's books as a legitimate area of study, but we are still looking through the lorgnettes of critical models now outworn in adult literature" (167). Theorizing of course enables us to articulate the value of children's literature or of Chicana literature; but as we have seen, theorizing that is not based on close literary analysis or that is not based on an appreciation of genre can lead to the subordination of these literatures for political reasons.

* * *

Cisneros addresses the home versus homelessness theme in an urban rather than pastoral setting. In the vignette "The Monkey Garden," she shows why the pastoral must be rejected—a rejection, certainly, of the pastoral image of Eden, perhaps a postlapsarian vision of Eden, for this garden is overgrown *and* decaying. The urban world has overtaken the pastoral world in that the garden becomes a junk yard where "Dead cars appeared overnight like mushrooms" (95).[4] In the garden, too, Esperanza, brick in hand, realizes that Sally does not want to be "saved" from "Tito's buddies." This realization results in a form of self-expulsion in that Esperanza now feels she no longer belongs in the garden: "I looked at my feet in their white socks and ugly round shoes. They seemed far away. They didn't seem to be my feet anymore. And the garden that had been such a good place to play didn't seem mine either" (98). It is time, she senses, for her to leave the garden and what it represents. She is changing, outgrowing that which kept her in the garden until now, and she expresses that awareness through a reference to her feet and shoes—one of many references to feet and shoes in Cisneros's book. Others may be found, for example, in "The Family of Little Feet" and "Chanclas" (a *chancla* is a type of slipper or old shoe), vignettes concerned with the confusion involved in the transition from childhood to adolescence.

Cisneros presents the image of the garden in order to reject it. Any attempt to return to an edenic past would be ironic for the female who seeks freedom from the patriarchal Genesis myth. Though Esperanza may not fully understand why, she nonetheless feels that she no longer belongs in the garden: "Who was it that said I was getting too old to play the games?" (96). Nor does she require a deity to evict her. The theme of exile from the garden—the recognition and rejection of what the garden represents—is specifically related to the home versus homelessness theme: the home Cisneros rejects is the patriarchal, edenic home.

The rejection of the patriarchal home has become an important theme in Chicana literature. For example, Estela Portillo Trambley also critiques the patriarchal myth in her short story "The Trees." Nina, "a confident city girl," marries the youngest of four sons of Don Teofilo Ayala, the head of a family that owns a large and very productive apple orchard. When the old patriarch dies, Nina worries about how the orchard will be divided among the brothers. She wishes to acquire the inheritance for herself and for her husband, Ismael (a name reminiscent of exile). By turning the brothers against each other, Nina eventually brings about the destruction of *that* garden—because she is greedy, to be sure, but also because she is opposed to the patriarchal world of which she is a victim. She was raped when she was a child; and as an adult she is expected to play the role of submissive housewife: "The family, with its elementary tie to the earth, had established a working patriarchal order. The father and sons lived for a fraternal cause, the apple orchards. Their women followed in silent steps, fulfilled in their women ways. If ambition or a sense of power touched the feminine heart, it was a silent touch. The lives were well patterned like the rows of apple trees and the trenches that fed them. Men and women had a separate given image until Nina came" (13). Although Portillo Trambley does not justify Nina's destructive behavior or encourage the reader to sympathize with Nina, she nonetheless shows how the patriarchal order can, through its obsessive adherence to a "fraternal cause," bring about its own destruction. After all, Nina is "an avenging angel come to the Garden of Eden" (16). In her critique of the Eden myth Portillo Trambley makes her protagonist, as Hamlet would say, both "scourge and minister." Like Cisneros, Portillo Trambley presents the patriarchal image of the garden to show why it must not only be rejected but also destroyed. This metaphorical significance of rejection/ destruction is fundamental to Cisneros's handling of the home versus homelessness theme: Esperanza understands that she must assert her independence if she is to find "A house all my own" (108).

In the vignette "Beautiful & Cruel," Esperanza declares that she will rebel against the traditional role expected of her by acting like a man: "I have begun my own quiet war. Simple. Sure. I am one who leaves the table like a man, without putting back the chair or picking up the plate" (89). Yet, only three vignettes later in "Red Clowns," which immediately follows "The Monkey Garden," Esperanza becomes a victim. She goes with Sally to the carnival, where Sally goes off with a boy and leaves Esperanza alone. What happens next is not clear, but it appears that Esperanza is raped, or if she is not, the experience is just as traumatic:

> Sally Sally a hundred times. Why didn't you hear me when I called? Why didn't you tell them to leave me alone? The one who grabbed me by the arm, he wouldn't let me go. He said I love you, Spanish girl, I love you, and pressed his sour mouth to mine.
>
> Sally, make him stop. I couldn't make them go away. I couldn't do anything but cry. I don't remember. It was dark. I don't remember. I don't remember. Please don't make me tell it all. (100)

The pattern seems similar to what happens to Nina; however, Esperanza will diverge from that pattern, we assume, for only two vignettes after "Red Clowns" Esperanza meets las comadres in the vignette "The Three Sisters." Esperanza will destroy the male myth, not by literally destroying the garden as Nina does, but by becoming a writer and writing about her past.

Cisneros's critique of patriarchal society—the forms of power through which it protects its "fraternal cause"—and her reaction against that society are evident through much of the book. The critique and the reaction are examples of what Gloria Anzaldúa refers to as "writing" that is "dangerous": "Writing is dangerous because we are afraid of what the writing reveals: the fears, the angers, the strengths of a woman under a triple or quadruple oppression. Yet in that very act lies our survival because a woman who writes has power. And a woman with power is feared" (171). Esperanza seeks to possess this kind of power. In the vignette "My Name" she declares that "the Chinese, like the Mexicans, don't like their women strong" (10). Although she has inherited her grandmother's name, Esperanza will not "inherit her place by the window" (11). Instead, she will "baptize" herself "something like Zeze the X," a name whose very sound conjures resistance, a cacophonous name that she feels will help her assert her power to avoid her grandmother's fate. Esperanza decides "not to grow up tame like the others who lay their necks on the threshold waiting for the ball and chain" ("Beautiful & Cruel" 88). Vowing to break away from what confines her makes Esperanza "dangerous" (a word Cisneros uses often in the book): "Them are dangerous," Mr. Benny points out to Esperanza and her friends. "You girls too young to be wearing shoes like that. Take them shoes off before I call the cops, but we just run" ("The Family of Little Feet" 41). Sally, too, is considered dangerous because of the type of clothes and shoes she wears, as Esperanza says to her: "I like your black coat and those shoes you wear, where did you get them? My mother says to wear black so young is dangerous, but I want to buy shoes just like yours, like your black ones made out of suede, just like those" ("Sally" 82). Esperanza is fascinated by what is deemed dangerous.

* * *

Throughout *The House on Mango Street*, the many references to children's literature are evidence of that genre's impact on Cisneros. In "Ghosts and Voices: Writing from Obsession," Cisneros tells of books and fairy tales that were especially significant to her as a child. One such book was Virginia Lee Burton's *The Little House*, which "was my own dream. And I was to dream myself over again in several books, to reinvent my world according to my own vision" (71). She mentions such favorite fairy tales as "Six Swans" and "Ugly Duckling," as well as the *Doctor Dolittle* series, *The Island of Blue Dolphins* series, the Alice books, and *Hitty: Her First 100 Years*, this last book being "a century account of a wooden doll who is whisked through different homes and owners but perseveres" (71). One can easily see, then, how the adult writer indeed writes "on behalf of adolescence."

In certain instances in *The House on Mango Street*, the references to children's literature also serve as metonyms through which Cisneros develops the home versus homelessness theme and the rejection of the patriarchal myth theme. For example, in the vignette "Edna's Ruthie," Esperanza tells how she had memorized "The Walrus and the Carpenter" from *Through the Looking-Glass*, and one day recited it to Ruthie, a friend, "because I wanted Ruthie to hear me" (69). In Tweedledee's poem the unsuspecting oysters are tricked and then eaten by the walrus and the carpenter. Esperanza's selection of this story is not accidental, as it bears special relevance to her vow not to be overpowered by the society in which she lives—her vow, that is, "not to grow up tame like the others who lay their necks on the threshold waiting for the ball and chain" (88).

Besides the Alice books, there is another text that Cisneros uses in her characterization of Ruthie. Esperanza describes Ruthie's whistling as "beautiful like the Emperor's nightingale" (68). This fairy tale serves as a metonym of the world in which Ruthie and Esperanza live. In Andersen's "The Nightingale," the emperor, one of the last people in his realm to know about the nightingale, finally recognizes and appreciates the beauty of its song. He cages the nightingale, however, so that it can sing only for the court. An artificial nightingale is later manufactured and brought to the court, which results in the loss of interest in the live nightingale; no one notices when the nightingale escapes back to the forest. But when the artificial nightingale breaks and the music is gone, the emperor begins to grow weak. With Death sitting on his chest and the demons of his past surrounding the emperor, the nightingale returns from the forest and rescues him through the beauty of its song. The nightingale then agrees to come and sing for him from time to time, though the emperor must promise not to tell anyone.

According to Esperanza—who perhaps got it from Ruthie herself—Ruthie was married and left Mango Street only to be forced to return and live with her mother: "She had lots of job offers when she was young, but she never took them. She got married instead and moved away to a pretty house outside the city. Only thing I can't understand is why Ruthie is living on Mango Street if she doesn't have to, why is she sleeping on a couch in her mother's living room when she has a real house all her own, but she says she's just visiting and next weekend her husband's going to take her home. But the weekends come and go and Ruthie stays" (69). Of course, Ruthie does not have "a real house all her own," and that is Cisneros's point. Like Andersen's nightingale, Ruthie is caged and ignored. For example, if she was indeed married, then she is ignored by her husband. Nor does her mother seem to show much affection for her: "Once some friends of Edna's came to visit and asked Ruthie if she wanted to go with them to play bingo. The car motor was running, and Ruthie stood on the steps wondering whether to go. Should I go, Ma? she asked the grey shadow behind the second-floor screen. I don't care, says the screen, go if you want. Ruthie looked at the ground. What do you think, Ma? Do what you want, how should I know? Ruthie looked at the ground some more. The car with the motor running waited fifteen minutes and then they left" (68). The image of Ruthie is of a female literally trapped and unable to escape Mango Street, to escape "her mother's living room," for that matter. Ruthie is only one of many symbols in *The House on Mango Street* of the trapped female.

For Esperanza, there is something at once sad and beautiful about Ruthie. Like Andersen's nightingale, Ruthie is much admired and loved because she is undemanding and unselfish. She "sees" beauty and, for Esperanza, she possesses beauty: "Ruthie sees lovely things everywhere. . . . When we brought out the deck of cards that night, we let Ruthie deal. . . . We are glad because she is our friend" (68-69). Interpreting the allusions to stories by Dodgson and Andersen enables us to understand the themes Cisneros addresses through the characterization of Ruthie: the homelessness and the victimization of the female.

Ruthie loves books and says she "used to write children's books

---

once," although now she seems unable to read (69), which suggests the possibility of losing the empowerment that comes through reading and writing. Books and paper give Esperanza the power to be dangerous and (possibly) to avoid Ruthie's fate.[5] She recognizes that through the power of books and paper she will make the prophecies of the old woman (la comadre) and of the young woman (Alicia) come true:

> One day I will pack my bags of books and paper. One day I will say good-bye to Mango. I am too strong for her to keep me here forever. One day I will go away.
>
> Friends and neighbors will say, What happened to that Esperanza? Where did she go with all those books and paper? Why did she march so far away?
>
> They will not know I have gone away to come back. For the ones I left behind. For the ones who cannot out. (110)

She says that she will leave and that she will come back. But these actions are beyond the confines of the narrative—a narrative fragment, that is, to be resolved by the reader.

Perhaps most important, the power Esperanza acquires through books and paper will give her the strength to return. This is the world of myth, but it is also the world of irony. Wolf makes a compelling argument for the distinction between children's literature and adult literature in terms of the myth/home-irony/homelessness dichotomies. But she also argues that in five books—Jarrell's *The Animal Family*, Norton's *The Borrowers*, Lively's *The House in Norham Gardens*, Fox's *One-Eyed Cat*, and Schlee's *Ask Me No Questions*—we can trace the movement from myth to irony. The five books "range in their portraits of houses from the romantic to the ironic" (Wolf 56). I suggest that this range may be seen specifically in *The House on Mango Street*.

Mango Street is a place where Esperanza may have at times felt joy and a sense of belonging, but it is also a place where she realizes that women are locked in their rooms by jealous and insecure husbands, a world in which there is violence, incest, and rape. She describes a harsh world from which she seeks escape, but a world to which she must return empowered as writer.

At the end of *The House on Mango Street* Esperanza recognizes, and Cisneros validates, the empowerment that comes through writing and remembering. Hence, the writer can find her freedom, can find her voice as writer, though she can only find that freedom and voice by honoring an injunction: You *will* come back, she is told. She may or may not go far away, but she will come back for herself and "for the others." Here, then, is yet another circle in the book that includes those outside the fictional narrative, those to whom the book is dedicated, and those who will read the book, thereby perpetuating the circular journey of the child/adult each time the text is read. There is indeed a circle that binds, that extends beyond the confines of the narrative to bind las mujeres. Dedicating her book "A las Mujeres/To the Women," *Cisneros* has come back "For the ones who cannot out." The book's dedication and the very last line of the book form a circle symbolic of remembering always to come back.

Notes

1. For a discussion of Freud's fort da theory, see Terry Eagleton (185-186).

2. For example, though urban settings are significant in Rudolfo Anaya's *Heart of Aztlan* and in Miguel Mendez's *Peregrines De Aztlan*, the pastoral remains the symbolic goal. That is, the pastoral image of Aztlan symbolizes the spiritual or psychological return to the place of origin, a paradise lost.

Though some works may not refer specifically to Aztlan, they nonetheless participate in a literary tradition concerning the protagonist's quest through the world of nature as symbolic of the struggle to find the self. Oscar Zeta Acosta's *Autobiography of a Brown Buffalo* involves Zeta's movement away from a city in California to the mountains of Idaho, to a city in Mexico, and finally back to a city in California (one finds a similar movement in Acosta's *The Revolt of the Cockroach People*, in the movement from Los Angeles to Acapulco and the mountains of Guerrero then back to Los Angeles). Ron Arias's *The Road to Tamazunchale* involves Fausto's fantasy of a movement away from Los Angeles to the mountains of Peru. Tomás Rivera's *Y No Se Lo Tragó La Tierra* involves a year in the life of a young boy in the world of the migrant workers, a setting that occurs as well in Raymond Barrio's *The Plum Plum Pickers*. Anaya's *Bless Me, Ultima* involves Antonio's movement through the sometimes dangerous and destructive pastoral of northern New Mexico. By no means exhaustive, this list is intended to suggest the tendency Chicano writers have of giving their male protagonists freedom of movement.

There are of course exceptions to the emphasis on the protagonist's journey through the pastoral. For example, Nash Candelaria's *Memories of the Alhambra* is set mainly in Los Angeles. Alejandro Morales' *The Brick People* and *Casas viejas y vino nuevo* are set in the barrios of large cities. Rolando Hinojosa's Klail City books are set in a small town along the Mexico-Texas border. Gary Soto's *Living up the Street* and Danny Santiago's/Daniel James's *Famous all over Town* are narratives set in cities, although some of Soto's stories have rural settings, and Santiago's/James's story involves Chato's journey from Los Angeles to rural/pastoral Mexico then back to Los Angeles.

3. One need only think of Denise Chávez's *The Last of the Menu Girls*, Lucha Corpi's *Delia's Song*, Mary Helen Ponce's *Taking Control*, Helena Viramontes' *The Moth and Other Stories*, and Estela Portillo Trambley's *Trini*, a work that traces the protagonist's movement from rural/pastoral to urban. These and other examples are narratives that in one way or another place the protagonists in realistic urban environments. Ana Castillo's epistolary novel, *The Mixquiahuala Letters*, does present protagonists who venture away from the city, though usually to other cities—from New York to San Francisco, or to the pyramids in Mexico, for example.

This concern with the urban experience is expressed not only in prose narratives but in Chicana poetry: For example, Lorna Dee Cervantes' *Emplumada*, Evangelina Vigil's *Thirty an' Seen a Lot*, Alma Villanueva's *Bloodroot* and *Mother, May I?*, Pat Mora's *Borders* and *Chants*, and the poetry of Corpi (*Palabras de mediodia/Noon Words*), Castillo (*Women Are Not Roses*), and Cisneros (*My Wicked, Wicked Ways*). Of course, the setting is not always as significant in poetry as it is in prose narratives, but when it is significant to a particular poem, it is often (though not always) an urban setting. For example, perhaps one of the most significant Chicana poems in recent years is Lorna Dee Cervantes' "Beneath the Shadow of the Freeway," a poem about three women—the grandmother, mother, and granddaughter—who live in a house next to a California freeway.

4. Elements of the pastoral might be seen as well in the vignette "Four Skinny Trees"—trees surrounded by concrete, trees that cling to the soil, trees that symbolize Esperanza's struggle to survive.

5. For two insightful discussions concerning Esperanza's empowerment as writer, see Yvonne Yarbro-Bejarano, "Chicana Literature from a Chicana Feminist Perspective," and Julián Olivares, "Sandra Cisneros' *The House on Mango Street* and the Poetics of Space."

Works Cited

Acosta, Oscar Zeta. *The Autobiography of a Brown Buffalo*. San Francisco: Straight Arrow Books, 1972.

_____. *The Revolt of the Cockroach People*. New York: Bantam Books, 1974.

Anaya, Rudolfo. *Bless Me, Ultima*. Berkeley: Tonatiuh-Quinto Sol International, 1972.

_____. *Heart of Aztlan*. Berkeley: Editorial Justa, Publications, 1976.

Andersen, Hans Christian. *Tales*. "The Emperor's Nightingale." Ed. Charles W. Eliot. Danbury, CT: Grolier, 1980.

Anzaldúa, Gloria. "Speaking in Tongues: A Letter to Third World Women Writers." In *This Bridge Called My Back*. Ed. Cherríe Moraga and Gloria Anzaldúa. New York: Kitchen Table/Women of Color Press, 1981, pp. 165-174.

Arias, Ron. *The Road to Tamazunchale*. Albuquerque: Pajarito Publications, 1978.

Barrio, Raymond. *The Plum Plum Pickers*. Sunnyvale, CA: Ventura Press, 1969.

Campbell, Joseph. *The Hero with a Thousand Faces*. Princeton: Princeton University Press, 1949.

Candelaria, Nash. *Memories of the Alhambra*. Palo Alto, CA: Cibola Press, 1977.

Castillo, Ana. *The Mixquiahuala Letters*. Binghamton, NY: Bilingual Press, 1986.

_____. *Women Are Not Roses*. Houston: Arte Público Press, 1984.

Cervantes, Lorna Dee. *Emplumada*. Pittsburgh: University of Pittsburgh Press, 1981.

Chambers, Aidan. "All of a Tremble to See His Danger." *Signal: Approaches to Children's Books*, 51 (September 1986), 193-212.

Chávez, Denise. *The Last of the Menu Girls*. Houston: Arte Público Press, 1986.

Cisneros, Sandra. "Ghosts and Voices: Writing from Obsession." *The Americas Review*, 15, no. 1 (Spring 1987), 69-73.

_____. *The House on Mango Street*. New York: Vintage Books, 1989.

_____. *My Wicked, Wicked Ways*. Berkeley: Third Woman Press, 1987.

Corpi, Lucha. *Delia's Song*. Houston: Arte Público Press, 1988.

_____. *Palabras de mediodia/Noon Words*. Berkeley: El Fuego de Aztlan Publications, 1980.

Eagleton, Terry. *Literary Theory: An Introduction*. Minneapolis: University of Minnesota Press, 1983.

Fox, Paula. *One-Eyed Cat*. Scarsdale, NY: Bradbury, 1984.

Frye, Northrop. *Anatomy of Criticism*. Princeton: Princeton University Press, 1957.

Higonnet, Margaret R. "Narrative Fractures and Fragments." *Children's Literature*, 15 (1987), 37-54.

Hinojosa, Rolando. *Klail City*. Houston: Arte Público Press, 1987.

_____. *This Migrant Earth*. Houston: Arte Público Press, 1987.

_____. *Dear Rafe*. Houston: Arte Público Press, 1990.

Jarrell, Randall. *The Animal Family*. New York: Pantheon, 1965.

Lively, Penelope. *The House in Norham Gardens*. New York: E. P. Dutton, 1974.

Meek, Margaret. "What Counts as Evidence in Theories of Children's Literature?"

In *Children's Literature: The Development of Criticism*. Ed. Peter Hunt. New York: Routledge, 1990, pp. 166-182.

Mora, Pat. *Borders*. Houston: Arte Público Press, 1984.

_____. *Chants*. Houston: Arte Público Press, 1984.

Morales, Alejandro. *The Brick People*. Houston: Arte Público Press, 1992.

_____. *Casas viejas y vino nuevo*. San Diego: Maize Press, 1981.

Norton, Mary. *The Borrowers*. New York: Harcourt, 1953.

Olivares, Julián. "Sandra Cisneros' *The House on Mango Street*, and the Poetics of Space." In *Chicana Creativity and Criticism*. Ed. María Hererra-Sobek and Helena María Viramontes. Houston: Arte Público Press, 1988, pp. 160-170.

Ponce, Mary Helen. *Taking Control*. Houston: Arte Público Press, 1987.

Portillo Trambley, Estela. *Rain of Scorpions*. Berkeley. Tonatiuh International, 1975.

_____. *Trini*. Binghamton, NY: Bilingual Press, 1986.

Rivera, Tomas. *Y No Se Lo Tragó La Tierra*. Houston: Arte Público Press, 1987.

Rodríguez, Juan. "*The House on Mango Street*, by Sandra Cisneros." *Austin Chronicle* (10 August 1984). Cited in Olivares, "Sandra Cisneros' *The House on Mango Street*, and the Poetics of Space." In *Chicana Creativity and Criticism*. Ed. María Hererra-Sobek and Helena María Viramontes. Houston: Arte Público Press, 1988, pp. 160-171.

Saldívar, Ramón. *Chicano Narrative: The Dialectics of Difference*. Madison: University of Wisconsin Press, 1990.

Santiago, Danny. *Famous all over Town*. New York: New American Library, 1983.

Schlee, Ann. *Ask Me No Questions*. New York: Holt, Rinehart and Winston, 1976.

Soto, Gary. *Living up the Street*. San Francisco: Strawberry Hill Press, 1985.

Vigil, Evangelina. *Thirty an' Seen a Lot*. Houston: Arte Público Press, 1982.

Villanueva, Alma Luz. *Bloodroot*. Austin: Place of Herons Press, 1982.

_____. *Mother, May I?* Pittsburgh: Motheroot, 1978.

Viramontes, Helena María. *The Moths and Other Stories*. Houston: Arte Público Press, 1985.

Wolf, Virginia L. "From the Myth to the Wake of Home: Literary Houses." *Children's Literature*, 18 (1990), 53-67.

Yarbro-Bejarano, Yvonne. "Chicana Literature from a Chicana Feminist Perspective." In *Chicana Creativity and Criticism*. Ed. María Hererra-Sobek and Helena María Viramontes. Houston: Arte Público Press, 1988, pp. 139-145.

RESOURCES

1954	Sandra Cisneros is born on December 20 in Chicago to Elvira Cordero Cisneros and Alfredo Cisneros del Moral, their third child of seven and only daughter. The family subsequently moves frequently around Chicago and often travels to Mexico to visit relatives.
1966	The Cisneros family buys a house in the Humboldt Park neighborhood of Chicago.
1976	Cisneros graduates from Loyola University, Chicago, with a bachelor's degree in English.
1978	Cisneros earns a master of fine arts degree in creative writing from the University of Iowa Writers' Workshop. In July, she is hired to teach at the Latino Youth Alternative High School.
1980	*Bad Boys* is published.
1981	Beginning in January, Cisneros works at Loyola University as a college recruiter and minority student counselor.
1982	Cisneros is awarded a National Endowment for the Arts Fellowship and uses the money to travel through Europe.
1983	Cisneros holds the position of artist in residence at the Foundation Michael Karolyi in Vence, France, for the spring term.
1984	*The House on Mango Street* is published by Arte Público Press. Cisneros is awarded the Texas Institute of Letters Dobie-Paisano Fellowship and moves to San Antonio, Texas, where she oversees the literary programs at the Guadeloupe Cultural Arts Center.
1985	*The House on Mango Street* wins the Before Columbus American Book Award. *The Rodrigo Poems* is published.
1987	*My Wicked, Wicked Ways* is published. Cisneros falls into a deep depression while spending a year as guest lecturer at California State University, Chico.

1988	Cisneros is awarded a second NEA Fellowship. She is appointed to the Roberta Holloway Lectureship at the University of California, Berkeley, and begins practicing Buddhism.
1991	*Woman Hollering Creek, and Other Stories* is published by Random House. Vintage Books reissues *The House on Mango Street*.
1992	*Woman Hollering Creek* wins the PEN Center West Award for best fiction. Cisneros makes San Antonio her permanent home when she buys a house in the city's King William district.
1994	*Loose Woman* is published.
1995	Cisneros is awarded a MacArthur Foundation Fellowship. She begins the Macondo Writing Workshop for writers engaging social issues in their work.
1997	Cisneros's father dies.
2002	*Caramelo* is published. Cisneros is awarded an honorary doctorate of humane letters from Loyola University.
2004	*Vintage Cisneros*, a collection of previously published novel excerpts, short stories, and poems, is published.
2007	Cisneros's mother dies.

Works by Sandra Cisneros

Long Fiction

The House on Mango Street, 1984
Caramelo: Or, Puro Cuento, 2002

Short Fiction

Woman Hollering Creek, and Other Stories, 1991

Poetry

Bad Boys, 1980
The Rodrigo Poems, 1985
My Wicked, Wicked Ways, 1987
Loose Woman, 1994

Children's Literature

Hairs = Pelitos, 1984

Miscellaneous

Vintage Cisneros, 2004

Bibliography

Brunk, Beth. "*En Otras Voces*: Multiple Voices in Sandra Cisneros' *The House on Mango Street.*" *Hispanófila* 133 (Sept. 2001): 137-50.

Dubb, Christina Rose. "Adolescent Journeys: Finding Female Authority in *The Rain Catchers* and *The House on Mango Street.*" *Children's Literature in Education* 38.3 (Sept. 2007): 219-32.

Gonzales-Berry, Erlinda, and Tey Diana Rebolledo. "Growing Up Chicano: Tomás Rivera and Sandra Cisneros." *Revista Chicano-Riqueña* 13 (Fall-Winter 1985): 109-19.

González, Myrna-Yamil. "Female Voices in Sandra Cisneros' *The House on Mango Street.*" *U.S. Latino Literature: A Critical Guide for Students and Teachers.* Ed. Harold Augenbraum and Margarite Fernández Olmos. Westport, CT: Greenwood Press, 2000. 101-12.

Gutiérrez-Jones, Leslie S. "Different Voices: The Re-*Bildung* of the Barrio in Sandra Cisneros' *The House on Mango Street.*" *Anxious Power: Reading, Writing, and Ambivalence in Narrative by Women.* Ed. Carol J. Singley and Susan Elizabeth Sweeney. Albany: State University of New York Press, 1993. 295-312.

Klein, Dianne. "Coming of Age in Novels by Rudolfo Anaya and Sandra Cisneros." *English Journal* 81.5 (Sept. 1992): 21-26.

Kuribayashi, Tomoko. "The Chicana Girl Writes Her Way In and Out: Space and Bilingualism in Sandra Cisneros' *The House on Mango Street.*" *Creating Safe Space: Violence and Women's Writing.* Ed. Julie Sharp and Tomoko Kuribayashi. Albany: State University of New York Press, 1998. 165-77.

McCracken, Ellen. "Sandra Cisneros' *The House on Mango Street*: Community-Oriented Introspection and the Demystification of Patriarchal Violence." *Breaking Boundaries: Latina Writing and Critical Readings.* Ed. Asunción Horno-Delgado et al. Amherst: University of Massachusetts Press, 1989. 62-71.

Matchie, Thomas. "Literary Continuity in Sandra Cisneros's *The House on Mango Street.*" *Midwest Quarterly* 37.1 (Autumn 1995): 67-79.

Mayock, Ellen C. "The Bicultural Construction of Self in Cisneros, Alvarez, and Santiago." *Bilingual Review* 23.3 (Sept.-Dec. 1998): 223-29.

Miriam-Goldberg, Caryn. *Sandra Cisneros: Latina Writer and Activist.* Berkeley Heights, NJ: Enslow, 1998.

Muske, Carol. "Breaking out of the Genre Ghetto." *Parnassus: Poetry in Review* 20.1-2 (1995): 409-11, 417-23.

Olivares, Julián. "Entering *The House On Mango Street.*" *Teaching American Ethnic Literatures.* Ed. John R. Maitino and David R. Peck. Albuquerque: University of New Mexico Press, 1996. 209-36.

_____. "Sandra Cisneros' *The House on Mango Street,* and the Poetics of

Space." *Chicana Creativity and Criticism: New Frontiers in American Literature.* 2nd ed. Ed. María Herrera-Sobek and Helena María Viramontes. Albuquerque: University of New Mexico Press, 1996. 233-44.

O'Reilly Herrera, Andrea. "'Chambers of Consciousness': Sandra Cisneros and the Development of the Self and the BIG *House on Mango Street.*" *Bucknell Review* 39.1 (1995): 191-204.

Quintana, Alvina E. *Home Girls: Chicana Literary Voices.* Philadelphia: Temple University Press, 1996.

Rivera, Carmen Haydée. *Border Crossings and Beyond: The Life and Works of Sandra Cisneros.* Santa Barbara, CA: Praeger, 2009.

Rodríguez Aranda, Pilar E. "On the Solitary Fate of Being Mexican, Female, Wicked and Thirty-three: An Interview with Writer Sandra Cisneros." *Americas Review* 18.1 (1990): 64-80.

Ryan, Kathleen J. "Teaching *The House on Mango Street*: Engaging Race, Class, and Gender in a White Classroom." *Academic Exchange* (Winter 2002): 187-92.

Saldívar, Ramón. *Chicano Narrative: The Dialectics of Difference.* Madison: University of Wisconsin Press, 1990.

Sanborn, Geoffrey. "Keeping Her Distance: Cisneros, Dickinson, and the Politics of Private Enjoyment." *Publications of the Modern Language Association* 116.5 (2001): 1334-48.

Sloboda, Nicholas. "A Home in the Heart: Sandra Cisneros's *The House on Mango Street.*" *Aztlán: A Journal of Chicano Studies* 22.2 (Spring 1997): 89-106.

Stavans, Ilan. "Una Nueva Voz." *Commonweal* 118.15 (13 Sept. 1991): 524-25.

Torres, Hector A. *Conversations with Contemporary Chicana and Chicano Writers.* Albuquerque: University of New Mexico Press, 2007.

Valdés, María Elena de. "The Critical Reception of Sandra Cisneros's *The House on Mango Street.*" *Gender, Self, and Society: Proceedings of the IV International Conference on the Hispanic Cultures of the United States.* Ed. Renate von Bardeleben. New York: Peter Lang, 1993. 287-300.

_____. "In Search of Identity in Cisneros's *The House on Mango Street.*" *Canadian Review of American Studies* 23.1 (Fall 1992): 55-72.

Wissman, Kelly. "'Writing Will Keep You Free': Allusions to and Recreations of the Fairy Tale Heroine in *The House on Mango Street.*" *Children's Literature in Education* 38 (2007): 17-34.

CRITICAL
INSIGHTS

About the Editor

María Herrera-Sobek (Ph.D., University of California, Los Angeles) is Associate Vice Chancellor for Diversity, Equity, and Academic Policy and Professor in the Department of Chicana and Chicano Studies at the University of California, Santa Barbara. Among the many awards and honors she has garnered is the Distinguished Alumnus Award for 2007 from the UCLA Department of Spanish and Portuguese. She became a Fellow of the American Folklore Society in 2000, served as a member of the editorial board of the publications of the Modern Language Association (2003-2005), and was elected Vice President of the International Association of Inter-American Studies (2009) at the University of Bielefeld, Germany. She has edited or coedited seventeen books and published more than 175 articles. Her publications include *The Bracero Experience: Elitelore Versus Folklore* (1979), *The Mexican Corrido: A Feminist Analysis* (1991), *Northward Bound: The Mexican Immigrant Experience in Ballad and Song* (1993), and *Chicano Folklore: A Handbook* (2006). She has presented her research at more than three hundred scholarly conferences both nationally and internationally in Germany, France, Spain, Russia, Italy, Sweden, Turkey, and Latin American countries. Among her current projects are the *Norton Anthology for Latino Literature*, of which she is an associate editor, and the *Encyclopedia for Latino Folklore*, of which she is the editor.

About *The Paris Review*

The Paris Review is America's preeminent literary quarterly, dedicated to discovering and publishing the best new voices in fiction, nonfiction, and poetry. The magazine was founded in Paris in 1953 by the young American writers Peter Matthiessen and Doc Humes, and edited there and in New York for its first fifty years by George Plimpton. Over the decades, the *Review* has introduced readers to the earliest writings of Jack Kerouac, Philip Roth, T. C. Boyle, V. S. Naipaul, Ha Jin, Ann Patchett, Jay McInerney, Mona Simpson, and Edward P. Jones, and published numerous now classic works, including Roth's *Goodbye, Columbus*, Donald Barthelme's *Alice*, Jim Carroll's *Basketball Diaries*, and selections from Samuel Beckett's *Molloy* (his first publication in English). The first chapter of Jeffrey Eugenides's *The Virgin Suicides* appeared in the *Review*'s pages, as well as stories by Rick Moody, David Foster Wallace, Denis Johnson, Jim Crace, Lorrie Moore, and Jeanette Winterson.

The Paris Review's renowned Writers at Work series of interviews, whose early installments include legendary conversations with E. M. Forster, William Faulkner, and Ernest Hemingway, is one of the landmarks of world literature. The interviews received a George Polk Award and were nominated for a Pulitzer Prize. Among the more than three hundred interviewees are Robert Frost, Marianne Moore, W. H. Auden, Elizabeth Bishop, Susan Sontag, and Toni Morrison. Recent issues feature conversations with Salman Rushdie, Joan Didion, Norman Mailer, Kazuo Ishiguro, Marilynne Robinson, Umberto Eco, Annie Proulx, and Gay Talese. In November 2009, Picador published the final volume of a four-volume series of anthologies of *Paris Review* interviews. *The New York Times* called the Writers at Work series "the most remarkable and extensive interviewing project we possess."

The Paris Review is edited by Philip Gourevitch, who was named to the post in 2005, following the death of George Plimpton two years earlier. A new editorial team has published fiction by André Aciman, Colum McCann, Damon Galgut, Mohsin Hamid, Uzodinma Iweala, Gish Jen, Stephen King, James Lasdun, Padgett Powell, Richard Price, and Sam Shepard. Poetry editors Charles Simic, Meghan O'Rourke, and Dan Chiasson have selected works by John Ashbery, Kay Ryan, Billy Collins, Tomaž Šalamun, Mary Jo Bang, Sharon Olds, Charles Wright, and Mary Karr. Writing published in the magazine has been anthologized in *Best American Short Stories* (2006, 2007, and 2008), *Best American Poetry*, *Best Creative Non-Fiction*, the Pushcart Prize anthology, and *O. Henry Prize Stories*.

The magazine presents two annual awards. The Hadada Award for lifelong contribution to literature has recently been given to Joan Didion, Norman Mailer, Peter Matthiessen, and, in 2009, John Ashbery. The Plimpton Prize for Fiction, awarded to a debut or emerging writer brought to national attention in the pages of *The Paris Review*, was presented in 2007 to Benjamin Percy, to Jesse Ball in 2008, and to Alistair Morgan in 2009.

The Paris Review was a finalist for the 2008 and 2009 National Magazine Awards in fiction, and it won the 2007 National Magazine Award in photojournalism. The *Los Angeles Times* recently called *The Paris Review* "an American treasure with true international reach."

Since 1999 *The Paris Review* has been published by The Paris Review Foundation, Inc., a not-for-profit 501(c)(3) organization.

The Paris Review is available in digital form to libraries worldwide in selected academic databases exclusively from EBSCO Publishing. Libraries can contact EBSCO at 1-800-653-2726 for details. For more information on *The Paris Review* or to subscribe, please visit: www.theparisreview.org.

Contributors

María Herrera-Sobek (Ph.D., University of California, Los Angeles) is Associate Vice Chancellor for Diversity, Equity, and Academic Policy and Professor in the Department of Chicana and Chicano Studies at the University of California, Santa Barbara. Her publications include *The Bracero Experience: Elitelore versus Folklore (1979)*; *The Mexican Corrido: A Feminist Analysis* (1991); *Northward Bound: The Mexican Immigrant Experience in Ballad and Song* (1993) and *Chicano Folklore: A Handbook* (2006). She has edited or coedited seventeen books and has published more than 175 articles. Among her current projects are the *Norton Anthology for Latino Literature*, of which she is an associate editor, and the *Encyclopedia for Latino Folklore*, of which she is the editor.

Gloria A. Duarte-Valverde is Professor of English and Director of First Year Experience at Angelo State University in San Angelo, Texas.

Chloë Schama is the author of *Wild Romance: A Victorian Story of a Marriage, a Trial, and a Self-Made Woman*. She has written for *The New Republic*, *The New York Sun*, and *The Guardian*.

Amelia María de la Luz Montes is Associate Professor of English and Ethnic Studies at the University of Nebraska-Lincoln as well as director of the university's Institute for Ethnic Studies. Her research interests center on transnational studies, and she is the editor of the Penguin edition of María Amparo Ruiz de Burton's *Who Would Have Thought It?*

Amy Sickels is an MFA graduate of Pennsylvania State University. Her fiction and essays have appeared or are forthcoming in *DoubleTake*, *Passages North*, *Bayou*, *The Madison Review*, *LIT*, *Natural Bridge*, and *The Greensboro Review*.

Felicia J. Cruz is Assistant Professor and Chair of the Department of Spanish at the College of St. Catherine in Minnesota.

Catherine Leen is a lecturer in the Department of Spanish at the National University of Ireland, Maynooth. Her research focuses on Latin American film and literature, and in 2007 she was the recipient of a Fulbright Scholarship.

Leslie Petty is Assistant Professor of English at Rhodes College in Tennessee, where she lectures primarily on nineteenth-century American literature and studies. She is the author of *Romancing the Vote: Feminist Activism in American Fiction, 1870-1920* (2000). Her articles and book reviews have appeared in such journals as *Women's Studies*, *MELUS*, *Southern Quarterly*, and *Journal of American History*.

Catrióna Rueda Esquibel is Associate Professor of Ethnic Studies at San Francisco State University. Her courses cover cultural literature, Chicana lesbian fiction, and race and gender in literature. She is the author of *With Her Machete in Her Hand: Reading Chicana Lesbians* (2006) and several book chapters, encyclopedia entries, and articles.

Michelle Scalise Sugiyama is a teacher at the Institute for Cognitive and Decision Sciences and in the English Department at the University of Oregon, Eugene. Her research interests include prehistory of narrative, art behavior, and storytelling. Her articles have appeared in publications such as *Human Nature, Evolution and Human Behavior, Philosophy and Literature*, and *Interdisciplinary Literary Studies*.

Robin Ganz is a literary critic, biographer, and teacher specializing in American multiethnic literature. She has published articles in the *Boston Globe*, the *San Francisco Chronicle*, and *MELUS* and is currently working on a book about author Philip Roth.

Stella Bolaki is Professor of English and American Literature at the University of Edinburgh. Her focus is on contemporary literature and multiethnic fiction, and she has published on such topics as cultural translation, narratives of community, and loss and mourning. She is currently a postdoctoral fellow at the Institute for Advanced Studies in the Humanities at the University of Edinburgh, where she is working on "Poetics, Identity, and Witnessing in Contemporary Narratives of Illness and Disability."

Maria Karafilis is Associate Professor of English at California State University, Los Angeles. She is the author of "The Traumatic Sublime and American Democracy" (2005) and "Trauma, Race, and the Unassimilated" (2003). Her most recent article, "The Jewish Ghetto in Mary Antin and Her Contemporaries," appears in the winter 2010 issue of *American Literary Realism*.

Annie O. Eysturoy is the author of *Daughters of Self-Creation: The Contemporary Chicana Novel* (1996).

Delia Poey is Professor of Modern Languages at Florida State University. She specializes in comparative literature and U.S. Latino literature, and she has published several books, including *Latino American Literature in the Classroom: The Politics of Transformation* (2002), *Out of the Mirrored Garden: New Fiction by Latin American Women* (1996), and *Little Havana Blues: A Cuban-American Literature Anthology* (1996).

Maria Antònia Oliver-Rotger is Assistant Professor at Universitat Pompeu Fabra in Barcelona, where she lectures on Latino authors. She is the author of *Battlegrounds and Crossroads: Social and Imaginary Space in Writings by Chicanas* (2003).

Jacqueline Doyle is Professor of English at California State University, East Bay. She has published nonfiction, flash fiction, and lyric prose in *Flashquake, Six Sentences, SoMa Literary Review, JuiceBox*, and *Glossolalia*.

James R. Giles is Professor of English at Northern Illinois University. He is the author of *Understanding Hubert Selby, Jr.* (1998) and *The Naturalistic Inner-City Novel in America* (1995) and coeditor of *The Dictionary of Literary Biography: American Novelists Since World War II*, volumes 143, 152, 173 (1994, 1995, 1996).

Reuben Sánchez is Professor of English at California State University, Fresno. His areas of specialization include Renaissance literature, the Bible, and Chicano literature, and he has published a variety of essays in such journals as *Children's Literature, Milton Studies, Milton Quarterly, Prose Studies*, and *Hamlet Studies*.

Acknowledgments

"Sandra Cisneros" by Gloria A. Duarte-Valverde. From *Cyclopedia of World Authors, Fourth Revised Edition*. Copyright © 2004 by Salem Press, Inc. Reprinted with permission of Salem Press.

"The *Paris Review* Perspective" by Chlöe Schama. Copyright © 2011 by Chlöe Schama. Special appreciation goes to Christopher Cox, Nathaniel Rich, and David Wallace-Wells, editors at *The Paris Review*.

"On the 'Simplicity' of Sandra Cisneros's *House on Mango Street*" by Felicia J. Cruz. From *Modern Fiction Studies* 47, no. 4 (Winter 2001): 910-946. Copyright © 2001 by the Purdue Research Foundation. Reprinted with permission of The Johns Hopkins University Press.

"The 'Dual'-ing Images of la Malinche and la Virgen de Guadalupe in Cisneros's *The House on Mango Street*" by Leslie Petty. From *MELUS: Journal of the Society for the Study of the Multi-Ethnic Literature of the United States* 25, no. 2 (Summer 2000): 119-132. Copyright © 2000 by *MELUS*. Reprinted with permission of the journal.

"Memories of Girlhood: Chicana Lesbian Fictions" by Catrióna Rueda Esquibel. From *Signs: Journal of Women in Culture and Society* 23, no. 3 (1998): 645-682. Copyright © 1998 by The University of Chicago Press. Reprinted with permission of The University of Chicago Press.

"Of Woman Bondage: The Eroticism of Feet in *The House on Mango Street*" by Michelle Scalise Sugiyama. From *The Midwest Quarterly* 41, no. 1 (1999): 9-20. Copyright © 1999 by *The Midwest Quarterly*. Reprinted with permission of *The Midwest Quarterly*.

"Sandra Cisneros: Border Crossings and Beyond" by Robin Ganz. From *MELUS: Journal of the Society for the Study of the Multi-Ethnic Literature of the United States* 19, no. 1 (Spring 1994): 19-29. Copyright © 1994 by *MELUS*. Reprinted with permission of the journal.

"'This Bridge We Call Home': Crossing and Bridging Spaces in Sandra Cisneros's *The House on Mango Street*" by Stella Bolaki. From *eSharp* 5 (2005): 1-19. Copyright © 2005 by *eSharp*. Reprinted with permission of the author.

"Crossing the Borders of Genre: Revisions of the *Bildungsroman* in Sandra Cisneros's *The House on Mango Street* and Jamaica Kincaid's *Annie John*" by Maria Karafilis. From *The Journal of the Midwest Modern Language Association* 31, no. 2 (1998): 63-78. Copyright © 1998 by the Midwest Modern Language Association. Reprinted with permission of the Midwest Modern Language Association.

"*The House on Mango Street*: A Space of Her Own" by Annie O. Eysturoy. From *Daughters of Self-Creation: The Contemporary Chicana Novel* (1996), pp. 89-112. Copyright © 1996 by the University of New Mexico Press. Reprinted with permission of the University of New Mexico Press.

Index

American Book Award, 3, 10, 37, 239
American Dream, 61, 68, 73, 108, 222
Annie John (Kincaid), 219; as anti-bildungsroman, 230
Anzaldúa, Gloria, 39, 66, 97, 134, 205, 207, 212, 239, 351, 397
Arteaga, Alfred, 215
Austin, J. L., 90, 282

Bachelard, Gaston, 254, 286, 306
Bad Boys (Cisneros), 10
Bakhtin, Mikhail, 77, 85, 90
Barrett, Michèle, 349, 356
Benjamin, Walter, 379
Bethel, Lorraine, 132
Betzig, Laura, 181
Bhabha, Homi K., 208
Biblical allusions, 107, 357, 373, 395
Bildungsroman, 6, 17, 43, 56, 205, 218, 239, 270, 298
Bilingualism, 48, 274
Birtha, Becky, 172
Bless Me, Ultima (Anaya), 44, 88, 266, 390
Bluest Eye, The (Morrison), 95
Borderlands/La Frontera (Anzaldúa), 206, 210, 279
Bourboulis, Photeine, 180
Bourdieu, Pierre, 109
Brady, Mary Pat, 32
Braendlin, Bonnie Hoover, 220
Breedlove, Pecola (*The Bluest Eye*), 99
Bremer, Sidney H., 364
Brunk, Beth, 49
Buckley, Jerome, 271

Calderón, Héctor, 278, 282
Campbell, Joseph, 383

Caramelo (Cisneros), 7, 11, 37
Castillo, Ana, 39, 173, 215, 403
Castillo, Debra, 290
Cather, Willa, 24
Catholicism, 114, 160, 173-174, 291, 302, 313, 315
Chambers, Aidan, 386
Chapa, Jorge, 23, 25
Chávez, Denise, 145, 312
Chicano movement, 38, 98, 278
Chicano nationalism, 23, 38
Chicano/a literature, 23, 39, 56, 131, 190, 201, 266, 390
Children's literature, 382
Cisneros, Sandra; childhood and early life, 9, 25, 190; early career, 11, 14, 196; education, 9, 66; as midwesterner, 21; and otherness, 27, 36, 66, 95, 196, 260, 326; poetry, 6, 10, 49, 195, 202, 330, 356, 378; on writing, 27, 65, 194, 201, 208, 330, 334, 356
Class issues. *See* Social class issues
Claudia MacTeer. *See* MacTeer, Claudia
Comadrazgo, 130, 162
Cordero, Esperanza (*The House on Mango Street*), 6, 28, 61, 75, 96, 118, 135, 160, 178, 211, 222, 239, 277, 289, 327, 365, 383; as Jesus Christ, 6; and mother, 118, 257, 331, 344; rape of, 126, 142, 249, 339, 375, 397
Coward, Rosalind, 298
Cruz, Felicia J., 51
Culler, Jonathan, 270
Culture wars, 42, 265

Daly, Martin, 188
Dasenbrock, Reed Way, 273